HENRY MILLER

THE BOOKS
IN MY LIFE

A NEW DIRECTIONS BOOK

*New Directions Books are published by James Laughlin
at Norfolk, Connecticut*

NEW YORK OFFICE—333 SIXTH AVENUE, NEW YORK 14

Printed in the Republic of Ireland

TO

LAWRENCE CLARK POWELL

(Librarian of the University of California at Los Angeles)

This is the first of a several-volume work. Included in the second volume will be a list of all the books Henry Miller can recall having read. There will also be an index of all literary references in Henry Miller's works.

CONTENTS

LIST OF ILLUSTRATIONS

QUOTATIONS FROM WRITERS

" All I have written now appears to me as so much straw."
(THOMAS AQUINAS on his deathbed.)

" When the artist has exhausted his materials, when the fancy
no longer paints, when thoughts are no longer apprehended, and
books are a weariness—he has always the resource *to live*."
(RALPH WALDO EMERSON.)

" All is marvellous for the poet, all is divine for the saint, all is
great for the hero ; all is wretched, miserable, ugly and bad for the
base and sordid soul."

(AMIEL.)

" Probably, even in our time, an artist might find his imagination
considerably stimulated and his work powerfully improved if he
knew that anything short of his best would bring him to the gallows,
with or without trial by jury . . ."

(HENRY ADAMS.)

" Après avoir pris un an de vacances (15 sept. '49—15 sept. '50),
me marier, un peu voyager en Suisse, Luxembourg, Hollande,
Angleterre, Belgique, soigner mes yeux, faire trois mois de radio,
déménager, me réinstaller à Paris—je me suis remis au travail,
hélas ! . . . Petit à petit je vais m'enfoncer dans cet univers qui
contient tous les autres comme une goutte d'eau des myriades de
microbes, la goutte d'encre qui coule de la plume . . . C'est
extraordinaire . . . et je n'arrive pas à m'y habituer ni . . . à y
croire ! "

(BLAISE CENDRARS in a letter dated Sept. 16, 1950.)

ACKNOWLEDGMENTS

To the *World Review*, London, for permission to reprint the chapter on Blaise Cendrars ; to *Survival*, New York, for the chapter on Rider Haggard.

GRATEFUL acknowledgment is herewith made to the following publishers and individuals for their kind permission to quote from the following works:

Blackie & Son Ltd., for *Life of G. A. Henty* by G. Melville Fenn.

Borden Publishing Co., for *The History of Magic* by Eliphas Levi.

Coward-McCann, Inc., for *Hill of Destiny* by Jean Giono.

C. W. Daniel Co., Ltd., for *The Absolute Collective* by Erich Gutkind.

James Ladd Delkin for *Zen* by Alan W. Watts.

Doubleday & Co., Inc., for *The Story of My Life* by Helen Keller.

Druid Press for *The Obstinate Cymric* by J. C. Powys.

E. P. Dutton & Co., Inc., for *Cosmic Consciousness* by R. M. Bunche and *Magicians, Seers and Mystics* by Maurice Magre.

Éditions Bernard Grasset for *Moravagine* by Blaise Cendrars.

Falcon Press for *Babu of Montparnasse* by C. L. Philippe.

Harcourt, Brace & Co., Inc., for *In Search of the Miraculous* by P. D. Ouspensky.

Hermann Hesse for his article which appeared in *Horizon*, Sept., 1946.

Houghton Mifflin Co., & Constable & Co., Ltd., for *Mont Saint Michel and Chartres* by Henry Adams.

Henry Holt & Co., Inc., for *Nature and Man* by Paul Weiss.

Alfred A. Knopf, Inc., for *Men of Good Will* by Jules Romain.

John Lane The Bodley Head for *Autobiography* by J. C. Powys.

Frieda Lawrence for *Studies in Classic American Literature*, and *Apocalypse*—both by D. H. Lawrence.

Le Cercle Du Livre for *Krishnamurti* by Carlo Suarès.

Les Éditions Denoël for *Le Lotissement du Ciel* and *Bourlinguer*—both by Blaise Cendrars.

Little, Brown & Co., for *Schliemann* by Emil Ludwig.

Longmans, Green & Co., Ltd., and A. P. Watt & Son for *The Days of My Life* by H. Rider Haggard.

The Macmillan Co., for *Dostoievsky* by Janko Lavrin.

W. W. Norton & Co., Inc., for *The Great Age of Greek Literature* by Edith Hamilton.

J. C. Powys for his book *Visions and Revisions*.

Random House for Deems Taylor's introduction to *Peter Ibbetson* and for *Anna Christie* by Eugene O'Neill.

Routledge and Kegan Paul Ltd., for *Politics of the Unpolitical* by Herbert Read.

Sylvan Press Ltd., for *From Puskin to Mayakovsky* by Janko Lavrin.

W. T. Symonds for an article by Erich Gutkind in *Purpose*, 1947.

The Viking Press Inc., for *Joy of Man's Desiring* and *Blue Boy*—both by Jean Giono, and the *Portable Sherwood Anderson*.

CREDIT FOR PHOTOS

1. Henry Miller in Studio, Big Sur (1950) by Flair, New York.

2. Blaise Cendrars (1950) by Robert Doisneau, Montrouge, France.

3. Xerxes Society.

4. Miller Family Portrait by Pach Bros., New York (circa 1902-03).

PREFACE

THE purpose of this book, which will run to several volumes in the course of the next few years, is to round out the story of my life. It deals with books as vital experience. It is not a critical study nor does it contain a program for self-education.

One of the results of this self-examination—for that is what the writing of this book amounts to—is the confirmed belief that one should read less and less, not more and more. As a glance at the Appendix will reveal, I have not read nearly as much as the scholar, the bookworm, or even the " well-educated " man—yet I have undoubtedly read a hundred times more than I should have read for my own good. Only one out of five in America, it is said, are readers of " books." But even this small number read far too much. Scarcely any one lives wisely or fully.

There have been and always will be books which are truly revolutionary—that is to say, inspired and inspiring. They are few and far between, of course. One is lucky to run across a handful in a lifetime. Moreover, these are not the books which invade the general public. They are the hidden reservoirs which feed the men of lesser talent who know how to appeal to the man in the street. The vast body of literature, in every domain, is composed of hand-me-down ideas. The question—never resolved, alas !— is to what extent it would be efficacious to curtail the overwhelming supply of cheap fodder. One thing is certain today—the illiterate are definitely not the least intelligent among us.

If it be knowledge or wisdom one is seeking, then one had better go direct to the source. And the source is not the scholar or philosopher, not the master, saint, or teacher, but life itself—direct experience of life. The same is true for art. Here, too, we can dispense with " the masters." When I say life I have in mind, to be sure, another kind of life than that we know today. I have in mind the sort which D. H. Lawrence speaks of in *Etruscan Places*.*

* Published by Martin Secker, London, 1932. See pages 88–93.

Or that Henry Adams speaks of when the Virgin reigned supreme at Chartres.

In this age, which believes that there is a short cut to everything, the greatest lesson to be learned is that the most difficult way is, in the long run, the easiest. All that is set forth in books, all that seems so terribly vital and significant, is but an iota of that from which it stems and which it is within everyone's power to tap. Our whole theory of education is based on the absurd notion that we must learn to swim on land before tackling the water. It applies to the pursuit of the arts as well as to the pursuit of knowledge. Men are still being taught to create by studying other men's works or by making plans and sketches never intended to materialize. The art of writing is taught in the classroom instead of in the thick of life. Students are still being handed models which are supposed to fit all temperaments, all kinds of intelligence. No wonder we produce better engineers than writers, better industrial experts than painters.

My encounters with books I regard very much as my encounters with other phenomena of life or thought. All encounters are configurate, not isolate. In this sense, and in this sense only, books are as much a part of life as trees, stars or dung. I have no reverence for them per se. Nor do I put authors in any special, privileged category. They are like other men, no better, no worse. They exploit the powers given them, just as any other order of human being. If I defend them now and then—as a class—it is because I believe that, in our society at least, they have never achieved the status and the consideration they merit. The great ones, especially, have almost always been treated as scapegoats.

To see myself as the reader I once was is like watching a man fighting his way through a jungle. To be sure, living in the heart of the jungle I learned a few things about the jungle. But my aim was never to live in the jungle—it was to get clear of it ! It is my firm conviction that it is not necessary to first inhabit this jungle of books. Life itself is enough of a jungle—a very real and a very instructive one, to say the least. But, you ask, may not books be a help, a guide, in fighting our way through the wilderness ? " N'ira pas loin," said Napoleon, " celui qui sait d'avance où il veut aller."

The principal aim underlying this work is to render homage

where homage is due, a task which I know beforehand is impossible of accomplishment. Were I to do it properly, I would have to get down on my knees and thank each blade of grass for rearing its head. What chiefly motivates me in this vain task is the fact that in general we know all too little about the influences which shape a writer's life and work. The critic, in his pompous conceit and arrogance, distorts the true picture beyond all recognition. The author, however truthful he may think himself to be, inevitably disguises the picture. The psychologist, with his single-track view of things, only deepens the blur. As author, I do not think myself an exception to the rule. I, too, am guilty of altering, distorting and disguising the facts—if " facts " there be. My conscious effort, however, has been—perhaps to a fault—in the opposite direction. I am on the side of revelation, if not always on the side of beauty, truth, wisdom, harmony and ever-evolving perfection. In this work I am throwing out fresh data, to be judged and analyzed, or accepted and enjoyed for enjoyment's sake. Naturally I cannot write about *all* the books, or even all the significant ones, which I have read in the course of my life. But I do intend to go on writing about books and authors until I have exhausted the importance (for me) of this domain of reality.

To have undertaken the thankless task of listing all the books I can recall ever reading gives me extreme pleasure and satisfaction. I know of no author who has been mad enough to attempt this. Perhaps my list will give rise to more confusion—but its purpose is not that. Those who know how to read a man know how to read his books. For these the list will speak for itself.

In writing of the " amoralisme " of Goethe, Jules de Gaultier, quoting Goethe, I believe, says : " La vraie nostalgie doit toujours être productrice et créer une nouvelle chose qui soit meilleure." At the core of this book there *is* a genuine nostalgia. It is not a nostalgia for the past itself, as may sometimes appear to be the case, nor is it a nostalgia for the irretrievable ; it is a nostalgia for moments lived to the fullest. These moments occurred sometimes through contact with books, sometimes through contact with men and women I have dubbed " living books." Sometimes it is a nostalgia for the companionship of those boys I grew up with and with whom one of the strongest bonds I had was—books. (Yet

13

here I must confess that, however bright and revivifying these memories, they are as nothing to the remembrance of days spent in the company of my former idols-in-the-flesh, those boys—still boys to me !—who went by the immortal names of Johnny Paul, Eddie Carney, Lester Reardon, Johnny and Jimmy Dunne, none of whom did I ever see with a book or associate with a book in the remotest way.) Whether it was Goethe who said it or de Gaultier, I too most firmly believe that true nostalgia must always be productive and conducive to the creation of new and better things. If it were merely to rehash the past, whether in the form of books, persons or events, my task would be a vain and futile one. Cold and dead as it may now seem, the list of titles given in the Appendix may prove for some kindred souls to be the key with which to unlock *their* living moments of joy and plenitude in the past.

One of the reasons I bother to write a preface, which is always something of a bore to the reader, one of the reasons I have rewritten it for the fifth and, I hope, the last time, is the fear that its completion may be frustrated by some unforeseen event. This first volume finished, I have immediately to set to work to write the third and last book of *The Rosy Crucifixion*, the hardest task I ever set myself and one which I have avoided for many a year. I would like, therefore, while time permits, to give a hint of some of the things I planned or hoped to write about in succeeding volumes.

Naturally, I had some sort of flexible plan in mind when I began this work. Unlike the architect, however, an author often discards his blueprint in the process of erecting his edifice. To the writer a book is something to be lived through, an experience, not a plan to be executed in accordance with laws and specifications. At any rate, whatever is left of my original plan has grown tenuous and complicated as a spider's web. It is only in bringing this volume to a close that I have come to realize how much I wish to say, and have to say, about certain authors, certain subjects, some of which I have already touched upon.* For example, no matter how often

---

* An American whose influence I may have minimized is Jack London. Glancing through his *Essays of Revolt*, edited by Leonard D. Abbott, I recalled the great thrill it gave me, a boy of fourteen, to merely hear the name *Jack*

14

I refer to him I have never said, and probably never will say, all that I mean to say about Elie Faure. Nor have I by any means exhausted the subject of Blaise Cendrars. And then there is Céline, a giant among our contemporaries, whom I have not even begun to approach. As for Rider Haggard, I shall certainly have more to say about him, in particular, his *Ayesha*, the sequel to *She*. When it comes to Emerson, Dostoievsky, Maeterlinck, Knut Hamsun, G. A. Henty, I know I shall never say my last word about *them*. A subject like *The Grand Inquisitor*, for example, or *The Eternal Husband*—my favorite of all Dostoievsky's works—would seem to demand separate books in themselves. Perhaps when I come to Berdyaev and that great flock of exalted Russian writers of the Nineteenth century, the men with the eschatological flair, I shall get round to saying some of the things I have been wanting to say for twenty years or more. Then there is the Marquis de Sade, one of the most maligned, defamed, misunderstood—deliberately and wilfully misunderstood—figures in all literature. Time I came to grips with him ! Back of him and overshadowing him stands the figure of Gilles de Rais, one of the most glorious, sinister, enigmatic figures in all European history. In the letter to Pierre Lesdain I said I had not yet received a good book on Gilles de Rais. In the meantime a friend has sent me one from Paris, and I have read it.

London. To us who hungered for life he was a shining light, adored as much for his revolutionary fervor as for his wild, adventurous life. How strange now to read, in Leonard Abbott's Introduction, that in the year 1905 (!) Jack London was proclaiming : " The revolution is here now. Stop it who can ! " How strange now to read the opening words of his famous speech on " Revolution," which he delivered to university students throughout America—*how did it ever happen ?*—telling of the seven million men and women then enrolled throughout the world in the army of revolt. Listen to Jack London's words :

" There has never been anything like this revolution in the history of the world. There is nothing analogous between it and the American Revolution or the French Revolution. It is unique, colossal. Other revolutions compare with it as asteroids compare with the sun. It is alone of its kind, the first world revolution in a world whose history is replete with revolutions. And not only this, for it is the first organized movement of men to become a world movement, limited only by the limits of the planet. This revolution is unlike all other revolutions in many respects. It is not sporadic. It is not a flame of popular discontent, arising in a day and dying down in a day . . ."

One of the first Americans, I presume, to make a fortune with the pen, Jack London resigned from the Socialist Party in 1916, accusing it of lacking fire and fight. One wonders what he would say today, were he alive, about " the Revolution."

It is just the book I was looking for ; it is called *Gilles de Rais et son temps* by George Meunier.*

Here are a few more books and authors I intend to dwell on in the future : Algernon Blackwood, author of *The Bright Messenger*, to my mind the most extraordinary novel on psychoanalysis, one which dwarfs the subject ; *The Path to Rome*, by Hilaire Belloc, an early favorite and a steadfast love : each time I read the opening pages, " Praise of This Book," I dance with joy ; Marie Corelli, a contemporary of Rider Haggard, Yeats, Tennyson, Oscar Wilde, who said of herself in a letter to the vicar of the parish church at Stratford-on-Avon : " With regard to the Scriptures, I do not think any *woman* has ever studied them so deeply and devoutly as I have, or, let me say, *more* deeply and devoutly." I shall certainly write about René Caillé, the first white man to enter Timbuctoo and get out alive ; his story, as related by Galbraith Welch in *The Unveiling of Timbuctoo*, is to my mind the greatest adventure story in modern times. And Nostradamus, Janko Lavrin, Paul Brunton, Péguy, Ouspensky's *In Search of the Miraculous*, *Letters from the Mahatmas*, Fechner's *Life After Death*, Claude Houghton's metaphysical novels, Cyril Connolly's *Enemies of Promise* (another book about books), the language of night, as Eugene Jolas calls it, Donald Keyhoe's book on the flying saucers, cybernetics and dianetics, the importance of nonsense, the subject of resurrection and ascension, and, among other things, a recent book by Carlo Suarès (the same who wrote on Krishnamurti), entitled *Le Mythe Judéo-Chrétien*.

I shall also—" why not ? " as Picasso says—expatiate on the subject of " pornography and obscenity " in literature. In fact, I have already written quite a few pages on this theme, which I have held over for the second volume. Meanwhile I am very much in need of authentic data. I should like to know, for example, what are the great pornographic books of all time. (I know but a very

---

* In Paris, about 1931 or 1932, Richard Thoma gave me a copy of his book on Gilles de Rais, called *Tragedy in Blue*. A few weeks ago I received a reprint of this book, published as an anonymous work and entitled *The Authorized Version—Book Three—The Book of Sapphire*. Rereading it, I was overcome with mortification that I could have forgotten the power and the splendor of this work. It is a poetic justification, I might almost say, or paean or dithyramb, only fifty-one pages long, unique in its genre, and true as only highly imaginative works can be. It is a breviary for the initiated. Apologies and congratulations, Dicko !

few.) Who *are* the writers who are still regarded as " obscene " ?
How widely are their books circulated and where chiefly ? In
what languages ? I can think of only three great writers whose
works are still banned in England and America, and then only
certain of their works, not all. I mean the Marquis de Sade (whose
most sensational work is still banned in France), Aretino and D. H.
Lawrence. What of Restif de la Bretonne, concerning whom
an American, J. Rives Childs, has compiled (in French) a formidable
tome of " témoignages et jugements " ? And what about that
first pornographic novel in the English language, *The Memoirs
of Fanny Hill* ? Why, if it is so " dull," has it not become a " classic "
by now, free to circulate in drug stores, railway stations and other
innocent places ? It is just two hundred years since it first appeared,
and it has never gone out of print, as every American tourist in
Paris well knows.

Curious, but of all the books I was searching for while writing
this first volume, the two I wanted most have not turned up :
The Thirteen Crucified Saviours, by Sir Godfrey Higgins, author
of the celebrated *Anacalypsis*, and *Les Cléfs de l'Apocalypse*, by
O. V. Milosz, the Polish poet who died not long ago at Fontaine-
bleau. Nor have I yet received a good book on the Children's
Crusades.

There are three magazines I forgot to mention when speaking of
good magazines : *Jugend*, *The Enemy* (edited by that amazing,
bright spirit, Wyndham Lewis), and *The Masque* of Gordon Craig

And now a word about the man to whom this book is dedicated
—Lawrence Clark Powell. It was on one of his visits to Big Sur
that this individual, who knows more about books than any one
I have ever had the good fortune to meet, suggested that I write
(for him if for no one else) a short book about my experience with
books. Some months later the germ, which had always been
dormant, took hold. After writing about fifty pages I knew that
I could never rest content with a summary account of the subject.
Powell knew it too, no doubt, but he was cunning or discreet
enough to keep it to himself. I owe Larry Powell a great deal.
For one thing, and it is a big thing to me because it means the
correction of a false attitude, I owe him my present ability to view
librarians as human beings, very live human beings, sometimes,

and capable of proving dynamic forces in our midst. Certainly no librarian could be more zealous than he in making books a vital part of our life, which they are not at present. Nor could any librarian have given me greater direct aid than he. Not a single question have I put to him which he has not answered fully and scrupulously. No request of any sort, in fact, has he ever turned down. Should this book prove to be a failure it will not be *his* fault.

Here I must add a few words about other individuals who extended their aid in one way or another. First and foremost, Dante T. Zaccagnini of Port Chester, New York. You, Dante, whom I have never met, how can I express to you my deep gratitude for all the arduous labors you performed—and voluntarily!—on my behalf? I blush to think what humdrum tasks some of them were. In addition you insisted on making me gifts of some of your most precious books—because you thought I had more need of them than you! And what helpful suggestions you made, what subtle corrections! All done with discretion, tact, humility and devotion. Words fail me.

It should be understood that when I began this task there were, I felt, several hundred books which I needed to borrow or to own. My only recourse, not having the money to buy them, was to make up a list of titles and disseminate it among my friends and acquaintances—*and*, among my readers. The men and women whose names I have given at the close of this volume supplied me with my wants. Many of these were simply readers whom I got to know through correspondence. The "friends" who could most afford to send me the books I so sorely needed, and whom I counted upon, failed to come through. An experience of this sort is always illuminating. The friends who fail you are always replaced by new ones who appear at the critical moment and from the most unexpected quarters...

One of the few rewards an author obtains for his labors is the conversion of a reader into a warm, personal friend. One of the rare delights he experiences is to receive exactly the gift he was waiting for from an unknown reader. Every sincere writer has, I take it, hundreds, perhaps thousands, of such unknown friends among his readers. There may be, and doubtless are, authors who have little need of their readers except as purchasers of their books. My case is somewhat different. I have need of every one. I am a borrower and a lender. I make use of any and all who volunteer their aid. I would be ashamed not to accept these gracious overtures. The latest one was from a student at Yale, Donald A. Schön. In filing a letter of mine to Professor Henri Peyre of the French Department there, a letter in which I had made an appeal for clerical help, this young man read my letter and spontaneously offered his services. (A grand gesture ! Sehr Schön !)

A case in point is the fortuitous emergence of John Kidis of Sacramento. A request for a signed photograph led to a brief interchange of letters followed by a visit and a shower of gifts. John Kidis (originally Mestakidis) is a Greek, which explains much. But it doesn't explain everything. I don't know which I appreciate the more, the armfuls of books (some of them very difficult to find) which he dumped on my desk or the never-ceasing flow of gifts, viz., sweaters and socks of pure wool and nylon, knitted by his mother, trousers, caps, and other articles of clothing picked up here and there, Greek pastries (such delicious delicacies !) prepared by his grandmother or his aunt, tins of Halva, jugs of rezina, toys for the children, writing materials (paper, envelopes of all kinds, post cards with my name and address printed on them, carbon paper, pencils, blotters), circulars and announcements, baptismal towels (his father is a priest), dates and nuts of all kinds, fresh figs, oranges, apples, even pomegranates (all from the mythical " farm "), to say nothing of the typing he did for me, or the printing (*The Waters Reglitterized*, for example), the water colors he bought, the paper and paints he supplied me with, the errands he volunteered to run, the books he sold for me (throwing out all his other stock-in-trade and setting himself up as " The House of Henry Miller "), the tires he bought for me, the music he offered to get me (records, sheet music, albums), and so on and so on ad infinitum. . . . How is one to account for such generosity ? How ever repay it ?

It goes without saying, I trust, that I shall welcome from the readers of this book any and all indications of error, omission, falsification or misjudgment. I am well aware that this book, because it is " about books," will go to many who have never read me before. I hope that they will spread the good word, not about *this* book, but about the books *they* love. Our world is rapidly drawing to a close ; a new one is about to open. If it is to flourish it will have to rest on deeds as well as faith. The word will have to become flesh.

There are few among us today who are able to view the immediate future with anything but fear and apprehension. If there is one book among all those I have recently read which I might signal as containing words of comfort, peace, inspiration and sublimity, it is Henry Adams' *Mont-Saint-Michel and Chartres.* Particularly the chapters dealing with Chartres and the cult of the Virgin Mary. Every reference to the " Queen " is exalted and commanding. Let me quote a passage—page 194*—which is in order :

> There she actually is—not in symbol or in fancy, but in person, descending on her errands of mercy and listening to each one of us, as her miracles prove, or satisfying our prayers merely by her presence which calms our excitement as that of a mother calms her child. She is there as Queen, not merely as intercessor, and her power is such that to her the difference between us earthly beings is nothing. Pierre Mauclerc and Philippe Hurepel and their men-at-arms are afraid of her, and the Bishop himself is never quite at his ease in her presence ; but to peasants, and beggars, and people in trouble, this sense of her power and calm is better than active sympathy. People who suffer beyond the formulas of expression—who are crushed into silence, and beyond pain—want no display of emotion —no bleeding heart—no weeping at the foot of the Cross —no hysterics—no phrases ! They want to see God, and to know that He is watching over His own.

There are writers, such as this man, who enrich us—and others who impoverish us. However it be, there is all the while a more important thing going on. All the while, whether we enrich or impoverish, we who write, we authors, we men of letters, we scribblers, are being supported, protected, maintained, enriched and endowed by a vast horde of unknown individuals—the men and women who watch and pray, so to speak, that we reveal the truth which is in us. How vast this multitude is no man knows. No one artist has ever reached the whole great throbbing mass

* From the Houghton, Mifflin Co. edition, Boston and New York, 1933.

of humanity. We swim in the same stream, we drink from the same source, yet how often or how deeply are we aware, we who write, of the common need ? If to write books is to restore what we have taken from the granary of life, from sisters and brothers unknown, then I say : " *Let us have more books !* "

In the second volume of this work I shall write, among other things, of Pornography and Obscenity, Gilles de Rais, Haggard's *Ayesha*, Marie Corelli, Dostoievsky's *Grand Inquisitor*, Céline, Maeterlinck, Berdyaev, Claude Houghton and Malaparte. The index of all references to all books and authors cited in all of my books will be included in the second volume.

HENRY MILLER.

I

THEY WERE ALIVE AND THEY SPOKE TO ME

I SIT in a little room, one wall of which is now completely lined with books. It is the first time I have had the pleasure of working with anything like a collection of books. There are probably no more than five hundred in all, but for the most part they represent my own choice. It is the first time, since I began my writing career, that I am surrounded with a goodly number of the books I have always longed to possess. The fact, however, that in the past I did most of my work without the aid of a library I look upon as an advantage rather than a disadvantage.

One of the first things I associate with the reading of books is the struggle I waged to obtain them. Not to own them, mind you, but to lay hands on them. From the moment the passion took hold of me I encountered nothing but obstacles. The books I wanted, at the public library, were always out. And of course I never had the money to buy them. To get permission from the library in my neighborhood—I was then eighteen or nineteen years of age—to borrow such a " demoralizing " work as *The Confession of a Fool*, by Strindberg, was just impossible. In those days the books which young people were prohibited from reading were decorated with stars—one, two or three—according to the degree of immorality attributed to them. I suspect this procedure still obtains. I hope so, for I know of nothing better calculated to whet one's appetite than this stupid sort of classification and prohibition.

What makes a book live? How often this question arises! The answer, in my opinion, is simple. A book lives through the passionate recommendation of one reader to another. Nothing can throttle this basic impulse in the human being. Despite the views of cynics and misanthropes, it is my belief that men will always strive to share their deepest experiences.

Books are one of the few things men cherish deeply. And the

better the man the more easily will he part with his most cherished possessions. A book lying idle on a shelf is wasted ammunition. Like money, books must be kept in constant circulation. Lend and borrow to the maximum—of both books and money ! But especially books, for books represent infinitely more than money. A book is not only a friend, it makes friends for you. When you have possessed a book with mind and spirit, you are enriched. But when you pass it on you are enriched threefold.

Here an irrepressible impulse seizes me to offer a piece of gratuitous advice. It is this : read as little as possible, not as much as possible ! Oh, do not doubt that I have envied those who drowned themselves in books. I, too, would secretly like to wade through all those books I have so long toyed with in my mind. But I know it is not important. I know now that I did not need to read even a tenth of what I have read. The most difficult thing in life is to learn to do only what is strictly advantageous to one's welfare, strictly vital.

There is an excellent way to test this precious bit of advice I have not given rashly. When you stumble upon a book you would like to read, or think you ought to read, leave it alone for a few days. But think about it as intensely as you can. Let the title and the author's name revolve in your mind. Think what you yourself might have written had the opportunity been yours. Ask yourself earnestly if it be absolutely necessary to add this work to your store of knowledge or your fund of enjoyment. Try to imagine what it would mean to forego this extra pleasure or enlightenment. Then, if you find you *must* read the book, observe with what extraordinary acumen you tackle it. Observe, too, that however stimulating it may be, very little of the book is really new to you. If you are honest with yourself you will discover that your stature has increased from the mere effort of resisting your impulses.

Indubitably the vast majority of books overlap one another. Few indeed are those which give the impression of originality, either in style or content. Rare are the unique books—less than fifty, perhaps, out of the whole storehouse of literature. In one of his recent autobiographical novels, Blaise Cendrars points out that Rémy de Gourmont, because of his knowledge and awareness of this repetitive quality in books, was able to select and read all

23

that is worth while in the entire realm of literature. Cendrars himself—who would suspect it ?—is a prodigious reader. He reads most authors in their original tongue. Not only that, but when he likes an author he reads every last book the man has written, as well as his letters and all the books that have been written about him. In our day his case is almost unparalleled, I imagine. For, not only has he read widely and deeply, but he has himself written a great many books. All on the side, as it were. For, if he is anything, Cendrars, he is a man of action, an adventurer and explorer, a man who has known how to " waste " his time royally. He is, in a sense, the Julius Caesar of literature.

The other day, at the request of the French publisher, Gallimard, I made up a list of the hundred books* which I thought had influenced me most. A strange list, indeed, containing such incongruous titles as *Peck's Bad Boy*, *Letters from the Mahatmas* and *Pitcairn Island*. The first named, a decidedly " bad " book, I read as a boy. I thought it worth including in my list because no other book ever made me laugh so heartily. Later, in my teens, I made periodical trips to the local library to paw the books on the shelf labelled "Humor." How few I found which were really humorous ! This is the one realm of literature which is woefully meagre and deficient. After citing *Huckleberry Finn*, *The Crock of Gold*, *Lysistrata*, *Dead Souls*, two or three of Chesterton's works, and *Juno and the Paycock*, I am hard put to it to mention anything outstanding in this category of humor. There are passages in Dostoievsky and in Hamsun, it is true, which still bring tears of laughter to my eyes, but they are only passages. The professional humorists, and their names are legion, bore me to death. Books on humor, such as Max Eastman's, Arthur Koestler's, or Bergson's, I also find deadly. It would be an achievement, I feel, if I could write just one humorous book before I die. The Chinese, incidentally, possess a sense of humor which is very close, very dear, to me. Particularly their poets and philosophers.

In books for children, which influence us the most—I mean fairy tales, legends, myths, allegories—humor is, of course, woefully absent. Horror and tragedy, lust and cruelty, seem to be the cardinal ingredients. But it is through the reading of these books that the

* See Appendix.

imaginative faculty is nourished. As we grow older, fantasy and imagination become increasingly rare to find. One is carried along on a treadmill which grows increasingly monotonous. The mind becomes so dulled that it takes a truly extraordinary book to rout one out of a state of indifference or apathy.

With childhood reading there is a factor of significance which we are prone to forget—the physical ambiance of the occasion. How distinctly, in after years, one remembers the feel of a favorite book, the typography, the binding, the illustrations, and so on. How easily one can localize the time and place of a first reading. Some books are associated with illness, some with bad weather, some with punishment, some with reward. In the remembrance of these events the inner and outer worlds fuse. These readings are distinctly " events " in one's life.

There is one thing, moreover, which differentiates the reading done in childhood from later reading, and that is the absence of choice. The books one reads as a child are thrust upon one. Lucky the child who has wise parents ! So powerful, however, is the dominion of certain books that even the ignorant parent can hardly avoid them. What child has not read *Sinbad the Sailor, Jason and the Golden Fleece, Ali Baba and the Forty Thieves*, the *Fairy Tales* of Grimm and Andersen, *Robinson Crusoe, Gulliver's Travels* and such like ?

Who also, I ask, has not enjoyed the uncanny thrill which comes later in life on rereading his early favorites ? Only recently, after the lapse of almost fifty years, I reread Henty's *Lion of the North*. What an experience ! As a boy, Henty was my favorite author. Every Christmas my parents would give me eight or ten of his books. I must have read every blessed one before I was fourteen. Today, and I regard this as phenomenal, I can pick up any book of his and get the same fascinating pleasure I got as a boy. He does not seem to be " talking down " to his reader. He seems, rather, to be on intimate terms with him. Everyone knows, I presume, that Henty's books are historical romances. To the lads of my day they were vitally important, because they gave us our first perspective of world history. *The Lion of the North*, for instance, is about Gustavus Adolphus and the Thirty Years' War. In it appears that strange, enigmatic figure—Wallenstein. When, just

25

the other day, I came upon the pages dealing with Wallenstein, it was as though I had read them only a few months ago. As I remarked in a letter to a friend, after closing the book, it was in these pages about Wallenstein that I first encountered the words "destiny" and "astrology." Pregnant words, for a boy, at any rate.

I began by speaking of my "library." Only lately I had the pleasure of reading about the life and times of Montaigne. Like ours, his was an age of intolerance, persecution, and wholesale massacres. I had often heard, to be sure, of Montaigne's withdrawal from active life, of his devotion to books, of his quiet, sober life, so rich in inward ways. There, of course, was a man who could be said to possess a library ! For a moment I envied him. If, I thought to myself, I could have in this little room, right at my elbow, all the books which I cherished as a child, a boy, a young man, how fortunate I would be ! It was always my habit to mark excessively the books I liked. How wonderful it would be, thought I, to see those markings again, to know what were my opinions and reactions in that long ago. I thought of Arnold Bennett, of the excellent habit he had formed of inserting at the back of every book he read a few blank pages whereon he might record his notes and impressions as he went along. One is always curious to know what one was like, how one behaved, how one reacted to thoughts and events, at various periods in the past. In the marginal annotations of books one can easily discover one's former selves.

When one realizes the tremendous evolution of one's being which occurs in a lifetime one is bound to ask : " Does life cease with bodily death ? Have I not lived before ? Will I not appear again on earth or perhaps on some other planet ? Am I not truly imperishable, as is all else in the universe ? " Perhaps, too, one may be impelled to ask himself a still more important question : " *Did I learn my lesson here on earth ?* "

Montaigne, I noticed with pleasure, speaks frequently of his bad memory. He says that he was unable to recall the contents, or even his impressions, of certain books, many of which he had read not once but several times. I feel certain, however, that he must have had a good memory in other respects. Most everyone has a faulty, spotty memory. The men who can quote copiously and accurately from the thousands of books they have read, who can relate the plot of a novel in detail, who can give names and dates of historical events, and so on, possess a monstrous sort of memory which has always seemed repellent to me. I am one of those who have a weak memory in certain respects and a strong one in others. In short, just the kind of memory which is useful for me. When I really wish to recall something I can, though it may take considerable time and effort. I know quietly that nothing is lost. But I know also that it is important to cultivate a " forgettery." The flavor, the savor, the aroma, the ambiance, as well as the value or non-value of a thing, I never forget. The only kind of memory I wish to preserve is the Proustian sort. To know that there is this infallible, total, exact memory is sufficient for me. How often it happens that, in glancing through a book read long ago, one stumbles on passages whose every word has a burning, inexhaustible, unforgettable resonance ? Recently, in completing the script of the second book of *The Rosy Crucifixion*, I was obliged to turn to my notes, made many years ago, on Spengler's *Decline of the West*. There were certain passages, a considerable number, I might say, of which I had only to read the opening words and the rest followed like music. The sense of the words had lost, in some instances, some of the importance I once attached to them, but not the words themselves. Every time I struck these passages, for I had read them again and again, the language became more redolent, more pregnant, more charged with that mysterious quality which every great author embeds in his language and which is the mark of his uniqueness. At any rate, so impressed was I by the vitality and hypnotic character of these Spenglerian passages that I decided to quote a number of them in their entirety. It was an experiment which I felt obliged to conduct, an experiment between myself and my readers. The lines I chose to quote had become my very own and I felt that they had to be transmitted. Were they not every bit as important in my life as the haphazard encounters, crises and events which I had described as my own ? Why not pass Oswald Spengler on intact also since he was an event in my life ?

I am one of those readers who, from time to time, copy out long passages from the books I read. I find these citations everywhere whenever I begin going through my belongings. They are never at my elbow, fortunately or unfortunately. Sometimes I spend whole days trying to recollect where I have secreted them. Thus, the other day, opening one of my Paris notebooks to look for something else, I stumbled on one of those passages which have lived with me for years. It is by Gautier from Havelock Ellis' Introduction to *Against the Grain*. It begins : " The poet of the *Fleurs du Mal* loved what is improperly called the style of decadence, and which is nothing else but art arrived at that point of extreme maturity yielded by the slanting suns of aged civilizations : an ingenious, complicated style, full of shades and of research, constantly pushing back the boundaries of speech, borrowing from all the technical vocabularies, taking color from all palettes and notes from all keyboards . . ." Then follows a sentence which always pops up like a flashing semaphore : " The style of decadence is the ultimate utterance of the Word, summoned to final expression and driven to its last hiding-place."

Utterances such as these I have often copied out in large letters and placed above my door so that, in leaving, my friends would be sure to read them. Some people have the opposite compulsion —they keep these precious revelations secret. My weakness is to shout from the rooftop whenever I believe I have discovered something of vital importance. On finishing a wonderful book, for example, I almost always sit down and write letters to my friends, sometimes to the author, and occasionally to the publisher. The experience becomes a part of my daily conversation, enters into the very food and drink I consume. I called this a weakness. Perhaps it is not. " Increase and multiply ! " commanded the Lord. E. Graham Howe, author of *War Dance*, put it another way, which I like even better. " Create and share!" he counseled. And, though reading may not at first blush seem like an act of creation, in a deep sense it is. Without the enthusiastic reader, who is really the author's counterpart and very often his most secret rival, a book would die. The man who spreads the good word augments not only the life of the book in question but the act of creation itself. He breathes spirit into other readers. He sustains the creative spirit everywhere. Whether he is aware of it or not, what he is doing is praising God's handiwork. For, the good reader, like the good author, knows that everything stems from the same source. He knows that he could not participate in the author's private experience were he not composed of the same substance through and through. And when I say author I mean Author. The writer is, of course, the best of all readers, for in writing, or " creating," as it is called, he is but reading and transcribing the great message of creation which the Creator in his goodness has made manifest to him.

In the Appendix the reader will find a list of authors and titles arranged in a frank and curious way.* I mention it because I think it important to stress at the outset a psychological fact about the reading of books which is rather neglected in most works on the subject. It is this : many of the books one lives with in one's mind are books one has never read. Sometimes these take on amazing importance. There are at least three categories of this order. The first comprises those books which one has every intention of reading some day but in all probability never will ; the second comprises those books which one feels he ought to have read, and which, some at least, he undoubtedly will read before he dies ; the third comprises the books one hears about, talks about, reads about, but which one is almost certain never to read because nothing, seemingly, can ever break down the wall of prejudice erected against them.

In the first category are those monumental works, classics mostly, which one is usually ashamed to admit he has never read : tomes one nibbles at occasionally, only to push them away, more than ever convinced that they are still unreadable. The list varies with the individual. For myself, to give a few outstanding names, they comprise the works of such celebrated authors as Homer, Aristotle, Francis Bacon, Hegel, Rousseau (excepting *Emile*), Robert Browning, Santayana. In the second category I include *Arabia Deserta*, the *Decline and Fall of the Roman Empire*, *The Hundred and Twenty Days of Sodom*, Casanova's *Memoirs*, Napoleon's *Memoirs*, Michelet's *History of the French Revolution*. In the third Pepys' *Diary*, *Tristram Shandy*, *Wilhelm Meister*, *The Anatomy of Melancholy*, *The Red and the Black*, *Marius the Epicurean*, *The Education of Henry Adams*.

Sometimes a chance reference to an author one has neglected to read or abandoned all thought of ever reading—a passage, say, in the work of an author one admires, or the words of a friend who is

* That is, those I have read and those I still hope to read.

also a book lover—is sufficient to make one run for a book, read it with new eyes and claim it as one's very own. In the main, however, the books one neglects, or deliberately spurns, seldom get read. Certain subjects, certain styles, or unfortunate associations connected with the very names of certain books, create a repugnance almost insuperable. Nothing on earth, for example, could induce me to tackle anew Spenser's *Faery Queen*, which I began in college and fortunately dropped because I left that institution in a hurry. Never again will I look at a line of Edmund Burke, or Addison, or Chaucer, though the last-named I think altogether worthy of reading. Racine and Corneille are two others I doubt if I shall ever look at again, though Corneille intrigues me because of a brilliant essay I read not long ago on *Phèdre* in *The Clown's Grail*.* On the other hand there are books which lie at the very foundations of literature but which are so remote from one's thinking and experience as to render them "untouchable." Certain authors, supposed to be the bulwark of our particular Western culture, are more foreign in spirit to me than are the Chinese, the Arabs, or primitive peoples. Some of the most exciting literary works spring from cultures which have not contributed directly to our development. No fairy tales, for example, have exercised a more potent influence over me than those of the Japanese, which I became acquainted with through the work of Lafcadio Hearn, one of the exotic figures in American literature. No stories were more seductive to me as a child than those drawn from the *Arabian Nights' Entertainment*. American Indian folklore leaves me cold, whereas the folklore of Africa is near and dear to me.† And, as I have said repeatedly, whatever I read of Chinese literature (barring Confucius) seems as if written by my immediate ancestors.

I said that sometimes it is an esteemed author who puts one on the track of a buried book. "What! He liked *that* book?" you say to yourself, and immediately the barriers fall away and the mind becomes not only open and receptive but positively aflame. Often it happens that it is not a friend of similar tastes who revives one's interest in a dead book but a chance acquaintance. Sometimes this

---

* By Wallace Fowlie. Sub-title : *A Study of Love in its Literary Expression* ; Dennis Dobson, Ltd., London, 1947.
† See Cendrars' *African Anthology*.

individual gives the impression of being a nitwit, and one wonders why he should retain the memory of a book which this person casually recommended, or perhaps did not recommend at all but merely mentioned in the course of conversation as being an "odd" book. In a vacant mood, at loose ends, as we say, suddenly the recollection of this conversation occurs, and we are ready to give the book a trial. Then comes a hock, the shock of discovery. *Wuthering Heights* is for me an example of this sort. From having heard it praised so much and so often, I had concluded that it was impossible for an English novel—by a woman !—to be that good. Then one day a friend, whose taste I suspected to be shallow, let drop a few pregnant words about it. Though I promptly proceeded to forget his remarks, the poison sank into me. Without realizing it, I nurtured a secret resolve to have a look at this famous book one day. Finally, just a few years ago, Jean Varda put it in my hands.★ I read it in one gulp, astounded as is everyone, I suspect, by its amazing power and beauty. Yes, one of the very great novels in the English language. And I, through pride and prejudice, had almost missed reading it.

Quite another story is that of *The City of God*. Many years ago I had, like everyone else, read the *Confessions* of St. Augustine. And it had made a deep impression. Then, in Paris, some one thrust upon me *The City of God*, in two volumes. I found it not only boring and deadly, but in parts monstrously ridiculous. An English bookseller, hearing from a mutual friend—to his surprise, no doubt— that I had read this work informed me that he could get a good price for it if I would only annotate it. I sat down to read it once again, taking elaborate pains to make copious remarks, usually derogatory, in the margins ; after spending a month or so at this vain task I dispatched the book to England. Twenty years later I received a post card from this same bookseller stating that he hoped to sell the copy in a few days—he had found a buyer for it at last. And that was the last I heard from him. Drôle d'histoire !

Throughout my life the word "confessions" in a title has always acted like a magnet. I mentioned Strindberg's *Confession of a Fool*. I should also have mentioned Marie Bashkirtseff's famous work

★ He also put into my hands another amazing book, *Hebdomeros*, by the painter, Giorgio di Chirico.

31

and the *Confessions of Two Brothers* by Powys. There are some very celebrated confessions, however, which I have never been able to wade through. One is Rousseau's, another is de Quincey's. Only recently I took another stab at Rousseau's *Confessions*, but after a few pages was forced to abandon it. His *Emile*, on the other hand, I fully intend to read—when I can find a copy with readable type. The little I did read of it had an extraordinary appeal.

I believe they are woefully mistaken who assert that the foundations of knowledge or culture, or any foundations whatsoever, are necessarily those classics which are found in every list of " best " books. I know that there are several universities which base their entire curricula on such select lists. It is my opinion that each man has to dig his own foundations. If one is an individual at all it is by reason of his uniqueness. Whatever the material which vitally affected the form of our culture, each man must decide for himself which elements of it are to enter into and shape his own private destiny. The great works which are singled out by the professorial minds represent *their* choice exclusively. It is in the nature of such intellects to believe that they are our appointed guides and mentors. It may be that, if left to our own devices, we would in time share their point of view. But the surest way to defeat such an end is to promulgate the reading of select lists of books—the so-called foundation stones. A man should begin with his own times. He should become acquainted first of all with the world in which he is living and participating. He should not be afraid of reading too much or too little. He should take his reading as he does his food or his exercise. The good reader will gravitate to the good books. He will discover from his contemporaries what is inspiring or fecundating, or merely enjoyable, in past literature. He should have the pleasure of making these discoveries on his own, in his own way. What has worth, charm, beauty, wisdom, cannot be lost or forgotten. But things can lose all value, all charm and appeal, if one is dragged to them by the scalp. Have you not noticed, after many heart-aches and disillusionments, that in recommending a book to a friend the less said the better ? The moment you praise a book too highly you awaken resistance in your listener. One has to know when to give the dose and how much—and if it is to be repeated or not. The gurus of India and Tibet, it is often pointed out, have for ages practiced the high art of *discouraging* their ardent would-be disciples. The same sort of strategy might well be applied where the reading of books is concerned. Discourage a man in the right way, that is, with the right end in view, and you will put him on the path that much more quickly. The important thing is not *which* books, *which* experiences, a man is to have, but what he puts into them of his own.

One of the most mysterious of all the intangibles in life is what we call influences. Undoubtedly influences come under the law of attraction. But it should be borne in mind that when we are pulled in a certain direction it is also because we pushed in that direction, perhaps without knowing it. It is obvious that we are not at the mercy of any and every influence. Nor are we always cognizant of the forces and factors which influence us from one period to another. Some men never know themselves or what motivates their behavior. Most men, in fact. With others the sense of destiny is so clear, so strong, that there hardly seems to be any choice : they create the influences needed to fulfill their ends. I use the word " create " deliberately, because in certain startling instances the individual has literally been obliged to create the necessary influences. We are on strange grounds here. My reason for introducing such an abstruse element is that, where books are concerned, just as with friends, lovers, adventures and discoveries, all is inextricably mixed. The desire to read a book is often provoked by the most unexpected incident. To begin with, everything that happens to a man is of a piece. The books he chooses to read are no exception. He may have read Plutarch's *Lives* or *The Fifteen Decisive Battles of the World* because a doting aunt thrust them under his nose. He may not have read them if he detested this aunt. Of the thousands of titles which come under one's ken, even early in life, how is it that one individual steers straight towards certain authors and another towards others ? The books a man reads are determined by what a man is. If a man be left alone in a room with a book, a single book, it does not follow that he will read it because he has nothing better to do. If the book bores him he will drop it, though he may go wellnigh mad for want of anything better to do. Some men, in reading, take the pains to look up every reference given in the footnotes ; others again never even glance at footnotes. Some men will undertake arduous journeys to read a book whose title alone has intrigued

C

them. The adventures and discoveries of Nicholas Flamel in connection with the Book of Abraham the Jew constitute one of the golden pages in literature.

As I was saying, the chance remark of a friend, an unexpected encounter, a footnote, illness, solitude, strange quirks of memory, a thousand and one things can set one off in pursuit of a book. There are times when one is susceptible to any and all suggestions, hints, intimations. And there are times again when it takes dynamite to put one afoot and astir.

One of the great temptations, for a writer, is to read when engaged in the writing of a book. With me it seems that the moment I begin a new book I develop a passion for reading too. In fact, due to some perverse instinct, the moment I am launched on a new book I itch to do a thousand different things—not, as is often the case, out of a desire to escape the task of writing. What I find is that I can write *and* do other things. When the creative urge seizes one—at least, such is my experience—one becomes creative in all directions at once.

It was in the days before I undertook to write, I must confess, that reading was at once the most voluptuous and the most pernicious of pastimes. Looking backward, it seems to me as if the reading of books was nothing more than a narcotic, stimulating at first but depressing and paralyzing afterwards. From the time I began in earnest to write, the reading habit altered. A new element crept into it. A fecundating element, I might say. As a young man I often thought, on putting a book down, that I could have done much better myself. The more I read the more critical I became. Hardly anything was good enough for me. Gradually I began to despise books—and authors too. Often the writers I had most adored were the ones I castigated mercilessly. There was always a fringe of authors, to be sure, whose magic powers baffled and eluded me. As the time approached for me to assert my own powers of expression I began to reread these "spellbinders" with new eyes. I read cold-bloodedly, with all the powers of analysis I possessed. In order, believe it or not, to rob them of their secret. Yes, I was then naïve enough to believe that I could discover what makes the clock tick by taking it apart. Vain and foolish though my behavior was, this period stands out, nevertheless, as one of the most rewarding of all

34

my bouts with books. I learned something about style, about the art of narration, about effects and how they are produced. Best of all, I learned that there really is a mystery involved in the creation of good books. To say, for example, that the style is the man, is to say almost nothing. Even when we have the man we have next to nothing. The way a man writes, the way he speaks, the way he walks, the way he does everything, is unique and inscrutable. The important thing, so obvious that one usually overlooks it, is not to wonder about such matters but to listen to what a man has to say, to let his words move you, alter you, make you more and more what you truly are.

The most important factor in the appreciation of any art is the practice of it. There is the wonder and intoxication of the child when it first encounters the world of books ; there is the ecstasy and despair of youth in discovering his " own " authors ; but greater than these, because combined with them are other more permanent and quickening elements, are the perceptions and reflections of a mature being who has dedicated his life to the task of creation. In reading Van Gogh's letters to his brother, one is struck by the vast amount of meditation, analysis, comparison, adoration and criticism he indulged in during the course of his brief and frenzied career as a painter. It is not uncommon, among painters, but in Van Gogh's case it reaches heroic proportions. Van Gogh was not only looking at nature, people, objects, but at other men's canvases, studying their methods, techniques, styles and approaches. He reflected long and earnestly on what he observed, and these thoughts and observations penetrated his work. He was anything but a primitive, or a " fauve." Like Rimbaud, he was nearer to being " a mystic in the wild state."

It is not altogether by accident that I have chosen a painter rather than a writer to illustrate my point. It happens that Van Gogh, without having any literary pretensions whatever, wrote one of the great books of our time, and without knowing that he was writing a book. His life, as we get it in the letters, is more revelatory, more moving, more a work of art, I would say, than are most of the famous autobiographies or autobiographical novels. He tells us unreservedly of his struggles and sorrows, withholding nothing. He displays his rare knowledge of the painter's craft, though he is acclaimed more for his passion and his vision than for his knowledge

35

of the medium. His life, in that it makes clear the value and the meaning of dedication, is a lesson for all time. Van Gogh is at one and the same time—and of how few men can we say this!—the humble disciple, the student, the lover, the brother of all men, the critic, the analyst, and the doer of good deeds. He may have been obsessed, or possessed rather, but he was not a fanatic working in the dark. He possessed, for one thing, that rare faculty of being able to criticize and judge his own work. He proved, indeed, to be a much better critic and judge than those whose business it unfortunately is to criticize, judge and condemn.

The more I write the more I understand what others are trying to tell me in their books. The more I write the more tolerant I grow with regard to my fellow writers. (I am not including "bad" writers, for with them I refuse to have any traffic.) But with those who are sincere, with those who are honestly struggling to express themselves, I am much more lenient and understanding than in the days when I had not yet written a book. I can learn from the poorest writer, provided he has done his utmost. Indeed, I have learned a very great deal from certain "poor" writers. In reading their works I have been struck time and again by that freedom and boldness which it is almost impossible to recapture once one is "in harness," once one is aware of the laws and limitations of his medium. But it is in reading one's favorite authors that one becomes supremely aware of the value of practicing the art of writing. One reads then with the right and the left eye. Without the least diminution of the sheer enjoyment of reading, one becomes aware of a marvellous heightening of consciousness. In reading these men the element of the mysterious never recedes, but the vessel in which their thoughts are contained becomes more and more transparent. Drunk with ecstasy, one returns to his own work revivified. Criticism is converted into reverence. One begins to pray as one never prayed before. One no longer prays for oneself but for Brother Giono, Brother Cendrars, Brother Céline—for the whole galaxy of fellow authors, in fact. One accepts the uniqueness of his fellow artist unreservedly, realizing that it is only through one's uniqueness that one asserts his commonness. One no longer asks for something *different* of his beloved author but for more of the same. Even the ordinary reader testifies to this longing. Does he not say, on finishing the last volume of his favorite author : " If only he had written a few more books ! " When, after an author is dead some time, a forgotten manuscript is dug up, or a bundle of letters, or an unknown diary, what a cry of exultation goes up ! What gratitude for even the tiniest posthumous fragment ! Even the perusal of an author's expense account gives us a thrill. The moment a writer dies his life suddenly becomes of momentous interest to us. His death often enables us to see what we could not see when he was alive—that his life and work were one. Is it not obvious that the art of resuscitation (biography) masks a profound hope and longing ? We are not content to let Balzac, Dickens, Dostoievsky remain immortal in their works—we want to restore them in the flesh. Each age strives to join the great men of letters with its own, to incorporate the pattern and significance of their lives in its own. Sometimes it seems as though the influence of the dead were more potent than the influence of the living. If the Saviour had not been resurrected, man would certainly have resurrected Him through grief and longing. That Russian author who spoke of the " necessity " of resurrecting the dead spoke truly.

They were alive and they spoke to me! That is the simplest and most eloquent way in which I can refer to those authors who have remained with me over the years. Is this not a strange thing to say, considering that we are dealing, in books, with signs and symbols ? Just as no artist has ever succeeded in rendering nature on canvas, so no author has ever truly been able to give us his life and thoughts. Autobiography is the purest romance. Fiction is always closer to reality than fact. The fable is not the essence of worldly wisdom but the bitter shell. One might go on, through all the ranks and divisions of literature, unmasking history, exposing the myths of science, devaluating aesthetics. Nothing, on deep analysis, proves to be what it seems or purports to be. Man continues to hunger.

They were alive and they spoke to me! Is it not strange to understand and enjoy what is incommunicable ? Man is not *communicating* with man through words, he is communing with his fellow man and with his Maker. Over and over again one puts down a book and one is speechless. Sometimes it is because the author seems " to have said everything." But I am not thinking of this sort of reaction. I am thinking that this business of becoming mute corresponds to something much deeper. It is from the silence that words are drawn, and it is to the silence that they return, if properly used. In the interval something inexplicable takes place : a man who is dead, let us say, resuscitates himself, takes possession of you, and in departing leaves you thoroughly altered. He did this by means of signs and symbols. Was this not magic which he possessed—perhaps still possesses ?

Though we know it not, we do possess the key to paradise. We talk a great deal about understanding and communicating, not only with our fellow man but with the dead, with the unborn, with those who inhabit other realms, other universes. We believe that there are mighty secrets to be unlocked. We hope that science will point the way, or if not, religion. We dream of a life in the distant future which will be utterly different from the one we now know ; we invest ourselves with powers unnameable. Yet the writers of books have ever given evidence not only of magical powers but of the existence of universes which infringe and invade our own little universe and which are as familiar to us as though we had visited them in the flesh. These men had no " occult " masters to initiate them. They sprang from parents similar to our own, they were the products of environments similar to our own. What makes them stand apart then ? Not the use of imagination, for men in other walks of life have displayed equally great powers of imagination. Not the mastery of a technique, for other artists practice equally difficult techniques. No, to me the cardinal fact about a writer is his ability to " exploit " the vast silence which enwraps us all. Of all artists he is the one who best knows that " in the beginning was the Word and the Word was with God and the Word *was* God." He has caught the spirit which informs all creation and he has rendered it in signs and symbols. Pretending to communicate with his fellow creatures, he has unwittingly taught us to commune with the Creator. Using language as his instrument, he demonstrates that it is not language at all but prayer. A very special kind of prayer, too, since nothing is demanded of the Creator. " Blessings on thee, O Lord ! " So it runs, no matter what the subject, what the idiom. " Let me exhaust myself, O Lord, in singing thy praises ! "

Is this not " the heavenly work " of which it has been spoken ?

Let us cease to wonder what they, the great, the illustrious ones, are doing in the beyond. Know that they are still singing hymns of praise. Here on earth they may have been practicing. *There* they are perfecting their song.

Once again I must mention the Russians, those obscure ones of the Nineteenth Century, who knew that there is only one task, one supreme joy—to establish the perfect life here on earth.*

---

* In 1880 Dostoievsky made a speech on " The Mission of Russia " in which he said : " To become a true Russian is to become the brother of all men, a universal man. . . . Our future lies in Universality, not won by violence, but by the strength derived from our great ideal—the reuniting of all mankind."

II

EARLY READING

It is only in the last few years that I have begun to reread—certain books. I can recall with accuracy the first books I singled out to reread : *The Birth of Tragedy, The Eternal Husband, Alice in Wonderland, The Imperial Orgy*, Hamsun's *Mysteries*. Hamsun, as I have often said, is one of the authors who vitally affected me *as writer*. None of his books intrigued me as much as *Mysteries*. In that period I spoke of earlier, when I began to take my favorite authors apart in order to discover their secret power of enchantment, the men I concentrated on were Hamsun first of all, then Arthur Machen, then Thomas Mann. When I came to reread *The Birth of Tragedy* I remember being positively stunned by Nietzsche's magical use of language. Only a few years ago, thanks to Eva Sikelianou, I became intoxicated once again with this extraordinary book.

I mentioned Thomas Mann. For a whole year I lived with Hans Castorp of *The Magic Mountain* as with a living person, as with a blood brother, I might even say. But it was Mann's skill as a writer of short stories, or novelettes, which most intrigued and baffled me during the "analytical" period I speak of. At that time *Death in Venice* was for me the supreme short story. In the space of a few years, however, my opinion of Thomas Mann, and especially of his *Death in Venice*, altered radically. It is a curious tale and perhaps worth recounting. It was like this . . . During my early days in Paris I made the acquaintance of a most engaging and provocative individual whom I believed to be a genius. John Nichols was his name. He was a painter. Like so many Irishmen, he also possessed the gift of gab. It was a privilege to listen to him, whether he were discussing painting, literature, music, or talking sheer nonsense. He had a flair for invective, and, when he waxed strong, his tongue was vitriolic. One day I happened to speak of my admiration for Thomas Mann and, before long, I found myself raving about *Death in Venice*. Nichols responded with jeers and contempt. In exasperation I told him I would get the book and read the story aloud to him. He admitted he had never read it and thought my proposal an excellent one.

I shall never forget this experience. Before I had read three pages Thomas Mann began to crumble. Nichols, mind you, had not said a word. But reading the story aloud, and to a critical ear, suddenly the whole creaking machinery which underlay this fabrication exposed itself. I, who thought I was holding in my hands a piece of pure gold, found myself looking at a piece of papier-mâché. Halfway through I flung the book on the floor. Later on I glanced through *The Magic Mountain* and *Buddenbrooks*, works I had regarded as monumental, only to find them equally meretricious.

This sort of experience, I must quickly add, has happened but seldom to me. There was one outstanding one—I blush to mention it!—and that was in connection with *Three Men in a Boat*. How on earth I had ever managed to find that book " funny " is beyond my comprehension. Yet I had, once. Indeed, I remember that I laughed until the tears came to my eyes. The other day, after a lapse of thirty years, I picked it up and started to read it again. Never have I tasted a shoddier piece of tripe. Another disappointment, though much milder, lay in store for me on rereading *The Triumph of the Egg*. It came near to being a rotten egg.* But once it had made me laugh and weep.

Oh, who was I, *what* was I, in those dreary days of long ago ?

What I started to say is that, in rereading, I find more and more that the books I long to read again are the ones I read in childhood and early youth. I mentioned Henty, bless his name ! There are others—like Rider Haggard, Marie Corelli, Bulwer-Lytton, Eugene Sue, James Fenimore Cooper, Sienkiewicz, Ouida (*Under Two Flags*), Mark Twain (*Huckleberry Finn* and *Tom Sawyer* particularly). Imagine not having read any of these men since boyhood ! It seems incredible. As for Poe, Jack London, Hugo, Conan Doyle, Kipling, it matters little if I never look at their works again.†

I should also like very much to reread those books which I used

---

* It should not be inferred from this that I have turned against Sherwood Anderson, who has meant so much to me. I have still a great admiration for his *Winesburg, Ohio* and *Many Marriages*.

† For some mysterious reason I do, however, intend to read *Toilers of the Sea*, which I missed when I was devouring Hugo.

to read aloud to my grandfather as he sat on his tailor's bench in our old home in the Fourteenth Ward in Brooklyn. One of these, I recall, was about our great " hero " (for a day)—Admiral Dewey. Another was about Admiral Farragut—probably about the battle of Mobile Bay, if there ever was such an engagement. Regarding this book I recall now that, in writing the chapter called " My Dream of Mobile " in *The Air-conditioned Nightmare*, I was actively aware of this tale of Farragut's heroic exploits. Without a doubt, my whole conception of Mobile was colored by this book I had read fifty years ago. But it was through the book on Admiral Dewey that I became acquainted with my first live hero, who was not Dewey but our sworn enemy, Aguinaldo, the Filipino rebel. My mother had hung Dewey's portrait, floating above the battleship Maine, over my bed. Aguinaldo, whose likeness is now dim in my mind, links up physically with that strange photograph of Rimbaud taken in Abyssinia, the one wherein he stands in prison-like garb on the banks of a stream. Little did my parents realize, in handing me our precious hero, Admiral Dewey, that they were nurturing in me the seeds of a rebel. Beside Dewey and Teddy Roosevelt, Aguinaldo stands out like a colossus. He was the first Enemy Number One to cross my horizon. I still revere his name, just as I still revere the names of Robert E. Lee and Toussaint L'Ouverture, the great Negro liberator who fought Napoleon's picked men and worsted them.

In this vein how can I forbear mentioning Carlyle's *Heroes and Hero Worship* ? Or Emerson's *Representative Men* ? And why not make room for another early idol, John Paul Jones ? In Paris, thanks to Blaise Cendrars, I learned what is not given in history books or biographies concerning John Paul Jones. The spectacular story of this man's life is one of those projected books which Cendrars has not yet written and probably never will. The reason is simple. Following the trail of this adventurous American, Cendrars amassed such a wealth of material that he was swamped by it. In the course of his travels, searching for rare documents and buying up rare books relating to John Paul Jones' myriad adventures, Cendrars confessed that he had spent more than tenfold the amount given him by the publishers in advance royalties. Following John Paul Jones' traces, Cendrars had made a veritable Odyssean voyage. He confessed finally that he would one day either write a huge tome on the subject or a very thin book, something which I understand perfectly.

The first person to whom I ventured to read aloud was my grandfather. Not that he encouraged it ! I can still hear him saying to my mother that she would regret putting all those books in my hands. He was right. My mother did regret it bitterly, later. It was my own mother, incidentally, whom I can scarcely recall ever seeing with a book in her hand, who told me one day when I was reading *The Fifteen Decisive Battles of the World* that she had read that book years ago herself—in the toilet. I was flabbergasted. Not that she had admitted to reading in the toilet, but that it should have been that book, of all books, which she had read there.

Reading aloud to my boyhood friends, particularly to Joey and Tony, my earliest friends, was an eye-opener for me. I discovered early in life what some discover only much later, to their disgust and chagrin, namely, that reading aloud to people can put them to sleep. Either my voice was monotonous, either I read poorly, or the books I chose were the wrong sort. Inevitably my audience went to sleep on me. Which did not discourage me, incidentally, from continuing the practice. Nor did these experiences alter the opinion I had of my little friends. No, I came quietly to the conclusion that books were not for everyone. I still hold to that view. The last thing on earth I would counsel is to make everyone learn to read. If I had *my* way, I would first see to it that a boy learned to be a carpenter, a builder, a gardener, a hunter, a fisherman. The practical things first, by all means, then the luxuries. And books *are* luxuries. Of course I expect the normal youngster to dance and sing from infancy. And to play games. I would abet these tendencies with might and main. But the reading of books can wait.

To play games . . . Ah, there is a chapter of life in a category all by itself. I mean, primarily, out-of-door games—the games which poor children play in the streets of a big city. I pass up the temptation to expand on this subject lest I write another, very different, kind of book !

However, boyhood is a subject I never tire of. Neither the remembrance of the wild and glorious games we played by day and night in the streets, nor the characters with whom I hobnobbed and whom I sometimes deified, as boys are prone to do. All my experiences I shared with my comrades, including the experience of reading. Time and again, in my writings, I have made mention of the amazing acumen we displayed in discussing the fundamental problems of life. Subjects such as sin, evil, reincarnation, good government, ethics and morality, the nature of the deity, Utopia, life on other planets—these were food and drink to us. My real education was begun in the street, in empty lots on cold November days, or on street corners at night, frequently with out skates on. Naturally, one of the things we were forever discussing was books, the books we were then reading and which we were not even supposed to know about. It sounds extravagont to say so, I know, but it does seem to me that only the great interpreters of literature can rival the boy in the street when it comes to extracting the flavor and essence of a book. In my humble opinion, the boy is much nearer to understanding Jesus than the priest, much closer to Plato, in his views on government, than the political figures of this world.

During this golden period of boyhood there was suddenly injected into my world of books a whole library, housed in a beautiful walnut bookcase with glass doors and movable shelves, of boys' books. They were from the collection of an Englishman, Isaac Walker, my father's predecessor, who had the distinction of being one of the first merchant tailors of New York. As I review them now in my mind, these books were all handsomely bound, the titles embossed usually in gold, as were the cover designs. The paper was thick and glossy, the type bold and clear. In short, these books were de luxe in every respect. Indeed, so elegantly forbidding was their appearance, that it took some time before I dared tackle them.

What I am about to relate is a curious thing. It has to do with my deep and mysterious aversion for everything English. I believe I am telling the truth when I say that the cause of this antipathy is deeply connected with the reading of Isaac Walker's little library. How profound was my disgust, on becoming acquainted with the contents of these books, may be judged by the fact that I have completely forgotten the titles. Just one lingers in my memory, and even this one I am not positive is correct : *A Country Squire*. The rest is a blank. The nature of my reaction I can put in a few words. For the first time in my life I sensed the meaning of melancholy and morbidity. All these elegant books seemed wrapped in a veil of thick fog.

England became for me a land shrouded in murky obscurity, in evil, cruelty and boredom. Not one ray of light issued from these musty tomes. It was the primordial slime, on all levels. Senseless and irrational though it be, this picture of England and the English lasted well into middle life, until, to be honest, I visited England and had the opportunity of meeting Englishmen on their own native heath.* (My first impression of London, I must however admit, corresponded closely to my boyhood picture of it ; it is an impression which has never been wholly dissipated.)

When I came to Dickens, these first impressions were, of course, corroborated and strengthened. I have very few *pleasant* recollections connected with the reading of Dickens. His books were sombre, terrifying in parts, and usually boring. Of them all, *David Copperfield* stands out as the most enjoyable, the most nearly human, according to my conception (then) of the word. Fortunately, there was one book which had been given me by a good aunt,† which served as a corrective to this morose view of England and the English people. The title of this book, if I remember rightly, was *A Boy's History of England*, by Ellis. I remember distinctly the pleasure this book gave me. There were, to be sure, the Henty books, which I was also reading, or had read just a little earlier, and from which I gained a wholly different notion of the English world. But the Henty books were concerned with historical exploits, whereas the books from Isaac Walker's collection dealt with the immediate past. Years later, when I came upon Thomas Hardy's works, I relived these boyish reactions —the bad ones, I mean. Sombre, tragic, full of mishaps and accidental or coincidental misfortunes, Hardy's books caused me once again to adjust my " human " picture of the world. In the end I was obliged to pass judgment on Hardy. For all the air of realism which permeated his books, I had to admit to myself that they were not " true to life." I wanted my pessimism " straight."

On returning to America from France I met two individuals who were passionately fond of an English author whom I had never heard

---

* On reading that delightful and singularly imaginative book, *Land Under England* by Joseph O'Neill—just a few years back—the old feeling about England cropped up again. But this is a book by an Irishman, and an unusual one it is.

† This good aunt, my father's sister, also gave me *The Autocrat at the Breakfast Table*, a brace of books by Samuel Smiles, and *Knickerbocker's History of New York*.

of—Claude Houghton. "A metaphysical novelist," he is often called. At any rate, Claude Houghton has done more than any Englishman, with the exception of W. Travers Symons—the first "gentleman" I ever met !—to alter profoundly my picture of England. I have by now read the majority of his works. Whether the performance is good or bad, Claude Houghton's books captivate me. Many Americans know *I Am Jonathan Scrivener*, which would have made a wonderful movie, as would some of his others. His *Julian Grant Loses His Way*, one of my favorites, and *All Change, Humanity !* are less well known—more's the pity.

But there is one of Claude Houghton's books—here I touch upon a subject I hope to enlarge on later—which seems to have been written especially *for me*. It is called *Hudson Rejoins the Herd*. In a lengthy letter to the author I explained why this seemed to be so. This letter will one day be made public.* What so startled me, in reading this book, was that it appeared to give a picture of my most intimate life during a certain crucial period. The outer circumstances were "disguised," but the inner ones were hallucinatingly real. I could not have done better myself. For a time I thought that Claude Houghton had in some mysterious way gained access to these facts and events in my life. In the course of our correspondence, however, I soon discovered that all his works are imaginative. Perhaps the reader will be surprised to learn that I should think such a coincidence "mysterious." Do not the lives and characters in fiction frequently correspond to actual counterparts ? Of course. But still I am impressed. Those who think they know me intimately should have a look at this book.

And now, for no reason, unless it be the afterglow of boyhood reminiscences, there leaps to mind the name of Rider Haggard. He is one of the authors on the list of A Hundred Books I made up for Gallimard. *There* was a writer who had me in his thrall ! The contents of his books are vague and fuzzy. At best I can recall only a few titles : *She, Ayesha, King Solomon's Mines, Allan Quatermain.* Yet when I think of them I get the same shivers as I do when I relive the meeting between Stanley and Livingstone in darkest Africa. I am certain that when I reread him, as I expect to do shortly, I shall

---

* Not to be confused with the "Letter" ; Argus Books, Inc., Mohegan Lake, New York, 1950.

find, as I did with Henty, that my memory will become amazingly alive and fecund.

This adolescent period over, it becomes increasingly difficult to strike an author capable of producing an effect anywhere near that created by Rider Haggard's works. For reasons now inscrutable, *Trilby* came close to doing so. *Trilby* and *Peter Ibbetson* are a unique brace of books. That they should have come from a middle-aged illustrator, renowned for his drawings in " Punch," is more than interesting. In the introduction to *Peter Ibbetson*, published by the Modern Library, Deems Taylor relates how, " walking one night in High Street, Bayswater, with Henry James, Du Maurier offered his friend an idea for a novel, and proceeded to unfold the plot of *Trilby*." " James," he says, " declined the offer." *Fortunately*, I should say. I can imagine with dread what Henry James would have made of such a subject.

Oddly enough, the man who put me on the track of Du Maurier also put into my hands Flaubert's *Bouvard et Pécuchet*, which I did not open until thirty years later. He had given this volume and the *Sentimental Education* to my father in payment of a small debt he owed. My father, of course, was disgusted. With the *Sentimental Education* goes a queer association. Somewhere Bernard Shaw says that certain books cannot be appreciated, and should therefore not be read, until one is past fifty. One of those he cited was this famous work of Flaubert. It is another of those books, like *Tom Jones* and *Moll Flanders*, which I intend one day to read, particularly since I have " come of age."

But to return to Rider Haggard . . . Strange that a book such as *Nadja*, by André Breton, should in any way be linked with the emotional experiences engendered in reading Rider Haggard's works. I think it is in *The Rosy Crucifixion* that I have dwelt at some length—or was it in *Remember to Remember*?—upon the spell which *Nadja* will always cast over me. Each time I read it I go through the same inner turmoil, the same rather terrifyingly delicious sensation that seizes one, for example, upon finding himself completely disoriented in the pitch blackness of a room with every square inch of which he is thoroughly familiar. I recall singling out a section of

the book which reminded me vividly of my first piece of prose, or at
least the first I was to submit to an editor.* (As I write, I realize that
this statement is not quite true, because my very first piece of prose
was an essay on Nietzsche's *Anti-Christ*, which I wrote for myself
in my father's shop. Also, the first piece of writing I ever submitted
to an editor antedates the aforementioned piece by a few years,
being a critical article which I sent to the *Black Cat* magazine and
which, to my amazement, was accepted and paid for to the tune of
$1.75, or something like that, this trifling remuneration being
sufficient at the time to set me on fire, to make me throw a brand
new hat into the gutter, where it was immediately crushed by a
passing truck.)

Why an author of the magnitude of André Breton should be linked
in my mind with Rider Haggard, of all authors, is something which
would require pages to explain. Perhaps the association is not so
far-fetched after all, considering the peculiar sources from which the
Surrealists gathered inspiration, nourishment and corroboration.
Nadja is still, to my way of thinking, a unique book. (The photos
which accompany the text have a value all their own.) At any rate, it
is one of the few books I have reread several times with no rupture
of the original spell. This in itself, I do believe, is sufficient to mark
it out.

The word I have deliberately withheld, speaking of Rider Haggard
and of *Nadja*, is "mystery." This word, both in the singular and
the plural, I have reserved in order to treat of my delightful, all-
engrossing associations with dictionary and encyclopaedia. Many
is the time I spent whole days at the public library looking up words
or subjects. Here again, to be truthful, I must say that *the* most
wonderful days were passed at home, with my boon companion
Joe O'Regan. Bleak, wintry days, when food was scarce and all
hope or thought of obtaining employment had vanished. Mingled
with the dictionary and encyclopaedia bouts are recollections of other
days or nights spent entirely in playing chess or ping pong, or
painting water colors which we turned out like monomaniacs.

One morning, scarcely out of bed, I turned to my huge Funk &
Wagnall's unabridged dictionary to look up a word which had come

---

* The man to whom I sent it was Francis K. Hackett, and never shall
I forget his discreet but encouraging reply, God bless him!

to my mind on awakening. As usual, one word led to another, for what is the dictionary if not the subtlest form of " circuit game " masquerading in the guise of a book ? With Joe at my side, Joe the eternal sceptic, a discussion ensued which lasted the entire day and night, the search for more and more definitions never slackening. It was because of Joe O'Regan, who had stimulated me so often to question all that I had blindly accepted, that my first suspicions about the value of the dictionary were aroused. Prior to this moment I had taken the dictionary for granted, much as one does the Bible. I had believed, as everyone does, that in obtaining a definition one got the meaning of, or shall I say the " truth," about a word. But that day, shifting from derivation to derivation, thereby stumbling upon the most amazing changes in meaning, upon contradictions and reversals of earlier meanings, the whole framework of lexico-graphy began to slither and slide. In reaching the earliest " origin " of a word I observed that one was up against a stone wall. Surely it was not possible that the words we were looking up had entered human language at the points indicated ! To get back only as far as Sanskrit, Hebrew or Icelandic (and what wonderful words stem from the Icelandic !) was nothing, in my opinion. History had been pushed back more than ten thousand years, and here were we, stranded at the vestibule, so to speak, of modern times. That so many words of metaphysical and spiritual connotation, freely employed by the Greeks, had lost all significance was in itself some-thing to give us pause. To be brief, it soon became apparent that the meaning of a word changed or disappeared entirely, or became the very opposite, according to the time, place, culture of the people using the term. The simple truth that life is what we make it, how we see it with our whole being, and not what is given factually, historically, or statistically, applies to language too. The one who seems least to understand this is the philologist. But let me get on—from dictionary to encyclopaedia . . .

It was only natural, in jumping from meaning to meaning, in observing the *uses* of the words we were tracking down, that for a fuller, deeper treatment we must have recourse to the encyclo-paedia. The defining process, after all, is one of reference and cross-reference. To know what a specific word means one has to know the words which, so to speak, hedge it in. The meaning

D

is never directly given ; it is inferred, implied, or distilled out. And this is probably because the original source is never known.

But the encyclopaedia ! Ah, there perhaps we would be on firm ground ! We would look up subjects, not words. We would discover whence arose these mystifying symbols over which men had fought and bled, tortured and killed one another. Now there is a wonderful article in the Encyclopaedia Britannica (the celebrated edition) on " Mysteries "* and, if one wishes to pass a pleasant, amusing and instructive day at the library, by all means start with a word such as " mysteries." It will lead you far and wide, it will send you home reeling, indifferent to food, sleep and other claims of the autonomic system. But you will never penetrate the mystery ! And if, as the good scholar usually does, you should be impelled to go from the " authorities " selected by the encyclopaedic know-alls to other " authorities " on the same subject, you will soon find your awe and reverence for the accumulated wisdom housed in encyclopaedias withering and crumbling. It is well that one should become méfiant in the face of this buried learning. Who, after all, are these pundits entombed in the encyclopaedias ? Are they the *final* authorities ? Decidedly not ! The final authority must always be oneself. These wizened pundits have " labored in the field," and they have garnered much wisdom. But it is neither divine wisdom nor even the sum of human wisdom (on any subject) which they offer us. They have worked like ants and beavers, and usually with as little humor and imagination as these humble creatures. One encyclopaedia selects *its* authorities, another *other* authorities. Authorities are always a drug on the market. When you have done with them you know a little about the subject of your quest and a great deal more about things of no account. More often than not you end up in despair, doubt and confusion. If you gain at all, it is in the sharper use of the questioning faculty, that faculty which Spengler extols and which he distinguishes as the chief contribution made him by Nietzsche.

The more I think of it the more I believe that the unwitting contribution made me by the makers of encyclopaedias was to foster the lazy, pleasurable pursuit of learning—the most foolish

* Even Annie Besant, I noticed just the other day, makes mention of this article, in her book *Esoteric Christianity*.

of all pastimes. To read the encyclopaedia was like taking a drug —one of those drugs of which they say that it has no evil effects, is non habit-forming. Like the sound, stable, sensible Chinese of old, I think the use of opium preferable. If one wishes to relax, to enjoy surcease from care, to stimulate the imagination—and what could be more conducive to mental, moral and spiritual health ?—then I would say the judicious use of opium is far better than the spurious drug of the encyclopaedia.

Looking back upon my days in the library—curious that I do not recall my *first* visit to a library !—I liken them to the days spent by an opium addict in his little cell. I went regularly for my " dose " and I got it. Often I read at random, whatever book came to hand. Sometimes I buried myself in technical works, or in handbooks, or the " curiosa " of literature. There was one shelf in the reading room of the New York 42nd Street library, I recall, which was packed with mythologies (of many countries, many peoples) and which I devoured like a starved rat. Sometimes, impelled as if by an ardent mission, I burrowed in nomenclatures alone. There were other times when it seemed imperative —and indeed it *was* imperative, so deep was my trance—to study the habits of moles or whales, or the thousand and one varieties of ophidians. A word like " ecliptic," encountered for the first time, might set me off on a chase that would last for weeks, leaving me stranded eventually in the stellar depths this side of Scorpio.

Here I must diverge to make mention of those little books which one stumbles on accidentally and which, so great is their impact, one esteems above whole rows of encyclopaedias and other compendiums of human knowledge. These books, microcosmic in size but monumental in effect, may be likened to precious stones hidden in the bowels of the earth. Like gems, these books have a crystalline or " primordial " character which gives them a simple, immutable and eternal quality. They are almost as limited in number and variety as crystals in nature. I will mention two at random which I came upon much later than the period I speak of but which illustrate my thought. The one is *Symbols of Revelation*, by Frederick Carter, whom I met in London under peculiar circumstances ; the other is *The Round*, by Eduardo Santiago, a pseudonym. I doubt if there are a hundred people in this world who would be interested in the latter book. It is one of the strangest I know of, though the subject, apocatastasis, is one of the perennial themes of religion and philosophy. One of the freakish things connected with this unique and limited edition of the work is the error in spelling made by the printer. At the top of every page, in bold type, it reads : APOCASTASIS. Something even more freakish, however, something which is apt to give the lovers of Blake the cold shivers, is the reproduction of William Blake's life mask (from the National Portrait Gallery, London) which is given on page 40.

Since I have spoken at some length of dictionary usage, of definitions and their failure to define, and since the average reader is not apt to recognize the import of such a word as apocatastasis, let me give the three definitions offered by Funk & Wagnall's unabridged dictionary :

" 1. Return to or toward a previous place or condition ; re-establishment ; complete restoration.

" 2. *Theology*. The final restoration to holiness and the favor of God of those who died impenitent.

" 3. *Astronomy*. The periodic return of a revolving body to the same point in its orbit."

In a footnote on page 4 Santiago gives the following from *Virgile* by J. Carcopino (Paris, 1930) :

" Apocatastasis is the word which the Chaldeans had already used to describe the return of the planets, on the celestial sphere, to the points symmetrical to their departure. It is also the word the Greek doctors employed to describe the return of the patient to health."

As for Frederick Carter's little book—*Symbols of Revelation*—it may be of interest to know that it was the author of this book who supplied D. H. Lawrence with invaluable material for the writing of *Apocalypse*. Without knowing, Carter has also given me, through his book, the material and inspiration with which I hope one day to write *Draco and the Ecliptic*. This, the seal or capstone to my " autobiographical novels," as they are called, I trust will prove to be a condensed, transparent, alchemical work, thin as a wafer and absolutely air-tight.

The greatest of all little books of course is the *Tao Teh Ch'ing*. I suppose it is not only an example of supreme wisdom but unique in its condensation of thought. As a philosophy of life it not only holds its own with the bulkier systems of thought propounded by other great figures of the past but, in my mind, surpasses them in every respect. It has one element which wholly sets it apart from other philosophies of life—*humor*. Aside from the celebrated follower of Lao-tse who comes a few centuries later, we do not meet with humor in these lofty regions again until we come to Rabelais. Rabelais, being a physician as well as a philosopher and imaginative writer, makes humor appear what in truth it is : the great emancipator. But beside the suave, sage, spiritual iconoclast of old China, Rabelais seems like an uncouth Crusader. The Sermon on the Mount is perhaps the only short piece of writing which can be compared with Lao-tse's miniature gospel of wisdom and health. It may be a more spiritual message than Lao-tse's, but I doubt that it contains greater wisdom. It is, of course, utterly devoid of humor.

Two little books of pure literature, which belong in a category all their own, to my way of thinking, are Balzac's *Seraphita* and Hermann Hesse's *Siddhartha*. *Seraphita* I first read in French, at a period when my French was none too good. The man who put the book in my hands employed that artful strategy I spoke of earlier : he said almost nothing about the book except that it was a book *for me*. Coming from him, this was incentive enough. It was indeed a book " for me." It came exactly at the right moment in my life and it had precisely the desired effect. I have since, if I may put it thus, " experimented " with it by handing it to people who were not ready to read it. I learned a great deal from these experiments. *Seraphita* is one of those books, and they are rare indeed, which make their way unaided. Either it " converts " a man or it bores and disgusts him. Propaganda can do nothing to make it more widely read. Indeed, its virtue lies in this, that never at any time will it be effectively read except by a chosen few. It is true that in the beginning of its career it had a wide vogue. Are we not all familiar with the exclamation of that young Viennese student who, accosting Balzac in the street, begged permission to kiss the hand that wrote *Seraphita* ? Vogues, however, soon die out, and it is fortunate they do, because only then does a book begin its real journey on the road to immortality.

Siddhartha I first read in German—after not having read any German for at least thirty years. It was a book I had to read at any cost because, so I was told, it was the fruit of Hesse's visit to India. It had never been translated into English* and it was difficult for me, at the time, to lay hands on the 1925 French version which had been published by Grasset in Paris. Suddenly I found myself with two copies of it, in German, one sent me by my translator, Kurt Wagenseil, the other sent by the wife of George Dibbern, author of *Quest*. I had hardly finished reading the original version when my friend Pierre Laleure, a bookseller in Paris, sent me several copies of the Grasset edition. I immediately reread the book in that language, discovering to my delight that I had missed nothing of the flavor or substance of the book because of my very rusty knowledge of German. Often since I have remarked to friends, and there is truth in the exaggeration, that had *Siddhartha* been obtainable only in Turkish, Finnish or Hungarian, I would have read and understood it just the same, though I know not a word of any of these outlandish tongues.

It is not quite accurate to say that I conceived an overwhelming desire to read this book because Hermann Hesse had been to India. It was the word Siddhartha, an epithet which I had always associated with the Buddha, that whetted my appetite. Long before I had accepted Jesus Christ, I had embraced Lao-tse and Gautama the Buddha. The Prince of Enlightenment ! Somehow, that appellation never seemed to fit Jesus. A man of sorrow—that was more my conception of the gentle Jesus. The word enlightenment struck a responsive chord in me ; it seemed to burn out those other words associated, rightly or wrongly, with the founder of Christianity. I mean words such as sin, guilt, redemption, and so on. To this day I still prefer the guru to a Christian saint or the best of the twelve disciples. About the guru there is, and always will be, this aura, so precious to me, of " enlightenment."

I should like to speak at length of *Siddhartha* but, as with *Seraphita*, I know that the less said the better. I shall therefore content myself with quoting—for the benefit of those who know how to read between the lines—a few words lifted from an autobiographical sketch by Hermann Hesse in the September, 1946, issue of *Horizon*, London.

* An English version is now promised by New Directions.

54

Another reproach they [his friends] levelled at me I also found to be quite just : they accused me of lacking in a sense of reality. Neither my writings nor my paintings do in actual fact conform to reality, and when I compose I often forget all the things that an educated reader demands of a good book—and above all I am lacking in a true *respect* for reality.

I see that inadvertently I have touched on one of the vices or weaknesses of the too passionate reader. Lao-tse says that " when a man with a taste for reforming the world takes the business in hand, it is easily seen that there will be no end to it." Only too true, alas ! Each time I feel impelled to advocate a new book—with all the powers that are in me—I create more work, more anguish, more frustration for myself. I have spoken of my letter-writing mania. I have told how I sit down, after closing a good book, and inform all and sundry about it. Admirable, you think ? Perhaps. But it is also sheer folly and waste of time. The very men I seek to interest—critics, editors, publishers—are the ones least affected by my enthusiastic howls. I have come to believe, in fact, that my recommendation is alone sufficient to cause editors and publishers to lose interest in a book. Any book which I sponsor, or for which I write a preface or review, seems to be doomed.* I think perhaps there is a profound and just law underlying the situation. As best I can put it, this unwritten law runs thus : " Do not tamper with the destiny of another, even if that other be nothing but a book." More and more, too, I understand what makes me act on these rash impulses. It is, sadly enough, the fact that I identify myself with the poor author whom I am trying to aid. (Some of these authors, to reveal a ridiculous aspect of the situation, have been dead a long time. They are aiding me, not I them !) Of course I always put it to myself this way : " What a pity that so-and-so or so-and-so has not read this book ! What joy it would give him ! What sustenance ! " I never stop to think that the books which others find on their own may serve equally well.

It was because of my overheated enthusiasm for such books

---

* An exception is *Really the Blues*, which, in the French version, carries a letter, in the form of a preface, under my signature. This book, I am told, is selling like hot cakes. However, I take no credit for this; it would have sold as well without my preface.

as *The Absolute Collective, Quest, Blue Boy, Interlinear to Cabeza de Vaca*, the *Diary* of Anaïs Nin (which still exists only in manuscript), and others, many others, that I began to plague the perverse and mercurial tribe of editors and publishers who dictate to the world what we shall or shall not read. Concerning two writers particularly, I have penned the most ardent, urgent letters imaginable. A schoolboy could not have been more enthusiastic and naïve than I. In writing one of these letters, I recall, I actually shed tears. It was addressed to the editor of a well-known pocket book edition. Do you suppose this individual was moved by my unrestrained emotion? It took him just about six months to answer, in that matter of fact, cold-blooded, hypocritical fashion which editors often employ, that "they" (always the dark horses) had come to the conclusion, with deep regret (the same old song), that my man was unsuitable for their list. Gratuitously they cited the excellent sales enjoyed by Homer (long dead) and William Faulkner, whom they had chosen to publish. The implication was—find us writers like these and we will jump to the bait! Fantastic as it may sound, it is nevertheless the truth. It is exactly how editors think.

However, this vice of mine, as I see it, is a harmless one compared with those of political fanatics, military humbugs, vice crusaders and other detestable types. In broadcasting to the world my admiration and affection, my gratitude and reverence, for two living French writers—Blaise Cendrars and Jean Giono—I fail to see that I am doing any serious harm. I may be guilty of indiscretion, I may be regarded as a naïve dolt, I may be criticized justly or unjustly for my taste, or lack of it; I may be guilty, in the highest sense, of "tampering" with the destiny of others; I may be writing myself down as one more "propagandist," but—how am I injuring anyone? I am no longer a young man. I am, to be exact, fifty-eight years of age. ("Je me nomme Louis Salavin.") Instead of growing more dispassionate about books, I find the contrary is taking place. Perhaps my extravagant statements do contain an element of insensitivity. But then I was never what is called "discreet" or "delicate." Mine is a rough touch—honest and sincere, in any case. And so, if I *am* guilty, I beg pardon in advance of my friends Giono and Cendrars. I beg them to disown me should I bring ridicule upon their heads. But I will not hold back my words. The course of the previous pages, the course of my whole life, indeed, leads me to this declaration of love and adoration.

III

BLAISE CENDRARS

CENDRARS was the first French writer to look me up, during my stay in Paris,* and the last man I saw on leaving Paris. I had just a few minutes before catching the train for Rocamadour and I was having a last drink on the terrasse of my hotel near the Porte d'Orléans when Cendrars hove in sight. Nothing could have given me greater joy than this unexpected last-minute encounter. In a few words I told him of my intention to visit Greece. Then I sat back and drank in the music of his sonorous voice which to me always seemed to come from a sea organ. In those last few minutes Cendrars managed to convey a world of information, and with the same warmth and tenderness which he exudes in his books. Like the very ground under our feet, his thoughts were honeycombed with all manner of subterranean passages. I left him sitting there in shirt-sleeves, never dreaming that years would elapse before hearing from him again, never dreaming that I was perhaps taking my last look at Paris.

I had read whatever was translated of Cendrars before arriving in France. That is to say, almost nothing. My first taste of him in his own language came at a time when my French was none too proficient. I began with *Moravagine*, a book by no means easy to read for one who knows little French. I read it slowly, with a dictionary by my side, shifting from one café to another. It was in the Café de la Liberté, corner of the rue de la Gaieté and the Boulevard Edgar Quinet, that I began it. I remember well the day. Should Cendrars ever read these lines he may be pleased, touched perhaps, to know that it was in that dingy hole I first opened his book.

Moravagine was probably the second or third book which I had attempted to read in French. Only the other day, after a lapse of about eighteen years, I reread it. What was my amazement to

* I lived in Paris from March, 1930, to June, 1939.

58

discover that whole passages were engraved in my memory !
And I had thought my French was null ! Here is one of the passages
I remember as clearly as the day I first read it. It begins at the top
of page 77 (Editions Grasset, 1926).

> I tell you of things that brought some relief at the start.
> There was also the water, gurgling at intervals, in the
> water-closet pipes. . . A boundless despair possessed me.
> (Does this convey anything to you, my dear Cendrars ?)

Immediately I think of two other passages, even more deeply
engraved in my mind, from *Une Nuit dans la Forêt*,* which I read
about three years later. I cite them not to brag of my powers of
memory but to reveal an aspect of Cendrars which his English
and American readers probably do not suspect the existence of.

> 1. I, the freest man that exists, recognise that there is
> always something that binds one : that liberty, independence do not exist, and I am full of contempt for, and at
> the same time take pleasure in, my helplessness.
> 2. More and more I realise that I have always led the
> contemplative life. I am a sort of Brahmin in reverse,
> meditating on himself amid the hurly-burly, who, with
> all his strength, disciplines himself and scorns existence.
> Or the boxer with his shadow, who, furiously, calmly,
> punching at emptiness, watches his form. What virtuosity,
> what science, what balance, the ease with which he accelerates ! *Later, one must learn how to take punishment with
> equal imperturbability.* I, I know how to take punishment
> and with serenity I fructify and with serenity destroy
> myself : in short, work in the world not so much to enjoy
> as to make others enjoy (it's others' reflexes that give
> me pleasure, not my own). Only a soul full of despair
> can ever attain serenity and, to be in despair, you must
> have loved a good deal and *still love the world.*†

These last two passages have probably been cited many times
already and will no doubt be cited many times more as the years
go by. They are memorable ones and thoroughly the author's
own. Those who know only *Sutter's Gold, Panama* and *On the
Trans-siberian,* which are about all the American reader gets to

* Editions du Verseau, Lausanne, 1929.
† Italics mine.

know, may indeed wonder on reading the foregoing passages why this man has not been translated more fully. Long before I attempted to make Cendrars better known to the American public (and to the world at large, I may well add), John Dos Passos had translated and illustrated with water colors *Panama, or the adventures of my seven uncles*.*

However, the primary thing to know about Blaise Cendrars is that he is a man of many parts. He is also a man of many books, many kinds of books, and by that I do not mean " good " and " bad " but books so different one from another that he gives the impression of evolving in all directions at once. An evolved man, truly. Certainly an evolved writer.

His life itself reads like the *Arabian Nights' Entertainment*. And this individual who has led a super-dimensional life is also a bookworm. The most gregarious of men and yet a solitary. (" O mes solitudes ! ") A man of deep intuition and invincible logic. The logic of life. Life first and foremost. Life always with a capital L. That's Cendrars.

To follow his career from the time he slips out of his parents' home in Neufchâtel, a boy of fifteen or sixteen, to the days of the Occupation when he secretes himself in Aix-en-Provence and imposes on himself a long period of silence, is something to make one's head spin. The itinerary of his wanderings is more difficult to follow than Marco Polo's, whose trajectory, incidentally, he seems to have crossed and recrossed a number of times. One of the reasons for the great fascination he exerts over me is the resemblance between his voyages and adventures and those which I associate in memory with Sinbad the Sailor or Aladdin of the Wonderful Lamp. The amazing experiences which he attributes to the characters in his books, and which often as not he has shared, have all the qualities of legend as well as the authenticity of legend. Worshipping life and the truth of life, he comes closer than any author of our time to revealing the common source of word and deed. He restores to contemporary life the elements of the heroic, the imaginative and the fabulous. His adventures have led him to nearly every region of the globe, particularly those regarded as

* See chapter 12, " Homer of the Trans-siberian," *Orient Express* ; Jonathan Cape & Harrison Smith, New York, 1922.

Blaise Cendrars

dangerous or inaccessible. (One must read his early life especially to appreciate the truth of this statement.) He has consorted with all types, including bandits, murderers, revolutionaries and other varieties of fanatic. He has tried out no less than thirty-six métiers, according to his own words, but, like Balzac, gives the impression of knowing every métier. He was once a juggler, for example—on the English music-hall stage—at the same time that Chaplin was making his début there ; he was a pearl merchant and a smuggler ; he was a plantation owner in South America, where he made a fortune three times in succession and lost it even more rapidly than he had made it. But read his life ! There is more in it than meets the eye.

Yes, he is an explorer and investigator of the ways and doings of men. And he has made himself such by planting himself in the midst of life, by taking up his lot with his fellow creatures. What a superb, painstaking reporter he is, this man who would scorn the thought of being called " a student of life." He has the faculty of getting "his story" by a process of osmosis ; he seems to seek nothing deliberately. Which is why, no doubt, his own story is always interwoven with the other man's. To be sure, he possesses the art of distillation, but what he is vitally interested in is the alchemical nature of all relationships. This eternal quest of the trans-mutative enables him to reveal men to themselves and to the world ; it causes him to extol men's virtues, to reconcile us to their faults and weaknesses, to increase our knowledge and respect for what is essentially human, to deepen our love and understanding of the world. He is the " reporter " par excellence because he combines the faculties of poet, seer and prophet. An innovator and initiator, ever the first to give testimony, he has made known to us the real pioneers, the real adventurers, the real discoverers among our contemporaries. More than any writer I can think of he has made dear to us " le bel aujourd'hui."

Whilst performing on all levels he always found time to read. On long voyages, in the depths of the Amazon, in the deserts (I imagine he knows them all, those of the earth, those of the spirit), in the jungle, on the broad pampas, on trains, trams, tramps and ocean liners, in the great museums and libraries of Europe, Asia and Africa, he has buried himself in books, has ransacked whole archives,

61

has photographed rare documents, and, for all I know, may have stolen invaluable books, scripts, documents of all kinds—why not, considering the enormity of his appetite for the rare, the curious, the forbidden ?

He has told us in one of his recent books how the Germans (les Boches !) destroyed or carried off, I forget which, his precious library, precious to a man like Cendrars who loves to give the most precise data when referring to a passage from one of his favorite books. Thank God, his memory is alive and functions like a faithful machine. An incredible memory, as will testify those who have read his more recent books—*La Main Coupée, l'Homme Foudroyé, Bourlinguer, Le Lotissement du Ciel, La Banlieue de Paris.*

On the side—with Cendrars it seems as though almost everything of account has been done " on the side "—he has translated the works of other writers, notably the Portuguese author, Ferreira de Castro (*Forêt Vierge*) and our own Al Jennings, the great outlaw and bosom friend of O. Henry.* What a wonderful translation is *Hors-la-loi* which in English is called *Through the Shadows with O. Henry.* It is a sort of secret collaboration between Cendrars and the innermost being of Al Jennings. At the time of writing it, Cendrars had not yet met Jennings nor even corresponded with him. (This is another book, I must say in passing, which our pocket book editors have overlooked. There is a fortune in it, unless I am all wet, and it would be comforting to think that part of this fortune should find its way into Al Jennings' pocket.)

One of the most fascinating aspects of Cendrars' temperament is his ability and readiness to collaborate with a fellow artist. Picture him, shortly after the first World War, editing the publications of La Sirène ! What an opportunity ! To him we owe an edition of *Les Chants de Maldoror*, the first to appear since the original private publication by the author in 1868. In everything an innovator, always meticulous, scrupulous and exacting in his demands, whatever issued from the hands of Cendrars at La Sirène is now a valuable collector's item. Hand in hand with this capability for collaboration goes another quality—the ability, or grace, to make the first overtures. Whether it be a criminal, a saint, a man of genius, a tyro with promise, Cendrars is the first to look him up, the first to herald him,

---

* Cendrars has also translated Al Capone's autobiography.

the first to aid him in the way the person most desires. I speak with justifiable warmth here. No writer ever paid me a more signal honor than dear Blaise Cendrars who, shortly after the publication of *Tropic of Cancer*, knocked at my door one day to extend the hand of friendship. Nor can I forget that first tender, eloquent review of the book which appeared under his signature in *Orbes* shortly there-after. (Or perhaps it was *before* he appeared at the studio in the Villa Seurat.)

There were times when reading Cendrars—and this is something which happens to me rarely—that I put the book down in order to wring my hands with joy or despair, with anguish or with despera-tion. Cendrars has stopped me in my tracks again and again, just as implacably as a gunman pressing a rod against one's spine. Oh, yes, I am often carried away by exaltation in reading a man's work. But I am alluding now to something other than exaltation. I am talking of a sensation in which all one's emotions are blended and confused. I am talking of knockout blows. Cendrars has knocked me cold. Not once, but a number of times. And I am not exactly a ham, when it comes to taking it on the chin ! Yes, mon cher Cendrars, you not only stopped *me*, you stopped the clock. It has taken me days, weeks, sometimes months, to recover from these bouts with you. Even years later, I can put my hand to the spot where I caught the blow and feel the old smart. You battered and bruised me ; you left me scarred, dazed, punch-drunk. The curious thing is that the better I know you—through your books—the more susceptible I become. It is as if you had put the Indian sign on me. I come forward with chin outstretched—" to take it." *I am your meat*, as I have so often said. And it is because I believe I am not unique in this, because I wish others to enjoy this uncommon experience, that I continue to put in my little word for you whenever, wherever, I can.

I incautiously said : " the better I know you." My dear Cendrars, I will never know you, not as I do other men, of that I am certain. No matter how thoroughly you reveal yourself I shall never get to the bottom of you. I doubt that anyone ever will, and it is not vanity which prompts me to put it this way. You are as inscrutable as a Buddha. You inspire, you reveal, but you never give yourself wholly away. Not that you withhold yourself ! No, encountering you, whether in person or through the written word, you leave the impression of having given all there is to give. Indeed, you are one of the few men I know who, in their books as well as in person, give that " extra measure " which means everything to us. You give all that *can* be given. It is not your fault that the very core of you forbids scrutiny. It is the law of your being. No doubt there are men less inquisitive, less grasping, less clutching, for whom these remarks are meaningless. But you have so refined our sensitivity, so heightened our awareness, so deepened our love for men and women, for books, for nature, for a thousand and one things of life which only one of your own unending paragraphs could catalogue, that you awaken in us the desire to turn you inside out. When I read you or talk to you I am always aware of your inexhaustible awareness : you are not just sitting in a chair in a room in a city in a country, telling us what is on your mind or in your mind, you make the chair talk and the room vibrate with the tumult of the city whose life is sustained by the invisible outer throng of a whole nation whose history has become your history, whose life is your life and yours theirs, and as you talk or write all these elements, images, facts, creations enter into your thoughts and feelings, forming a web which the spider in you ceaselessly spins and which spreads in us, your listeners, until the whole of creation is involved, and we, you, them, it, everything, have lost identity and found new meaning, new life . . .

Before proceeding further, there are two books on Cendrars which I would like to recommend to all who are interested in knowing more about the man. Both are entitled *Blaise Cendrars*. One is by Jacques-Henry Levèsque (Editions de la Nouvelle Critique, Paris, 1947), the other by Louis Parrot (Editions Pierre Seghers, Paris, 1948), finished on the author's deathbed. Both contain bibliographies, excerpts from Cendrars' works, and a number of photographs taken at various periods of his life. Those who do not read French may glean a surprising knowledge of this enigmatic individual from the photographs alone. (It is amazing what spice and vitality French publishers lend their publications through the insertion of old photographs. Seghers has been particularly enterprising in this respect. In his series of little square books, called *Poètes d'Aujourd'hui*,* he has given us a veritable gallery of contemporary and near contemporary figures.)

* Distributed in the United States by New Directions.

Yes, one can glean a lot about Cendrars just from studying his physiognomy. He has probably been photographed more than any contemporary writer. In addition, sketches and portraits of him have been made by any number of celebrated artists, including Modigliani, Apollinaire, Léger. Flip the pages of the two books I just mentioned —Levèsque's and Parrot's ; take a good look at this " gueule " which Cendrars has presented to the world in a thousand different moods. Some will make you weep ; some are almost hallucinating. There is one photo of him taken in uniform during the days of the Foreign Legion when he was a corporal. His left hand, holding a butt which is burning his fingers, protrudes from beneath the cape ; it is a hand so expressive, so very eloquent, that if you do not know the story of his missing arm, this will convey it unerringly. It is with this powerful and sensitive left hand that he has written most of his books, signed his name to innumerable letters and post cards, shaved himself, washed himself, guided his speedy Alfa-Romeo through the most dangerous terrains ; it is with this left hand that he has hacked his way through jungles, punched his way through brawls, defended himself, shot at men and beasts, clapped his copains on the back, greeted with a warm clasp a long lost friend and caressed the women and animals he has loved. There is another photo of him taken in 1921 when he was working with Abel Gance on the film called *La Roue*, the eternal cigarette glued to his lips, a tooth missing, a huge checkered cap with an enormous peak hanging over one ear. The expression on his face is something out of Dostoievsky. On the opposite page is a photo taken by Raymone in 1924, when he was working on *l'Or (Sutter's Gold)*. Here he stands with legs spread apart, his left hand sliding into the pocket of his baggy pantaloons, a mégot to his lips, as always. In this photo he looks like a healthy cocky young peasant of Slavic origin. There is a taunting gleam in his eye, a sort of frank, good-natured defiance. " Fuck you, Jack, I'm fine . . . *and you ?* " That's what it conveys, his look. Another, taken with Levèsque at Tremblay-sur-Maulne, 1926, captures him square in the prime of life. Here he seems to be at his peak physically ; he emanates health, joy, vitality. In 1928 we have the photo which has been reprinted by the thousands. It is Cendrars of the South American period, looking fit, sleek almost, well garbed, his conk crowned by a handsome fedora with its soft brim upturned. He has

65

a burning, faraway look in the eyes, as if he had just come back from the Antarctic. (I believe it was in this period that he was writing, or had just finished, *Dan Yack*, the first half of which [*Le Plan de l'Aiguille*] has only recently been issued in translation by an English publisher.*) But it is in 1944 that we catch a glimpse of le vieux Légionnaire—photo by Chardon, Cavaillon. Here he reminds one of Victor MacLaglan in the title rôle of *The Informer*. This is the period of *l'Homme Foudroyé*, for me one of his major books. Here he is the fully developed earth man composed of many rich layers—roustabout, tramp, bum, panhandler, mixer, bruiser, adventurer, sailor, soldier, tough guy, the man of a thousand-and-one hard, bitter experiences who never went under but ripened, ripened, ripened. Un homme, quoi ! There are two photos taken in 1946, at Aix-en-Provence, which yield us tender, moving images of him. One, in which he leans against a fence, shows him surrounded by the urchins of the neighbourhood : he is teaching them a few sleight of hand tricks. The other catches him walking through a shadowed old street which curves endearingly. His look is meditative, if not triste. It is a beautiful photograph, redolent of the atmosphere of the Midi. One walks with him in his pensive mood, hushed by the unseizable thoughts which envelop him . . . I force myself to draw rein. I could go on forever about the " physiognomic " aspects of the man. His is a mug one can never forget. It's *human*, that's what. Human like Chinese faces, like Egyptian, Cretan, Etruscan ones.

Many are the things which have been said against this writer . . . that his books are cinematic in style, that they are sensational, that he exaggerates and deforms à outrance, that he is prolix and verbose, that he lacks all sense of form, that he is too much the realist or else that his narratives are too incredible, and so on ad infinitum. Taken altogether there is, to be sure, a grain of truth in these accusations, but let us remember—*only a grain !* They reflect the views of the paid critic, the academician, the frustrated novelist. But supposing, for a moment, we accepted them at face value. Will they hold water ? Take his cinematic technique, for example. Well, are we not living in the age of the cinema ? Is not this period of history more fantastic, more " incredible," than the simulacrum of it which we see unrolled

* Title : *Antarctic Fugue* ; Pushkin Press, London, 1948.

66

on the silver screen ? As for his sensationalism—have we forgotten Gilles de Rais, the Marquis de Sade, the *Memoirs* of Casanova ? As for hyperbole, what of Pindar ? As for prolixity and verbosity, what about Jules Romains or Marcel Proust ? As for exaggeration and deformation, what of Rabelais, Swift, Céline, to mention an anomalous trinity ? As for lack of form, that perennial jackass which is always kicking up its heels in the pages of literary reviews, have I not heard cultured Europeans rant about the " vegetal " aspect of Hindu temples, the façades of which are studded with a riot of human, animal and other forms ? Have I not seen them twisting their lips in distaste when examining the amazing efflorescences embodied in Tibetan scrolls ? No taste, eh ? No sense of proportion ? No control ? C'est ca. De la mesure avant tout ! These cultured nobodies forget that their beloved exemplars, the Greeks, worked with Cyclopean blocks, created monstrosities as well as apotheoses of harmony, grace, form and spirit ; they forget perhaps that the Cycladic sculpture of Greece surpassed in abstraction and simplification anything which Brancusi or his followers ever attempted. The very mythology of these worshippers of beauty, whose motto was " Nothing to the extreme," is a revelation of the " monstrous " aspect of their being.

Oui, Cendrars is full of excrescences. There are passages which swell up out of the body of his text like rank tumors. There are detours, parentheses, asides, which are the embryonic pith and substance of books yet to come. There is a grand efflorescence and exfoliation, and there is also a grand wastage of material in his books. Cendrars neither cribs and cabins, nor does he drain himself completely. When the moment comes to let go, he lets go. When it is expedient or efficacious to be brief, he is brief and to the point— like a dagger. To me his books reflect his lack of fixed habits, or better yet, his ability to break a habit. (A sign of real emancipation !) In those swollen paragraphs, which are like une mer houleuse and which some readers, apparently, are unable to cope with, Cendrars reveals his oceanic spirit. We who vaunt dear Shakespeare's madness, his elemental outbursts, are we to fear these cosmic gusts ? We who swallowed the *Pantagruel* and *Gargantua*, via Urquhart, are we to be daunted by catalogues of names, places, dates, events ? We who produced the oddest writer in any tongue—Lewis Carroll—

67

are we to shy away from the play of words, from the ridiculous, the grotesque, the unspeakable or the " utterly impossible " ? It takes a *man* to hold his breath as Cendrars does when he is about to unleash one of his triple-page paragraphs without stop. *A man ?* A deep-sea diver. A whale. A whale of a man, precisely.

What *is* remarkable is that this same man has also given us some of the shortest sentences ever written, particularly in his poems and prose poems. Here, in staccato rhythm—let us not forget that before he was a writer he was a musician !—he deploys a telegraphic style. (It might also be called " telesthetic.") One can read it as fast as Chinese, with whose written characters his vocables have a curious affinity, to my way of thinking. This particular technique of Cendrars' creates a kind of exorcism—a deliverance from the heavy weight of prose, from the impedimenta of grammar and syntax, from the illusory intelligibility of the merely communicative in speech. In *l'Eubage*, for example, we discover a sibylline quality of thought and utterance. It is one of his curious books. An extreme. Also a departure and an end. Cendrars is indeed difficult to classify, though why we should want to classify him I don't know. Sometimes I think of him as " a writer's writer," though he is definitely not that. But what I mean to say is that a writer has much to learn from Cendrars. In school, I remember, we were always being urged to take as models men like Macaulay, Coleridge, Ruskin, or Edmund Burke—even de Maupassant. Why they didn't say Shakespeare, Dante, Milton, I don't know. No professor ever believed, I dare say, that any of us brats would turn out to be writers one day. They were failures themselves, hence teachers. Cendrars has made it clear that the only teacher, the only model, is life itself. What a writer learns from Cendrars is to follow his nose, to obey life's commands, to worship no other god but life. Some interpreters will have it that Cendrars means " the dangerous life." I don't believe Cendrars would limit it thus. He means *life* pure and simple, in all its aspects, all its ramifications, all its bypaths, temptations, hazards, what not. If he is an adventurer, he is an adventurer in all realms of life. What interests him is *every* phase of life. The subjects he has touched on, the themes he has pursued, are encyclopaedic. Another sign of " emancipation," this all-inclusive absorption in life's myriad manifestations. It is often when he seems most " realistic," for

68

example, that he tends to pull all the stops on his organ. The realist is a meagre soul. He sees what is in front of him, like a horse with blinders. Cendrars' vision is perpetually open ; it is almost as if he had an extra eye buried in his crown, a skylight open to all the cosmic rays. Such a man, you may be sure, will never complete his life's work, because life will always be a step ahead of him. Besides, life knows no completion, and Cendrars is one with life. An article by Pierre de Latil in *La Gazette des Lettres*, Paris, August 6, 1949, informs us that Cendrars has projected a dozen or more books to be written within the next few years. It is an astounding program, considering that Cendrars is now in his sixties, that he has no secretary, that he writes with his left hand, that he is restless underneath, always itching to sally forth and see more of the world, that he actually detests writing and looks upon his work as forced labor. He works on four or five books at a time. He will finish them all, I am certain. I only pray that I live to read the trilogy of " les souvenirs humains " called *Archives de ma tour d'ivoire*, which will consist of : *Hommes de lettres, Hommes d'affaires* and *Vie des hommes obscurs*. Particularly the last-named . . .

I have long pondered over Cendrars' confessed insomnia. He attributes it to his life in the trenches, if I remember rightly. True enough, no doubt, but I surmise there are deeper reasons for it. At any rate, what I wish to point out is that there seems to be a connection between his fecundity and his sleeplessness. For the ordinary individual sleep is *the* restorative. Exceptional individuals—holy men, gurus, inventors, leaders, men of affairs, or certain types of the insane—are able to do with very little sleep. They apparently have other means of replenishing their dynamic potential. Some men, merely by varying their pursuits, can go on working with almost no sleep. Others, like the yogi and the guru, in becoming more and more aware and therefore more alive, virtually emancipate themselves from the thrall of sleep. (Why sleep if the purpose of life is to enjoy creation to the fullest ?) With Cendrars, I have the feeling that in switching from active life to writing, and vice versa, he replenishes himself. A pure supposition on my part. Otherwise I am at a loss to account for a man burning the candle at both ends and not consuming himself. Cendrars mentions somewhere that he is of a line of long-lived antecedents. He has certainly squandered his hereditary patrimony regally. *But*—he shows no signs of cracking up. Indeed, he seems to have entered upon a period of second youth. He is confident that when he reaches the ripe age of seventy he will be ready to embark on new adventures. It will not surprise me in the least if he does ; I can see him at ninety scaling the Himalayas or embarking in the first rocket to voyage to the moon.

But to come back to the relation between his writing and his sleeplessness . . . If one examines the dates given at the end of his books, indicating the time he spent on them, one is struck by the rapidity with which he executed them as well as by the speed with which (all good-sized books) they succeed one another. All this implies one thing, to my mind, and that is " obsession." To write one has to be possessed and obsessed. What is it that possesses and obsesses Cendrars ? *Life.* He is a man in love with life—et c'est tout. No matter if he denies this at times, no matter if he vilifies the times or excoriates his contemporaries in the arts, no matter if he compares his own recent past with the present and finds the latter lacking, no matter if he deplores the trends, the tendencies, the philosophies and behavior of the men of our epoch, he is the one man of our time who has proclaimed and trumpeted the fact that *today* is profound and beautiful. And it is just because he has anchored himself in the midst of contemporary life, where, as if from a conning tower, he surveys all life, past, present and future, the life of the stars as well as the life of the ocean depths, life in miniscule as well as the life grandiose, that I seized upon him as a shining example of the right principle, the right attitude towards life. No one can steep himself in the splendors of the past more than Cendrars ; no one can hail the future with greater zest ; but it is the present, the eternal present, which he glorifies and with which he allies himself. It is such men, and only such men, who are in the tradition, who carry on. The others are backward lookers, idolaters, or else mere wraiths of hopefulness, bonimenteurs. With Cendrars you strike ore. And it is because he understands the present so profoundly, accepts it and is one with it, that he is able to predict the future so unerringly. Not that he sets himself up as a soothsayer ! No, his prophetic remarks are made casually and discreetly ; they are buried often in a maze of unrelated material. In this he often reminds me of the good physician. He knows how to take the pulse. In fact, he knows all the pulses, like the Chinese physicians of old. When he says of certain men that they are sick, or of certain artists that they are corrupt or fakes, or of politicians in general that they are crazy, or of military men that they are criminals, he knows whereof he speaks. It is the magister in him which is speaking.

He has, however, another way of speaking which is more endearing to me. He can speak with tenderness. Lawrence, it will be remembered, originally thought of calling the book known as *Lady Chatterley's Lover* by the title "Tenderness." I mention Lawrence's name because I remember vividly Cendrars' allusion to him on the occasion of his memorable visit to the Villa Seurat. "You must think a lot of Lawrence," he said questioningly. "I do," I replied. We exchanged a few words and then I recall him asking me fair and square if I did not believe Lawrence to be overrated. It was the metaphysical side of Lawrence, I gathered, that was not to his liking, that was "suspect," I should say. (And it was just at this period that I was engrossed in this particular aspect of Lawrence !) I am sure, at any rate, that my defense of Lawrence was weak and unsustained. To be truthful, I was much more interested in hearing Cendrars' view of the man than in justifying my own. Often, later, in reading Cendrars this word "tenderness" crossed my lips. It would escape involuntarily, rouse me from my reverie. Futile though it be, I would then indulge in endless speculation, comparing Lawrence's tenderness with Cendrars'. They are, I now think, of two distinct kinds. Lawrence's weakness is man, Cendrars' men. Lawrence longed to know men better ; he wanted to work in common with them. It is in *Apocalypse* that he has some of the most moving passages—on the withering of the "societal" instinct. They create real anguish in us—for Lawrence. They make us realize the tortures he suffered in trying to be "a man among men." With Cendrars I detect no hint of such deprivation or mutilation. In the ocean of humanity Cendrars swims as blithely as a porpoise or a dolphin. In his narratives he is always together with men, one with them in deed, one with them in thought. If he is a solitary, he is nevertheless fully and completely a man. He is also the brother of all men. Never does he set himself up as superior to his fellow man. Lawrence thought himself superior, often, often—I think that is undeniable—and very often he was anything but. Very often it is a lesser man who

71

" instructs " him. Or shames him. Lawrence had too great a love for " humanity " to understand or get along with his fellow man.

It is when we come to their respective fictional characters that we sense the rift between these two figures. With the exception of the self portraits, given in *Sons and Lovers*, *Kangaroo*, *Aaron's Rod* and such like, all Lawrence's characters are mouthpieces for his philosophy or the philosophy he wishes to depose. They are ideational creatures, moved about like chess pieces. They have blood in them all right, but it is the blood which Lawrence has pumped into them. Cendrars' characters issue from life and their activity stems from life's moving vortex. They too, of course, acquaint us with his philosophy of life, but obliquely, in the elliptic manner of art.

The tenderness of Cendrars exudes from all pores. He does not spare his characters ; neither does he revile or castigate them. His harshest words, let me say parenthetically, are usually reserved for the poets and artists whose work he considers spurious. Aside from these diatribes, you will rarely find him passing judgment upon others. What you do find is that in laying bare the weaknesses or faults of his subjects he is unmasking, or endeavoring to unmask, their essential heroic nature. All the diverse figures—human, all too human—which crowd his books are glorified in their basic, intrinsic being. They may or may not have been heroic in the face of death ; they may or may not have been heroic before the tribunal of justice ; but they *are* heroic in the common struggle to assert and uphold their own primal being. I mentioned a while ago the book by Al Jennings which Cendrars so ably translated. The very choice of this book is indicative of my point. This mite of a man, this outlaw with an exaggerated sense of justice and honor who is " up for life " (but eventually pardoned by Theodore Roosevelt), this terror of the West who wells over with tenderness, is just the sort of man Cendrars *would* choose to tell the world about, just the sort of man he *would* uphold as being filled with the dignity of life. Ah, how I should like to have been there when Cendrars eventually caught up with him, in Hollywood of all places ! Cendrars has written of this " brief encounter " and I heard of it myself from Al Jennings' own lips when I met him by chance a few years ago—in a bookshop there in Hollywood.

In the books written since the Occupation, Cendrars has much to say about the War—the First War, naturally, not only because it was less inhuman but because the future course of his life, I might say, was decided by it. He has also written about the Second War, particularly about the fall of Paris and the incredible exodus preceding it. Haunting pages, reminiscent of *Revelation*. Equalled in war literature only by St. Exupéry's. *Flight to Arras*. (See the section of his book, *Le Lotissement du Ciel*, which first appeared in the *revue*, *Le Cheval de Troie*, entitled: *Un Nouveau Patron pour l'Aviation*.)* In all these recent books Cendrars reveals himself more and more intimately. So penetrative, so naked, are these glimpses he permits us that one instinctively recoils. So sure, swift and deft are these revelations that it is like watching a safecracker at work. In these flashes stand revealed the whole swarm of intimates whose lives dovetail with his own. Exposed through the lurid searchlight of his Cyclopean eye they are caught in the flux and surveyed from every angle. Here there is "completion" of a sort. Nothing is omitted or altered for the sake of the narrative. With these books the "narrative" is stepped up, broadened out, the supports and buttresses battered away, in order that the book may become part of life, swim with life's currents, and remain forever identical with life. Here one comes to grips with the men Cendrars truly loves, the men he fought beside in the trenches and whom he saw wiped out like rats, the Gypsies of the Zone whom he consorted with in the good old days, the ranchers and other figures from the South American scene, the porters, concierges, tradesmen, truck drivers, and "people of no account" (as we say), and it is with the utmost sympathy and understanding that he treats these latter. What a gallery! Infinitely more exciting, in every sense of the word, than Balzac's gallery of "types." This is the real *Human Comedy*. No sociological studies, à la Zola. No satirical puppet show, à la Thackeray. No pan-humanity, à la Jules Romains. Here in these latter books, though minus the aim and purpose of the great Russian, but perhaps with another aim which we will understand better later, at any rate, with equal amplitude, violence, humor, tenderness and religious—yes, religious—fervor, Cendrars gives us the French equivalent of Dostoievsky's outpourings in such works as *The Idiot*, *The Possessed*, *The Brothers Karamazov*.

* Editions Denoël, Paris, 1949.

A production which could only be realized, consummated, in the ripe middle years of life.

Everything now forthcoming has been digested a thousand times. Again and again Cendrars has pushed back—where ? into what deep well ?—the multiform story of his life. This heavy, molten mass of experience raw and refined, subtle and crude, digested and predigested, which had been lodging in his entrails like a torpid and amorphous dinosaur idly flapping its rudimentary wings, this cargo destined for eventual delivery at the exact time and the exact place, demanded a touch of dynamite to be set off. From June, 1940, to the 21st of August, 1943, Cendrars remained awesomely silent. Il s'est tu. Chut ! Motus ! What starts him writing again is a visit from his friend Edouard Peisson, as he relates in the opening pages of *l'Homme Foudroyé*. En passant he evokes the memory of a certain night in 1915, at the front—" la plus terrible que j'ai vécue." There were other occasions, one suspects, before the critical visit of his friend Peisson, which might have served to detonate the charge. But perhaps on these occasions the fuse burned out too quickly or was damp or smothered under by the weight of world events. But let us drop these useless speculations. Let us dive into Section 17 of *Un Nouveau Patron Pour l'Aviation* . . .

This brief section begins with the recollection of a sentence of Rémy de Gourmont's : " And it shows great progress that, where women prayed before, cows now chew the cud . . . " In a few lines comes this from Cendrars' own mouth :

> Beginning on May 10th, Surrealism descended upon earth : not the works of absurd poets who pretend to be such and who, at most, are but sou-realistes since they preach the subconscious, but the work of Christ, the only poet of the sur-real . . .
> If ever I had faith, it was on that day that grace should have touched me . . .

Follow two paragraphs dealing in turbulent, compressed fury with the ever execrable condition of war. Like Goya, he repeats : " *J'ai vu.*" The second paragraph ends thus :

> The sun had stopped. The weather forecast announced an anti-cyclone lasting forty days. It couldn't be ! For

which reason everything went wrong : gear-wheels
would not lock, machinery everywhere broke down :
the dead-point of everything.

The next five lines will ever remain in my memory :

No, on May 10th, humanity was far from adequate
to the event. Lord ! Above, the sky was like a backside
with gleaming buttocks and the sun an inflamed anus.
What else but shit could ever have issued from it ?
And modern man screamed with fear . . .

This man of August the 21st, 1943, who is exploding in all
directions at once, had of course already delivered himself of a wad
of books, not least among them, we shall probably discover one
day, being the ten volumes of *Notre Pain Quotidien* which he composed intermittently over a period of ten years in a chateau outside
Paris, to which manuscripts he never signed his name, confiding the
chests containing this material to various safety vaults in different
parts of South America and then throwing the keys away. (*" Je
voudrais rester l'Anonyme*," he says.)

In the books begun at Aix-en-Provence are voluminous notes,
placed at the ends of the various sections. I will quote just one, from
Bourlinguer (the section on Genoa), which constitutes an everlasting
tribute to the poet so dear to French men of letters :

Dear Gerard de Nerval, man of the crowd, night-
walker, slang-ist, impenitent dreamer, neurasthenic lover
of the Capital's small theatres and the vast necropoli of
the East : architect of Solomon's Temple, translator of
Faust, personal secretary to the Queen of Sheba, Druid of
the 1st and 2nd class, sentimental vagabond of the Ile-de-
France, last of the Valois, child of Paris, lips of gold, you
hung yourself in the mouth of a sewer after shooting your
poems up to the sky and now your shade swings ever
before them, ever larger and larger, between Notre-
Dame and Saint-Merry, and your fiery Chimearas range
this square of the heavens like six dishevelled and terrifying
comets. By your appeal to the New Spirit you for ever
disturbed our feeling today : and nowadays men could
not go on living without this anxiety :
' The Eagle has already passed : the New Spirit calls
me . . .' (Horus, str. III, v. 9)

On page 244, in the same body of notes, Cendrars states the following : " The other day I was sixty and it is only today, as I reach the end of the present tale, that I begin to believe in my vocation of writer . . ." Put that in your pipe and smoke it, you lads of twenty-five, thirty and forty years of age who are constantly belly-aching because you have not yet succeeded in establishing a reputation. Be glad that you are still alive, still *living* your life, still garnering experience, still enjoying the bitter fruits of isolation and neglect !

I would have liked to dwell on many singular passages in these recent books replete with the most astounding facts, incidents, literary and historic events, scientific and occult allusions, curiosa of literature, bizarre types of men and women, feasts, drunken bouts, humorous escapades, tender idylls, anecdotes concerning remote places, times, legends, extraordinary colloquies with extraordinary individuals, reminiscences of golden days, burlesques, fantasies, myths, inventions, introspections and eviscerations . . . I would have liked to speak at length of that singular author and even more singular man, Gustave Le Rouge, the author of 312 books which the reader has most likely never heard of, the variety, nature, style and contents of which Cendrars dwells on con amore; I would like to have given the reader some little flavor of the closing section, *Vendetta*, from *l'Homme Foudroyé*, which is direct from the lips of Sawo the Gypsy ; I would like to have taken the reader to La Cornue, chez Paquita, or to that wonderful hideout in the South of France where, hoping to finish a book in peace and tranquility, Cendrars abandons the page which he had slipped into the typewriter after writing a line or two and never looks at it again but gives himself up to pleasure, idleness, reverie and drink ; I would like to have given the reader at least an inkling of that hair-raising story of the " homunculi " which Cendrars recounts at length in *Bourlinguer* (the section called " Gênes "), but if I were to dip into these extravaganzas I should never be able to extricate myself.

I shall jump instead to the last book received from Cendrars, the one called *La Banlieue de Paris*, published by La Guilde du Livre, Lausanne. It is illustrated with 130 photographs by Robert Doisneau, sincere, moving, unvarnished documents which eloquently supplement the text. De nouveau une belle collaboration. (Vive les collaborateurs, les vrais !) The text is fairly short—fifty large pages.

But haunting pages, written sur le vif. (From the 15th of July to the 31st of August, 1949.) If there were nothing more noteworthy in these pages than Cendrars' description of a night at Saint-Denis on the eve of an aborted revolution this short text would be worth preserving. But there are other passages equally sombre and arresting, or nostalgic, poignant, saturated with atmosphere, saturated with the pullulating effervescence of the sordid suburbs. Mention has often been made of Cendrars' rich vocabulary, of the poetic quality of his prose, of his ability to incorporate in his rhapsodic passages the montrous jargon and terminology of science, industry, invention. This document, which is a sort of retrospective elegy, is an excellent example of his virtuosity. In memory he moves in on the suburbs from East, South, North, and West, and, as if armed with a magic wand, resuscitates the drama of hope, longing, failure, ennui, despair, frustration, misery and resentment which devours the denizens of this vast belt. In one compact paragraph, the second in the section called "Nord," Cendrars gives a graphic, physical summary of all that makes up the hideous suburban terrain. It is a bird's-eye view of the ravages which follow in the wake of industry. A little later he gives us a detailed description of the interior of one of England's war plants, "a shadow factory," which is in utter contrast to the foregoing. It is a masterful piece of reportage in which the cannon plays the rôle of vedette. But in paying his tribute to the factory, Cendrars makes it clear where he stands. It is the one kind of work he has no stomach for. "Mieux vaut être un vagabond," is his dictum. In a few swift lines he volplanes over the eternal bloody war business and, with a cry of shame for the Hiroshima "experiment," he launches the staggering figures of the last war's havoc tabulated by a Swiss review for the use and the benefit of those who are preparing the coming carnival of death. They belong, these figures, just as the beautiful arsenals belong and the hideous banlieue. And finally, for he has had them in mind throughout, Cendrars asks: "What of the children? Who are they? Whence do they come? Where are they going?" Referring us back to the photos of Robert Doisneau, he evokes the figures of David and Goliath—to let us know what indeed the little ones may have in store for us.

No mere document, this book. It is something I should like to own in a breast-pocket edition, to carry with me should I ever wander forth again. Something to take one's bearings by . . .

It has been my lot to prowl the streets, by night as well as day, of these God-forsaken precincts of woe and misery, not only here in my own country but in Europe too. In their spirit of desolation they are all alike. Those which ring the proudest cities of the earth are the worst. They stink like chancres. When I look back on my past I can scarcely see anything else, smell anything else but these festering empty lots, these filthy, shrouded streets, these rubbish heaps of jerries indiscriminately mixed with the garbage and refuse, the forlorn, utterly senseless household objects, toys, broken gadgets, vases and pisspots abandoned by the poverty-stricken, hopeless, helpless creatures who make up the population of these districts. In moments of high fettle I have threaded my way amidst the bric-a-brac and shambles of these quarters and thought to myself : What a poem ! What a documentary film ! Often I recovered my sober senses only by cursing and gnashing my teeth, by flying into wild, futile rages, by picturing myself a benevolent dictator who would eventually " restore order, peace and justice." I have been obsessed for weeks and months on end by such experiences. But I have never succeeded in making music of it. (And to think that Erik Satie, whose domicile Robert Doisneau gives us in one of the photos, to think that this man also " made music" in that crazy building is something which makes my scalp itch.) No, I have never succeeded in making music of this insensate material. I have tried a number of times, but my spirit is still too young, too filled with repulsion. I lack that ability to recede, to assimilate, to pound the mortar with a chemist's skill. But Cendrars *has* succeeded, and that is why I take my hat off to him. Salut, cher Blaise Cendrars ! You are a musician. Salute ! And glory be ! We have need of the poets of night and desolation as well as the other sort. We have need of comforting words—and you give them—as well as vitriolic diatribes. When I say " we " I mean all of us. Ours is a thirst unquenchable for an eye such as yours, an eye which condemns without passing judgment, an eye which wounds by its naked glance and heals at the same time. Especially in America do " we " need your historic touch, your velvety backward sweep of the plume. Yes, we need it perhaps more than anything you have to offer us. History has passed over our scarred, terrains vagues at a gallop. It has left us a few names, a few absurd monuments—and a veritable chaos of bric-a-brac. The one race which inhabited these shores and which did not mar the work of God was the redskins. Today they occupy the wastelands. For their "protection" we have organized a pious sort of concentration camp. It has no barbed wires, no instruments of torture, no armed guards. We simply leave them there to die out . . .

But I cannot end on this dolorous note, which is only the backfire of those secret rumblings which begin anew whenever the past crops up. There is always a rear view to be had from these crazy edifices which our minds inhabit so tenaciously. The view from Satie's back window is the kind I mean. Wherever in the "zone" there is a cluster of shabby buildings, there dwell the little people, the salt of the earth, as we say, for without them we would be left to starve, without them that crust which is thrown to the dogs and which we pounce on like wolves would have only the savor of death and revenge. Through those oblong windows from which the bedding hangs I can see my pallet in the corner where I have flopped for the night, to be rescued again in miraculous fashion the next sundown, always by a "nobody," which means, when we get to understand human speech, by an angel in disguise. What matter if with the coffee one swallows a mislaid emmenagogue? What matter if a stray roach clings to one's tattered garments? Looking at life from the rear window one can look down at one's past as into a still mirror in which the days of desperation merge with the days of joy, the days of peace, and the days of deepest friendship. Especially do I feel this way, think this way, when I look into my *French* backyard. There all the meaningless pieces of my life fall into a pattern. I see no waste motion. It is all as clear as "The Cracow Poem" to a chess fiend. The music it gives off is as simple as were the strains of "Sweet Alice Ben Bolt" to my childish ears. More, it is beautiful, for as Sir H. Rider Haggard says in his autobiography: "The naked truth is always beautiful, even when it tells of evil."

My dear Cendrars, you must at times have sensed a kind of envy in me for all that you have lived through, digested, and vomited forth transformed, transmogrified, transubstantiated. As a child you played by Virgil's tomb; as a mere lad you tramped across Europe, Russia, Asia, to stoke the furnace in some forgotten hotel in Pekin; as a young man, in the bloody days of the Legion, you elected to remain a corporal, no more ; as a war victim you begged for alms in your own dear Paris, and a little later you were on the bum in New York, Boston, New Orleans, Frisco . . . You have roamed far, you have idled the days away, you have burned the candle at both ends, you have made friends and enemies, you have dared to write the truth, you have known how to be silent, you have pursued every path to the end, and you are still in your prime, still building castles in the air, still breaking plans, habits, resolutions, because *to live* is your primary aim, and you *are* living and will continue to live both in the flesh and in the roster of the illustrious ones. How foolish, how absurd of me to think that I might be of help to *you*, that by putting in my little word for you here and there, as I said before, I would be advancing your cause. You have no need of *my* help or of anyone's. Just living your life as you do you automatically aid us, all of us, everywhere where life is lived. Once again I doff my hat to you. I bow in reverence. I have not the right to salute you because I am not your peer. I prefer to remain your devotee, your loving disciple, your spiritual brother in der Ewigkeit.

You always close your greetings with " ma main amie." I grasp that warm left hand you proffer and I wring it with joy, with gratitude, and with an everlasting benediction on my lips.

IV

RIDER HAGGARD

SINCE mentioning Rider Haggard's name, his book, *She*, has fallen into my hands. I have now read about two-thirds of it, my first glance at the book since the year 1905 or 1906, as best I remember. I feel impelled to relate, as quietly and restrained as I can, the extraordinary reactions which I am now experiencing as a result of this second reading. To begin with, I must confess that not until I came to Chapter 11, "The Plain of Kôr," did I have the faintest recollection of reading a word of this startling book before. I was certain, nevertheless, that the moment I encountered that mysterious creature called Ayesha (She) my memory would come alive. It has fallen out just as I anticipated. As with *The Lion of the North*, referred to earlier, so in *She* I rediscover the emotions which first overcame me upon coming face to face with a "femme fatale." (*The* femme fatale !) Ayesha, the true name of this ageless beauty,★ this lost soul who refuses to die until her beloved returns to earth again, occupies a position—at least, in my mind—comparable to the Sun in the galaxy of immortal lovers, all of them cursed with a deathless beauty. In this starry firmament Helen of Troy is but a pale moon. Indeed, and only today can I say it with certitude, Helen was never real to me. Ayesha is more than real. She is superreal, in every sense of that maligned word. About her personage the author has spun a web of such proportions that it almost deserves the appellation "cosmogonic." Helen is legendary, mythical— de la littérature. Ayesha is of the eternal elements, both discarnate and incarnate. She is of the dark mothers, of which mysterious race we get hints and echoes in Germanic literature. But before I babble on about the wonders of this narrative, which dates from the next to the last decade of the Nineteenth Century, let me speak of certain revelations concerning my own character and identity which are connected with it.

★ Also the name of Mahomet's second and favorite wife.

As I write this book I keep jotting down the titles of books I have read, as they return to memory. It is a game which has taken complete possession of me. The reasons for it I have already begun to perceive. The primary one is that I am rediscovering my own identity which, unknown to me, had been smothered or stifled in the pages of certain books. That is to say, in finding myself, through certain authors who acted as my intermediaries, I had also (without knowing it) lost myself. And this must have happened over and over again. For, what happens to me every day now is this : the mere recollection of a forgotten title brings to life not only the aura of the book's untouchable personality but the knowledge and the reality of my former selves. I need not add that something approaching awe, dread, consternation is beginning to take hold of me. I am coming to grips with myself in a wholly new and unexpected way. It is almost as if I were embarked on that journey to Tibet I have so frequently alluded to and which I have less and less need to make as times goes on and I myself go on, crab-wise, as seems to be my destiny.

Not for naught, I perceive more and more profoundly, have I clung to childhood memories ; not for naught have I attached such importance to " the boys in the street," our life together, our gropings for truth, our struggle to understand the perverse order of society in which we found ourselves enmeshed and from whose grip we vainly sought to free ourselves.

Just as there are two orders of human knowledge, two kinds of wisdom, two traditions, two everything, so in boyhood we came to realize that there were two sources of instruction : the one which we discovered ourselves and secretly strove to guard, and the other which we learned about in school and which impressed us as not only dull and futile, but diabolically false and perverted. The one kind of instruction nourished us, the other undermined us. And I mean this " literally and in every sense," to use Rimbaud's expression.

Every genuine boy is a rebel and an anarch. If he were allowed to develop according to his own instincts, his own inclinations, society would undergo such a radical transformation as to make the adult revolutionary cower and cringe. His would probably not be a comfortable or benevolent pattern of organization, but

it would reflect justice, splendor and integrity. It would accelerate
the vital pulse of life, abet and augment life. And what could be
more terrifying to adults than such a prospect ?

" A bas l'histoire ! " (Rimbaud's words.) Do you begin to see
the pregnancy of them ?

The books which we recommended to one another on the q.t.,
the books which we devoured stealthily at all hours of the day and
night—and in the weirdest places sometimes !—these books which
we discussed in the empty lot, or on a street corner under an arc
light, or at the edge of a cemetery, or in an icehouse of our own
construction or a cave dug into a hillside, or in any secret place of
gathering, for we always met as a clan, as blood brothers, as members of a secret order—The Order of Youth Defending the Traditions
of Youth !—these books were part of our daily instruction, part
of our Spartan discipline and our spiritual training. They were
the heritage of anterior orders, inconspicuous groups like ourselves,
who from earliest times fought to keep alive and to prolong, if
possible, the golden age of youth. We were not aware then that
our elders, some of them at least, looked back on this hallowed
period of their lives with envy and longing ; we had no suspicion
that our glorious dynasty would be referred to as " the period of
conflict." We did not know that we were little primitives, or
archaic heroes, saints, martyrs, gods or demigods. *We knew that
we were*—and that was sufficient. We wanted a voice in the government of our affairs ; we did not want to be treated as embryonic
adults. For most of us, neither father nor mother were objects
of veneration, much less of idolatry. We opposed their dubious
authority as best we could—and at great odds, it goes without
saying. Our law, and it was the only voice of authority we truly
respected, was the law of life. That we understood this law was
revealed by the games we played, that is, by the way we played
them and the inferences we drew from the way the various players
entered into them. We established genuine hierarchies ; we passed
judgment according to our various levels of understanding, our
various levels of being. We were conscious of the peak as well
as of the base of the pyramid. We had faith, reverence and discipline. We created our own ordeals and tests of power and fitness.
We abided by the decisions of our superiors, or our chief. He

was a king who manifested the dignity and the power of his rank
—and he never ruled a day beyond his time !

I speak of these facts with some emotion because it amazes me
that adults should ever forget them, as I see they do. We all
experience a thrill when, having put the past behind us, we suddenly
find ourselves among the " primitives." I mean now the true
primitive : early man. The study of anthropology has one great
merit—it permits us to live again as youths. The true student of
primitive peoples has respect, deep respect, for these " ancestors "
who exist side by side with us but who do not " grow up." He
finds that man in the early stages of his development is in no wise
inferior to man in the later stages ; some have even found early
man to be superior, in most respects, to late man. " Early " and
" late " are here used according to the vulgar acceptation of the
terms. We know nothing, in truth, about the origin of early man
or whether, indeed, he was young or decadent. And we know
little about the origin of " homo sapiens," though we pretend
much. There is a gap between the farthest reaches of history and
the relics and evidences of prehistoric man, branches of which,
such as the Cro-Magnon, baffle us by the evidences of their intelligence and aesthetic sensibility. The wonders which we constantly
expect the archaeologist to unearth, the links in our very slender
thread of knowledge about our own species, are supplied incessantly
and in the most amazing ways by those whom we refer to con-
descendingly as " imaginative " writers. I limit myself to these
latter for the moment since the others, sometimes termed " occult "
or " esoteric " writers, are still less accredited. They are for " second
childhood " (sic).

Rider Haggard is one of those imaginative writers who
undoubtedly fed from many streams. We think of him now as a
writer of boys' books, content to let his name fade into oblivion.
Perhaps only when our scientific explorers and investigators stumble
upon the truths revealed through imagination will we recognize
the true stature of such a writer.

" *What is imagination ?* " asks Rider Haggard in the midst of
his narrative. And he answers : " Perhaps it is a shadow of the
intangible truth, perhaps it is the soul's thought ! "

It was in the imagination that Blake lived entirely. It was imagination which led a humble grocery boy (Schliemann), fired by his reading of Homer, to go in search of Troy, Tiryns and Mycenae. And what of Jacob Boehme ? What of that intrepid Frenchman, Caillé, the first white man to enter Timbuctoo and come out alive ? What an epic !

Curious, but just about the time that I first became acquainted with the mysteries of Egypt, the dazzling history of Crete, the bloody annals of the House of Atreus, just when I am overwhelmed by my first contact with such themes as reincarnation, split personality, the Holy Grail, resurrection and immortality, and so on, via such "romancers" as Herodotus, Tennyson, Scott, Sienkiewicz, Henty, Bulwer-Lytton, Marie Corelli, Robert Louis Stevenson and others, many others, all these so-called legends, myths and superstitious beliefs were beginning to take substance in fact. Schliemann, Sir Arthur Evans, Frazer, Frobenius, Annie Besant, Madame Blavatsky, Paul Radin, a whole flock of courageous pioneers had been busy unveiling the truth in one realm after another, all interlocked, all contributory in breaking the spell of defeat and paralysis in which the doctrines of the Nineteenth Century held us. The new century opens with promise and splendor ; the past comes alive again, but tangibly, substantially, and with almost greater reality than the present.

When I stood amid the ruins of Knossos and of Mycenae did my thoughts turn to school books, to my penal instructors and the enchanting tales they told us ? No. I thought of the stories I had read as a child ; I saw the illustrations of those books I had thought buried in oblivion ; I thought of our discussions in the street and the amazing speculations we had indulged in. I recalled my own private speculation about all these exciting, mysterious themes connected with past and future. Looking out over the plain of Argos from Mycenae, I lived over again—and how vividly ! —the tale of the Argonauts. Gazing upon the Cyclopean walls of Tiryns I recalled the tiny illustration of the wall in one of my wonder books—it corresponded exactly with the reality confronting me. Never, in school, had a history professor even attempted to make living for us these glorious epochs of the past which every child enters into naturally as soon as he is able to read. With what childlike faith does the hardy explorer pursue his grim task ! We learn nothing from the pedagogues. The true educators are the adventurers and wanderers, the men who plunge into the living plasm of history, legend, myth.

A moment ago I spoke of the world youth might create, if given a chance. I have noticed repeatedly how frightening to parents is the thought of educating a child according to their own private notions. As I write I recall a momentous scene connected with this subject which passed between the mother of my first child and myself. It was in the kitchen of our home, and it followed upon some heated words of mine about the futility and absurdity of sending the child to school. Thoroughly engrossed, I had gotten up from the table and was pacing back and forth in the little room. Suddenly I heard her ask, almost frantically : " *But where would you begin ? How ?* " So deep in thought was I that the full import of her words came to me bien en retard. Pacing back and forth, head down, I found myself up against the hall door just as her words penetrated my consciousness. And at that very moment my eyes came to rest on a small knot in the panel of the door : How would I begin ? Where ? " *Why there ! Anywhere !* " I bellowed. And pointing to the knot in the wood I launched into a brilliant, devastating monologue that literally swept her off her feet. I must have carried on for a full half hour, hardly knowing what I was saying but swept along by a torrent of ideas long pent up. What gave it paprika, so to speak, was the exasperation and disgust which welled up with the recollection of my experiences in school. I began with that little knot of wood, how it came about, what it meant, and thence found myself treading, or rushing, through a veritable labyrinth of knowledge, instinct, wisdom, intuition and experience. Everything is so divinely connected, so beautifully interrelated—how could one possibly be at a loss to undertake the education of a child ? Whatever we touch, see, smell or hear, from whatever point we begin, we are on velvet. It is like pushing buttons that open magical doors. It works by itself, creates its own traction and momentum. There is no need to " prepare " the child for his lesson : the lesson itself is a kind of enchantment. The child longs to know ; he literally hungers and thirsts. And so does the adult, if we could but dissipate the hypnotic thrall which subjugates him.

To what lengths the teacher may go, to what heights he may rise, what powers he may draw on, we have but to turn to the story of Helen Keller's awakening to learn. There was a great teacher, this Miss Sullivan. A pupil deaf, dumb and blind—what a task to confront ! The miracles she accomplished were born of love and patience. Patience, love, understanding. But above all, *patience*. Whoever has not read the amazing life of Helen Keller has missed one of the great chapters in the history of education.

When I came to read of Socrates and of the Peripatetic schools, when later in Paris I roamed through the precincts haunted by Dante (the university curricula were then conducted out of doors . . . there is a street in this district, near Notre Dame, named after the very straw they slept on, these ardent students of the Middle Ages), when I read of the origins of our postal system and the part played in it by university students (who were the runners), when I thought of that lifelike education I had unwittingly received in such places as Union Square and Madison Square, where the soapbox orators held forth, when I recalled the heroic rôles, which in truth were *educational* rôles, played by such figures of the public square as Elizabeth Gurley Flynn, Carlo Tresca, Giovanitti, Big Bill Haywood, Jim Larkin, Hubert Harrison and such like, I was more than ever convinced that as boys, *on our own*, we were on the right track : we had sensed that education was a *vital* process, one acquired in the midst of life by living and wrestling with life. I felt closer then to Plato, Pythagoras, Epictetus, Dante and all the ancient illustrious ones than ever before or since. When my Hindu messenger boys in the telegraph company told me of Tagore's famous "Shantiniketan," when I read of Ramakrishna's bright abode, when I thought of Saint Francis and the birds, I knew that the world was wrong and that education as it is conducted today is disastrous. We who have sat behind closed doors on hard benches in foul rooms under stern eyes, hostile eyes, we have been betrayed, stunted, martyrized. A bas les écoles ! Vive le plein air ! Once again, I say, I plan to read *Emile*. What matter if Rousseau's theories proved a fiasco ? I shall read him as I read the works of Ferrer, Montessori, Pestalozzi and all the others. Anything to put a spike in our present system which turns out dolts, jackasses, tame ducks, weathervanes, bigots and blind leaders of the blind. If needs be, let us take to the jungle !

Behold the lot of man ! Certainly it shall overtake us, and we shall sleep. Certainly, too, we shall awake and live again, and again shall sleep, and so on and so on, through periods, spaces, and times, from aeon unto aeon, till the world is dead, and the worlds beyond the world are dead, and naught liveth save the Spirit that is Life . . .

Thus speaks Ayesha in the tombs of Kôr.

A boy wonders mightily over such a phrase as the last—" and naught liveth save the Spirit that is Life." If he was sent to church as well as to school, he heard much about the Spirit from the pulpit. But from the pulpit such talk falls on deaf ears. It is only when one becomes awake—twenty, thirty, forty years later—that the words of the Gospel acquire depth and meaning. The Church is wholly unrelated to the other activities of a boy's life. All that remains of this discipline, this instruction, is the awesome, majestic sound of the English language when it was in flower. The rest is jumble and confusion. There is no initiation, such as the common " savage " receives. Nor can there be any spiritual blossoming. The world of the chapel and the world outside are distinct and utterly apart. The language and behavior of Jesus do not conform to sense until one has passed through sorrow and travail, until one has become desperate, lost, utterly forsaken and abandoned.

That there is something beyond, above, and anterior to earthly life, every boy instinctively divines. It is only a few years since he himself lived wholly in the Spirit. He has an identity which manifests itself at birth. He struggles to preserve this precious identity. He repeats the rituals of his primitive forbears, he relives the struggles and ordeals of mythical heroes, he organizes his own secret order—to preserve a sacred tradition. Neither parents, teachers nor preachers play any part in this all-important domain of youth. Looking back upon myself as a boy, I feel exactly like a member of the lost tribe of Israel. Some, like Alain-Fournier in *The Wanderer*, are never able to desert this secret order of youth. Bruised by every contact with the world of adults, they immolate themselves in dream and reverie. Especially in the realm of love are they made to suffer. Occasionally they leave us a little book, a testament of the true and ancient faith, which we read with dim eyes, marvelling over its sorcery, aware, but too late, that we are looking at ourselves, that we are weeping over our own fate.

More than ever do I believe that at a certain age it becomes imperative to reread the books of childhood and youth. Else we may go to the grave not knowing who we are or why we lived.

> A stonyhearted mother is our earth, and stones are the bread she gives her children for their daily food. Stones to eat and bitter water for their thirst, and stripes for tender nurture.

A boy wonders if it be truly thus. Such thoughts fill him with anguish and dismay. He wonders again when he reads that " out of good cometh evil and out of evil good." Familiar though it be, coming from the mouth of Ayesha the thought troubles him. Of such matters he has heard little that was not mere echo. He surmises that he is indeed in some mysterious fane.

But it is when Ayesha explains that it is not by force but by terror that she reigns, when she exclaims—"*My empire is of the imagination*"—it is then a boy is startled to the core. *The imagination?* He has not heard yet of " the undenominated legislators of the world." Well he has not. There is a mightier thought here, something which lifts us above the world and all question of dominion over it. There is the hint—at least for a boy !—that if man only dared to *imagine* the dazzling possibilities life offers he would realize them to the full. There creeps over him a suspicion, even if fleeting, that age, death, evil, sin, ugliness, crime and frustration are but limitations conceived by man and imposed by man upon himself and his fellow man . . . In this fleeting moment one is shaken to the roots. One begins to question everything. The result, needless to say, is that he is covered with mockery and ridicule. " Thou art foolish, my son ! " That is the refrain.

There will come similar confrontations with the written word, more and more of them, as time goes on. Some will be even more shattering, more impenetrable. Some will send him reeling to the brink of madness. And ever and always none to offer a helping hand. No, the farther one advances the more one stands alone. One becomes like a naked infant abandoned in the wilderness.

Finally one runs amok or one conforms. At this juncture the drama surrounding one's "identity" is played out for good and all. At this point the die is cast irrevocably. One joins up—or one takes to the jungle. From boy to wage earner, husband, father, then judge—it all seems to take place in the twinkle of an eye. One does one's best—that age-old excuse. Meanwhile life passes us by. Our backs ever bent to receive the lash, we have only to murmur a few words of gratitude and our persecutors accept our reverence. Only one hope remains—to become oneself tyrant and executioner. From "The Place of Life," where one took his stance as a boy, one passes over into the Tomb of Death, the only death which man has a right to avoid and evade : *living death*.

"There is one being, one law and one faith, as there is only one race of man," says Eliphas Levi in his celebrated work, *The History of Magic*.

I would not be rash enough to say that a boy understands such a statement but I will say that he is much nearer to understanding it than the so-called "wise" adult. The boy prodigy, Arthur Rimbaud—that sphinx of modern literature—we have reason to believe was obsessed by this idea. In a study devoted to him* I dubbed him "The Columbus of Youth." I felt that he had pre-empted this domain. Because of his refusal to surrender the vision of truth which he had glimpsed as a mere boy he turned his back on poetry, broke with his confrères, and, in accepting a life of brute toil, literally committed suicide. In the hell of Aden he asks : "*What am I doing here ?*" In the famous *Lettre d'un Voyant* we have intimations of a thought which Levi has expressed thus : "It may be understood in a day to come that seeing is actually speaking and that the consciousness of light is a twilight of eternal life in being." It is in this singular twilight that many boys live their days. Is it any wonder then that certain books, originally intended for adults, should be appropriated by boys ?

Speaking of the Devil, Levi says : "We would point out that whatsoever has a name exists ; speech may be uttered in vain, but in itself it cannot be vain, and it has a meaning invariably." The ordinary adult finds it difficult to accept such a statement.

---

* Serialized in the annual anthologies, *New Directions* IX and *New Directions* XI.

Even the writer, particularly the "cultured" writer, for whom presumably the "word" is sacred, finds this thought unpalatable. A boy, on the other hand, if such a statement were explained to him, would find truth and meaning in it. For him nothing is "in vain"; neither is anything too incredible, too monstrous, for him to swallow. Our children are at home in a world which seems to terrify and stupefy us. I am not thinking altogether of the sadistic trend which has come to the fore; I am thinking rather of the unknown worlds, microcosmic and macrocosmic, whose impingement on our own quaking world of feeble reality has now become oppressive and menacing. Our grown-up boys, the scientists, prate about the imminent conquest of the moon; our children have already voyaged far beyond the moon. They are ready, at a moment's notice, to take off for Vega—and beyond. They beg our supposedly superior intellects to furnish them with a new cosmogony and a new cosmology. They have grown intolerant of our naïve, limited, antiquated theories of the universe.

If Rimbaud may be said to have broken his heart with chagrin because of his failure to win his contemporaries over to a new—and *truly modern*—view of man, if he surrendered all desire to establish a new heaven and a new earth, we now know why. The time was not ripe. Nor is it yet, apparently. (Though we should beware more and more of all "seeming" obstacles, hindrances and barriers.) The rhythm of time has been accelerated almost beyond comprehension. We are moving towards the day, and with frightening speed, when past, present and future will appear as one. The millennium ahead will not resemble, in duration, any like period in the past. It may be like the wink of an eye.

But to return to *She* . . . The chapter in which Ayesha is consumed in the flame of life—an extraordinary piece of writing!— is burned into my being. It was at this point in the narrative that I came awake—and remembered. It was because of this gruesome, harrowing event that the book remained with me all these years. That I had difficulty in summoning it from the depths of memory I attribute to the naked horror which it inspired. In the brief space which Haggard takes to describe her death one lives through the whole gamut of devolution. It is not death indeed which he describes but reduction. One is privileged, as it were, to assist at the spectacle of Nature reclaiming from her victim the secret which had been stolen from her. By observing the process in reverse the sense of awe which lies at the very roots of our being is enhanced. Prepared to witness a miracle, we are made to participate in a fiasco beyond human comprehension. It is at the Place of Life, let me remind the reader, that this unique death takes place. Life and death, Haggard tells us, are very close together. What he probably meant us to understand is that they are twins, and that only once is it given us to experience the miracle of life, only once the miracle of death : what happens in between is like the turning of a wheel, a perpetual rotation about an inner void, a dream that never ends, the activity of the wheel having nothing to do with the movement engendering it.

The deathless beauty of Ayesha, her seeming immortality, her wisdom which is ageless, her powers of sorcery and enchantment, her dominion over life and death, as Rider Haggard slowly but deftly reveals this mysterious being to us, might well serve as a description of the soul of Nature. That which sustains Ayesha, and at the same time consumes her, is the faith that she will eventually be reunited with her beloved. And what could the Beloved be but the holy Spirit ? No less a gift than this could suffice a soul endowed with her matchless hunger, patience and fortitude. The love which alone can transform the soul of Nature is divine love. Time counts for naught when spirit and soul are divorced. The splendor of neither can be made manifest except through union. Man, the only creature possessed of a dual nature, remains a riddle unto himself, keeps revolving on the wheel of life and death, until he pierces the enigma of identity. The drama of love, which is the highest he may enact, carries within it the key to the mystery. One law, one being, one faith, one race of man. Aye ! " To die means to be cut off, not to cease being." In his inability to surrender to life, man cuts himself off. Ayesha, seemingly deathless, had thus cut herself off by renouncing the spirit which was in her. The beloved Kallikrates, her twin soul, unable to bear the splendor of her soul when he gazes upon it for the first time, is killed by Ayesha's own will. The punishment for this incestuous murder is arrestation. Ayesha, invested with beauty, power, wisdom and youth, is doomed to wait until her Beloved assumes flesh once again. The generations of time which pass in the interval are like the period separating one incarnation from another. Ayesha's Devachan is the Caves of Kôr. There she is as remote from life as the soul in limbo. In this same dread place Kallikrates too, or rather the preserved shell of her immortal love, passes the interval. His image is with her constantly. Possessive in life, Ayesha is equally possessive in death. Jealousy, manifesting itself in a tyrannical will, in an insatiable love of power, burns in her with the brightness of a funeral pyre. She has all time, seemingly, in which to review her past, to weigh her deeds, her thoughts, her emotions. An endless time of preparation for the one lesson she has yet to learn—the lesson of love. Godlike, she is yet more vulnerable than the merest mortal. Her faith is born of despair, not of love, not of understanding. It is a faith which will be tested in cruelest fashion. The veil which wraps her round, the veil which no mortal man has penetrated—her divine virginity, in short— will be removed, torn from her, at the crucial moment. Then she will stand revealed to herself. Then, open to love, she will move forward in spirit as well as soul. Then she will be ready for the miracle of death, that death which comes but once. With the coming of this final death she will enter the deathless realm of being. Isis, to whom she had sworn eternal devotion, will be no more. Devotion, transformed by love, merges with understanding, then death, then divine being. That which always was, always will be, now is eternally. Nameless, timeless, indefinable, the nature of one's true identity is thus swallowed up in the manner of the dragon swallowing its tail.

To summarize thus briefly the salient features of this great romance, especially perhaps to offer interpretation of his theme, is to do an injustice to the author. But there is a duality in Rider Haggard which intrigues me enormously. An earth-bound individual, conventional in his ways, orthodox in his beliefs, though full of curiosity and tolerance, endowed with great vitality and practical wisdom, this man who is reticent and reserved, English to the core, one might say, reveals through his "romances" a hidden nature, a hidden being, a hidden lore which is amazing. His method of writing these romances—at full speed, hardly stopping to think, so to speak—enabled him to tap his unconscious with freedom and depth. It is as if, by virtue of this technique, he found the way to project the living plasm of previous incarnations. In spinning his tales he permits the narrator to philosophize in a loose way, thus permitting the reader to obtain glimpses and flashes of his true thoughts. His story-teller's gift, however, is too great for him to allow his deepest reflections to assume the cloying form and dimensions which would break the spell of the recital.

With these brief sidelights on the author for the reader who may not know *She* or the sequel called *Ayesha*, let me proceed to expose some of the mysterious filaments by which a boy, this particular boy, myself, was bound and doubtless formed in ways beyond his knowing. I have said that Helen of Troy was never real to me. Certainly I read of her before I happened upon *She*. Everything relating to the golden legends of Troy and Crete was part of my childhood legacy. Through the tales interwoven with the legend and romance of King Arthur and his Knights of the Round Table I had become acquainted with other legendary and deathless beauties, notably Isolt. The awesome deeds of Merlin and other hoary wizards were also familiar to me. I had presumably steeped myself in tales dealing with the rites of the dead, as practiced in Egypt and elsewhere. I mention all this to indicate that the collision with Rider Haggard's subject matter was not in the nature of a first shock. I had been prepared, if I may put it that way. But perhaps because of his skill as a narrator, perhaps because he had struck just the right tone, the right level of understanding for a boy, the force of these combined factors permitted the arrow to reach its destined target for the first time. I was pierced through and through—in the Place of Love, in the Place of Beauty, in the Place of Life. It was at the Place of Life that I received the mortal wound. Just as Ayesha had dealt death to her beloved instead of life, thereby condemning herself to a prolonged purgatorial existence, so had I been dealt a " little " death, I suspect, on closing this book some forty-five years ago. Gone, seemingly forever, were my visions of Love, of Eternal Beauty, of Renunciation and Sacrifice, of Life Eternal. Like Rimbaud, however, in referring to the visions of the poet-seer, I may exclaim : " *But I saw them !* " Ayesha, consumed by the devouring flame, at the very source and fount of life, took with her into limbo all that was sacred and precious

94

to me. *Only once is it given to experience the miracle of life.* The import of this dawns slowly, very slowly, upon me. Again and again I revolt against books, against raw experience, against wisdom itself, as well as Nature and God knows what all. But I am always brought back, sometimes at the very edge of the fateful precipice.

"Whoever has not become fully alive in this life will not become so through death."* I believe this to be the hidden note in all religious teachings. "To die," as Gutkind says, "means to be *cut off*, not to cease." Cut off from what ? From everything : from love, participation, wisdom, experience, but above all, from the very source of life.

Youth is one kind of aliveness. It is not the only kind, but it is vitally linked to the world of spirit. To worship youth instead of life itself is as disastrous as to worship power. Only wisdom is eternally renewable. But of life-wisdom contemporary man knows little. He has not only lost his youth, he has lost his innocence. He clings to illusions, ideals, beliefs.

In the chapter called "What We Saw," which affects me as deeply now as it did long ago, the narrator, after watching Ayesha consumed by the flame of life, reflects thus : "Ayesha locked up in her living tomb, waiting from age to age for the coming of her lover, worked but a small change in the order of the world. But Ayesha, strong and happy in her love, clothed with immortal youth, godlike beauty and power, and the wisdom of the centuries, would have revolutionized society, and even perchance have changed the destinies of Mankind." And then he adds this sentence, upon which I have pondered long : "Thus she opposed herself to the eternal law, and, strong though she was, by it was swept back into nothingness . . ."

One immediately thinks of the great figures in myth, legend and history who attempted to revolutionize society and thereby alter the destiny of man : Lucifer, Prometheus, Akhnaton, Ashoka, Jesus, Mahomet, Napoleon . . . One thinks especially of Lucifer, the Prince of Darkness, the most shining revolutionary of all. Each one paid for his "crime." Yet all are revered. The rebel, I firmly believe, is closer to God than the saint. To him is given dominion over the dark forces which we must obey before we

* *The Absolute Collective,* by Erich Gutkind.

95

can receive the light of illumination. The return to the source, the only revolution which has meaning for man, is the whole goal of man. It is a revolution which can occur only in his being. This is the true significance of the plunge into life's stream, of becoming fully alive, awakening, recovering one's complete identity.

Identity ! This is the word which, on rereading Rider Haggard, has come to haunt me. It is the riddle of identity which caused such books as *Louis Lambert, Seraphita, Interlinear to Cabeza de Vaca, Siddhartha,* to exercise dominion over me. I began my writing career with the intention of telling the truth about myself. What a fatuous task ! What can possibly be more fictive than the story of one's life ? " We learn nothing by reading [Winckelman]," said Goethe, " we *become* something." Similarly I might say—we reveal nothing of ourselves by telling the truth, but we do sometimes *discover* ourselves. I who had thought to *give* something found that I had *received* something.

Why the emphasis, in my works, on crude, repetitious experience of life ? Is it not dust in the eye ? Am I revealing myself or finding myself ? In the world of sex I seem alternately to lose and to find myself. It is all seeming. The conflict, which if not hidden is certainly smothered, is the conflict between Spirit and Reality. (*Spirit and Reality*, incidentally, is the title of a book by a blood brother whom I have discovered only recently.) For a long time *reality* for me was Woman. Which is equivalent to saying—Nature, Myth, Country, Mother, Chaos. I expatiate—to the reader's amazement, no doubt—on a romance called *She*, forgetting that I dedicated the cornerstone of my autobiography to " Her." How very much there was of " She " in " Her " ! In place of the great Caves of Kôr I described the bottomless black pit. Like " She," " Her " also strove desperately to give me life, beauty, power and dominion over others, even if only through the magic of words. " Her's " too was an endless immolation, a waiting (in how awful a sense !) for the Beloved to return. And if " Her " dealt me death in the Place of Life, was it not also in blind passion, out of fear and jealousy ? What was the secret of Her terrible beauty, Her fearful power over others, Her contempt for Her slavish minions, if not the desire to expiate Her crime ? *The crime ?* That she had robbed me of my identity at the very moment when I was about to recover it. In Her I lived as truly as the image

96

of the slain Kallikrates lived in the mind, heart and soul of Ayesha. In some strange, twisted way, having dedicated myself to the task of immortalizing Her, I convinced myself that I was giving Her Life in return for Death. I thought I could resurrect the past, thought I could make it live again—*in truth*. Vanity, vanity ! All I accomplished was to reopen the wound that had been inflicted upon me. The wound still lives, and with the pain of it comes the remembrance of what I was. I see very clearly that I was not this, not that. The " notness " is clearer than the " isness." I see the meaning of the long Odyssey I made ; I recognize *all* the Circes who held me in their thrall. I found my father, both the one in the flesh and the unnameable one. And I discovered that father and son are one. More, immeasurably more : I found at last that all is one.

At Mycenae, standing before the grave of Clytemnestra, I relived the ancient Greek tragedies which nourished me more than did the great Shakespeare. Climbing down the slippery stairs to the pit, which I described in the book on Greece, I experienced the same sensation of horror which I did as a boy when descending into the bowels of Kôr. It seems to me that I have stood before many a bottomless pit, have looked into many a charnel house. But what is more vivid still, more awe-inspiring, is the remembrance that, whenever in my life I have gazed too long upon Beauty, particularly the beauty of the female, I have always experienced the sensation of fear. Fear, and a touch of horror too. What is the origin of this horror ? The dim remembrance of being other than I now am, of being fit (once) to receive the blessings of beauty, the gift of love, the truth of God. Why, do we not sometimes ask ourselves, why the fatidical beauty in the great heroines of love throughout the ages ? Why do they seem so logically and naturally surrounded by death, bolstered by crime, nourished by evil ? There is a sentence in *She* which is strikingly penetrative. It comes at the moment when Ayesha, having found her Beloved, realizes that physical union must be postponed yet a while. " As yet I may not mate with thee, for thou and I are different, and the very brightness of my being would burn thee up, and perchance destroy thee." (I would give anything to know what I made of these words when I read them as a boy !)

97

G

No matter how much I dwell on the works of others I come back inevitably to the one and only book, the book of myself.

"Can I be," says Miguel de Unamuno, "as I believe myself or as others believe me to be ? Here is where these lines become a confession in the presence of my unknown and unknowable me, unknown and unknowable for myself. Here is where I create the legend wherein I must bury myself."

These lines appear in the fly-leaf to *Black Spring*, a book which came nearer to being myself, I believe, than any book I have written before or since. The book which I had promised myself to create as a monument to Her, the book in which I was to deliver the "secret," I did not have the courage to begin until about eight years ago. And then, having begun it, I put it aside for another five years. *Tropic of Capricorn* was intended to be the cornerstone of this monumental work. It is more like a vestibule or ante-chamber. The truth is that I wrote this dread book* in my head when jotting down (in the space of about eighteen continuous hours) the complete outline or notes covering the subject matter of this work. I made this cryptic skeleton of the magnum opus during a period of brief separation—from "Her." I was completely possessed and utterly desolate. It is now almost twenty-three years to the dot that I laid out the plan of the book. I had no thought whatever then of writing anything but this one grand book. It was to be the Book of My Life—my life with Her. Of what stupendous, unimaginable detours are our lives composed ! All is voyage, all is quest. We are not even aware of the goal until we have reached it and become one with it. To employ the word reality is to say myth and legend. To speak of creation means to bury oneself in chaos. We know not whence we come nor whither we go, nor even who we are. We set sail for the golden shores, sped on sometimes like "arrows of longing," and we arrive at our destination in the full glory of realization—or else as unrecognizable pulp from which the essence of life has been squashed. But let us not be deceived by that word "failure" which attaches itself to certain illustrious names and which is nothing more than the written seal and symbol of martyrdom. When the good Dr. Gachet wrote to brother Theo that the expression "love of art" did not apply

* *The Rosy Crucifixion.*

98

in Vincent's case, that his was rather a case of "martyrdom" to his art, we realize with full hearts that Van Gogh was one of the most glorious "failures" in the history of art. Similarly, when Professor Dandieu states that Proust was "the most living of the dead," we understand immediately that this "living corpse" had walled himself in to expose the absurdity and the emptiness of our feverish activity. Montaigne from his "retreat" throws a beam of light down the centuries. *The Failure*, by Papini, incited me enormously and helped to erase from my mind all thought of failure. If Life and Death are very near together, so are success and failure.

It is our great fortune sometimes to misinterpret our destiny when it is revealed to us. We often accomplish our ends despite ourselves. We try to avoid the swamps and jungles, we seek frantically to escape the wilderness or the desert (one and the same), we attach ourselves to leaders, we worship the gods instead of the One and Only, we lose ourselves in the labyrinth, we fly to distant shores and speak with other tongues, adopt other customs, manners, conventions, but ever and always are we driven towards our true end, concealed from us till the last moment.

V

JEAN GIONO

I<small>T</small> was in the rue d'Alésia, in one of those humble stationery stores which sell books, that I first came across Jean Giono's works. It was the daughter of the proprietor—bless her soul!—who literally thrust upon me the book called *Que ma joie demeure!* (*The Joy of Man's Desiring*). In 1939, after making a pilgrimage to Manosque with Giono's boyhood friend, Henri Fluchère, the latter bought for me *Jean le Bleu* (*Blue Boy*), which I read on the boat going to Greece. Both these French editions I lost in my wanderings. On returning to America, however, I soon made the acquaintance of Pascal Covici, one of the editors of the Viking Press, and through him I got acquainted with all that has been translated of Giono—not very much, I sadly confess.

Between times I have maintained a random correspondence with Giono, who continues to live in the place of his birth, Manosque. How often I have regretted that I did not meet him on the occasion of my visit to his home—he was off then on a walking expedition through the countryside he describes with such deep poetic imagination in his books. But if I never meet him in the flesh I can certainly say that I have met him in the spirit. And so have many others throughout this wide world. Some, I find, know him only through the screen versions of his books—*Harvest* and *The Baker's Wife*. No one ever leaves the theatre, after a performance of these films, with a dry eye. No one ever looks upon a loaf of bread, after seeing *Harvest*, in quite the same way as he used to ; nor, after seeing *The Baker's Wife*, does one think of the cuckold with the same raucous levity.

But these are trifling observations . . .

A few moments ago, tenderly flipping the pages of his books, I was saying to myself : " Tenderize your finger tips ! Make yourself ready for the great task ! "

For several years now I have been preaching the gospel—of

Jean Giono. I do not say that my words have fallen upon deaf ears, I merely complain that my audience has been restricted. I do not doubt that I have made myself a nuisance at the Viking Press in New York, for I keep pestering them intermittently to speed up the translations of Giono's works. Fortunately I am able to read Giono in his own tongue and, at the risk of sounding immodest, *in his own idiom*. But, as ever, I continue to think of the countless thousands in England and America who must wait until his books are translated. I feel that I could convert to the ranks of his ever-growing admirers innumerable readers whom his American publishers despair of reaching. I think I could even sway the hearts of those who have never heard of him—in England, Australia, New Zealand and other places where the English language is spoken. But I seem incapable of moving those few pivotal beings who hold, in a manner of speaking, his destiny in their hands. Neither with logic nor passion, neither with statistics nor examples, can I budge the position of editors and publishers in this, my native land. I shall probably succeed in getting Giono translated into Arabic, Turkish and Chinese before I convince his American publishers to go forward with the task they so sincerely began.

Flipping the pages of *The Joy of Man's Desiring*—I was looking for the reference to Orion "looking like Queen Anne's lace"—I noticed these words of Bobi, the chief figure in the book :

> I have never been able to show people things. It's curious, I have always been reproached for it. They say ·
> 'No one sees what you mean.'

Nothing could better express the way I feel at times. Hesitatingly I add—Giono, too, must often experience this sense of frustration. Otherwise I am unable to account for the fact that, despite the incontrovertible logic of dollars and cents with which his publishers always silence me, his works have not spread like wildfire on this continent.

I am never convinced by the sort of logic referred to. I may be silenced, but I am not convinced. On the other hand, I must confess that I do not know the formula for "success," as publishers use the term. I doubt if they do either. Nor do I think a man like Giono would thank me for making him a commercial success.

He would like to be read more, certainly. What author does not ? Like every author, he would especially like to be read by those who see what he means.

Herbert Read paid him a high tribute in a paper written during the War. He referred to him as the " peasant-anarchist." (I am sure his publishers are not keen to advertise such a label !) I do not think of Giono, myself, either as peasant or anarchist, though I regard neither term as pejorative. (Neither does Herbert Read, to be sure.) If Giono is an anarchist, then so were Emerson and Thoreau. If Giono is a peasant, then so was Tolstoy. But we do not begin to touch the essence of these great figures in regarding them from these aspects, these angles. Giono ennobles the peasant in his narratives ; Giono enlarges the concept of anarchism in his philosophic adumbrations. When he touches a man like our own Herman Melville, in the book called *Pour Saluer Melville* (which the Viking Press refuses to bring out, though it was translated for them), we come very close to the real Giono—and, what is even more important, close to the real Melville. This Giono is a poet. His poetry is of the imagination and reveals itself just as forcibly in his prose. It is through this function that Giono reveals his power to captivate men and women everywhere, regardless of rank, class, status or pursuit. This is the legacy left him by his parents, particularly, I feel, by his father, of whom he has written so tenderly, so movingly, in *Blue Boy*. In his Corsican blood there is a strain which, like the wines of Greece when added to French vintages, lend body and tang to the Gallic tongue. As for the soil in which he is rooted, and for which his true patriotism never fails to manifest itself, only a wizard, it seems to me, could relate cause to effect. Like our own Faulkner, Giono has created his own private terrestrial domain, a mythical domain far closer to reality than books of history or geography. It is a region over which the stars and planets course with throbbing pulsations. It is a land in which things " happen " to men as aeons ago they happened to the gods. Pan still walks the earth. The soil is saturated with cosmic juices. Events " transpire." Miracles occur. And never does the author betray the figures, the characters, whom he has conjured out of the womb of his rich imagination. His men and women have their prototypes in the legends of provincial France, in the songs of the troubadors, in the daily doings of humble, unknown peasants, an endless line of them, from Charlemagne's day to the very present. In Giono's works we have the sombreness of Hardy's moors, the eloquence of Lawrence's flowers and lowly creatures, the enchantment and sorcery of Arthur Machen's Welsh settings, the freedom and violence of Faulkner's world, the buffoonery and licence of the medieval mystery plays. And with all this a pagan charm and sensuality which stems from the ancient Greek world.

> If we look back on the ten years preceding the outbreak of the war, the years of steep incline into disaster, then the significant figures in the French scene are not the Gides and the Valérys, or any competitor for the laurels of the Académie, but Giono, the peasant-anarchist, Bernanos, the integral Christian, and Bréton, the super-realist. These are the significant figures, and they are positive figures, creative because destructive, moral in their revolt against contemporary values. Apparently they are disparate figures, working in different spheres, along different levels of human consciousness ; but in the total sphere of that consciousness their orbits meet, and include within their points of contact nothing that is compromising, reactionary or decadent ; but contain everything that is positive, revolutionary, and creative of a new and enduring world.*

Giono's revolt against contemporary values runs through all his books. In *Refusal to Obey*, which appeared in translation only in James Cooney's little magazine, *The Phoenix*, so far as I know, Giono spoke out manfully against war, against conscription, against bearing arms. Such diatribes do not help to make an author more popular in his native land. When the next war comes such a man is marked : whatever he says or does is reported in the papers, exaggerated, distorted, falsified. The men who have their country's interest most at heart are the very ones to be vilified, to be called " traitors," " renegades " or worse. Here is an impassioned utterance made by Giono in *Blue Boy*. It may throw a little light on the nature of his revolt. It begins :

* *Politics of the Unpolitical*, by Herbert Read, Routledge, London, 1946.

I don't remember how my friendship for Louis David began. At this moment, as I speak of him, I can no longer recall my pure youth, the enchantment of the magicians and of the days. I am steeped in blood. Beyond this book there is a deep wound from which all men of my age are suffering. This side of the page is soiled with pus and darkness . . .

If you (Louis) had only died for honorable things ; if you had fought for love or in getting food for your little ones. But, no. First they deceived you and then they killed you in the war.

What do you want me to do with this France that you have helped, it seems, to preserve, as I too have done ? What shall we do with it, we who have lost all our friends ? Ah ! If it were a question of defending rivers, hills, mountains, skies, winds, rains, I would say, 'Willingly. That is our job. Let us fight. All our happiness in life is there.' No, we have defended the sham name of all that. When I see a river, I say 'river' ; when I see a tree, I say 'tree' ; I never say 'France.' That does not exist.

Ah ! How willingly would I give away that false name that one single one of those dead, the simplest, the most humble, might live again ! Nothing can be put into the scales with the human heart. They are all the time talking about God ! It is God who gave the tiny shove with His finger to the pendulum of the clock of blood at the instant the child dropped from its mother's womb. They are always talking about God, when the only product of His good workmanship, the only thing that is godlike, the life that He alone can create, in spite of all your science of bespectacled idiots, that life you destroy at will in an infamous mortar of slime and spit, with the blessing of all your churches. What logic !

There is no glory in being French. There is only one glory : in being alive.

When I read a passage like this I am inclined to make extravagant statements. Somewhere I believe I said that if I had to choose between France and Giono I would choose Giono. I have the same feeling about Whitman. For me Walt Whitman is a hundred, a thousand, times more *America* than America itself. It was the great Democrat himself who wrote thus about our vaunted democracy :

We have frequently printed the word Democracy. Yet
I cannot too often repeat that it is a word the real gist of
which still sleeps, quite unawakened, notwithstanding
the resonance and the many angry tempests out of which
its syllables have come, from pen and tongue. It is a great
word, whose history, I suppose, remains unwritten, because
that history has yet to be enacted.*

No, a man like Giono could never be a traitor, not even if he
folded his hands and allowed the enemy to overrun his country. In
Maurizius Forever, wherein I devoted some pages to his *Refusal to
Obey*, I put it thus, and I repeat it with even greater vehemence :
" I say there is something wrong with a society which, because it
quarrels with a man's views, can condemn him as an arch-enemy.
Giono is not a traitor. Society is the traitor. Society is a traitor to
its fine principles, its empty principles. Society is constantly looking
for victims—and finds them among the glorious in spirit."

What was it Goethe said to Eckermann ? Interesting indeed that
the " first European " should have expressed himself thus : " Men
will become more clever and more acute ; but not better, happier,
and stronger in action—or at least only at epochs. I foresee the time
when God will break up everything for a renewed creation. I am
certain that everything is planned to this end, and that the time and
hour in the distant future for occurrence of this renovating epoch are
already fixed . . . "

The other day someone mentioned in my presence how curious
and repetitive was the rôle of the father in authors' lives. We had
been speaking of Joyce, of Utrillo, of Thomas Wolfe, of Lawrence,
of Céline, of Van Gogh, of Cendrars, and then of Egyptian myths
and of the legends of Crete. We spoke of those who had never
found their father, of those who were forever seeking a father. We
spoke of Joseph and his brethren, of Jonathan and David, of the
magic connected with names such as the Hellespont and Fort
Ticonderoga. As they spoke I was frantically searching my memory
for instances where the mother played a great rôle. I could think
only of two, but they were truly illustrious names—Goethe and da
Vinci. Then I began to speak of *Blue Boy*. I looked for that extraordinary passage, so meaningful to a writer, wherein Giono tells
what his father meant to him.

* From *Democratic Vistas*.

If I have such love for the memory of my father, it begins, if I can never separate myself from his image, if time cannot cut the thread, it is because in the experience of every single day I realize all that he has done for me. He was the first to recognize my sensuousness. He was the first to see, with his gray eyes, that sensuousness that made me touch a wall and imagine the roughness like porous skin. That sensuousness that prevented me from learning music, putting a higher price on the intoxication of listening than on the joy of being skillful, that sensuousness that made me like a drop of water pierced by the sun, pierced by the shapes and colors in the world, bearing in truth, like a drop of water, the form, the color, the sound, the sensation, physically in my flesh . . .

He broke nothing, tore nothing in me, stifled nothing, effaced nothing with his moistened finger. With the prescience of an insect he gave the remedies to the little larva that I was : one day this, the next day that ; he weighted me with plants, trees, earth, men, hills, women, grief, goodness, pride, all these as remedies, all these as provision, in prevision of what might be a running sore, but which, thanks to him, became an immense sun within me.

Towards the close of the book, the father nearing his end, they have a quiet talk under a linden tree. " Where I made a mistake," says his father, " was when I wanted to be good and helpful. You will make a mistake, like me."

Heart-rending words. Too true, too true. I wept when I read this. I weep again in recalling his father's words. I weep for Giono, for myself, for all who have striven to be " good and helpful." For those who are still striving, even though they know in their hearts that it is a " mistake." What we know is nothing compared to what we feel impelled to do out of the goodness of our hearts. Wisdom can never be transmitted from one to another. And in the ultimate do we not abandon wisdom for love ?

There is another passage in which father and son converse with Franchesc Odripano. They had been talking about the art of healing.

' When a person has a pure breath,' my father said, ' he can put out wounds all about him like so many lamps.'

But I was not so sure. I said, ' If you put out all the lamps, Papa, you won't be able to see any more.'

At that moment the velvet eyes were still and they were looking beyond my glorious youth.

'That is true,' he replied, 'the wounds illumine. That is true. You listen to Odripano a good deal. He has had experience. If he can stay young amongst us it is because he is a poet. Do you know what poetry is? Do you know that what he says is poetry? Do you know that, son? It is essential to realize that. Now listen. I, too, have had my experiences, and I tell you that you must put out the wounds. If, when you get to be a man, you know these two things, poetry and the science of extinguishing wounds, then you *will* be a man.'

I beg the reader's indulgence for quoting at such length from Giono's works. If I thought for one moment that most everyone was familiar with Giono's writings I would indeed be embarrassed to have made these citations. A friend of mine said the other day that practically everyone he had met knew Jean Giono. " You mean his books? " I asked. " At least some of them," he said. " At any rate, they certainly know what he stands for." " That's another story," I replied. " You're lucky to move in such circles. I have quite another story to tell about Giono. I doubt sometimes that even his editors have read him. *How to read*, that's the question."

That evening, glancing through a book by Holbrook Jackson,[*] I stumbled on Coleridge's four classes of readers. Let me cite them :

1. Sponges, who absorb all they read, and return it nearly in the same state, only a little dirtied.

2. Sand-glasses, who retain nothing, and are content to get through a book for the sake of getting through the time.

3. Strain-bags, who retain merely the dregs of what they read.

4. Mogul diamonds, equally rare and valuable, who profit by what they read, and enable others to profit by it also.

Most of us belong in the third category, if not also in one of the first two. Rare indeed are the mogul diamonds ! And now I wish to make an observation connected with the lending of Giono's books. The few I possess—among them *The Song of the World* and *Lovers are never Losers*, which I see I have not mentioned—have been loaned over and over again to all who expressed a desire to become acquainted with Jean Giono. This means that I have not only handed them to a considerable number of visitors but that I have wrapped and mailed the books to numerous others, to some in foreign lands as

[*]*The Reading of Books*, Scribner's, New York, 1947.

well. To no author I have recommended has there been a response such as hailed the reading of Giono. The reactions have been virtually unanimous. " Magnificent ! Thank you, thank you ! " that is the usual return. Only one person disapproved, said flatly that he could make nothing of Giono, and that was a man dying of cancer. I had lent him *The Joy of Man's Desiring*. He was one of those "successful " business men who had achieved everything and found nothing to sustain him. I think we may regard his verdict as exceptional. The others, and they include men and women of all ages, all walks of life, men and women of the most diverse views, the most conflicting aims and tendencies, all proclaimed their love, admiration and gratitude for Jean Giono. They do not represent a " select " audience, they were chosen at random. The one qualification which they had in common was a thirst for good books . . .

These are my private statistics, which I maintain are as valid as the publisher's. It is the hungry and thirsty who will eventually decide the future of Giono's works.

There is another man, a tragic figure, whose book I often thrust upon friends and acquaintances : Vaslav Nijinsky. His *Diary* is in some strange way connected with *Blue Boy*. It tells me something about writing. It is the writing of a man who is part lucid, part mad. It is a communication so naked, so desperate, that it breaks the mold. We are face to face with reality, and it is almost unbearable. The technique, so utterly personal, is one from which every writer can learn. Had he not gone to the asylum, had this been merely his baptismal work, we would have had in Nijinsky a writer equal to the dancer.

I mention this book because I have scanned it closely. Though it may sound presumptuous to say so, it is a book for writers. I cannot limit Giono in this way, but I must say that he, too, feeds the writer, instructs the writer, inspires the writer. In *Blue Boy* he gives us the genesis of a writer, telling it with the consummate art of a practiced writer. One feels that he is a " born writer." One feels that he might also be a painter, a musician (despite what he says). It is the " Storyteller's Story," l'histoire de l'histoire. It peels away the wrappings in which we mummify writers and reveals the embryonic being. It gives us the physiology, the chemistry, the physics, the biology of that curious animal, the writer. It is a textbook dipped

108

in the magic fluid of the medium it expounds. It connects us with the source of all creative activity. It breathes, it palpitates, it renews the blood stream. It is the kind of book which every man who thinks he has at least one story to tell could write but which he never does, alas. It is the story which authors are telling over and over again in myriad disguises. Seldom does it come straight from the delivery room. Usually it is washed and dressed first. Usually it is given a name which is not the true name.

His sensuousness, the development of which Giono attributes to his father's delicate nurturing, is without question one of the cardinal features of his art. It invests his characters, his landscapes, his whole narrative. " Let us refine our finger tips, our points of contact with the world . . . " Giono has done just this. The result is that we detect in his music the use of an instrument which has undergone the same ripening process as the player. In Giono the music and the instrument are one. That is his special gift. If he did not become a musician because, as he says, he thought it more important to be a good listener, he has become a writer who has raised listening to such an art that we follow his melodies as if we had written them ourselves. We no longer know, in reading his books, whether we are listening to Giono or to ourselves. We are not even aware that we are listening. We live through his words and in them, as naturally as if we were respiring at a comfortable altitude or floating on the bosom of the deep or swooping like a hawk with the down-draught of a canyon. The actions of his narratives are cushioned in this terrestrial effluvium ; the machinery never grinds because it is perpetually laved by cosmic lubricants. Giono gives us men, beasts and gods— in their *molecular* constituency.* He has seen no need to descend to the atomic arena. He deals in galaxies and constellations, in troupes, herds, and flocks, in biological plasm as well as primal magma and plasma. The names of his characters, as well as the hills and streams which surround them, have the tang, the aroma, the vigor and the spice of strong herbs. They are autochthonous names, redolent of the Midi. When we pronounce them we revive the memory of other times ; unknowingly we inhale a whiff of the African shore. We suspect that Atlantis was not so distant either in time or space.

* *Et bien mieux qu' Ossendowski !*

It is a little over twenty years now since Giono's *Colline*, published in translation as *Hill of Destiny*, by Brentano's, New York, made the author known at once throughout the reading world. In his introduction to the American edition, Jacques le Clercq, the translator, explains the purpose of the *Prix Brentano*, which was first awarded to Jean Giono.

> For the French public, the *Prix Brentano* owes its importance to various novel features. To begin with, it is the first American Foundation to crown a French work and to insure the publication of that work in America. The mere fact that it comes from abroad—*l'étranger, cette postérité contemporaine*"—arouses a lively interest ; again, the fact that the jury was composed of foreigners gave ample assurance that there could be no *propagande de chapelle* here, no manoeuvres of cliques such as must necessarily attend French prize-awards. Finally the material value of the prize itself proved of good augur.

Twenty years since ! And just a few months ago I received two new books from Giono—*Un Roi Sans Divertissement* and *Noé*—the first two of a series of twenty. A series of " *Chroniques*," he calls them. He was thirty years old when *Colline* won the *Prix Brentano*. In the interval he has written a respectable number of books. And now, in his fifties, he has projected a series of twenty, of which several have already been written. Just before the war started he had begun his celebrated translation of *Moby Dick*, a labor of several years, in which he was aided by two capable women whose names are given along with his as translators of the book. An immense undertaking, since Giono is not fluent in English. But, as he explains in the book which followed—*Pour Saluer Melville*—*Moby Dick* was his constant companion for years during his walks over the hills. He had lived with the book and it had become a part of him. It was inevitable that he should be the one to make it known to the French public. I have read parts of this translation and it seems to me an inspired one. Melville is not one of my favorites. *Moby Dick* has always been a sort of bête noir for me. But in reading the French version, which I prefer to the original, I have come to the conclusion that I will some day read the book. After reading *Pour Saluer Melville*, which is a poet's interpretation of a poet—" a pure invention," as Giono himself says in a letter—I was literally beside myself. How often it is the "foreigner" who teaches us to appreciate our own authors ! (I think immediately of that wonderful study of Walt Whitman by a Frenchman who virtually dedicated his life to the subject. I think, too, of what Baudelaire did to make Poe's name a by-word throughout all Europe.) Over and over again we see that the understanding of a language is not the same as the understanding of language. It is always communion versus communication. Even in translation some of us understand Dostoievsky, for example, better than his Russian contemporaries—or, shall I say, better than our present Russian contemporaries.

I noticed, in reading the Introduction to *Hill of Destiny*, that the translator expressed apprehension that the book might offend certain "squeamish" American readers. It is curious how askance French authors are regarded by Anglo-Saxons. Even some of the good Catholic writers of France are looked upon as "immoral." It always reminds me of my father's anger when he caught me reading *The Wild Ass' Skin*. All he needed was to see the name Balzac. That was enough to convince him that the book was "immoral." (Fortunately he never caught me reading *Droll Stories !*) My father, of course, had never read a line of Balzac. He had hardly read a line of any English or American author, indeed. The one writer he confessed to reading—c'est inoui, mais c'est vrai !—was John Ruskin. *Ruskin !* I nearly fell off the chair when he blurted this out. I did not know how to account for such an absurdity, but later I discovered that it was the minister who had (temporarily) converted him to Christ who was responsible. What astounded me even more was his admission that he had enjoyed reading Ruskin. That still remains inexplicable to me. But of Ruskin another time.

In Giono's books, as in Cendrars' and so many, many French books, there are always wonderful accounts of eating and drinking. Sometimes it is a feast, as in *The Joy of Man's Desiring*, sometimes it is a simple repast. Whatever it be, it makes one's mouth water. (There still remains to be written, by an American for Americans, a cookbook based on the recipes gleaned from the pages of French literature.) Every cinéaste has observed the prominence given by French film directors to eating and drinking. It is a feature conspicuously absent in American movies. When we have such a scene it is seldom real, neither the food nor the participants. In France, whenever two or more come together there is sensual as well as spiritual communion. With what longing American youths look at these scenes. Often it is a repast al fresco. Then are we even more moved, for truly we know little of the joy of eating and drinking outdoors. The Frenchman "loves" his food. We take food for nourishment or because we are unable to dispense with the habit. The Frenchman, even if he is a man of the cities, is closer to the soil than the American. He does not tamper with or refine away the products of the soil. He relishes the homely meals as much as the creations of the gourmet. He likes things fresh, not canned or refrigerated. And almost every Frenchman knows how to cook. I have never met a Frenchman who did not know how to make such a simple thing as an omelette, for example. But I know plenty of Americans who cannot even boil an egg.

Naturally, with good food goes good conversation, another element completely lacking in our country. To have good conversation it is almost imperative to have good wine with the meal. Not cocktails, not whisky, not cold beer or ale. Ah, the wines ! The variety of them, the subtle, indescribable effects they produce ! And let me not forget that with good food goes beautiful women— women who, in addition to stimulating one's appetite, know how to inspire good conversation. How horrible are our banquets for men only ! How we love to castrate, to mutilate ourselves ! How we really loathe all that is sensuous and sensual ! I believe most earnestly that what repels Americans more than immorality is the pleasure to be derived from the enjoyment of the five senses. We are not a " moral " people by any means. We do not need to read *La Peau* by Malaparte to discover what beasts are hidden beneath our chivalric uniforms. And when I say " uniforms " I mean the garb which disguises the civilian as well as that which disguises the soldier. We are men in uniform through and through. We are not individuals, neither are we members of a great collectivity. We are neither democrats, communists, socialists nor anarchists. We are an unruly mob. And the sign by which we are known is vulgarity.

There is never vulgarity in even the coarsest pages of Giono. There may be lust, carnality, sensuality—but not vulgarity. His characters may indulge in sexual intercourse occasionally, they may even be said to " fornicate," but in these indulgences there is never anything horripilating as in Malaparte's descriptions of American soldiers abroad. Never is a French writer obliged to resort to the mannerisms of Lawrence in a book such as *Lady Chatterley's Lover*. Lawrence should have known Giono, with whom he has much in common, by the way. He should have travelled up from Vence to the plateau of Haute-Provence where describing the setting of *Colline*, Giono says : " an endless waste of blue earth, village after village lying in death on the lavender tableland. A handful of men, how pitifully few, how ineffectual ! And, crouching amid the grasses, wallowing in the reeds—the hill, like a bull." But Lawrence was then already in the grip of death, able nevertheless to give us *The Man Who Died* or *The Escaped Cock*. Still enough breath in him, as it were, to reject the sickly Christian image of a suffering Redeemer and restore the image of man in flesh and blood, a man content just to live, just to breathe. A pity he could not have met Giono in the early days of his life. Even the boy Giono would have been able to divert him from some of his errors. Lawrence was forever railing against the French, though he enjoyed living in France, it would seem. He saw only what was sick, what was " decadent," in the French. Wherever he went he saw that first—his nose was too keen. Giono so rooted in his native soil, Lawrence so filled with wanderlust. Both proclaiming the life abundant : Giono in hymns of life, Lawrence in hymns of hate. Just as Giono has anchored himself in his " region," so has he anchored himself in the tradition of art. He has not suffered because of these restrictions, self-imposed. On the contrary, he has flowered. Lawrence jutted out of his world and out of the realm of art. He wandered over the earth like a lost soul, finding peace nowhere. He exploited the novel to preach the resurrection of man, but himself perished miserably. I owe a great debt to D. H. Lawrence. These observations and comparisons are not intended as a rejection of the man, they are offered merely as indications of his limitations. Just because I am also an Anglo-Saxon, I feel free to stress his faults. We have all of us a terrible need of France. I have said it over and over again. I shall probably do so until I die.

Vive la France ! Vive Jean Giono !

It was just five months ago that I put aside these pages on Jean Giono, knowing that I had more to say but determined to hold off until the right moment came. Yesterday I had an unexpected visit from a literary agent whom I knew years ago in Paris. He is the sort of individual who on entering a house goes through your library first, fingering your books and manuscripts, before looking at you. And when he does look at you he sees not *you* but only what is exploitable in you. After remarking, rather asininely, I thought, that his one aim was to be of help to writers, I took the cue and mentioned Giono's name.

" There's a man you could do something for, if what you say is true," I said flatly. I showed him *Pour Saluer Melville*. I explained that Viking seemed to have no desire to publish any more of Giono's books.

" And do you know why ? " he demanded.

I told him what they had written me.

" That's not the real reason," he replied, and proceeded to give me what he " knew " to be the real reason.

" And even if what you say is true," said I, " though I don't believe it, there remains this book which I want to see published. It is a beautiful book. I love it."

" In fact," I added, " my love and admiration for Giono is such that it doesn't matter a damn to me what he does or what he is said to have done. I know my Giono."

He looked at me quizzically and, as if to provoke me, asserted : " There are *several* Gionos, you know."

I knew what he was implying but I answered simply : " I love them all."

That seemed to stop him in his tracks. I was certain, moreover, that he was not as familiar with Giono as he pretended to be. What he wanted to tell me, undoubtedly, was that the Giono of a certain period was much better than the Giono of another. The " better " Giono would, of course, have been *his* Giono. This is the sort of small talk which keeps literary circles in a perpetual ferment.

When *Colline* appeared it was as if the whole world recognized this man Giono. This happened again when *Que ma joie demeure* came out. It probably happened a number of times. At any rate, whenever this happens, whenever a book wins immediate universal acclaim, it is somehow taken for granted that the book is a true reflection of the author. It is as though until that moment the man did not exist. Or perhaps it is admitted that the man existed but the writer did not. Yet the writer exists even before the man, paradoxically. The man would never have become what he did unless there was in him the creative germ. He lives the life which he will record in words. He dreams his life before he lives it ; he dreams it *in order to live it*.

In their first " successful " work some authors give such a full image of themselves that no matter what they say later this image endures, dominates, and often obliterates all succeeding ones. The same thing happens sometimes in our first encounter with another individual. So strongly does the personality of the other register itself in such moments that ever afterwards, no matter how much the person alters, or reveals his other aspects, this first image is the one which endures. Sometimes it is a blessing that one is able to retain this original full image ; other times it is a rank injustice inflicted upon the one we love.

That Giono is a man of many facets I would not think of denying. That, like all of us, he has his good side and his bad side, I would not deny either. In Giono's case it happens that with every book he produces he reveals himself fully. The revelation is given in every sentence. He is always himself and he is always giving of himself. This is one of the rare qualities he possesses, one which distinguishes him from a host of lesser writers. Moreover, like Picasso, I can well imagine him saying : " Is it necessary that everything I do prove a masterpiece ? " Of him, as of Picasso, I would say that the " masterpiece " was the creative act itself and not a particular work which happened to please a large audience and be accepted as the very body of Christ.

Supposing you have an image of a man and then one day, quite by accident, you come upon him in a strange mood, find him behaving or speaking in a way you have never believed him capable of. Do you reject this unacceptable aspect of the man or do you incorporate it in a larger picture of him ? Once he revealed himself to you completely, you thought. Now you find him quite other. Are *you* at fault or is *he* ?

I can well imagine a man for whom writing is a life's task revealing so many aspects of himself, as he goes along, that he baffles and bewilders his readers. And the more baffled and bewildered they are by the protean character of his being, the less qualified are they, in my opinion, to talk of "masterpieces" or of "revelation." A mind open and receptive would at least wait until the last word had been written. That at least. But it is the nature of little minds to kill a man off before his time, to arrest his development at that point which is most comfortable for one's peace of mind. Should an author set himself a problem which is not to the liking or the understanding of your little man, what happens? Why, the classic avowal: "He's not the writer he used to be!" Meaning, always, "he's not the writer *I know*."

As creative writers go, Giono is still a comparatively young man. There will be more ups and downs, from the standpoint of carping critics. He will be dated and re-dated, pigeonholed and re-pigeonholed, resurrected and re-resurrected—until the final dead line. And those who enjoy this game, who identify it with the art of interpretation, will of course undergo many changes themselves—in themselves. The diehards will make sport of him until the very end. The tender idealists will be disillusioned time and again, and will also find their beloved again and again. The skeptics will always be on the fence, if not the old one another one, but on the fence.

Whatever is written about a man like Giono tells you more about the critic or interpreter than about Giono. For, like the song of the world, Giono goes on and on and on. The critic perpetually pivots around his rooted, granulated self. Like the girouette, he tells which way the wind is blowing—but he is not of the wind nor of the airs. He is like an automobile without spark plugs.

A simple man who does not boast of his opinions but who is capable of being moved, a simple man who is devoted, loving and loyal is far better able to tell you about a writer like Giono than the learned critics. Trust the man whose heart is moved, the man whose withers can still be wrung. Such men are with the writer when he orders his creation. They do not desert the writer when he moves in ways beyond their understanding. Becoming is their silence and instructive. Like the very wise, they know how to hold themselves in abeyance.

"Each day," says Miguel de Unamuno, "I believe less and less in

the social question, and in the political question, and in the moral
question, and in all the other questions that people have invented in
order that they shall not have to face resolutely the only real question
that exists—the *human* question. So long as we are not facing this
question, all that we are now doing is simply making a noise so that
we shall not hear it."

Giono is one of the writers of our time who faces this human
question squarely. It accounts for much of the disrepute in which he
has found himself. Those who are active on the periphery regard
him as a renegade. In their view he is not playing the game. Some
refuse to take him seriously because he is " only a poet." Some admit
that he has a marvellous gift for narrative but no sense of reality.
Some believe that he is writing a legend of his region and not the
story of our time. Some wish us to believe that he is only a dreamer.
He is all these things and more. He is a man who never detaches
himself from the world, even when he is dreaming. Particularly
the world of human beings. In his books he speaks as father, mother,
brother, sister, son and daughter. He does not depict the human
family against the background of nature, he makes the human family
a part of nature. If there is suffering and punishment, it is because
of the operation of divine law through nature. The cosmos which
Giono's figures inhabit is strictly ordered. There is room in it for all
the irrational elements. It does not give, break or weaken because the
fictive characters who compose it sometimes move in contradiction
of or defiance to the laws which govern our everyday world.
Giono's world possesses a reality far more understandable, far more
durable than the one we accept as world reality. Tolstoy expressed
the nature of this other deeper reality in his last work :

> This then is everything that I would like to say : I
> would say to you that we are living in an age and under
> conditions that cannot last and that, come what may, we are
> obliged to choose a new path. And in order to follow it, it is
> not necessary for us to invent a new religion nor to discover
> new scientific theories in order to explain the meaning of
> life or art as a guide. Above all it is useless to turn back
> again to some special activity ; it is necessary to adopt one
> course alone to free ourselves from the superstitions of false
> Christianity and of state rule.
> Let each one realize that he has no right, nor even the

possibility, to organize the life of others ; that he should
lead his own life according to the supreme religious law
revealed to him, and as soon as he has done this, the present
order will disappear ; the order that now reigns among
the so-called Christian nations, the order that has caused
the whole world to suffer, that conforms so little to the
voice of conscience and that renders humanity more
miserable every day. Whatever you are : ruler, judge,
landlord, worker, or tramp, reflect and have pity on your
soul. No matter how clouded your brain has become
through power, authority and riches, no matter how
maltreated and harassed you are by poverty and humilia-
tion, remember that you possess and manifest, as we all
do, a divine spirit which now asks clearly : ' Why do
you martyrize yourself and cause suffering to everyone
with whom you come in contact ? ' Understand, rather,
who you really are, how truly insignificant and vulnerable
is the being you call you, and which you recognize in your
own shape, and to what extent, on the contrary, the real
you is immeasurably your spiritual self—and having understood this, begin to live each moment to accomplish your
true mission in life revealed to you by a universal wisdom,
the teachings of Christ, and your own conscience. Put the
best of yourself into increasing the emancipation of your
spirit from the illusions of the flesh and into love of your
neighbor, which is one and the same thing. As soon as
you begin to live this way you will experience the joyous
feeling of liberty and well-being. You will be surprised to
find that the same exterior objectives which preoccupied
you and which were far from realization, will no longer
stand in the way of your greatest possible happiness. And
if you are unhappy—I know you are unhappy—ponder
upon what I have stated here. It is not merely imagined
by me but is the result of the reflections and beliefs of the
most enlightened human hearts and spirits ; therefore,
realize that this is the one and only way to free yourself
from your unhappiness and to discover the greatest possible
good that life can offer. This then is what I would like to
say to my brothers, before I die.*

Notice that Tolstoy speaks of " the greatest possible happiness "
and " the greatest possible good." I feel certain that these are the
two goals which Giono would have humanity attain. Happiness !
Who, since Maeterlinck has dwelt at any length on this state of

* *The Law of Love and the Law of Violence.*

being ? Who talks nowadays of " the greatest good " ? To talk of happiness and of the good is now suspect. They have no place in our scheme of reality. Yes, there is endless talk of the political question, the social question, the moral question. There is much agitation, but nothing of moment is being accomplished. Nothing *will* be accomplished until the human being is regarded as a whole, until he is first looked upon as a human being and not a political, social or moral animal.

As I pick up Giono's last book—*Les Ames Fortes*—to scan once again the complete list of his published works, I am reminded of the visit I made to his home during his absence. Entering the house I was instantly aware of the profusion of books and records. The place seemed to be overflowing with spiritual provender. In a bookcase, high up near the ceiling, were the books he had written. Even then, eleven years ago, an astounding number for a man of his age. I look again, now, at the list as it is given opposite the title page of his last work, published by Gallimard. How many I have still to read ! And how eloquent are the titles alone ! *Solitude de la Pitié, Le Poids du Ciel, Naissance de l'Odyssée, Le Serpent d'Etoiles, Les Vraies Richesses, Fragments d'un Déluge, Fragments d'un Paradis, Présentation de Pan* . . . A secret understanding links me to these unknown works. Often, at night, when I go into the garden for a quiet smoke, when I look up at Orion and the other constellations, all so intimate a part of Giono's world, I wonder about the contents of these books I have not read, which I promise myself I will read in moments of utter peace and serenity, for to " crowd them in " would be an injustice to Giono. I imagine him also walking about in his garden, stealing a look at the stars, meditating on the work in hand, bracing himself for renewed conflicts with editors, critics and public. In such moments it does not seem to me that he is far away, in a country called France. He is in Manosque, and between Manosque and Big Sur there is an affinity which abolishes time and space. He is in that garden where the spirit of his mother still reigns, not far from the manger in which he was born and where his father who taught him so much worked at the bench as a cobbler. His garden has a wall around it ; here there is none. That is one of the differences between the Old World and the New. But there is no wall between Giono's spirit and my own. That is what draws me to him—the openness of his spirit. One feels it the moment one opens his books. One tumbles in drugged, intoxicated, rapt.

Giono gives us the world he lives in, a world of dream, passion and reality. It is French, yes but that would hardly suffice to describe it. It is of a certain region of France, yes, but that does not define it. It is distinctly Jean Giono's world and none other. If you are a kindred spirit you recognize it immediately, no matter where you were born or raised, what language you speak, what customs you have adopted, what tradition you follow. A man does not have to be Chinese, nor even a poet, to recognize immediately such spirits as Lao-tse and Li Po. In Giono's work what every sensitive, full-blooded individual ought to be able to recognize at once is "the song of the world." For me this song, of which each new book gives endless refrains and variations, is far more precious, far more stirring, far more poetic, than the "Song of Songs." It is intimate, personal, cosmic, untrammeled—and ceaseless. It contains the notes of the lark, the nightingale, the thrush ; it contains the whir of the planets and the almost inaudible wheeling of the constellations ; it contains the sobs, cries, shrieks and wails of wounded mortal souls as well as the laughter and ululations of the blessed ; it contains the seraphic music of the angelic hosts and the howls of the damned. In addition to this pandemic music Giono gives the whole gamut of color, taste, smell and feel. The most inanimate objects yield their mysterious vibrations. The philosophy behind this symphonic production has no name : its function is to liberate, to keep open all the sluices of the soul, to encourage speculation, adventure and passionate worship.

"Be what thou art, only be it to the utmost !" That is what it whispers.

Is this French ?

·VI

INFLUENCES

I HAVE already mentioned that in the Appendix I am listing all the books I can recall ever reading. There are a number of reasons why I am doing this. One is that I enjoy playing games, and this is one of the oldest of games : the pursuit game. A better reason is that I have never once seen a list of the books read by any of my favorite authors. I would give anything, for example, to know *all* the titles of those books which Dostoievsky devoured, or Rimbaud. But there is a more important reason still, and it is this : people are always wondering what *were* an author's influences, upon what great writer or writers did he model himself, who offered the most inspiration, which ones affected his style most, and so on. I intend presently to give the line of my descent, in as strictly chronological order as possible. I shall give specific names and I shall include a few men and women (some of them not writers at all) whom I regard as "living books," meaing by this that they had (for me) all the weight, power, prestige, magic and sorcelry which are attributed to the authors of great books. I shall also include a few "countries" ; they are, all of them, countries I have penetrated only through reading, but they are as alive for me and have affected my thought and behavior as much as if they were books.

But to come back to the list . . . I wish to emphasize the fact that I am listing both good and bad books. With respect to some I must confess that I am unable to say which were good for me and which bad. If I were to offer my own criterion of good and bad with respect to books, I would say—those which are alive and those which are dead. Certain books not only give a sense of life, sustain life, but, like certain rare individuals, *augment life*. Some authors long dead are less dead than the living, or, to put it another way, "the most alive of the dead." *When* these books were written, *who* wrote them matters little. They will breathe the flame of life until books are no more. To discuss *which* books belong in this category, to dispute the reasons pro and con, are futile, in my opinion. On this subject each man is his own best judge. He is right, for himself. We need not agree as to the source of a man's inspiration or the degree of his vitality ; it is enough to know and to recognize that he *is* inspired, that he *is* thoroughly alive.

Despite what I have just said, there will be endless speculation as to which authors, which books, influenced me most. I cannot hope to arrest these speculations. Just as each man interprets an author's work in his own limited way, so will the readers of this book, on scanning my list, draw their own conclusions as to my "true" influences. The subject is fraught with mystery, and I leave it a mystery. I know, however, that this list will give extraordinary pleasure to some of my readers, perhaps chiefly to the readers of a century hence. Impossible as it is to recall *all* the books one has read, I am nevertheless reasonably sure that I shall be able to give at least half. I repeat, I do not regard myself as a great reader. The few men I know who have read widely, and whom I have sounded out on the extent of their reading, startle me by their replies. Twenty to thirty thousand books, I perceive, is a fair average for a cultured individual of our time. As for myself, I doubt if I have read more than five thousand, though I may well be in error.

When I look over my list, which never ceases to grow, I am appalled by the obvious waste of time which the reading of most of these books entailed. It is often said of writers that "all is grist for the mill." Like all sayings, this one too must be taken with a grain of salt. A writer needs very little to stimulate him. The fact of being a writer means that more than other men he is given to cultivating the imagination. Life itself provides abundant material. Superabundant material. The more one writes the less books stimulate. One reads to corroborate, that is, to enjoy one's own thoughts expressed in the multifarious ways of others.

In youth one's appetite, both for raw experience and for books, is uncontrolled. Where there is excessive hunger, and not mere appetite, there must be vital reason for it. It is blatantly obvious that our present way of life does not offer proper nourishment. If it did I am certain we would read less, work less, strive less. We would not need substitutes, we would not accept vicarious modes of existence. This applies to all realms : food, sex, travel, religion, adventure. We get off to a bad start. We travel the broad highway with one foot in the grave. We have no definite goal or purpose, nor the freedom of being without goal or purpose. We are, most of us, sleepwalkers, and we die without ever opening our eyes.

If people enjoyed deeply everything they read there would be no excuse for talking this way. But they read as they live—aimlessly, haphazardly, feebly and flickeringly. If they are already asleep, then whatever they read only plunges them into a deeper sleep. If they are merely lethargic, they become more lethargic. If they are idlers, they become worse idlers. And so on. Only the man who is wide awake is capable of enjoying a book, of extracting from it what is vital. Such a man enjoys whatever comes into his experience, and, unless I am horribly mistaken, makes no distinction between the experiences offered through reading and the manifold experiences of everyday life. The man who thoroughly enjoys what he reads or does, or even what he says, or simply what he dreams or imagines, profits to the full. The man who *seeks* to profit, through one form of discipline or another, deceives himself. It is because I am so firmly convinced of this that I abhor the issuance of lists of books for those who are about to enter life. The advantages to be derived from this sort of self-education are even more dubious, to my way of thinking, than the supposed advantages to be obtained from ordinary methods of education. Most of the books given on such lists cannot begin to be understood and appreciated until one has lived and thought for himself. Sooner or later the whole kit and caboodle has to be regurgitated.

And now here are *names* for you. Names of those whose influence I *am* aware of and which, through my writings, I have testified to again and again.* To begin with, let me say that *everything* which came within the field of my experience influenced me. Those who do not find themselves mentioned should know that I include them too. As for the dead, they knew in advance, doubtless, that they would put their seal on me. I mention them only because it is in order.

First of all come the books of childhood, those dealing with legend, myth, tales of imagination, all of them saturated with

* See Appendix for reference to authors and books touched on in my writings, as well as to complete essays on certain ones.

mystery, heroism, supernaturalism, the marvelous and the impossible, with crime and horror of all sorts and all degrees, with cruelty, with justice and injustice, with magic and prophecy, with perversion, ignorance, despair, doubt and death. These books affected my whole being : they formed my character, my way of looking at life, my attitude towards woman, towards society, laws, morals, government. They determined the *rhythm* of my life. From adolescence on, the books I read, particularly those I adored or was enslaved by, affected me only partially. That is, some affected the man, some the writer, some the naked soul. This perhaps because my being had already become fragmented. Perhaps too because the substance of adult reading cannot possibly affect the whole man, his whole being. There are exceptions, to be sure, but they are rare. At any rate, the whole province of childhood reading belongs under the sign of anonymity ; those who are curious will discover the titles in the Appendix. I read what other children read. I was not a prodigy, nor did I make special demands. I took what was given me and I swallowed it. The reader who has followed me thus far has by this time gleaned the nature of my reading. The books read in boyhood I have also touched upon already, signalling such names as Henty first and foremost, Dumas, Rider Haggard, Sienkiewicz and others, most of them quite familiar. Nothing unusual about this period, unless that I read too much.

Where the specific influences commence is at the brink of manhood, that is, from the time I first dreamed that I too might one day become " a writer." The names which follow may be regarded then as the names of authors who influenced me as a man and as a writer, the two becoming more and more inseparable as time went on. From early manhood on my whole activity revolved about, or was motivated by, the fact that I thought of myself, first potentially, then embryonically, and finally manifestly, as a writer. And so, if my memory serves me right, here is my genealogical line : Boccaccio, Petronius, Rabelais, Whitman, Emerson, Thoreau, Maeterlinck, Romain Rolland, Plotinus, Heraclitus, Nietzsche, Dostoievsky (and other Russian writers of the Nineteenth Century), the ancient Greek dramatists, the Elizabethan dramatists (excluding Shakespeare), Theodore Dreiser, Knut Hamsun, D. H. Lawrence, James Joyce, Thomas Mann, Elie Faure, Oswald Spengler, Marcel

Proust, Van Gogh, the Dadaists and Surrealists, Balzac, Lewis Carroll, Nijinsky, Rimbaud, Blaise Cendrars, Jean Giono, Céline, everything I read on Zen Buddhism, everything I read about China, India, Tibet, Arabia, Africa, and of course the Bible, the men who wrote it and especially the men who made the King James version, for it was the language of the Bible rather than its "message" which I got first and which I will never shake off.

What were the subjects which made me seek the authors I love, which permitted me to be influenced, which formed my style, my character, my approach to life? Broadly these : the love of life itself, the pursuit of truth, wisdom and understanding, mystery, the power of language, the antiquity and the glory of man, eternality, the purpose of existence, the oneness of everything, self-liberation, the brotherhood of man, the meaning of love, the relation of sex to love, the enjoyment of sex, humor, oddities and eccentricities in all life's aspects, travel, adventure, discovery, prophecy, magic (white and black), art, games, confessions, revelations, mysticism, more particularly the mystics themselves, the varieties of faith and worship, the marvelous in all realms and under all aspects, for "there is only the marvelous and nothing but the marvelous."

Have I left out some items? Fill them in yourself! I was, and still am, interested in everything. Even in politics—when regarded from "the perspective of the bird." But the struggle of the human being to emancipate himself, that is, to liberate himself from the prison of his own making, that is for me the supreme subject. That is why I fail, perhaps, to be completely "the writer." Perhaps that is why, in my works, I have given so much space to sheer experience of life. Perhaps too, though the critics so often fail to perceive it, that is why I am powerfully drawn to the men of wisdom, the men who have experienced life to the full and who give life—artists, religious figures, pathfinders, innovators and iconoclasts of all sorts. And perhaps—why not say it?—that is why I have so little respect for literature, so little regard for the accredited authors, so little appreciation of the transitory revolutionaries. For me the only true revolutionaries are the inspirers and activators, figures like Jesus, Lao-tse, Gautama the Buddha, Akhnaton, Ramakrishna, Krishnamurti. The yardstick I employ is life : how men stand in relation to life. Not whether they succeeded in overthrowing a government, a social order, a religious form, a moral code, a system of education, an economic tyranny. Rather, how did they affect life itself? For, what distinguishes the men I have in mind is that they did not impose their authority on man; on the contrary, they sought to destroy authority. Their aim and purpose was to open up life, to make man hungry for life, to exalt life—and to refer all questions back to life. They exhorted man to realize that he had all freedom in himself, that he was not to concern himself with the fate of the world (which is not his problem) but to solve his own individual problem, which is a question of liberation, nothing else.

And now for "the living books" . . . Several times I have said that there were men and women who came into my experience, at various times, whom I regard as "living books." I have explained why I refer to them in this fashion. I shall be even more explicit now. They stay with me, these individuals, as do the good books. I can open them up at will, as I would a book. When I glance at a page of their being, so to speak, they talk to me as eloquently as they did when I met them in the flesh. The books they left me are their lives, their thoughts, their deeds. It was the fusion of thought, being and act which made each of these lives singular and inspiring to me. Here they are, then, and I doubt that I have forgotten a single one: Benjamin Fay Mills, Emma Goldman, W. E. Burghardt Dubois, Hubert Harrison, Elizabeth Gurley Flynn, Jim Larkin, John Cowper Powys, Lou Jacobs, Blaise Cendrars. A curious assemblage indeed. All but one are, or were, known figures. There are others, of course, who without knowing it played an important rôle in my life, who helped to open the book of life for me. But the names I have cited are the ones I shall always revere, the ones I feel forever indebted to.

The Xerxes Society
(*circa* 1910 or 1911, *Henry Miller is on the extreme right
of the second row*)

VII

LIVING BOOKS

Lou Jacobs, that one unknown figure, I can recall at will merely by saying *Asmodeus, or The Devil on Two Sticks*. Curious that a book I never read should be the magic touchstone. The book was always there on the shelf, in his little flat. Several times I picked it up, scanned a page or two, then put it down. For almost forty years now I have kept in the back of my head this unread *Asmodeus*. Next to it, on the same shelf, was *Gil Blas*, which I never read either.

Why do I feel compelled to talk of this unknown man ? Because, among other things, he taught me to laugh at misfortune. It was during a period of dire woe that I made his acquaintance. Everything was black, black, black. No egress. No hope of egress. I was more a prisoner than a man serving a life sentence in the penitentiary.* Living then with my first mistress, the unofficial janitor of the three-storey house in which we shared a flat with a young man dying of tuberculosis and a trolley conductor who was our star boarder, strictly surveilled by the ogress who owned the house, without funds, without work, with no knowledge of what I wanted to do or could do, convinced that I had no talent—twelve lines with a pencil were sufficient to corroborate the suspicion—trying to save the life of the young man, who was my mistress' son, hiding away from friends and parents, eating my heart out with remorse for having surrendered the girl I loved (my first love !), the slave of sex, the girouette who veered with the slightest breeze, lost, utterly lost, I discovered one day on the floor below this man Lou Jacobs, who forthwith became my Guide, my Comforter, my Bright Green Wind. No matter what the hour, what the

* " And a night comes when all is over, when so many jaws have closed upon us that we no longer have the strength to stand, and our meat hangs upon our bodies as though it had been masticated by every mouth. A night comes when man weeps and woman is emptied." (From *Bubu of Montparnasse* by Charles-Louis Philippe.)

occasion, no matter if Death were knocking at the door, Lou Jacobs could laugh and make me laugh with him. "*For all your ills laughter !*"

I had then only a furtive acquaintance with Rabelais, if my memory serves me right. But Lou Jacobs was his intimate, I am certain. He knew all who brought joy as well as those who had known sorrow. Whenever he passed Shakespeare's statue in the park he doffed his hat. "Why not ?" he would say. He could recite the lamentations of Job and give me the remedy in the next breath. ("What is man, that thou art mindful of him ? and the son of man, that thou visitest him ?")

He always appeared to be doing nothing, nothing at all. The door was ever open to any and every one. Conversation began at once—*instanter*. Usually he was half-crocked, a state beyond which he never appeared to progress, or degenerate, if you prefer. His skin was like parchment, the face seamed with fine wrinkles, the abundant head of hair always oily, tousled, and falling over his eyes. He might have been a centenarian, though I doubt if he was a day over sixty.

His "job" was that of certified public accountant, for which he was well paid. He seemed to have no ambition of any sort. A game of chess, if you wished it, was to him as good a way of passing the time as any other pursuit. (He played the most unorthodox, the most erratic, eccentric, brilliant game imaginable.) He slept little, was always thoroughly alive and awake, jovial, full of banter and raillery, outwardly mocking but inwardly reverencing, inwardly adoring and worshipping.

Books ! Never a title I mentioned but he had read the book. And he was honest. The impression he left with me was that he had read *everything* worth reading. In talking he always came back to Shakespeare and the Bible. In this he reminded me of Frank Harris, who also talked incessantly of Shakespeare and the Bible, or rather of Shakespeare and Jesus.

Without being in the least aware of it, I was receiving from this man my first real schooling. It was the indirect method of education. As with the ancients, his technique consisted in indicating that "it" was not this, not that. Whatever "it" was, and of course it was the all, he taught me never to approach it head on, never to name or define. The oblique method of art. First and last things. But no first and no last. Always from the center outward. Always the spiral motion : never the straight line, never sharp angles, never the impasse or cul-de-sac.

Yes, Lou Jacobs possessed a wisdom I am only *beginning* to acquire. He had the faculty of looking upon everything as an open book. He had ceased reading to discover the secrets of life ; he read for sheer enjoyment. The essence of all he read had permeated his entire being, had become one with his total experience of life. " There are not more than a dozen basic themes in all literature," he once said to me. But then he quickly added that each man had his own story to tell, and that it was unique. I suspected that he, too, had once endeavored to write. Certainly no one could express himself better or more clearly. His wisdom, however, was the sort that is not concerned with the imparting of it. Though he knew how to hold his tongue, no man enjoyed conversation more than he. Moreover, he had a way of never closing a subject. He was content to skirmish and reconnoiter, to throw out feelers, to dangle clues, to give hints, to suggest rather than to inform. Whether one wished it or not, he compelled his listener to think for himself. I can't recall ever once receiving advice or instruction from him, yet everything which issued from his mouth constituted advice and instruction . . . if one knew how to take it !

In Maeterlinck's works, particularly a book such as *Wisdom and Destiny*, there are inspiring references to great figures of the past (in life and in literature) who weathered adversity with noble equanimity. Such books are no longer in favor, I fear. We do not turn for comfort, consolation or renewed courage to authors like Maeterlinck any longer. Nor to Emerson, with whom his name is often linked. Their spiritual pabulum is suspect nowadays. Dommage ! The truth is, we really have no great authors to turn to these days—if we are in search of eternal verities. We have surrendered to the flux. Our hopes, feeble and flickering, seem to be completely centered on political solutions. Men are turning away from books, which is to say, from writers, from " intellectuals." An excellent sign—if only they were turning from books to life ! But are they ? Never was the fear of life so rampant. The fear of life has replaced the fear of death. Life and death have come

I

to mean the same thing. Yet never did life hold more promise than now. Never before in the history of man was the issue so clear —the issue between creation and annihilation. Yes, by all means throw away your books ! Especially if they obscure the issue. Life itself was never more an open book than at this present moment. *But, can you read the Book of Life ?*

("What are you doing there on the floor ?"
"I am teaching the alphabet to the ants.")

It's a strange thing, but outrageously noticeable latterly, that the only gay, youthful spirits among us are the "old dogs." They continue blithely with their work of creation no matter what dire forebodings poison the air. I think of certain painters principally, men who already have an immense body of work behind them. Perhaps their vision of things was never dimmed by the reading of many books. Perhaps their very choice of profession safeguarded them against a bleak, sterile, morbid view of the universe. Their signs and symbols are of another order from the writer's or thinker's. They deal in forms and images, and images have a way of remaining fresh and vivid. I feel that the painter looks at the world more directly. At any rate, these veterans whom I have in mind, these gay old dogs, have a youthful gaze. Whereas our young in years see with a dim, blurred vision ; they are filled with fear and fright. The thought which haunts them day and night is—will this world be snuffed out before we have had a chance to enjoy it ? And there is no one who dares to tell them that even if the world were snuffed out tomorrow, or the day after, it would not really matter—since the life they crave to enjoy is imperishable. Nor does any one tell them that the destruction of this planet, or its preservation and everlasting glory, hinges on their own thoughts, their own deeds. The individual has now become identified, involuntarily, with society. Few are able to see any longer that society is made up of *individuals*. Who is an individual any longer ? What is an individual ? And what is society, if it is no longer the sum or aggregate of the individuals which constitute it ?

I remember, more than thirty years ago it was, reading Carlyle's *Heroes and Hero Worship* on my way to and from work each day.

It was in the elevated train that I read him. One day a thought he enunciated moved me so profoundly that when I looked up from the page I had difficulty recognizing the all too familiar figures surrounding me. I was in another world—but completely. Something he had said—what it was I no longer remember—had shaken me to the roots of my being. Then and there I had the conviction that my fate, or destiny, would be different from those about me. I suddenly saw myself lifted out—ejected !—from the circle which imprisoned me. A momentary feeling of pride and exaltation, of vanity too no doubt, accompanied this revelation, but it soon vanished, soon gave way to a state of quiet acceptance and deep resolution, awakening at the same time a stronger sense of communion, a much more human bond between myself and my neighbor.

Carlyle is another writer of whom not much is said nowadays. "Too much fustian," no doubt. Too fuliginous. Besides, we no longer worship heroes, or, if we do make use of the word, it is to distinguish those who are on a level with ourselves. Lindbergh, for example, was a tremendous hero—for a day. We have no permanent pantheon in which our heroes may be placed, adored and reverenced. Our pantheon is the daily rag, which is erected and destroyed from day to day.

One of the reasons why so few of us ever act, instead of reacting, is because we are continually stifling our deepest impulses. I can illustrate this thought by choosing, for example, the way in which most of us read. If it is a book which excites and stimulates us to thought, we race through it. We cannot wait to know what it is leading to ; we want to grasp, to possess, the hidden message. Time and again, in such books, we stumble on a phrase, a passage, sometimes a whole chapter, so stimulating and provocative that we scarcely understand what we are reading, so charged is our mind with thoughts and associations of our own. How seldom do we interrupt the reading in order to surrender ourselves to the luxury of our own thoughts ! No, we stifle and suppress *our* thoughts, pretending that we will return to them when we have finished the book. We never do, of course. How much better and wiser it would be, how much more instructive and enriching, if we proceeded at a snail's pace ! What matter if it took a year, instead of a few days, to finish the book ?

131

"But I haven't time to read books that way!" it will be objected. "I have other things to do. I have duties and responsibilities."

Precisely. Whoever speaks thus is the very one for whom these words are intended. Whoever fears to neglect his duties by reading leisurely and thoughtfully, by cultivating his own thoughts, will neglect his duties anyway, and for worse reasons. Perhaps it was intended that you lose your job, your wife, your home. If the reading of a book can stir you so deeply as to make you forget your responsibilities, then those responsibilities could not have had much meaning for you. Then you had higher responsibilities. If you had trusted your own inner promptings you would have followed through to firmer ground, to vantage ground. But you were afraid a voice might whisper: "Turn here! Knock there! Enter by this door!" You were afraid of being deserted and abandoned. You thought of security instead of new life, new fields of adventure and exploration.

This is merely an example of what may happen, or not happen, in reading a book. Extend it to the multitudinous opportunities which life constantly offers and it is easy to see why men fail not only to become heroes but even plain individuals. The way one reads a book is the way one reads life. Maeterlinck, whom I referred to a moment ago, writes as profoundly and engagingly about insects, flowers, stars, even space itself, as he does about men and women. For him the world is a continuous, interactive, interchanging whole. There are no walls or barriers. There is no death anywhere. A moment of time is as rich and complete as ten thousand years. Truly, a luxurious kind of thinking!

But let me get back to my "bright green wind" . . . I got off on Maeterlinck and Carlyle because there was something in Lou Jacobs' character which reminded me of both these men. Perhaps I detected beneath his gaiety and bright insouciance a hint of the sombre and the tragic. He was a man, I must say, whom no one knew much about, who appeared to have no intimates, and who never talked about himself. When he left his office at four in the afternoon no one on God's earth could predict where his feet would lead him before he arrived home for dinner. Usually he stopped off at a bar or two, where he might have regaled himself by conversing with a jockey, a prizefighter, or a broken-down pimp. He was certainly more in his element with such people than with the more respectable members of society. Sometimes he would wander down to the fish market and lose himself in contemplation of the creatures of the deep, not forgetting however to bring home an assortment of oysters, clams, shrimps, eels or whatever else pleased his fancy. Or he might wander into a second-hand bookshop, not so much to find a rare old book as to talk to some old crony of a bookdealer, for he loved the talk of books even more than books themselves. But no matter with what fresh experiences he was charged, when you encountered him after dinner he was always free, ready to take any stance, and open to any suggestion. It was in the evening I always saw him. Usually, when I entered, I found him sitting at the window, gazing down upon the passing show. As with Whitman, everything seemed to be of equal and absorbing interest to him. I never knew him to be ill, never saw him in a bad mood. He might just have lost his last cent, but never would anyone have suspected it.

I spoke of the way he played chess. Never did an opponent intimidate me more than he. To be sure, I was not then, nor am I now, a good player. Probably not even as good as Napoleon. When, for instance, Marcel Duchamp once invited me to play a game with him, I forgot everything I knew about the game because of my unholy respect for his knowledge of it. With Lou Jacobs it was worse. I could never arrive at any conclusions about his knowledge of the game. What defeated me with him was his utter nonchalance. " Would you like me to give you a queen or two rooks or a knight and two bishops ? " He never uttered these words but they were implied by his manner. He would open in any old fashion, as though out of contempt for my ability, though it was never that ; he had contempt for no one. No, he did it probably merely to enjoy himself, to see what liberties he could take, to see how far he could stretch a point. It seemed to make no difference to him whether he were winning or losing the game ; he played with the ease and assurance of a wizard, enjoying the false moves as well as the brilliant ones. Besides, what could it possibly mean to a man like him to lose a game of chess, or ten games, or a hundred ? " I'll be playing it in paradise," he seemed to be saying. " Come on, let's have fun ! Make a bold move, a rash move !" Of course the more rashly he played the more cautious I grew. I suspected him of being a genius. And was he not a genius to thus bewilder and confuse me ?

The way he played chess was the way he played the game of life. Only the "old dogs" can do it. Lao-tse was one of these gay old dogs. Sometimes, when the image of Lao-tse seated on the back of a water buffalo crosses my mind, when I think of that steady, patient, kindly, penetrating grin of his, that wisdom so fluid and benevolent, I think of Lou Jacobs sitting before me at the chessboard. Ready to play the game anyway you liked. Ready to rejoice over his ignorance or to beam with pleasure at his own tomfoolery. Never malicious, never petty, never envious, never jealous. A great comforter, yet remote as the dog star. Always bowing himself out of the picture, yet the farther he retreated the closer he was to you. All those sayings from Shakespeare or from the Bible with which he sprinkled his talk, how much more instructive were they than the weightiest sermon ! He never lifted a finger for emphasis, never raised his voice to make a point ; everything of moment was expressed by the laughing wrinkles which cracked his parched face when he spoke. The sound of his laughter only the "ancient ones" could reproduce. It came from on high, as if tuned in to our earthly vibrations. It was the laughter of the gods, the laughter which heals, which, sustained by its own unimpeded wisdom of life, splinters and shatters all learning, all seriousness, all morality, all pretense and artifice.

Let me leave him there, his face cracked with wrinkles, his laughter echoing through the chandeliers of hell. Let me think of him as he stood bowing me out of an evening, a nightcap in his hand, the ice faintly tinkling in the glass, his eyes bright as beads, his mustache moist with whisky, his breath divinely perfumed with garlic, onion, leek and alcohol. He was not of this time nor of any time that I know. He was the perfect misfit, the contented fool, the artful teacher, the great comforter, the mysteriously anonymous one. And he was not any one of these alone but all together. Hail, bright spirit ! What a book of life you were !

And now to speak of another "living book," this one a *known* figure. This man is still alive, thank the Lord, and living a rich, peaceful life in a corner of Wales. I mean John Cowper Powys, or, as he dubs himself in his *Autobiography*,* "Prester John."

It was only a few years after Lou Jacobs disappeared out of my life that I encountered this famous author and lecturer. I met him after one of his lectures at the Labour Temple, on Second Avenue in New York.

A few months ago, having discovered his whereabouts through a friend, I acted upon an impulse and wrote him a long-deferred letter of homage. It was a letter I should have written twenty years ago at least. I would have been a much richer man today had I done so. For, to get a letter from "Prester John" is something of an event in one's life.

This man, whose lectures I attended frequently, whose books I devoured hungrily, I met just once in the flesh. It took all the courage I then possessed to go up to him after the lecture and say a few words of appreciation, to shake his hand and then flee with tail between my legs. I had an unholy veneration for the man. Every word he uttered seemed to go straight to the mark. All the authors I was then passionate about were the authors he was writing and lecturing about. He was like an oracle to me.

Now that I have found him again, now that I hear from him regularly, it is as if I had recovered my youth. He is still "the master" to me. His words, even today, have the power of bewitching me. At this very moment I am deep in his *Autobiography*, a most nourishing, stimulating book of 652 close-packed pages. It is the sort of biography I revel in, being utterly frank, truthful, sincere, and containing a superabundant wealth of trivia (most illuminating!) as well as the major events, or turning points, in one's life. "If all the persons who wrote autobiographies would dare to put down the things that in their life have caused them their most intense misery, it would be a much greater boon than all these testy justifications of public actions," says the author. Like Céline, Powys has the faculty of telling of his misfortunes with humor. Like Céline, he can speak of himself in the most derogatory terms, call himself a fool, a clown, a weakling, a coward, a degenerate, even a "sub-human" being, without in the least

* Published by John Lane, The Bodley Head, London, 1934.

diminishing his stature. His book is full of life-wisdom, revealed not so much through big incidents as little ones.

It is in his sixtieth year that the book is written. There are two passages, out of many, many, that I should like to quote, which reveal something of the man that is particularly precious to me. Here is one : " What is it that we all lose as we get older ? It is something in life itself. Yes, it is *in* life, but it is a much deeper thing—no ! not exactly deeper ; I mean it is of a more precious substance—than what we think of as ' life ' as we grow older. Now I am inclined to think that to a quite unusual extent I have retained to my sixtieth year the attitude of my early boyhood ; and such being the case I am tempted to hold the view that the more obstinately I exploit this childishness and take my stand on this childishness the wiser—if the less human—my mature life will be." The other runs as follows : " My whole life can be divided in two halves ; the first up to the time I was forty ; and the second *after* the time I was forty. During the first half I struggled desperately to evoke and to arrange my feelings according to what I admired in my favorite books ; but during the second half I struggled to find out what my real feelings were and to refine upon them and to balance them and to harmonize them, according to no one's method but my own."

But to get back to the man I know—from the lecture platform. It was John Cowper Powys, descendant of the poet Cowper, son of an English clergyman, with Welsh blood in his veins and the fire and magic which invests all the Gaelic spirits, who first enlightened me about the horrors and sublimities connected with the House of Atreus. I remember most vividly the way he wrapped himself in his gown, closed his eyes and covered them with one hand, before launching into one of those inspired flights of eloquence which left me dizzy and speechless. At the time I thought his pose and gestures sensational, the expression perhaps of an over-dramatic temperament. (He is, of course, an actor, John Cowper Powys, but not on *this* stage, as he himself points out. He is rather a kind of Spenglerian actor.) The oftener I listened to him, however, the more I read his works, the less critical I became. Leaving the hall after his lectures, I often felt as if he had put a spell upon me. A wondrous spell it was, too. For, aside from the celebrated experience with Emma Goldman in San Diego, it was my first intimate experience, my first real contact, with the living spirit of those few rare beings who visit this earth. Powys, needless to say, had his own select luminaries whom he raved about. I use the word "raved" advisedly. I had never before heard any one *rave* in public, particularly about authors, thinkers, philosophers. Emma Goldman, equally inspired on the platform, and often Sibylline in utterance, gave nevertheless the impression of radiating from an intellectual center. Warm and emotional though she was, the fire she gave off was an electrical one. Powys fulminated with the fire and smoke of the soul, or the depths which cradle the soul. Literature was for him like manna from above. He pierced the veil time and again. For nourishment he gave us wounds, and the scars have never healed.

Fatidical, if I remember rightly, was one of his favorite adjectives. Why I should mention it now I don't know, unless it was charged with mysterious sunken associations which once had tremendous significance for me. At any rate, his blood was saturated with racial myths and legends, with memories of magical feats and superhuman exploits. His hawk-like features, reminiscent of our own Robinson Jeffers, gave me the impression of confronting a being whose ancestry was different than ours, older, more obscure, more pagan, much more pagan than our historical forbears. To me he seemed preeminently at home in the Mediterranean world, that is the pre-Mediterranean world of Atlantis. In short, he was "in the tradition." Lawrence would have said of him that he was an "aristocrat of the spirit." That is why, probably, he stands out in my memory as one of the few men of culture I have known who could also be called "democratic"—democratic in Whitman's sense of the word. What he had in common with us inferior beings was a superlative regard for the rights and privileges of the individual. All *vital* questions were of interest to him. It was this broad yet passionate curiosity which enabled him to wrest from "dead" epochs and "dead" letters the universal human qualities which the scholar and pedant lose sight of. To sit at the feet of a living man, a contemporary, whose thoughts, feelings and emanations were kindred in spirit to those of the glorious figures of the past was a great privilege. I could visualize this representative of ours discoursing ably and familiarly with such spirits as Pythagoras, Socrates, or Abélard;

I could never thus visualize John Dewey, for example, or Bertrand Russell. I could appreciate and respect the intricacies of *this* mind, something I am incapable of when it comes to Whitehead or Ouspensky. My own limitations, undoubtedly. But, there are men who convince me in a few brief moments of their roundedness—I know no better word to describe that quality which I believe embraces, sums up, and epitomizes all that is truly human in us. John Cowper Powys was a rounded individual. He illumined whatever he touched, always relating it to the central fires which nourish the cosmos itself. He was an " interpreter " (or poet) in the highest sense of the word.

There are other more gifted men of our time, more brilliant perhaps, more profound, possibly, but neither their proportions nor their aspirations conform with this thoroughly human world in which Powys takes his stance and has his being. On the closing page of the *Autobiography*, which I could not resist glancing at, there stands this paragraph which is so revelatory of the inner, essential Powys : " The astronomical world is *not* all there is. We are in touch with other dimensions, other levels of life. And from among the powers that spring from these *other levels* there rises up one Power, all the more terrible because it refuses to practice cruelty, a Power that is neither Capitalist, nor Communist, nor Fascist, nor Democratic, nor Nazi, a Power *not of this world at all*, but capable of inspiring the individual soul with the wisdom of the serpent and the harmlessness of the dove."

It is not at all surprising to me to discover that in the declining years of his life Powys has found time to give us a book on Rabelais as well as a book on Dostoievsky, two poles of the human spirit. It is an unusual interpreter of the human spirit who can weigh and balance two such diverse beings. In the whole realm of literature it is difficult for me to think of two greater extremes than Rabelais and Dostoievsky, both of whom I still worship. No writers could be more mature than these two ; none reveal more eloquently the eternal youth of the spirit. Curious that I should think of it at this moment, but I doubt that Rimbaud, the very symbol of youth, ever heard of his contemporary, Dostoievsky. This is one of the mysterious and anomalous features of the modern age which boasts of its extended means of communication. It is in the Nineteenth Century particularly, this century so rich in demonic, prophetic and extremely individualistic figures, that we are often astounded to learn that one great figure did not know of the other's existence. Let the reader confirm this fact for himself. It is undeniable and of vast significance. Rabelais, a man of the Renaissance, knew his contemporaries. The men of the Middle Ages, despite all imagined inconveniences, communicated with one another and paid attendance upon one another. The world of learning then formed a huge web, the filaments of which were durable and electric. *Our* writers, the men who should be expressing and shaping world trends, give the impression of being incommunicado. Their significance, their influence, at any rate, is virtually nil. The men of intellect, the writers, the artists of today, are stranded on a reef which each successive breaker threatens to pound into annihilation.

John Cowper Powys belongs to that breed of man which is never extinguished. He belongs to the chosen few, who, despite the cataclysms which rock the world, always find themselves in the Ark. The covenant which he established with his fellowmen constitutes the warrant and guaranty of his survival. How few there are who have discovered this secret ! The secret, shall I say, of incorporating oneself in the living spirit of the universe. I have referred to him as " a living book." What is that but to say he is all flame, all spirit ? The book which comes alive is the book which has been penetrated through and through by the devouring heart. Until it is kindled by a spirit as flamingly alive as the one which gave it birth a book is dead to us. Words divested of their magic are but dead hieroglyphs. Lives devoid of quest, enthusiasm, of give and take, are as meaningless and barren as dead letters. To encounter a man whom we can call a living book is to arrive at the very fount of creation. He makes us witness of the consuming fire which rages throughout the universe entire and which gives not warmth alone nor enlightenment, but enduring vision, enduring strength, enduring courage.

VIII

THE DAYS OF MY LIFE

I HAVE just received from my friend Lawrence Powell the two volumes of Rider Haggard's autobiography,* a work I have been awaiting with the greatest impatience. I no more than unwrapped the volumes, hurriedly scanned the table of contents, when I sat down with feverish expectancy to read Chapter Ten—on *King Solomon's Mines* and *She*.

During the few weeks which have elapsed since reading *She* my thoughts have never ceased to revolve about the genesis of this "romance." Now that I have the author's own words before me I am literally astounded. Here is what he says :

> I remember that when I sat down to the task my ideas as to its development were of the vaguest. The only clear notion that I had in my head was that of an immortal woman inspired by an immortal love. All the rest shaped itself round this figure. And it came—it came faster than my poor aching hand could set it down.

This is virtually all he has to say about the conception of this remarkable work. "The whole romance," he states, "was completed in a little over six weeks. Moreover, it was never rewritten, and the manuscript carries but few corrections. The fact is that it was written at white heat, almost without rest, and that is the best way to compose."

But perhaps I should add the following, which may contain a surprise for the lovers of this extraordinary tale :

> Well do I recall taking the completed manuscript to the office of my literary agent, Mr. A. P. Watt, and throwing it on the table with the remark : 'There is what I shall be remembered by.' Well do I recall also visiting Mr. Watt at his office, which was then at 2 Paternoster Square, and finding him out. As the business was urgent, and I did

* *The Days of My Life*, An Autobiography, by Sir H. Rider Haggard ; Longmans, Green & Co., Ltd., London, 1926.

not wish to have to return, I sat down at his table, asked for some foolscap, and in the hour or two that I had to wait wrote the scene of the destruction of She in the Fire of Life. This, however, was of course a little while—it may have been a few days—before I delivered the manuscript.

It was twenty years later, Haggard points out—"the time that I had always meant to elapse"—that the sequel called *Ayesha*, or *The Return of She*, was written.

As for the title, *She*, so evocative, so utterly unforgettable, here is the origin of it, in his own words : " *She*, if I remember aright, was taken from a certain rag doll, so named, which a nurse at Bradenham used to bring out of some dark recess in order to terrify those of my brothers and sisters who were in her charge."

Could anything be more disappointing, or more thrilling, at the same time, than these bald, meagre facts ? Where imaginative works are concerned I suppose they are classic. If time permits, I intend to run down the " facts " about other great works of the imagination. Meanwhile, and particularly because I am informed that there has been a revival of interest in Rider Haggard's works, I think it pertinent to quote a letter written to the author by no less a person than Walter Besant. Here it is :

12, Gayton Crescent,
Hampstead
January 2, 1887.

My dear Haggard,
    While I am under the spell of ' Ayesha,' * which I have only just finished, I must write to congratulate you upon a work which most certainly puts you at the head—a long way ahead—of all contemporary imaginative writers. If fiction is best cultivated in the field of pure invention then you are certainly the first of modern novelists. *Solomon's Mines* is left far behind. It is not only the central conception that is so splendid in its audacity, but it is your logical and pitiless working out of the whole thing in its inevitable details that strikes me with astonishment.
    I do not know what the critics will say about it. Probably they will not read more than they can help and then will let you off with a few general expressions. If the critic is a woman she will put down this book with the remark

* Meaning *She*.

that it is impossible—almost all women have this feeling towards the marvellous.

Whatever else you do, you will have *She* always behind you for purposes of odious comparison. And whatever critics say the book is bound to be a magnificent success. Also it will produce a crop of imitators. And all the little conventional storytellers will be jogged out of their grooves —until they find new ones . . .

The book was indeed a great success, as the reports of sales from his publisher testify, not to speak of the letters which poured in on the author from all parts of the world, some of them from well-known figures in the literary world. Haggard himself says that " in America it was pirated by the hundred thousand."

She was written in his thirtieth year, some time between the beginning of February, 1886, and the 18th of March, that same year. He began it about a month after finishing *Jess*. It was a remarkable creative period, as the following indicates :

> It would seem, therefore, that between January, 1885, and March 18, 1886, with my own hand, and unassisted by any secretary, I wrote *King Solomon's Mines*, *Allan Quatermain*, *Jess* and *She*. Also I followed my own profession, spending many hours of each day studying in chambers, or in Court, where I had some devilling practice, carried on my usual correspondence, and attended to the affairs of a man with a young family and a certain landed estate.

As I have often bitterly complained about the burden of answering the thousands of letters I receive, I think the following observations by Haggard may not be without interest " to all and sundry " :

> A little later on the work grew even harder, for to it was added the toil of an enormous correspondence hurled at me by every kind of person from all over the earth. If I may judge by those which remain marked with a letter A for ' answered,' I seem to have done my best to reply to all these scribes, hundreds of them, even down to the autograph hunter, a task which must have taken up a good part of every day, and this in addition to all my other work. No wonder that my health began to give out at last, goaded as I was at that period of my life by constant and venomous attacks.

In *The Rosy Crucifixion*, where I dwell at length on my relations with Stanley, my first friend, there are frequent and usually mocking references to Stanley's love of romances. It was nothing less than a good "romance" which Stanley always hoped to write one day. At this point in time I am better able to understand and appreciate his heart-felt desire. Then I merely looked upon him as another Pole—full of romantic nonsense.

I don't seem able to recall any discussion with him about Rider Haggard, though I do remember that we spoke now and then of Marie Corelli. Between the ages of ten and eighteen we saw almost nothing of each other, and before that the "discussion" of books must have been altogether negligible. It was when Stanley discovered Balzac—*The Wild Ass' Skin* first of all—and soon after other European writers, such as Pierre Loti, Anatole France, Joseph Conrad, that we began to talk books, and in earnest. To be honest, I doubt if I then understood clearly what Stanley meant by "romances." To me the word was associated with claptrap, with all that is unreal. I never suspected the part that "reality" played in this realm of pure imagination.

There is a most interesting dream, a recurrent one, which Rider Haggard describes at some length. It ends thus :

> I see . . . myself, younger than I am now, wearing some sort of white garments and bending over the desk at work, with papers spread before me. At the sight a kind of terror seizes me lest this fair place should be but a scented purgatory where, in payment for my sins, I am *doomed to write fiction for ever and a day!*
> 'At what do I work'? I ask, alarmed, of the guide, who, shining steadily, stands at my side and shows me all.
> 'You write the history of a world' (or was it 'of *the* world'?—I am not sure), is the answer . . .

A world or *the* world, what difference does it make ? The point is, as William James hints in his Introduction to Fechner's *Life After Death*, that "God has a history." The imagination makes of all worlds *one*, and in this world of Reality man plays the central rôle, for here man and God are one and all is divine. When Haggard voices the hope that in another life the subject of his toil may prove to be not fiction but history ("which I love"), when he adds that

143

" in all the worlds above us there must be much history to record (and much good work to do)," he is saying, I feel, that the proper subject for a writer is the endless story of creation. The history of man is bound up with the history of God, and the history of God is the revelation of the eternal mystery of creation.

"I think I am right," says Haggard, " in saying that no one has ever written a really first-class romance dwelling solely, for example, upon the utterly alien life of another world or planet with which human beings cannot possibly have any touch."

True or not, it is nevertheless indisputable that certain authors have made such use of the imagination as to make the realities of this, *our world*, seem incredible. Perhaps it is not necessary to visit distant worlds in order to grasp the essential truths of the universe, or to understand its order and functioning. Books which do not belong to great literature, books which do not command " the grand style," often bring us closer to the mystery of life. They treat of the fundamental experience of man, of his " unalterable " human nature, in quite another way from that of the classical writers. They speak of this common fund which binds us not only to one another but to God. They speak of man as an integral part of the universe and not as a " sport of creation." They speak of man as though to him alone it were given to discover the Creator. They link man's destiny with the destiny of all creation ; they do not make him a victim of fate or an " object of redemption." In glorifying man they glorify the whole universe. They may not speak in the grand manner, as I have just said. They are less interested in language than in subject matter, more interested in ideas than in the thoughts which clothe them. As a consequence, they often appear to be poor writers, they lend themselves to ridicule and caricature. Nothing is easier to make sport of than the yearning for the sublime. Often, be it noted, this yearning is masked or concealed ; often the author himself is not aware of what he seeks or what he states in veiled fashion.

What is the subject matter of these oft despised books ? Briefly, the web of life and death ; the pursuit of identity through the drama of identification ; the terrors of initiation ; the lure of indescribable visions ; the road to acceptance ; the redemption of the creature world and the transformation of Nature ; the final loss of memory, in God. Into the texture of such books is woven all that is symbolic and everlasting—not stars and planets but the deeps between them ; not other worlds and their possibly fantastic inhabitants but the ladders that reach to them ; not laws and principles but ever unfolding circles of creation and the hierarchies which constitute them.

As to the drama which informs these works, it has nothing to do with the individual versus society, nothing to do with the " conquest of bread," nor has it even ultimately to do with the conflict between good and evil. *It has to do with freedom.* For not a line could have been written by the men I have in mind if man had ever known freedom or even what is meant by it. Here truth and freedom are synonymous. In these works the drama begins only when man voluntarily opens his eyes. This act, the sole one which may be said to have heroic significance, displaces all the sound and fury of historical substance. Outward bound, man is at last able to look inward with grace and certitude. No longer looking at life from the world plane, man ceases to be the victim of chance or circumstance : he " elects " to follow his vision, to become one with the imagination. From this moment on he begins to travel ; all previous voyages were but circumnavigation.

The names of these precious books ?

I will answer you in the words of Gurdjieff as given by Ouspensky—" If you understood everything you have read in your life, you would already know what you are looking for now."*

This statement is one to be pondered over again and again. It reveals the true connection between books and life. It tells one *how* to read. It proves—to me, at any rate—something I have reiterated a number of times, to wit, that the reading of books is for the joy of corroboration, and that *that* is the final discovery we make about books. As for true reading—a procedure which never ends—that can be done with anything : a blade of grass, a flower, a horse's hoof, the eyes of a child when smitten with wonder or ecstasy, the mien of a real warrior, the form of a pyramid, or the serene composure graven on the statue of every Buddha. If the questioning faculty is not dead, if the sense of wonder is not atrophied, if there be real hunger and not mere appetite or craving, one cannot help

---

* *In Search of the Miraculous,* by P. D. Ouspensky ; Harcourt, Brace & Co., Inc., New York, 1949. Routledge & Co., Ltd., London.

K

but read as he runs. The whole universe must then become an open book.

This joyous reading of life or books does not imply the abatement of the critical faculty. On the contrary. To make full surrender to author or Author implies the exaltation of the critical faculty. In railing against the use of the word "constructive" in connection with literary criticism, Powys writes thus :

> O that word 'constructive' ! How, in the name of the mystery of genius, can criticism be anything else than an an idolatry, a worship, a metamorphosis, a love affair !*

Ever and again the moving finger points to the inmost self, not in warning but in love. The handwriting on the wall is neither mysterious nor menacing to the one who can interpret it. Walls fall away, and with them our fears and reluctances. But the last wall to give way is the wall which hems the ego in. Who reads not with the eyes of the Self reads not at all. The inner eye pierces all walls, deciphers all scripts, transforms all "messages." It is not a reading or appraising eye, but an informing eye. It does not receive light from without, it sheds light. Light and joy. Through light and joy is the world opened up, revealed for what it is : ineffable beauty, unending creation.

* *Visions and Revisions,* by John Cowper Powys ; G. Arnold Shaw, New York, 1915.

146

IX

KRISHNAMURTI

SOMEONE has said that " the world has never known her greatest men." If we could know their lives and works we might indeed have " a biography of God on earth."

Beside the inspired writings, of which there is an abundance, the creations of the poets seem pale. First come the gods, then the heroes (who incarnate the myth), then the seers and prophets, and then the poets. The concern of the poet is to restore the splendor and magnificence of the ever reviving past. The poet senses almost beyond endurance the enormous deprivation which afflicts mankind. For him " the magic of words " convey something which is totally lost to the ordinary individual. Ever a prisoner of the realm from which he springs, his province is one which the ordinary man never explores and from which he seems debarred by birth. The immortality which is reserved for the poet is the vindication of his unswerving allegiance to the Source from which he derives his inspiration.

> Listen to Pico della Mirandola : In the midst of the world, the Creator said to Adam, I have placed thee, so thou couldst look around so much easier, and see all that is in it. I created thee as a being neither celestial nor earthly, neither mortal nor immortal alone, so that thou shouldst be thy own free moulder and overcomer ; thou canst degenerate to animal, and through thyself be reborn to godlike existence . . .

Is this not the essence and purpose of human existence in a nutshell ? *In the midst of the world* the Creator placed man. The " anthropocentric " viewpoint, say our sad, learned men. Looking round and about them they see nothing but *dreck*. To them life is a tale told by an idiot, signifying nothing. Indeed, if we follow their thought to the end, the very substance of our mother, the Earth, is nothingness. Stripping the cosmos of spirit, they have finally succeeded in demolishing the very ground on which they take their stand : solid matter. They speak to us through a void of hypothesis and conjecture. Never will they understand that " the world is a generalized form of the spirit, its symbolic picture."* Though they speak as if " every rock has a tale written on its wrinkled and weathered face," they refuse to read what is written ; they impose their own feeble stories of creation upon myths and legends embedded in truth and reality. They reckon in light years, with the signs and symbols of their priestly caste, but they are alarmed when it is asserted that a superior order of men, superior orders of civilisation, flourished as recent as one hundred thousand years ago. Where *man* is concerned, the ancients have accorded him a greater antiquity, a greater intelligence and understanding, than our men of little faith whose vanity is bolstered by pretentious learning.

All this by way of saying that the books I most enjoy reading are those which put me in rapport with the incredible nature of man's being. Nothing attributed to the power and glory of man is too much for me to swallow. Nothing which concerns the story of our earth and the marvels it holds is too preposterous for me. The more disgusted I grow with what is called " history " the more exalted my opinion of man becomes. If I am passionate about the lives of individual artists, in whatever field, I am still more passionate about man as a whole. In my brief experience as reader of the written word I have been given to assist at marvels which surpass all understanding. Even if these were but the " imaginings " of inspired writers, their reality is in no way impugned. We are this day on the threshold of a world in which nothing men dare to think or believe is impossible of fruition. (Men have thought the same in certain moments in the past, but only as in a dream, from the deeps or the unconscious, as it were.) We are being told every day, for example, that the prosaic, practical minds which direct the affairs of certain departments of our government are seriously working to perfect the means of reaching the moon—and even planets more distant—within the next fifty years. (A very modest estimate !) What lies behind these plans and projects is another matter. Are " we " thinking of defending the planet Earth or of attacking the inhabitants of other planets ? Or are we thinking of abandoning this abode in which there seems to be no

* Novalis.

solution to our ills ? Be assured, whatever the reason, however
daring our plans, the motive is not a lofty one.

This effort to conquer space is, however, only one of many
heretofore " impossible dreams " which our men of science promise
to explode. The readers of the daily newspaper or of the popular
science magazines can discourse eloquently on these subjects, though
they themselves know next to nothing of the elements of science
which lie at the root of these once wild and incredible theories,
plans and projects.

Woven into the life of Nicolas Flamel is the story of the Book of
Abraham the Jew. The discovery of this book and the effort made
to penetrate the secret it contained is a tale of earthly adventure of the
highest order. " At the same time," says Maurice Magre,* " that he
[Flamel] was learning how to make gold out of any material, he
acquired the wisdom of despising it in his heart." As in any chapter
on the famous alchemists, there is in this one also astounding and, if
we were open-minded, most illuminating statements. I wish to
quote just one paragraph, if for no other reason than to suggest the
reverse of what I insinuated above. The passage concerns two
eminent alchemists of the Seventeenth Century ; the reader may, if
he likes, choose to regard them as " exceptions."

> It is probable that they attained the most highly
> developed state possible to man, that they accomplished
> the transmutation of their soul. While still living they
> were members of the spiritual world. They had regenerated
> their being, performed the task of man. They were twice
> born. They devoted themselves to helping their fellow-
> men ; this they did in the most useful way, which does
> not consist in healing the ills of the body or in improving
> men's physical state. They used a higher method, which
> in the first instance can be applied only to a small number,
> but eventually affects all. They helped the noblest minds
> to reach the goal which they had reached themselves.
> They sought such men in the towns through which they
> passed, and, generally, during their travels. They had
> no school and no regular teaching, because their teaching
> was on the border of the human and the divine. But they
> knew that a word sown at a certain time in a certain soul

* *Magicians, Seers and Mystics*, by Maurice Magre ; E. P. Dutton & Co.
New York, 1932.

would bring results a thousand times greater than those
which could accrue from the knowledge gained through
books or ordinary science.

The marvels I speak of are of all sorts. Sometimes they are just
thoughts or ideas ; sometimes they are extraordinary beliefs or
practices ; sometimes they are in the nature of physical quests ;
sometimes they are sheer feats of language ; sometimes they are
systems ; sometimes they are discoveries or inventions ; sometimes
they are the record of miraculous events ; sometimes they are the
embodiments of wisdom, the source of which is suspect ; sometimes
they are accounts of fanaticism, persecution and intolerance ; sometimes they take the form of Utopias ; sometimes they are superhuman feats of heroism ; sometimes they are deeds, or things, of
unbelievable beauty ; sometimes they are chronicles of all that is
monstrous, evil and perverted.

To give an inkling of what I have in mind I am stringing together
pell-mell a series of touchstones : Joachim of Floris, Gilles de Rais,
Jacob Boehme, the Marquis de Sade, the *I-Ching*, the Palace of
Knossos, the Albigensians, Jean-Paul Richter, the Holy Grail,
Heinrich Schliemann, Joan of Arc, the Count of St. Germain, the
Summa Theologica the great Uighur Empire, Apollonius of Tyana,
Madame Blavatsky, St. Francis of Assisi, the legend of Gilgamesh,
Ramakrishna, Timbuctoo, the Pyramids, Zen Buddhism, Easter
Island, the great Cathedrals, Nostradamus, Paracelsus, the Holy
Bible, Atlantis and Mu, Thermopylae, Akhnaton, Cuzco, The
Children's Crusade, Tristan and Isolt, Ur, the Inquisition, *Arabia
Deserta*, King Solomon, the Black Death, Pythagoras, Santos
Dumont, *Alice in Wonderland*, the Naacal Library, Hermes Trisme-
gistus, the White Brotherhood, the atom bomb, Gautama the
Buddha.

There is a name I have withheld which stands out in contrast
to all that is secret, suspect, confusing, bookish and enslaving :
Krishnamurti. Here is one man of our time who may be said to be
a master of reality. He stands alone. He has renounced more than
any man I can think of, except the Christ. Fundamentally he is so
simple to understand that it is easy to comprehend the confusion
which his clear, direct words and deeds have entailed. Men are
reluctant to accept what is easy to grasp. Out of a perversity deeper

than all Satan's wiles, man refuses to acknowledge his own God-given rights : he demands deliverance or salvation by and through an intermediary ; he seeks guides, counsellors, leaders, systems, rituals. He looks for solutions which are in his own breast. He puts learning above wisdom, power above the art of discrimination. But above all, he refuses to work for his own liberation, pretending that first " the world " must be liberated. Yet, as Krishnamurti has pointed out time and again, the world problem is bound up with the problem of the individual. Truth is ever present, Eternity is here and now. *And salvation ?* What is it, O man, that you wish to save ? Your petty ego ? Your soul ? Your identity ? Lose it and you will find yourself. Do not worry about God—God knows how to take care of Himself. Cultivate your doubts, embrace every kind of experience, keep on desiring, strive neither to forget nor to remember, but assimilate and integrate what you have experienced.

Roughly, this is Krishnamurti's way of speaking. It must be revolting at times to answer all the petty, stupid questions which people are forever putting to him. Emancipate yourself ! he urges. No one else will, because no one else can. This voice from the wilderness is, of course, the voice of a leader. But Krishnamurti has renounced that rôle too.

It was Carlo Suarès' book on Krishnamurti* which opened my eyes to this phenomenon in our midst. I first read it in Paris and since then have reread it several times. There is hardly another book I have read so intently, marked so copiously, unless it be *The Absolute Collective*. After years of struggle and search I found gold.

I do not believe this book has been translated into English, nor do I know, moreover, what Krishnamurti himself thinks of it. I have never met Krishnamurti, though there is no man living whom I would consider it a greater privilege to meet than he. His place of residence, curiously enough, is not so very far from my own. However, it seems to me that if this man stands for anything it is for the right to lead his own life, which is surely not to be at the beck and call of every Tom, Dick and Harry who wishes to make his acquaintance or obtain from him a few crumbs of wisdom.

* *Krishnamurti* ; Editions Adyar, Paris, 1932. This work has now been replaced by another, entitled *Krishnamurti et l'unité humaine* ; Le Cercle du Livre, Paris, 1950.

"You can never know me," he says somewhere. It is enough to know what he represents, what he stands for in being and essence.

This book by Carlo Suarès is invaluable. It is replete with Krishnamurti's own words culled from speeches and writings. Every phase of the latter's development (up to the year the book was published) is set forth—and lucidly, cogently, trenchantly. Suarès discreetly keeps in the background. He has the wisdom to let Krishnamurti speak for himself.

In pages 116 to 119 of Suarès' book the reader may find for himself the text of which I herewith give the substance . . .

After a long discussion with a man in Bombay, the latter says to Krishnamurti : What you speak of could lead to the creation of supermen, men capable of governing themselves, of establishing order in themselves, men who would be their own masters absolute. But what about the man at the bottom of the ladder, who depends on external authority, who makes use of all kinds of crutches, who is obliged to submit to a moral code which may, in reality, not suit him ?

Krishnamurti answers : See what happens in the world. The strong, the violent, the powerful ones, the men who usurp and wield power over others, are at the top ; at the bottom are the weak and gentle ones, who struggle and flounder. By contrast think of the tree, whose strength and glory derives from its deep and hidden roots ; in the case of the tree the top is crowned by delicate leaves, tender shoots, the most fragile branches. In human society, at least as it is constituted today, the strong and the powerful are supported by the weak. In Nature, on the other hand, it is the strong and the powerful who support the weak. As long as you persist in viewing each problem with a perverted, twisted mind you will accept the actual state of affairs. I look at the problem from another point of view . . . Because your convictions are not the result of your own understanding you repeat what is given by authorities ; you amass citations, you pit one authority against another, the ancient against the new. To that I have nothing to say. But if you envisage life from a standpoint which is not deformed or mutilated by authority, not bolstered by others' knowledge, but from one which springs from your own sufferings, from *your* thought, *your* culture, *your* understanding, *your* love, then you will understand what

I say—" car la méditation du coeur est l'entendement " . . . Personally, and I hope you will understand what I say now, *I have no belief and I belong to no tradition.** I have always had this attitude towards life. It being a fact that life varies from day to day, not only are beliefs and traditions useless to me, but, if I were to let myself be enchained by them, they would prevent me from understanding life . . . You may attain liberation, no matter where you are or what the circumstances surrounding you, but this means that you must have the strength of genius. For genius is, after all, the ability to deliver oneself from the circumstances in which one is enmeshed, the ability to free oneself from the vicious circle . . . You may say to me—I have not that kind of strength. That is my point of view exactly. In order to discover your own strength, *the power which is in you,* you must be ready and willing to come to grips with every kind of experience. And that is just what you refuse to do !

This sort of language is naked, revelatory and inspiring. It pierces the clouds of philosophy which confound our thought and restores the springs of action. It levels the tottering superstructures of the verbal gymnasts and clears the ground of rubbish. Instead of an obstacle race or a rat trap, it makes of daily life a joyous pursuit. In a conversation with his brother Theo, Van Gogh once said : " Christ was so infinitely great because no furniture or any other stupid accessories ever stood in his way." One feels the same way about Krishnamurti. *Nothing stands in his way.* His career, unique in the history of spiritual leaders, reminds one of the famous Gilgamesh epic. Hailed in his youth as the coming Savior, Krishnamurti renounced the rôle that was prepared for him, spurned all disciples, rejected all mentors and preceptors. He initiated no new faith or dogma, questioned everything, cultivated doubt (especially in moments of exaltation), and, by dint of heroic struggle and perseverance, freed himself of illusion and enchantment, of pride, vanity, and every subtle form of dominion over others. He went to the very source of life for sustenance and inspiration. To resist the wiles and snares of those who sought to enslave and exploit him demanded eternal vigilance. He liberated his soul, so to say, from the underworld and the overworld, thus opening to it " the paradise of heroes."

Is it necessary to define this state ?

* Italics mine.

There is something about Krishnamurti's utterances which makes the reading of books seem utterly superfluous. There is also another, even more striking, fact connected with his utterances, as Suarès aptly points out, namely, that "the clearer his words the less his message is understood."

Krishnamurti once said : "I am going to be vague expressly ; I could be altogether explicit, but it is not my intention to be so. For, once a thing is defined, it is dead " . . . No, Krishnamurti does not define, neither does he answer Yes or No. He throws the questioner back upon himself, forces him to seek the answer in himself. Over and over he repeats : " I do not ask you to believe what I say . . . I desire nothing of you, neither your good opinion, your agreement, nor that you follow me. I ask you not to *believe* but to *understand* what I say." *Collaborate with life !*—that is what he is constantly urging. Now and then it is a veritable lashing he inflicts—upon the self-righteous. What, he asks, have you accomplished with all your fine words, your slogans and labels, your books ? How many individuals have you made happy, not in a transitory but in a lasting sense ? And so on. "It's a great satisfaction to give oneself titles, names, to isolate oneself from the world and think oneself different from others ! But, if all that you say is true, have you saved a single fellow creature from sorrow and pain ? "

All the protective devices—social, moral, religious—which give the illusion of sustaining and aiding the weak so that they may be guided and conducted towards a better life, are precisely what prevent the weak from profiting by direct experience of life. Instead of naked and immediate experience, men seek to make use of protections and thus are mutilated. These devices become the instruments of power, of material and spiritual exploitation. (Suarès' own interpretation.)

One of the salient differences between a man like Krishnamurti and artists in general lies in their respective attitudes towards their rôles. Krishnamurti points out that there is a constant opposition between the creative genius of the artist and his ego. The artist imagines, he says, that it is his ego which is great or sublime. This ego wishes to utilize for its own profit and aggrandizement the moment of inspiration wherein it was in touch with the eternal, a moment, precisely, in which the ego was absent, replaced by the residue of its own living experience. It is one's intuition, he maintains, which should be the sole guide. As for poets, musicians, all artists, indeed, they should develop anonymity, should become detached from their creations. But for most artists it is just the contrary—they want to see their signatures attached to their creations. In short, as long as the artist clings to individualism, he will never succeed in rendering his inspiration or his creative power permanent. The quality or condition of genius is but the first phase of deliverance.

I am not a translator; I have had difficulty transcribing and condensing the foregoing observations and reflections. Nor am I attempting to give the whole of Krishnamurti's thought as revealed in Carlo Suarès' book. I was led to speak of him because of the fact that, however solidly Krishnamurti may be anchored in reality, he has unwittingly created for himself a myth and a legend. People simply will not recognize that a man who has made himself, simple, forthright and truthful is not concealing something much more complex, much more mysterious. Pretending that what they most ardently wish is to extricate themselves from the cruel difficulties in which they find themselves, what they really adore is to make everything difficult, obscure and capable of realization only in a distant future. That their difficulties are of their own making is the last thing they will admit usually. Reality, if for one moment they allow themselves to be persuaded it exists—in everyday life—is always referred to as "harsh" reality. It is spoken of as that which stands opposed to divine reality, or, we might say, a soft, hidden paradise. The hope that we may one day awaken to a condition of life utterly different from that which we experience daily makes men willing victims of every form of tyranny and suppression. Man is stultified by hope and fear. The myth which he lives from day to day is the myth that he may one day escape from the prison which he has created for himself and which he attributes to the machinations of others. Every true hero has made reality his own. In liberating himself, the hero explodes the myth which binds us to past and future. This is the very essence of myth —that it veils the wondrous here and now.

This morning I discovered on the shelf another book on Krishnamurti which I had forgotten that I possessed. It had been given to me by a friend on the eve of a long journey. I had put the book away without ever opening it. This preamble is to thank my friend for the great service he has rendered me—and to inform the reader who does not know French of another excellent interpretation of Krishnamurti's life and work. The book is called *Krishnamurti* (" Man is his own liberator "), by Ludowic Réhault.* Like the Suarès book, it too contains abundant citations from Krishnamurti's speeches and writings. The author, now dead, was a member of the Theosophical Society, "whose tendencies," he states in the preface, "I am far from approving, but to whose grand tenets of Evolution, Reincarnation and Karma I heartily subscribe." And then there comes this statement : " I wish to inform my readers that I am not for Krishnamurti, I am with him."

Since I know of no living man whose thought is more inspiring and fecundating, since I know of no living man who is more free of opinion and prejudice, *and*, because I find from personal experience that he is constantly being misquoted, misinterpreted, misunderstood, I regard it as important and opportune, even at the risk of boring the reader, to linger longer on the subject of Krishnamurti. In Paris, where I first heard of him, I had a number of friends who were forever talking about " the Masters." None of them, to my knowledge, were members of any group, cult or sect. They were just earnest seekers after the truth, as we say. And they were all artists. The books which they were reading were at that time unfamiliar to me—I mean the works of Leadbeater, Steiner, Besant, Blavatsky, Mabel Collins and such like. Indeed, hearing them quote from these sources, I often laughed in their faces. (To this day, I must confess, Rudolf Steiner's language still excites my sense of ridicule.) In the heat of argument I was now and then termed "a spiritual bum." Because I have not the makings of a " follower," these friends, all ardent souls, all consumed by a desire to convert, regarded me as " their meat." In anger, sometimes, I would tell them never to come near me again—unless they could talk about other things. But the morrow would find them at my door, as if nothing had happened.

The one quality which they had in common, I must say

* Christopher Publishing House, Boston, 1939.

immediately, was their utter helplessness. They were out to save me, but they could not save themselves. Here I must confess that later on, what they talked about, what they quoted from the books, what they were striving with might and main to make known to me, was not as silly and preposterous as I once thought. Not by any means! But what prevented me from "seeing things in the right light" was, as I say, their peculiar inability to profit from this wisdom they were so eager to impart. I was merciless with them, something I have never regretted. I think it may have done some good to remain as adamant as I did. It was only after they ceased bothering me that I was truly able to become interested in "all this nonsense." (Should any of them happen to read these lines they will know that, despite everything, I am indebted to them.) But the truth remains that they were doing exactly what "the Masters" discountenanced. "It is of no value," says Krishnamurti, "who is speaking, the value lies in the full significance of what is said." Naturally, to understand the full significance of what is said, to make it one's own, depends entirely on the individual. I recall an English teacher in school who was forever shouting at us: "*Make it your own!*" He was a vain, pretentious coxcomb, a real jackass, if ever there was one. Had he made one little thing of all that he had read and pompously recommended to us "his own" he would not have been teaching English literature: he would have been writing it, or assuming that he was truly humble, he would, as teacher, mentor, guide and what not, have inspired in us a love of literature—which he most certainly did not!

But to come back to "the Masters" . . . In the *International Star Bulletin* of November, 1929, Krishnamurti is quoted thus: "You are all immensely interested in the Masters, whether they exist or not, and what my view is with regard to them. I will tell you my view. To me it is of very little importance whether they exist or whether they do not exist, because when you have to walk to the camp or to the station from here, there are people ahead of you, nearer the station, people who have started earlier. What is more important—to get to the station or to sit down and worship the man who is ahead of you?"

In his book on Krishnamurti, Réhault points out that Krishnamurti's attitude towards, or vision of, the Masters never altered essentially. What had changed was "his outlook on those who seek the Masters and invoke them in season and out with a ridiculous and unseemly familiarity." He quotes an earlier statement (1925) of Krishnamurti's : "We all believe that the Masters exist, that they are somewhere, and are concerned about us ; but this belief is not living enough, not real enough, to make us change. The goal of evolution is to make us like the Masters who are the apotheosis, the perfection of humanity. As I have said, the Masters are a reality. For me at least they are one."

The tremendous consistency between these *apparently* clashing references to the Masters is typical of Krishnamurti's ever evolving attitude towards life. His shift of emphasis from the fact of the Masters' existence to the purpose of their existence is a demonstration of his vigilance, alertness and indefatigable efforts to come to grips with essentials.

> Why do you bother about the Masters ? The essential is that you should be free and strong, and you can never be free and strong if you are a pupil of another, if you have gurus, mediators, Masters over you. You cannot be free and strong if you make me your Master, your guru. I don't want that . . .

Only a few months after making this definitive, unequivocal statement (April, 1930), badgered again for an answer to the question "Do Adepts, Masters exist ? " he replies : "It is unessential to me. I am not concerned with it . . . I am not trying to evade the question . . . I do not deny that they exist. In evolution there must be a difference between the savage and the most cultured. But what value has it to the man who is held in the walls of a prison ? . . . I should be foolish to deny the gamut of experience which is what you call evolution. You care more about the man who is ahead of you than about yourself. You are willing to worship someone far away, not yourself or your neighbor. There may be Adepts, Masters, I do not deny it, but I cannot understand what value it has to you as an individual."

A few years later he is reported as saying : "Do not desire happiness. Do not seek truth. Do not seek the ultimate." Except to quibblers and falsifiers, there is no variance here from the eternal issue which he has marked out. "You seek truth," he says again, "as if it were the opposite of what you are."

If such clear, forthright words do not incite and awaken, nothing will.

"*Man is his own liberator!*" Is this not the ultimate teaching? It has been said again and again, and it has been proved again and again by great world figures. *Masters?* Undoubtedly. Men who espoused life, not principles, laws, dogmas, morals, creeds. "Really great teachers do not lay down laws, they want to set man free." (Krishnamurti.)

What distinguishes Krishnamurti, even from the great teachers of the past, the masters and the exemplars, is his absolute nakedness. The one rôle he permits himself to play is—himself, a human being. Clad only in the frailty of the flesh, he relies entirely upon the spirit, which is one with the flesh. If he has a mission it is to strip men of their illusions and delusions, to knock away the false supports of ideals, beliefs, fetishes, every kind of crutch, and thus render back to man the full majesty, the full potency, of his humanity. He has often been referred to as " the World Teacher." If any man living merits the title, he does. But to me the important thing about Krishnamurti is that he imposes himself upon us not as a teacher, nor even as a Master, but as *a man.*

> Find out for yourself, he says, what are the possessions and ideals that you do not desire. By knowing what you do not want, by elimination, you will unburden the mind, and only then will it understand the essential which is ever there.

X

THE PLAINS OF ABRAHAM

" *When you're ready, Griswold, fire !* "*

I THINK it was in the book called *With Dewey at Manila Bay*, which I spoke of earlier and which, if my memory serves me right, appeared about the same time that the Spanish-American War ended (the poor Spaniards, they never had a chance !) : I think it was right out of Dewey's mouth—or could it have been Admiral Sampson's ?—that this command sprang, to stay with me until I go to the grave. An idiotic thing to remember, but, like that other one—" Wait until you see the whites of their eyes !" —it remains. Of course a great deal more remains (of the reading of a book) than what the memory releases. But it remains eternally curious what one person remembers and another forgets.

The remains . . . As if we were talking of cadavers !

I awoke the other morning, my mind still in a whirl from the continuous effort to recall titles, authors, names of places, events and the most seemingly insignificant data, and what do you suppose I found myself dwelling on ? The Plains of Abraham ! Yes, my mind was full of Montcalm and Wolfe fighting it out up there towards the roof of the world. The French and Indian War, I believe we call it. Seven long years of fighting. It was probably this battle on the Plains of Abraham, which my weak memory places somewhere in the vicinity of Quebec, that decided the fate of the French in North America. I must have studied this bloody war in detail, in school. In fact, I'm sure I did. And what remains ? *The Plains of Abraham.* To be more accurate, more precise, it boils down to a clump of images which could be put in the hollow of a shell. I see Montcalm dying—or was it Wolfe ?—in the open air, surrounded by his bodyguard and a cluster of Indians with

* According to Gregory Mason, author of *Remember the Maine*, Dewey's words were : " You may fire when ready, Gridley."

bald knobs from which a few feathers protrude, long feathers, buried deep in the scalp. Eagles' feathers probably. Montcalm is making a dying speech, one of those historic "last words," such as—"I regret that I have but one life to give for my country." I no longer remember his words but it seems to me he was saying —"The tide is going against us." What matter, anyway ? In a few moments he will be dead, a thing of history. And Canada, except for the Eastern sliver, will be English—worse luck for us ! But how is it that I visualize a huge bird perched on his shoulder ? Whence that bird of ill omen ? Perhaps it is the same bird which got caught in the netting over the cradle in which lay the infant James Ensor, the bird which haunted him all his life. There it is, at any rate, large as life and dominating the infinitude of background in my imaginary picture. For some obscure reason the site of this famous battleground makes a woeful impression upon me : the sky seems to press down on it with all its impalpable weight. Not much space there between land and sky. The heads of the brave warriors seem to brush the cloudless vault of heaven. The battle over, the French will descend the steep face of the promontory by rope ladder. They will take to the rapids in canoes, a handful at a time, the English above raking them mercilessly with grapeshot. As for Montcalm, being a nobleman by birth, and a general, his remains will be removed from the scene with all the honors of war. Night falls rapidly, leaving the helpless Indians to look out for themselves. The British, now having a clear field, romp all over Canada. With stakes and cord the border is marked out. "We" have nothing to fear any more : our neighbors are our own kith and kin . . .

If this battle isn't included in the fifteen decisive battles of the world it should be. Anyway, I could think of nothing this morning I speak of but battles and battlefields. There was Teddy, at the head of his Rough Riders, storming San Juan Hill ; there was poor old Morro Castle being pounded to bits by our heavy guns, and the chain which locked the Spanish fleet in just a rusty old iron chain. Yes, and there was Aguinaldo leading his rebel forces (Igorotes largely) through the swamps and jungles of Mindanao, a price upon his head. With Admirals Dewey and Sampson goes Admiral Schley, who remains in my memory as a kindly, sensible

sort of man, not too bloodthirsty, not too great a strategist, but
" just right." The opposite extreme from John Brown the Liberator,
man of Ossawatomie and Harper's Ferry, the man who attributed
his grand fiasco to the fact that he had been too considerate of
the enemy. A chivalrous fanatic, John Brown. One of the brightest
stars in the whole firmament of our brief history. Our nearest of
kin to the incomparable Saladin. (*Saladin !* All during the last
war I thought of Saladin. What a gracious prince, compared to
the " butchers " on both sides in this last war ! How is it we have
forgotten all about him ?) Imagine, if we had two men of the
calibre of John Brown and Saladin fighting the corruption of the
world ! Would we need more ? John Brown swore that with
the right men—two hundred would be enough, he said—he could
lick the whole United States. He wasn't far from the mark, either,
when he made that boast.

Yes, thinking of the lofty, solemn ground of the Plains of Abraham,
I got to thinking of another battleground : Platea. This last I
saw with my own eyes. But at the time I forgot that it was there
the Greeks had put to the sword over three hundred thousand
Persians. A considerable number, for those times ! As I recall
the spot, it was perfect for " mass slaughter." When I came upon
it, from Thebes, the level ground was sown with wheat, barley,
oats. From a distance it resembled a huge game board. In the
dead center, as in the Chinese game of chess, the king was pinned.
Technically the game was over. But then followed the slaughter
—*comme d'habitude.* What would war be without slaughter ?

Places of slaughter ! My mind roamed afield. I recalled our own
War Between the States, now known as the Civil War. Some of
these terrible scenes of battle I had visited ; some I knew by heart,
having heard and read about them so often. Yes, there was Bull
Run, Manassas, the Battle of the Wilderness, Shiloh, Missionary
Ridge, Antietam, Appomatox Court House, and of course—
Gettysburg. Pickett's charge : the maddest, most suicidal charge
in history. So one is always told. The Yankees cheering the Rebels
for their courage. And waiting (as always) until " we " came
just a little closer, until they could see the whites of " our " eyes.
I thought of the Charge of the Light Brigade—" On rode the six
hundred ! " (To the tune of forty-nine verses and everlasting death.)

I thought of Verdun, the Germans climbing over their own dead piled man high and higher. Marching in full regalia, in strict order, as if on parade. The General Staff not caring how many men it took to capture Verdun, but never capturing it. Another " strategic error," as they say so glibly in books on military tactics. What a price we have paid for these errors ! All history now. Nothing accomplished, nothing gained, nothing learned. Just blunders. And wholesale death. Only generals and generalissimos are permitted to make such horrible " mistakes." Still, we keep turning them out. Never tire of making new generals, new admirals—or new wars. " Fresh wars," we say. I often wonder what is " fresh " about war.

If you wonder sometimes why some of our celebrated contemporaries are unable to sleep, or sleep fitfully, just revive some of these bloody battles. Try to imagine yourself back in the trenches or clinging to an overturned man-of-war ; try to picture the " dirty Japs " coming out of their hiding places aflame from head to foot ; try to recall the bayonet exercises, first with stuffed sacks and then with the soft resistant flesh of the enemy, who is au fond your brother in the flesh. Think of all the foul words in all the tongues of Babel, and when you have mouthed them all, ask yourself if in the thick of it you were able to summon a single word capable of conveying what you were experiencing. One can read *The Red Laugh, The Red Badge of Courage, Men in War* or *J'ai Tué*, and in the reading of them derive a certain aesthetic enjoyment— despite the horripilating nature of these books. This is one of the strange, strange things about the written word, that you can live the dread thing in your mind and not only not go mad but feel somewhat exhilarated, often healed. Andreyev, Crane, Latzko, Cendrars—these men were artists as well as murderers. Somehow, I can never think of a general as an artist. (An admiral possibly, but a general never.) For me a general *must* have the hide of a rhinoceros, otherwise he would be nothing more than an adjutant or a commissary sergeant. . . . Pierre Loti, was he not an officer in the French Navy ? Strange that he should pop into my head. But the Navy, as I said, offers one a thin chance of preserving the little humanity which is left us. Loti, in the image which is preserved from youthful readings, seems so cultured, so refined— a bit of a gymnast also, if I remember rightly. How could he possibly *kill* ? To be sure, there wasn't much guts in his writings. But he left one book which I cannot put aside as mere romantic balderdash, though possibly it is : I mean *Disenchanted*. (To think that just the other day a Dominican monk, who came to visit me, had met in the flesh the "heroine" of this tender romance !) Anyway, with Pierre Loti goes Claude Farrère, both relics now, like the Monitor and the Merrimac.

Thinking of Thermopylae, Marathon, Salamis, I recall an illustration in a juvenile book I read long ago. It was a picture of the brave Spartans, supposedly on the eve of their last stand, combing their long hair. They knew they would die to the last man, yet (or because of this fact) they were combing their hair. The long strands fell to the waist—and they were plaited, I believe. This, in my childish mind, gave them an effeminate appearance. The impression remains. On my expedition through the Peloponnesos, with Katsimbalis (the "Colossus") I was dumbfounded to learn that not one poet, artist or scientist had come out of the Peloponnesos. Only warriors, lawgivers, athletes—and obedient clods.

Thucydides' *History of the Peloponnesian War* is admittedly a masterpiece. It is a book I have never been able to finish, but I esteem it nevertheless. It is one of those books which should be read with attention at this moment in history. "Thucydides is pointing out what war is, why it comes to pass, what it does, and, unless men learn better ways, must continue to do."*

Twenty-seven years of war—and nothing accomplished, nothing gained. (Except the usual destruction.)

> The Athenians and the Spartans fought for one reason only—because they were powerful, and therefore were compelled (the words are Thucydides' own) to seek more power. They fought not because they were different—democratic Athens and oligarchical Sparta—but because they were alike. The war had nothing to do with differences in ideas or with considerations of right and wrong. Is democracy right and the rule of the few over the many wrong ? To Thucydides the question would have seemed an evasion of the issue. There was no right power. Power, whoever wielded it, was evil, the corrupter of men.†

* *The Great Age of Greek Literature*, by Edith Hamilton ; W. W. Norton, New York, 1942.
† Ibid.

In the opinion of this author, " Thucydides was the first probably to see, certainly to put into words, this new doctrine which was to become the avowed doctrine of the world." The doctrine, namely, that in power politics it is not only necessary, but right, for the state to seize every opportunity for self-advantage.

As for Sparta, how modern is the description of this State seen through Plutarch's eyes :

> In Sparta, the citizens' way of life was fixed. In general, they had neither the will nor the ability to lead a private life. They were like a community of bees, clinging together around the leader and in an ecstasy of enthusiasm and selfless ambition belonging wholly to their country.

When you're ready, Griswold, fire !

Three thousand, five thousand, ten thousand years of history —and the readiness and ability to make war is still the supreme annihilating day-to-day fact of our lives. We have not advanced a step, despite all the sound, irrefutable, analytical treatises and diatribes on the subject. Almost as soon as we are able to read, the history of our glorious country is put in our hands. It is a story written in bloodshed, telling of lust, greed, hatred, envy, persecution, intolerance, theft, murder and degradation. As children we thrill to read of the massacre of the Indians, the persecution of the Mormons, the crushing defeat of the rebellious South. Our first heroes are soldiers, usually *generals*, of course. To the Northerner, Lincoln is almost a Christ-like figure. To the Southerner, Robert E. Lee is the embodiment of grace, chivalry, valor and wisdom. Both men led their followers to slaughter. Both fought for the right. The Negro, who was the cause of the trouble, is still a slave and a pariah.

" Everything we are taught is false," said Rimbaud. As always, he meant literally everything. As soon as one begins to look deeply into any subject one realizes how very little is known, how very, very much is conjecture, hypothesis, surmise and speculation. Wherever one penetrates profoundly one is confronted by the triple-headed spectre of prejudice, superstition, authority. When it comes to vital instruction, almost everything that has been written for our edification can be junked.

As we grow older we learn how to read the myths, fables and legends which entranced us in childhood. We read biography more and more—and the philosophy of history rather than history itself. We care less and less for facts, more and more for pure flights of the imagination and intuitive apprehension of the truth. We discover that the poet, whatever his medium, is the only true inventor. Into this single type are merged all the heroes we at one time or another worshipped. We observe that man's only real enemy is fear, and that all imaginative acts (all heroism) are inspired by the desire and the unflinching resolve to conquer fear —in whatever form it manifests itself. The hero-as-poet epitomizes the inventor, the pioneer, the pathfinder, the truth seeker. He it is who slays the dragon and opens the gates of paradise. That we persist in situating this paradise in a beyond is not the fault of the poet. The same belief and worship which inspire the vast majority are mirrored by an inner absence of faith and reverence. The poet-as-hero inhabits reality : he seeks to establish this reality for all mankind. The purgatorial condition which prevails on earth is the caricature of the one and only reality ; and it is because the poet-hero refuses to acknowledge any but the true reality that he is always slain, always sacrificed.

I said a moment ago that our first heroes are soldiers. In a large sense this is true. True, if we mean by "soldier" one who acts on his own authority, one who fights for the good, the beautiful and the true in obedience to the dictates of his own conscience. In this sense even the gentle Jesus could be called "a good soldier." So could Socrates and other great figures whom we never think of as soldiers. The great pacifists must then be ranked as mighty soldiers. But this conception of the soldier derives from attributes formerly reserved for the hero. The only good soldier, strictly speaking, is the hero. The rest are tin soldiers. What is the hero then ? The incarnation of man "in his frailty" battling against insuperable odds. To be more exact, this is a residual impression left us through the heroic legends. When we examine the lives of that order of heroes known as saints and sages, we perceive very clearly that the odds are not insuperable, that the enemy is not society, that the gods are not against man, and, what is more important, we perceive that the reality which the latter strive to assert, establish and maintain is not at all a wishful reality but one which is ever present, only hidden by man's wilful blindness.

Before we come to adore such a figure as Richard the Lion-Hearted we have already been enthralled and subjugated by the more sublime figure of King Arthur. Before we come to the great Crusader we have had for company, in our rarest moments, the very real, very vivid personages known as Jason, Theseus, Ulysses, Sinbad, Aladdin, and such like. We are already familiar with historical figures such as the great King David, Joseph in Egypt, Daniel who braved the lions' den, and with lesser figures such as Robin Hood, Daniel Boone, Pocahontas. Or we may have fallen under the spell of purely literary creations, such as Robinson Crusoe, Gulliver, or Alice—for Alice, too, was in quest of reality and proved her courage poetically by stepping through the looking glass.

Whatever their provenance, all these early spellbinders were also "spacebinders." Even some of the historical figures seem to possess the faculty of dominating time and space. All were sustained and fortified by miraculous powers which they either wrested from the gods or developed through the cultivation of native ingenuity, cunning or faith. The moral underlying most of these stories is that man is really free, that he only begins to use his God-given powers when the belief that he possesses them becomes unshakable. Ingenuity and cunning appear again and again as basic qualities of the intellect. Perhaps it is only one little trick which the hero is given to know, but it more than suffices for all he does not know, never will know, never need know. The meaning is obvious. To jump clear of the clockwork we must employ whatever means are in our possession. It is not enough to believe or to know : we must act. And I mean act, not activity. (The " acts " of the Apostles, for example.) The ordinary man is involved in action, the hero acts. An immense difference.

Yes, long before we are filled with adoration for the incarnations of courage and stout-heartedness we have been impregnated with the spirit of more sublime types, men in whom intellect, heart and soul were welded in triumphant unison. And how can we overlook, in mentioning these truly masculine figures, the regal types of womanhood that were attracted to them ? Only back in this dim past do we seem to find women who are the equal and counterpart of the great in spirit. What disillusionment awaits us as we advance into history and biography !

Alexander, Caesar, Napoleon—can we compare these conquerors with men like King David, the great King Arthur, or Saladin ? How fortunate we are to taste the supernatural and the supra-sensual at the threshold of our institutional life ! That terrible episode in European history, known as the Children's Crusade, is it not being enacted over and over by those whom we bring into the world without thought or concern for their true welfare ? Almost from the start our children abandon us in favor of the true guides, the true leaders, the true heroes. They know instinctively that we are their jailers, their tyrannical masters, from whom they must flee at the earliest moment or else slay us alive. " Little primitives," we call them some times. Yes, but one might also say—" little saints," "little wizards," " little warriors." Or, tout court—" little martyrs."

" *Everything we are taught is false.*" Yes, but that is not all. For not believing " their " falsehoods we are relentlessly and mercilessly punished ; for not accepting " their " vile surrogates we are humiliated, insulted and injured ; for struggling to free ourselves from " their " strangling clutches we are shackled and manacled. O, the tragedies that are enacted daily in every home ! We beg to fly, and they tell us that only angels have wings. We beg to offer ourselves on the altar of truth, and they tell us that Christ is the truth, the way and the life. And if, accepting Him, demanding to follow Him literally and to the bitter end, we are laughed and jeered at. At every turn fresh confusion is heaped upon us. We know not where we stand nor why we should act thus instead of so. For us the question why is ever evaded. Ours to obey, not to ask the reason why. We begin in chains and we end in chains. Stones for bread, logarithms for answers. In despair we turn to books, confide in authors, take refuge in dreams.

Do not consult me, O miserable parents ! Do not beseech my aid, O forlorn and abandoned youths ! I know you are suffering. I know how you suffer and why you suffer. It has been thus since the beginning of time, or at least since we know anything about man. There is no redress. Even to be creative is but alleviation and palliation. One must free himself unaided. " To become as little children." Every one bows his head in silence when this utterance is repeated. But no one truly believes it. And parents will always be the last to believe.

The autobiographical novel, which Emerson predicted would grow in importance with time, has replaced the great confessions. It is not a mixture of truth and fiction, this genre of literature, but an expansion and deepening of truth. It is more authentic, more veridical, than the diary. It is not the flimsy truth of facts which the authors of these autobiographical novels offer but the truth of emotion, reflection and understanding, truth digested and assimilated. The being revealing himself does so on all levels simultaneously.

That is why books like *Death on the Installment Plan* and the *Portrait of the Artist as a Young Man* catch us in the very bowels. The sordid facts of miseducated youth acquire, through the hate, rage and revolt of men like Céline and Joyce, a new significance. As to the disgust which these books inspired when they first appeared, we have the testimony of some very eminent men of letters. *Their* reactions are also significant and revelatory. We know where *they* stand as regards truth. Though they speak in the name of Beauty, we are certain that Beauty is not their concern. Rimbaud, who took Beauty upon his knees and found her ugly, is a far more reliable criterion. Lautréamont, who blasphemed more than any man in modern times, was much closer to God than those who shudder and wince at his blasphemies. As for the great liars, the men whose every word is flouted because they invent and fantasticate, who could be more staunch and eloquent advocates of truth than they ?

Truth is stranger than fiction because reality precedes and includes imagination. What constitutes reality is unlimited and undefinable. Men of little imagination name and classify, the great ones are content to forego this game. For the latter, vision and experience suffice. They do not even try to tell what they have seen and felt, for their province is the ineffable. The great visions which have come down to us in words are but the pale, jeweled reflections of indescribable happenings. Great events may be soul-stirring, but great visions transfix one. As a saint—that is to say, as a wretched sinner struggling with his conscience—Augustine is magnificent ; as a theologian he is dull, overwhelmingly dull. As teacher and lover Abélard is magnificent, for in both realms he was in his element. He never became a saint ; he was content to remain a man. Héloise is the true saint, but the Church has never admitted it. The Church is a human institution which often mistakes the criminal for the saint and vice versa.

When we come to Montezuma we are in a totally different world. Again we have lustre and inner radiance. Again there is splendor, magnificence, beauty, imagination, dignity and true nobility. Again the awesome bright ambiance of the gods. What a ruffian is Cortez ! Cortez and Pizarro—they make our hearts bleed with disgust. In their exploits man touches nadir. They stand out as the supreme vandals of all time.

Prescott's monumental work,* which we usually happen upon in adolescence, is one of those terrifying and illuminating creations which put the seal of doom on our youthful dreams and aspirations. We of this continent, we adolescents who had been drugged and hypnotized by the heroic legends of history books (which begin only *after* the bloody preface written by the Conquistadores), we learn with a shock that this glorious continent was forced open with inhuman violence. We learn that the " fountain of youth " is a pretty symbol masking a hideous story of lust and greed. The lust for gold is the foundation on which this empire of the New World rests. Columbus followed a dream, but not his men, not the swashbuckling bandits who followed after him. Through the mists of history Columbus now seems like a quiet, serene madman. (The reverse of Don Quixote.) What all unwittingly he set in motion, what one eminent British writer calls " the American horror,"† has the quality and content of nightmare. With every

---

* *The Conquest of Mexico* and *Peru.*

† " It is a very hard thing to escape *the American horror* ; and quite impossible, I suppose, to explain to those who don't see what it is that the victims of it see. The horror can be very big. But it can also be very small. Most things of this sort can be detected by their smell ; and I think this particular horror is usually found—like the inside of an American coffin after the embalming process has run its course—to smell of a mixture of desolate varnish and unspeakable decomposition. The curious thing about it is that it is a horror that can only be felt by imaginative people. It is more than a mere negation of all that is mellow, lovely, harmonious, peaceful, organic, satisfying. It is not a negation at all ! It is a terrifying positive. I think at its heart lies a sort of lemur-like violence of gruesome vulgarity. It certainly loves to dance a sort of " danse macabre " of frantic self-assertion. It has something that is antagonistic to the very essence of what the old cultures have been training to us for ten thousand years." (John Cowper Powys in his *Autobiography*.)

new boatload came fresh vandals, fresh assassins. Vandals and assassins who were not content simply to plunder, pillage, rape and exterminate the living, but like devils incarnate fell upon the earth itself, violated it, annihilated the gods who protected it, destroyed every last trace of culture and refinement, never ceasing in their depredations until confronted by their own frightening ghosts.

The story of Cabeza de Vaca (in North America), and that is why I speak of it over and over, breathes the magic of redemption. It is a heartbreaking story as well as an inspiring one. This scape-goat of a Spaniard really expiates the crimes of his predatory pre-decessors. Naked, abandoned, hunted, persecuted, enslaved, for-saken even by the God he had perfunctorily worshipped, he is driven to the last ditch. The miracle occurs when, ordered by his captors (the Indians) to pray for them, to heal them of their ills or die, he obeys. It is a miracle indeed which he performs—at the bidding of his captors. He who was as dust is lifted up, glorified. The power to heal and restore, to create peace and harmony, does not vanish. Cabeza de Vaca moves through the wilderness of what is now Texas like the risen Christ. Reviewing his life in Spain, as a " European," as a faithful servant of his Majesty the Emperor, he realizes the utter emptiness of that life. Only in the wilderness, abandoned to a cruel fate, was he able to come face to face with his Creator and his fellow creatures. Augustine found Him "in the vast halls of his memory." De Vaca, like Abraham, found Him " in the direct conversation."

If only our history had taken its direction at this crucial point ! If only this Spaniard, in all the might and the glory that was revealed unto him, had become the forerunner of the American to come ! But no, this inspiring figure, this true warrior, is almost buried from sight. Ringed in light, he is nevertheless absent from the chronicles our children are given to read. A few men have written of him. A very few. One of these, Haniel Long, has interpreted for us de Vaca's own historic document. It is an " Interlinear " of the first order. The true and essential narrative has been exhumed and rendered with poetic licence. Like a powerful beacon, it sheds illumination upon the bloody confusion, the atrocious nightmare, of our beginnings here in this land of the red Indian.

XI

THE STORY OF MY HEART

SOME few years before sailing for Paris I had occasional meetings with my old friend Emil Schnellock in Prospect Park, Brooklyn. We used to stroll leisurely over the downs in the summer evenings, talking of the fundamental problems of life and eventually about books. Though our tastes were quite divergent, there were certain authors, such as Hamsun and D. H. Lawrence, for whom we had a common enthusiasm. My friend Emil had a most lovable way of deprecating his knowledge and understanding of books ; pretending to be ignorant or obtuse, he would ply me with questions which only a sage or a philosopher could answer. I remember this short period vividly because it was an exercise in humility and self-control on my part. The desire to be absolutely truthful with my friend caused me to realize how very little I knew, how very little I could reveal, though he has always maintained that I was a guide and a mentor to him. In brief, the result of these communions was that I began to doubt all that I had blithely taken for granted. The more I endeavored to explain my point of view the more I floundered. He may have thought I acquitted myself well, but not I. Often, on parting from him, I would continue the inner debate interminably.

I suspect that I was rather arrogant and conceited at this time, that I had all the makings of an intellectual snob. Even if I did not have all the answers, as we say, I must have given the illusion of being thus endowed. Talk came easily to me ; I could always spin a glittering web. Emil's sincere, direct questions, always couched in the most humble spirit, punctured my vanity. There was something very artful about these innocent questions of his. They made clear to me that he not only knew a lot more than he pretended but that he sometimes knew much more than I did myself. If he read far less than I, he read with much greater attention and, as a result, he retained much more than I ever did. I used to think

172

his memory astounding, and it was indeed, but, as I discovered later, it was the fruit of patience, love, devotion. He had, moreover, a gift which I only learned the value of much later, namely, the ability to discover in *every* author that which is valuable and lasting. By comparison I was ruthless and intolerant. There were certain authors I absolutely could not stomach : I ruled them out as being beneath one's attention. Ten years, perhaps twenty years later, I might confess to my good friend Emil that I had found something of merit in them, an admission which often took him by surprise because, influenced by my dogmatic assertions, he had in the meantime come to suspect that he had overrated these authors. There was always this amusing and sometimes bewildering *décalage* where our opinions of authors were concerned.

There was one author whom he recommended to me with great warmth—it must have been a good twenty years ago. Knowing nothing about him or the little book he had written, never having heard the name before, I made a mental note of it and passed on. For some reason, at the time Emil mentioned it to me, I got the impression that it was a " sentimental " narrative. *The Story of my Heart*, it was called, and the author was English. Richard Jefferies, no less. Meant nothing to me. I would read it some day—when I had nothing better to do.

It is strange—I have touched on this before, I know—that even if one does forget the title and author of a book once recommended one does not forget the aura which accompanied the recommendation. A little word or phrase, an extra touch of warmth or zeal, keeps a certain vague remembrance alive in the back of one's head. We ought always to be alert to these smouldering vibrations. No matter if the person recommending the book be a fool or an idiot, we should always be ready to take heed. Of course my friend Emil was neither a fool nor an idiot. He was of an unusually warm nature, tender, sympathetic and believing. That something " extra " which he had imparted on this occasion never ceased working in me.

Here let me digress a moment to speak of something which has been on my mind frequently of late. It has to do with the recollection of a certain " fat boy," whose name I like to think was Louis, because there is something about the name Louis which describes this type to a tee. (" Je me nomme Louis Salavin ! ") Now Louis,

173

I recalled just the other day, was the one who usually presided over our discussions of life and books in the vacant lot at the corner. He was a fat boy, as I said, and if I were to search for *the* word to categorize him, I would choose *déclassé*. (Or, let us say—"outlander.") I mean that this Louis, like all his tribe, had neither background nor milieu, neither home, parents, relatives, traditions, customs or fixed habits. Detached and apart, he mingled with the world only in obedience to a sublime kind of condescension. It was natural that he should possess the oracular gift. I can see this Louis of ours all over again, perched like a stuffed vulture atop the fence which closed off the lot. It is the month of November and a huge bonfire is blazing. We have all contributed our mite to the feast— chippies, raw potatoes, onions, carrots, apples, whatever could be grabbed off. Soon we will be standing by Louis' feet, munching our bit and warming up for the discussion which is certain to ensue. This particular day I remember that we touched on *The Mysteries of Paris.** It was a strange world for us kids, this world of Eugene Sue who, it is said, was one of Dostoievsky's favorite authors. We were much more at home in the imaginary worlds of the writers of romance. Louis listened benignly and directed the discussion with an invisible wand. Now and then he put in a cryptic word or two. It was as if Moses spake. Nobody ever questioned Louis' veracity. " I have spoken "—that was the tone of his " dicta."

What precisely Louis said is completely lost to me. All that remains is the tone of authority, the certitude behind his words. There was an additional quality, almost like grace, which Louis conveyed to us in these moments. It was approval—or benediction, if you like. " Continue your meanderings," he seemed to say. " Follow out every clue, every gossamer thread. Eventually you will know." If we had doubts, he urged us to cultivate them. If we passionately, blindly believed, he also approved. " It's your show," he seemed to insinuate. Just as de Sade says : " Your body is yours alone ; you are the only person in the world who has a right to take pleasure from it and to permit whoever you will to get pleasure from it . . . "†

It was the mind Louis was interested in. Not " our " minds, or any

* (See the end of this chapter for a note on Eugène Sue.)
† *La Philosophie dans le boudoir.*

particular mind, but Mind. It was as though Louis were revealing to us the essential nature of mind. Not thought, but mind. There was mystery attached to mind. Any one could grapple with thought, but *mind . . .?* So it mattered not to Louis what the " truth " might be as regards the problems we were then confronting for the first time in our young lives. Louis was trying to make us understand that it was all a game, so to speak. A very high game too. His replies, or observations, cryptic though they were, had for us all the import of revelation. They gave an importance hitherto unknown to the questioner rather than the question. *Who is it that asks ? Whence comes this question ? Why ?*

> Divine or die—such was the terrible dilemma proposed by the sphinx to the candidates for Theban royalty. The reason is that the secrets of science are actually those of life ; the alternatives are to reign or to serve, to be or not to be. The natural forces will break us if we do not put them to use for the conquest of the world. There is no mean between the height of kinghood and the abyss of the victim state, unless we are content to be counted among those who are nothing because they ask not why or what they are.*

It now seems undeniable to me that Louis, even as a mere youth, had divined some extraordinary secret of life. The pleroma was about him. Just to be in his presence was to partake of a fullness indescribable. He never pretended to be the possessor of great knowledge or wisdom. He preferred our company to that of the boys his own age. Did he know—it seems quite possible !—that these latter were already " lost," abandoned to the world ? At any rate, without in the least suspecting it, Louis had assumed the rôle of hierophant.

How much more we learned from Louis than from our appointed instructors ! I realize it now when I think of another boy my own age, whom I liked exceedingly, and who used to go out of his way every day to walk home with me from school. Joe Maurer was his name. I had tremendous respect for his intellect as well as his character. He and the French boy, Claude de Lorraine, whom I

* *The History of Magic*, by Eliphas Lévi (Alphonse Louis Constant) ; William Rider & Son, Ltd., London, 1922.

have spoken of elsewhere, were virtually models for me throughout this period. One day I made the mistake of introducing my friend Joe Maurer to Louis. Until that moment I had not the least suspicion that in the very being of Joe Maurer there existed a grave flaw. It was while listening to Louis, who had gone into a monologue, that I saw written all over Joe Maurer's face—DOUBT. Then I was made witness of a dreadful event : the incineration of my dear young skeptic. In that flood-like smile of compassion which Louis could summon on occasion I saw little Joe Maurer consumed to a crisp. Louis had put the torch to that petty, vaunting intellect which had so impressed me. He had turned on him the full power of Mind—and there was nothing left (for me) of my comrade's intellect, character or being.

Seeing Louis now, in my mind's eye, astride the fence billeted with announcements—huge flaming posters—of coming events (*Rebecca of Sunnybrook Farm*, *Way Down East*, *The Wizard of Oz*, Barnum & Bailey's Circus, Burton Holmes' Travelogues, Houdini, Gentleman Jim Corbett, *Pagliacci*, Maude Adams in the eternal *Peter Pan*, and so on), seeing Louis perched there like a rotund wizard, a lad of sixteen yet so immeasurably superior to us, so distant and yet so close, so serious and yet so carefree, so absolutely sure of himself and yet so unconcerned about his own person, his own fate, I ask myself—*what ever became of Louis ?* Did he disappear from our ranks to become the dominant character of some strange, occult book ? Has he, under the cloak of anonymity perhaps, written works which I have read and marveled over ? Or did he take off, at an early age, for Arabia, Tibet, Abyssinia—to disappear from " the world " ? Such as Louis never meet with an ordinary end.

A moment ago he was as alive to me as when I was a boy of ten standing in the vacant lot at the corner. I am certain he is still very much alive. It would not be at all remarkable if one day he announced himself here at Big Sur. All those other lads I played with and who were so very, very close to me, it then seemed, I never expect to hear of. Once I thought it strange that our paths should never cross again. Not any more. There are a handful who remain with you always—" even unto the end of the world."

But *Louis !* what was he doing in that grotesque body ? Why had he assumed such a disguise ? Was it to protect himself against

176

fools and ignoramuses ? Louis, Louis, what I would not give to know your real identity !

My friend Emil, it is high time to acknowledge my debt to you. How in the name of heaven could I possibly have avoided reading this book for so long ? Why did you not *shout* the title in my ears ? Why were you not more insistent ? Here is a man who speaks my inmost thoughts. He is the iconoclast I feel myself to be yet never fully reveal. He makes the utmost demands. He rejects, he scraps, he annihilates. What a seeker ! What a daring seeker ! When you read the following passage I wish you would try to recall those talks we had in Prospect Park, try to remember, if you can, the nature of my fumbling answers to those " deep " questions you propounded . . .

> The mind is infinite and able to understand everything that is brought before it ; there is no limit to its understanding.* The limit is the littleness of the things and the narrowness of the ideas which have been put for it to consider. For the philosophies of old time past and the discoveries of modern research are as nothing to it. They do not fill it. When they have been read, the mind passes on, and asks for more. The utmost of them, the whole together, make a mere nothing. These things have been gathered together by immense labor, labor so great that it is a weariness to think of it ; but yet, when all is summed up and written, the mind receives it all as easily as the hand picks flowers. It is like one sentence read and gone.†

Emil, reading Richard Jefferies, I suddenly recall my *sublime*—forgive me if I call it that—yes, my sublime impatience. *What are we waiting for ? Why are we marking time ?* Was not that *me* all over ? It used to annoy you, I know, but you were tolerant of me. You would ask me a question and I would reply with a bigger one. For the life of me I could not understand, and would not understand, why we did not scrap everything immediately and begin afresh. That is why, when I came across certain utterances from the lips of

---

* Curious that Lautréamont said almost the same : " Nothing is incomprehensible."

† This and other citations are taken from the Haldeman-Julius reprint of Jefferies' *Story of My Heart*.

M

Louis Lambert—*another Louis !*—I nearly jumped out of my skin. I was suffering then exactly as he had suffered.

I am not altogether convinced that there are many who suffer for the reasons intimated and to the degree which Louis Lambert tells us he suffered. Time and again I have hinted that there is a tyrant in me which continues to assert that society must one day be governed by its true masters. When I read Jefferies' statement : " In twelve thousand written years the world has not yet built itself a House, nor filled a Granary, nor organized itself for its own comfort "—this old tyrant which refuses to be smothered rises up again. Time and again, touching on certain books, certain authors, recalling the tremendous impact of their utterances—men like Emerson, Nietzsche, Rimbaud, Whitman, the Zen masters especially—I think with fury and resentment (still !) of those early teachers into whose hands we were entrusted. There was our principal at " dear old 85," for example. What a bundle of vanity and conceit ! He walks in one day, while we're studying arithmetic, begs the teacher to let him take over, and in the space of a few minutes goes to the blackboard and draws the figure eight lying on its side. " What does *that* signify ? " he asks. An impressive silence. No one knows, of course. Whereupon he announces sententiously : " Boys, that is the sign for infinity ! " Nothing further said about it. An egg lying on its side—nothing more. A little later, in High School, comes Dr. Murchisson, another mathematician and an ex-commander of the Navy. A living monument to discipline, this bird. " Never ask why ! Obey ! " That's Commander Murchisson. One day I plucked up the courage to ask why we studied geometry. (It seemed an utterly senseless, useless study to me.) For answer he tells me that it is good discipline for the mind. Is that an answer, I ask you ? Then, by way of punishment for my temerity and impudence, he makes me memorize a speech he has written for me, which I am to deliver before the whole school. It is about battle-ships, the various types there are, the kinds of armament they carry, their varying speeds and the effectiveness of their broadsides. Do you wonder that I still nourish a healthy contempt for this old master ? Then there was " Bulldog " Grant, the Latin teacher . . . our *first* Latin teacher. (Why I chose to study Latin is still a mystery to me.) Anyway, the man was an absolute conundrum to us. One moment

178

he would be apoplectic with rage, positively beside himself, " hop-
ping mad," as we say, the veins standing out like cords at the
temples, the perspiration rolling down his puffed red-apple cheeks.
Why ? Because some one had used the wrong gender or employed
the ablative instead of the vocative. The next moment he would be
wreathed in smiles, telling us a joke, a risqué one usually. Every day
he began the session by calling the roll, as if it were the most important thing on God's earth. Then, to warm us up he would bid us
rise, clear our throats, and yell at the top of our lungs : " Hic, haec,
hoc . . . huius, huius, huius . . . huic, huic, huic . . . " right
through to the end. This and the conjugation of the verb " amo "
are all I retain of the first three years of Latin. Instructive, what !
Later, under another Latin teacher named Hapgood, a good egg, by
the way, one who had a real love for his bloody Vergil, we used to
receive a surprise visit now and then from the principal, Dr. Paisley.
To this day, I tell you, the latter remains for me the symbol incarnate
of the pedagogue. In addition to being a blunderbuss and dunderhead
he was an arch-tyrant. Just to be near him was to be filled with fear,
terror and dread. Bloodless he was, with a heart of stone. His little
game—get this !—was to break in on us at some unexpected moment,
march to the head of the room on tiptoes, and, pretending that he
wished to keep his hand in, beg dear Professor Hapgood (who had
no choice in the matter) to let him take over for a few minutes.
Plunking himself in the master's chair, he picks up the book (the
Aeneid) which he undoubtedly knew by heart, scans it intently as
though puzzling it out, then quietly asks the professor (with his eyes
on us) where we were. Hm ! He riffles the pages, chooses a passage
which he reads to himself, then picks on one of us to rattle off the
translation. Naturally, terrified of him as we all were, what little
ability his poor victim had vanished like smoke. But Dr. Paisley
seemed not at all surprised or displeased ; on the contrary, he reacted
as though this—this utter blankness of mind—were entirely natural
and customary. All he was waiting for was to give us *his* version of
the translation. He would do it falteringly, as if *groping* his way
through the bloody text. Sometimes he would look up, and
addressing the air above us, would ask if we didn't perhaps prefer
this rendition to *that*. None of us gave a fuck which way he interpreted the passage. All we were praying for was that he would leave

179

as soon as possible. He gave off the odor, I must add, of camphor, arnica and embalming fluid. He was the very corpse of learning . . . There is one more I must mention—Doc Payne. He was a testy chap but likable in a way, especially out of class. He smoked a lot, we observed, and was as eager for the class to be dismissed as we ourselves. It meant a few puffs on the sly for him. Anyway, he taught us ancient, medieval and modern history—one after another, just like that. To him history was dates, battles, peace treaties, names of generals, statesmen, diplomats—" all the rats," so to speak. Because he was more human than the rest I can't forgive him for the " omissions." What do I mean ? Just this. Never once, at the beginning of a semester, did he give us a bird's-eye view of what we were in for. Never once did it occur to him to " orient " us in this vast muddle of dates, names, places, etc. If he expatiated at all, it was on some campaign long forgotten, some " decisive battle " of the world. I can see him all over again, with chalk in hand—red, white and blue—designating by chicken tracks the positions of the opposing armies. Very important for us to know why at a certain moment the cavalry was unleashed, or why the center gave way, or why some other fool manoeuvre took place. He never enlarged upon the character, temperament, genius (military or otherwise) of the leaders of these great conflicts. He never gave us his own précis of the causes of the various wars. We followed the books he handed us, and if we had any ideas of our own, we smothered them. It was more important to have the right date, the exact terms of the treaty under discussion, than to have a wide, general, integrated picture of the whole subject. He might have said, on opening the book of ancient history, for example, and here I take the liberty of adlibbing : " Boys, young men, in the year 9,763 B.C. the world found itself in a peculiar state of stasis. The grass and grains on either bank of the Iriwaddy were virtually extinct. The Chinese, just beginning to feel their oats, were on the march. The Minoan civilization of Crete and her colonies presented no threat to the other up-and-coming nations of the world. The rudiments of every invention now known were already in existence. The arts flourished everywhere, as they had for unknown ages in the past. The principal religions were such and such. No one knows why at this precise moment in history certain definite movements began to take place. In the East there was such and such an alignment of forces ; in the West another. Suddenly a figure appeared named Hochintuxityscy ; almost nothing is known about this great figure, except that he initiated a wave of new life . . ." You see what I mean. He could have drawn for us on that blackboard which was a perpetual vexation a map of the then world, and on the rear blackboard a map of the world as it is today. He could have made some boxes, by means of vertical and horizontal lines, and in them placed a few salient names, dates, events—to give us our bearings. He could have drawn a tree and on its limbs and branches shown the evolution of the arts, sciences, religions and metaphysical ideas throughout history. He could have told us that with recent times history has become the metaphysics of history. He could have shown us how and why the greatest of historians differ with one another. He could have done *something* more, I say, than force us to memorize names, dates, battles and so on. He could even have ventured to give us a picture of the next hundred years— or asked us to describe the future in our own terms. But he never did. And so I say : " Damn him and all history books ! " From the study of history, mathematics, Latin, English literature, botany, physics, chemistry, art I have gotten nothing but anguish, desperation and confusion. From four years in High School I retain nothing but the remembrance of the fleeting pleasure evoked by the reading of *Ivanhoe* and *Idylls of the King.* From grammar school I remember only one little episode—in the arithmetic class again. This is all I got out of eight years of primary instruction It was this . . . Our teacher, Mr. MacDonald, a gaunt, sombre person with almost no sense of humor and easily given to anger, asked me a direct question one day which I was unable to answer. Being rather fond of me, I suppose, he took the pains of going to the blackboard and explaining the problem thoroughly. (It probably had to do with fractions.) When he had finished he turned to me and said : " Now, Henry, do you understand ? " And I answered, " No, sir." Upon which the class burst into an uproar. I was left to stand there, feeling like the veriest idiot. Suddenly, however, this Mr. MacDonald turned on the class furiously and ordered the boys to be quiet. " Instead of laughing at him," he said, " I want you boys to take an example from Henry. Here is a boy who wants to know. He has the courage to say he does not understand. Remember this ! And try to do likewise, instead of pretending that you understand when you don't." That little lesson sank deep. It not only salved my wounded pride, it taught me true humility. All my life, whether as a result of this or not, I know not, I have been able to say, in critical moments : " No, I don't understand. Explain it again, if you will." Or, if I am asked a question which I really cannot answer I can say without blushing, without a sense of shame or guilt : " I'm sorry, but I don't know the answer." And what a relief it is to speak thus ! It is in such moments that the real answer usually comes—after one has confessed his ignorance or inability. The answer is always there, but we must put ourselves in readiness to receive it. We should know, however, that there are people to whom one must never put certain questions. The answer is not in them ! Among these people is the whole body of instructors to whom we are delivered from infancy hand and soul. These definitely do not know the answers. Nor, what is worse, do they know how to make us seek the answers in ourselves.

" If the eye is always watching, and the mind on the alert, ultimately chance supplies the solution," says Jefferies. True. But what is here termed chance is something of our own creation.

Suddenly I recall the name and presence of Dr. Brown. Dr. Brown was our " guest speaker " at the close of every grammar school period. I *must* speak of Dr. Brown because I would not for a minute have him, dead or alive, imagine that I include him in the category of nobodies mentioned above. Dr. Brown always appeared, just as vacation was about to begin, on wings of love. In fact, you felt that they were still fluttering, his wings, when he rose from his seat on the platform and made ready to say a few words. It was as though Dr. Brown knew each and every one of us intimately and was enveloping us in his all-enfolding mantle of love. His words came forth with palpitating warmth. He had just returned, it always seemed, from Asia, Africa or Europe, and he wanted us to be the first with whom to share his glorious experiences. That was the impression he gave, and I have no doubt it was genuine. He was a man who loved boys. What office he filled I no longer remember. He may have been a school superintendent ; he was probably also a deacon of the church. No matter. He was a man, he had a big heart, and he brimmed over with love. Nowadays we call such talks as Dr.

Brown gave "inspirational." Men are paid to turn them on or off at will. The effect of course is nil ; we all recognize the caricature. Dr. Brown was a truly inspired individual. All that he had read, and he was a man of great culture, all he had seen on his trips round the world, for he was a veritable globe-trotter, he had assimilated and woven into the very texture of his being. He was like a well-soaked sponge. One little squeeze of the fingers and he oozed water. When he rose to speak he was so full, so charged, that for a good few moments he was unable to begin. Once launched, his mind sparked in all directions at once. He was sensitive to the slightest pressure : he could detect instantly the nature of our longing, and respond to it immediately. In a quarter of an hour of this kind of communication he " instructed " us as we had never been instructed during the weeks and months of class. If he had been a teacher instead of our " guest speaker " he would, undoubtedly, have been dismissed in short order. He was too big for the system—for any system. He spoke from the heart, not the head. I need hardly repeat that no one ever spoke to us thus—not even the pastor. No, the pastor emanated a kind of vague, prescribed love which was like milk and water. He really did not give a damn about any one personally. He was interested in saving souls (supposedly) but there was damned little soul stuff in him. Dr. Brown reached our souls through our hearts. He had a sense of humor, a grand sense of humor—one of the infallible signs of liberation. When he got through—his speech was always too short for us—it was as if we had been given a bubble bath. We were relaxed, refreshed, silky inside and out. What's more, we felt a courage unknown before, a new kind of courage—I might almost say a " metaphysical " courage. We felt brave before the world because the good Dr. Brown had given us back our kingship. We were boys still—he never tried to pretend that we were " young men "—but we had become boys whose eyes swam with visions, whose appetite for life had increased. We were ready for hard tasks, valiant tasks.

I feel that I may now resume my theme with a clear conscience. . . . The little book which Richard Jefferies calls his " autobiography" is, to use the abused word once again, an inspirational work. In the whole of literature there are very few such works. Much that is styled inspirational is not at all ; it is what men who " specialize " in the subject would like us to believe is so. I mentioned Emerson. Never in my life have I met anyone who did not agree that Emerson is an inspiring writer. One may not accept his thought in toto, but one comes away from a reading of him purified, so to say, and exalted. He takes you to the heights, he gives you wings. He is daring, very daring. In our day he would be muzzled, I am certain. There are other men, such as Orage and Ralph Waldo Trine (among others) who are styled inspirational writers. They have undoubtedly been such to great numbers of people. But will they abide ? The reader may smile, knowing the sort of individual I am, that I should even mention such a name as R. W. Trine.* Am I mocking ? I am not. To each his due. At certain stages of one's evolution certain individuals stand forth as teachers. Teachers in the true sense— those who open our eyes. There are those who open our eyes and there are those who lift us out of ourselves. The latter are not interested in foisting upon us new beliefs but in aiding us to penetrate reality more deeply, " to make progress," in other words, " in the science of reality." They proceed first by levelling all the superstructures of thought. Second they point to something beyond thought, to the ocean of mind, let us say, in which thought swims. And last they force us to think for ourselves. Says Jefferies, for example, in the midst of his confession :

> Now, today, as I write, I stand in exactly the same position as the Caveman. Written tradition, systems of culture, modes of thought, have for me no existence. If ever they took any hold of my mind it must have been very slight ; they have long ago been erased.

That is a mighty utterance. An heroic utterance. Who can repeat it honestly and sincerely ? Who is there that even aspires to make such an utterance ? Jefferies tells us towards the end of his book how he had tried again and again to put into written words the thoughts which had taken possession of him. Repeatedly he failed. And no wonder, for what he succeeded in giving us finally, fragmentary though he confesses it to be, is almost a defiance of thought. Explaining how, " under happy circumstances," he did at last begin (in 1880), he states that he got no further than to write down a few notes.

* See my book *Plexus* for a long burlesque on *In Tune with the Infinite*.

" Even then," he says, " I could not go on, but I kept the notes (I had destroyed all former beginnings), and in the end, two years afterwards, commenced this book." He speaks of it as " only a fragment, and a fragment scarcely hewn." Then he adds, and this I think worth underscoring : " Had I not made it personal I could scarcely have put it into any shape at all . . . I am only too conscious of its imperfections, for I have as it were seventeen years of conscious-ness of my own inability to express this the idea of my life."

In this same small paragraph he makes an assertion which is very dear to me and which is the only stop that can be offered to critics. Speaking of the inadequacy of words to express ideas—and by this he means, of course, ideas which lay beyond the habitual realms of thought—attempting briefly to give his own definition of such moot terms as soul, prayer, immortality, and declaring these to be deficient still, he concludes : " I must leave my book as a whole to give its own meaning to its words."

Perhaps the key to this amazing little book is the sentence which runs thus : " No thought which I have ever had has satisfied my soul." The story of his life begins therefore with the realization of his soul's hunger, his soul's quest. All that preceded this became as nought. " Begin wholly afresh. Go straight to the sun, the im-mense forces of the universe, to the Entity unknown ; go higher than a god ; deeper than prayer ; and open a new day." Sounds like D. H. Lawrence. I wonder now if Lawrence ever read Jefferies. There is not only a similarity of thought but of accent and rhythm. But then we find this same idiosyncrasy of speech, in English at any rate, whenever we come upon an original thinker. The iconoclast always exhorts us in short, staccato sentences. It is as if he were transmitting telegraphically from a distant, higher station. It is an utterly different rhythm from that of the prophets, who are filled with woe and lamentation, with objurgation and malediction. Some-how, whether we accept the commands or not, we are stirred ; our feet go through the motion of marching forward, our chests heave, as if drawing in fresh draughts of oxygen, our eyes lift to capture the fleeting vision.

And now let us get to " the Fourth Idea," which is really the epitome of his soul's longing. He begins thus :

Three things only have been discovered of that which concerns the inner consciousness since before written history began. Three things only in twelve thousand written, or sculptured, years, and in the dumb, dim time before then. Three ideas the Cavemen primeval wrested from the unknown, the night which is round us still in daylight—the existence of the soul, immortality, the deity. These things found, prayer followed as a sequential result. Since then nothing further has been found in all the twelve thousand years, as if men had been satisfied and had found these to suffice. They do not suffice me. I desire to advance further, and to wrest a fourth, and even still more than a fourth, from the darkness of thought. I want more ideas of soul-life. I am certain there are more yet to be found. A great life—an entire civilization—lies just outside the pale of common thought. Cities and countries, inhabitants, intelligences, culture—an entire civilization. Except by illustrations drawn from familiar things, there is no way of indicating a new idea. I do not mean actual cities, actual civilization. Such life is different from any yet imagined. A nexus of ideas exists of which nothing is known—a vast system of ideas—a cosmos of thought. There is an Entity, a Soul-Entity, as yet unrecognized. These, rudely expressed, constitute my Fourth Idea. It is beyond, or beside, the three discovered by the Cavemen ; it is in addition to the existence of the soul ; in addition to immortality ; and beyond the idea of the deity. I think there is something more than existence.

In the same decade in which Jefferies enunciates these ideas, or better, this appeal for new, deeper, richer, more encompassing ideas, Madame Blavatsky put forth two astounding tomes into which entered a labor so prodigious that men are still cracking their skulls over them. I refer to *The Secret Doctrine* and *Isis Unveiled*. If they accomplished nothing more, these two books, they certainly put to rout the idea of the caveman's contribution to our culture. Drawing from every imaginable source, Madame Blavatsky amasses a wealth of material to prove the everlasting continuity of esoteric wisdom. According to this view, there never was a time when side by side with the " caveman," and even greatly anterior to him, there did not exist superior beings, and by superior I mean superior in every sense of the word. Certainly superior to those whom we today consider as such. Indeed, it is not even a question with her, or those who hold with her, of isolated superior beings but rather of whole great blazing civilizations the existence of which we do not even suspect.

Whether Jefferies knew of such views and rejected them I know not. I don't imagine it would have mattered any to him if he had been convinced that the only three ideas wrested from the unknown came to us via the mages of forgotten epochs or via the cavemen, as he says. I can see him sweeping the whole glittering array of knowledge off the boards. He would still be able to affirm that these three ideas are all we have—and what matter when they were put into circulation or by whom. What he strives magnificently to make us understand, make us realize, make us accept, is that these ideas came from a source which has never dried up and never will dry up ; that we are marking time, withering, ossifying, giving ourselves up to death, so long as we rest content with these precious three and make no effort to swim back to the source.

Filled with consuming wonder, awe and reverence for life, never able to get enough of sea, air and sky, realizing " the crushing hopelessness of books," determined to think things out for himself, it is not at all extraordinary consequently to find him declaring that the span of human life could be prolonged far beyond anything we imagine possible today. Indeed, he goes further, much further, and like a true man of spirit asserts that " death is not inevitable to the ideal man. He is shaped for a species of physical immortality." He begs us to ponder seriously on what might happen " if the entire human race were united in their efforts to eliminate causes of decay."

A few paragraphs further on he says, and with what justification :

> The truth is, we die through our ancestors, we are murdered by our ancestors. Their dead hands stretch forth from the tomb and drag us down to their mouldering bones. We in our turn are now at this moment preparing death for our unborn posterity. *This day those that die do not die in the sense of old age, they are slain.**

Every revolutionary figure, whether in the field of religion or the field of politics, knows this only too well. " *Begin wholly afresh !* " It is the old, old cry. But to slay the ghosts of the past

* Italics mine.

187

has thus far been an insuperable task for humanity. " A hen is only an egg's way of making another egg," said Samuel Butler. One wonders whose way it is that causes man to continue turning out misfits, that makes him, surrounded and invested as he is by the most potent and divine powers, satisfied to remain no more than he has been and still is. Imagine what man is capable of, in his ignorance and cruelty, to provoke from the lips of the Marquis de Sade upon his first release from prison (after almost thirteen years spent in solitary confinement) these terrible words : " . . . All my feelings are extinguished. I have no longer any taste for anything, I like nothing any more ; the world which foolishly I so wildly regretted seems to me so boring . . . and so dull . . . I have never been more misanthropic than I am now that I have returned among men, and if I seem peculiar to others, they can be assured that they produce the same effect on me . . . " The plaint of this unfortunate individual is today voiced by millions. From all quarters of the globe there rises a wail of distress. Worse, a wail of utter despair.

" When," asks Jefferies (in 1882 !), " will it be possible to be certain that the capacity of a single atom has been exhausted ? At any moment some fortunate incident may reveal a fresh power." Today we know—and how shamefully we have utilized it !—the power which resides in the atom. And it is today more than ever before that man roams hungry, naked, abandoned.

" *Begin afresh !* " The East rumbles. Indeed, the people of the East are at last making an heroic effort to shake off the fetters which bind them to the past. And what is the result ? We of the West tremble in fear. We would hold them back. *Where* is progress ? *Who* possesses enlightenment ?

There is a sentence in Jefferies' little book which literally jumps from the page—at least for me. " A reasoning process has yet to be invented by which to go straight to the desired end." To which statement I can hear the critical-minded objecting : " Excellent indeed, but why doesn't he invent it ? " Now it is one of the virtues of the men who inspire us that they always leave the way open. They suggest, they stimulate, they point. They do not take us by the hand and lead us. On the other hand I might say that there are men who are this very moment striving to show us how to accomplish this end. Now they are virtually unknown, but when the time comes they will stand revealed. We are not drifting blindly, however much it may seem so. But perhaps I ought to give the whole of Jefferies' thought here, for he has voiced it in a way which is unforgettable . . .

This hour, rays or undulations of more subtle mediums are doubtless pouring on us over the wide earth, unrecognized, and full of messages and intelligence from the unseen.* Of these we are this day as ignorant as those who painted the papyri were of light. There is an infinity of knowledge yet to be known, and beyond that an infinity of thought. No mental instrument even has yet been invented by which researches can be carried direct to the object. Whatever has been found has been discovered by fortunate accident ; in looking for one thing another has been chanced on. A reasoning process has yet to be invented by which to go straight to the desired end. For now the slightest particle is enough to throw the search aside, and the most minute circumstance sufficient to conceal obvious and brilliantly shining truths . . . At present the endeavor to make discoveries is like gazing at the sky up through the boughs of an oak. Here a beautiful star shines clearly ; here a constellation is hidden by a branch ; a universe by a leaf. Some mental instrument or organon is required to enable us to distinguish between the leaf which may be removed and a real void ; when to cease to look in one direction, and to work in another . . . I feel that there are infinities to be known, but they are hidden by a leaf . . .

Begin afresh ! Take another tack ! Or, as Claude Houghton says : " *All Change, Humanity !* " Or, as Klakusch says, in *The Maurizius Case*, " Stop, world of humans, and attack the problem from another angle ! " Again and again a voice within us commands us to get out of the rut, to leave bag and baggage, to change cars, change direction. Now and then an individual obeys the secret summons and undergoes what men call a conversion. But never does a whole world lift itself by the bootstraps and take a leap into the blue.

Things that have been miscalled supernatural appear to me simple, says Jefferies, more natural than nature, than earth, than sea or sun . . . It is matter which is the

* Very close to Maeterlinck's thought, as voiced in *The Magic of the Stars.*

supernatural, and difficult of understanding . . . Matter
is beyond understanding, mysterious, impenetrable ; I
touch it easily, comprehend it, no.   Soul, mind—the
thought, the idea—is easily understood, it understands
itself and is conscious.   The supernatural miscalled, the
natural in truth, is the real.   To me everything is supernatural. How strange that condition of mind which cannot
accept anything but the earth, the sea, the tangible
universe !   Without the misnamed supernatural these to
me seem incomplete, unfinished. Without soul all these are
dead. Except when I walk by the sea, and my soul is by it,
the sea is dead. Those seas by which no man has stood—
by which no soul has been—whether on earth or the
planets, are dead. No matter how majestic the planet rolls
in space, unless a soul be there it is dead.

Unless a soul be there it is dead. The man of today should be better
able to comprehend this than Jefferies' contemporaries. For him this
planet is virtually extinct already.

Around 1880 English novelists of imagination—the writers
of " romances "—began to introduce into their works the so-called
and miscalled " supernatural " element.   Theirs was a revolt against
the fateful tendency of the times, the bitter fruits of which we of
this generation are tasting. What is the gap, in thought or feeling,
between these writers (today regarded as ridiculous and misguided)
and our metaphysical scientists who struggle vainly to express a
larger, deeper, more significant view of the universe ?   It is a
common observation nowadays that the man in the street accepts
the " miracles " of science in a matter of fact way.   Every day of
his life the common man makes use of what men in other ages
would have deemed miraculous means.   In the range of invention,
if not in *powers* of invention, the man of today is nearer to being a
god than at any time in his history.   (So we like to believe !)   Yet
never was he less godlike. He accepts and utilizes the miraculous
gifts of science unquestioningly ; he is without wonder, without
awe, reverence, zest, vitality or joy. He draws no conclusions from
the past, has no peace or satisfaction in the present, and is utterly
unconcerned about the future. He is marking time. That is about
the most we can say for him.

We must, however, also say this—his *conception* of time, and of

190

space, together with other deeply embedded notions, such as the sacred doctrine of causality, the good work, progress, purpose, duty and so forth, have been killed *for him* by the scientist, the philosopher, the inventor, the big boss and the militarist. Precious little is left of the universe he was born into. Yet it is all there, every bit of it, and it will accompany him as he journeys backward or forward. His concepts only have been altered. Not his way of thinking. Not his thinking faculty, or his thinking powers. To the most baffling degree he remains immune and impervious to all that happens round and about him. He is not participating, he is being dragged along by the scalp. He initiates nothing, unless it be more reaction. What an image he presents, modern man ! A frightened and bewildered, a confused and bedeviled wretch, being dragged by the scalp, as I said, to some high, awesome place where all is about to be revealed to him, but where, whimpering and shuddering, he will be sent hurtling into the void. It is thus, and thus only, that I see him entering the great arcanum of truth and wisdom. How else could it be ? He himself has locked all doors ; he himself has kicked away all supports ; he himself has *elected* (if we may thus dignify him) to be flung into " the cauldron of rebirth." Sublime, ignominious spectacle. Punishment and salvation in one.

What, we ask, could or would constitute a " miracle " for man in this supine state ? Would it be a miracle to spare him his just fate ? Would it be a miracle if, just as he were going over the brink, his eyes were suddenly opened? What *does* modern man expect, if anything, in the way of miracles ? The only miracle I can possibly think of would be for him to beg, at the last moment, for a chance to begin afresh.

Is it not baffling that this species of man who believes so solidly in concrete reality, and only in concrete reality, can talk of the moon, or planets even more distant, as though they were only points of departure in his imminent physical exploration of the universe ; that he can think of communicating with unknown beings in the starry spheres or, what is more curious, think of how to defend himself against possible invasion by them ; that he can visualize himself abandoning this planet Earth and taking up a new mode of life somewhere in the heavens, and realize (mentally, at least) that such a change of residence would alter his physical age, structure and being, would make him over so completely, in short, that he would be unrecognizable to himself ? Is it not baffling, I say, that such thoughts do not terrify him—neither uprooting from his native planet, nor change of time, rhythm, metabolism, nor acquaintance with beings far, far stranger than any he has ever imagined ? And yet, yes—*and yet*, to get him to love and respect his neighbor, to endeavor to understand his fellow man, to share with him his possessions, his joys and sorrows, to get him to make provision for his progeny, to eliminate enmity, rivalry, jealousy, to create and respect a few simple laws—for his own welfare—to cease struggling for a bare existence and enjoy life, to concentrate on the elimination (not just the cure) of disease, old age, misery, loneliness—oh, so many, many things !—to get him to welcome new ideas and not be frightened of them, to get him to throw off superstition, bigotry, intolerance and all the other bogus claims which have him by the throat . . . no, towards these vital ends he refuses stubbornly to make a single step. He would rather walk out on his true problems, would rather desert the planet and his fellow creatures. Could there be a worse " renegade " ? Is it any wonder that, anticipating the advent of his glorious " new day " in the bosom of the stellar deep, he is already filled with dread that his new neighbors may resent his coming ? What, after all, can he possibly bring the denizens of these yet unknown worlds ? What but disaster and ruin. His pride tells him he is superior to these otherworld creatures, but his heart speaks differently. Perhaps there where time is of another order, where atmosphere and ambiance are one, " they " have been expecting the approach of this dread event. Perhaps nowhere in the vast swarms of habitable planets are there beings filled with the conceit, pride, arrogance, ignorance and insensitivity of our earthly creatures. So at least Marie Corelli conjectures again and again. Et elle a raison ! No, such as we are today, we may not be at all welcome in these starry abodes. If we have not found heaven within, it is a certainty we will not find it without. But there is the possibility—a desperate, almost forlorn hope—that, having caught a glimpse " out there " of order, peace and harmony, we who call ourselves men will recoil to this hell on earth and begin afresh.

All through great literature runs the idea of the circuitous voyage. Whatever man sets out to find, to whatever point in time or space he flings his weary body, in the end he comes home, home to himself. That the voyage to the moon will soon become fact I have not the slightest doubt. The voyage to more distant realms will also be realized before long. Time is no longer a factor. Time is being rolled up, like a carpet. Between man and his desires, in the brief interval ahead, there may quite possibly be no lapse of time. Like Franz Werfel's characters in *Star of the Unborn*,★ we may discover how to point the needle to the place we would be in and find ourselves there—instantaneously. Why not? If the mind can make the leap, so can the body. We have only to learn how. We have only to *desire* it, and it will be thus. The history of human thought and of human accomplishments corroborates this truth. At present man refuses to believe, or dares not believe, that things may come about in this fashion. Between the thought and the goal he cushions himself with inventions. He *makes* wings, but he still refuses " to take wing." Thought, however, is already on the wing. The Mind which contains all, and is all, is winging him on ahead of himself. At this very moment man is so infinitely farther ahead in thought than in being that it is as if he were distended, like a comet. The man of today lives in the tail of his own comet-like self. The tail of this monstrous distended self works havoc as it passes through new and utterly unpredictable realms. One part of man longs for the moon and other seizable worlds, never dreaming that another part of him is already traversing more mysterious, more spectacular realms.

Is it that man must make the circuit of the whole heavens before coming home to himself? Perhaps. Perhaps he must repeat the symbolic act of the great dragon of creation—coil and twist, twine and intertwine, until at last he succeeds in putting tail in mouth.

The true symbol of infinity is the full circle. It is also the symbol of fulfillment. And fulfillment is man's goal. Only in fulfillment will he find reality.

Aye, we must go full swing. *Home*—where is it if not everywhere and nowhere at the same time? When he is in possession of

★ The Viking Press, New York, 1946.

193

his soul, then will man be fully alive, caring nothing for immortality and knowing nothing of death.

To begin wholly afresh may mean coming alive at last !

————————

A Note on Eugène Sue

A letter from Pierre Lesdain of Belgium offers the following about Eugene Sue :

" Vous m'avez demandé des éclaircissements sur Eugène Sue. Je ne suis pas un lecteur assidu de Sue ; j'ai lu *Les Mystères de Paris*, dans ma tendre jeunesse et puis, jamais plus rien. Voici la liste des livres d'Eugène Sue :

Kernock le Pirate, 1830
Plick et Plock, 1831
Atar-Gull, 1831
La Salamandre, 1832
La Vigie de Koat-Ven, 1833
Arthur, 1833
Historie de la Marine française (5 vols.), 1835
Cécile, 1835
Latréaumont (2 vols.), 1837
Jean Cavalier (2 vols.), 1840
Deux Histoires, 1840
Le Marquis de Létorière
Le Morne au Diable (2 vols.), 1840
Mathilde (6 vols.), 1841
Le Commandeur de Malte, 1841
Les Mystères de Paris (10 vols.), 1842–43
Pauli Monti, 1842
Thérèse Dunoyer, 1842
Le Juif Errant (10 vols.), 1844–45
Martin ou l'Enfant trouvé, 1847
Le Républicain des Campagnes, 1848
Le Berger de Kravan
Les Sept Péchés Capitaux (16 vols.)
Les Mystères du Peuple, ou, Histoire d'une famille à travers les âges (16 vols.)
Les Enfants de l'Amour (6 vols.), 1852
Fernand Duplessis (6 vols.)
Le Marquis d'Amalfi (2 vols.), 1853
Gilbert et Gilberte (7 vols.), 1853
La famille Jouffroy (7 vols.), 1854
Le Fils de Famille (7 vols.), 1856
Les Secrets de l'Oreiller (7 vols.), 1858

Cette liste est étourdissante, elle me donne le vertige. Et que reste-t-il de l'oeuvre, immense, quant au poids-papier des volumes et à leur nombre, qui témoigne d'une luxuriance tropicale ? Il n'en reste rien. A peine le nom de l'auteur, nom prédestiné, qui provoque à la plaisanterie facile. Mais on ne lit plus rien d'Eugène Sue. Il est dans le domaine public, et aucun journal ne pense jamais à reprendre un de ses romans comme feuilleton. Avant la guerre de 1940, je ne sais plus très bien quel écrivain suisse—de talent—a voulu publier un " condensé " des *Mystères de Paris*. (L'ancêtre des " condensés," peut-être.) Sans succès, je crois. O la parole de l'Ecclésiaste !

Car Eugène Sue de son vivant a connu la gloire comme peu d'écrivains au monde, une gloire tapageuse, une gloire d'idole de la foule. On raconte qu'Eugène Sue, garde national, comme tout autre citoyen en ce temps là, ne s'était pas présenté pour prendre son tour de faction. Condamnation automatique. Pour se venger l'écrivain refuse de donner au journal la suite de celui de ses romans qui y passait en feuilleton et que les lecteurs attendaient avidement. Il y a presque une petite émeute à Paris et le Ministre doit lever la punition d'Eugène Sue.

Eugène Sue a-t-il eu réellement une influence sur Balzac et Dostoievski ? C'est très vite dit ; le prouver serait beaucoup plus long. Le succès d'Eugène Sue a incité peut-être Balzac et Dostoievski à situer leurs romans dans les milieux semblables à ceux dont Eugène Sue exploitait les particularités et la nouveauté, en ce temps là. Les personnages du roman, français, jusqu'alors, étaient factices, d'imagination pure, créés par jeu—comme *Gil Blas* qui n'a rien de spécifiquement espagnol . . . Il y a sur cette classe de la société des romans d'une psychologie aiguë et profonde tels *La Princesse de Clèves*, ou bien *Les Liaisons Dangéreuses*, mais il fallait, comme Madame de La Fayette ou Choderlos de Laclos, avoir été " nourri dans le sérail " pour en " connaître les detours."

Eugène Sue n'est pas un romancier profond. Il a une imagination débordante, c'est quelque chose, bien sûr, mais pas assez pour venir frapper à la porte de la postérité, confiant qu'elle l'ouvrira. L'imagination d'Eugène Sue qui frappait si fort ses contemporains, nous fait sourire souvent et, quelquefois, franchement éclater. La fin du fin pour Eugène Sue était d'amener dans un roman, le plus fréquemment qu'il se pouvait, un genre de dissertation morale, ce qu'il appelait ses utopies. Par exemple : on ne devrait plus exécuter les condamnés à mort ; pour les chatier de leurs crimes, il serait préférable de leur percer les yeux. Le procédé à la longue devient intolérable et crispant . . .

Eugène Sue est né en 1804 ; mort en 1857. Son père était médecin ; l'impératrice Josephine fut sa marraine. Il abandonne ses études avant la rhétorique ; étudie la médecine sous son père, qui le fait embarquer comme chirurgien à bord d'un bateau. (Les premières oeuvres littéraires d'Eugène Sue sont maritimes.) Son père lui laissa en mourant une fortune d'un million (francs de l'époque). Je ne sais pas si Eugène Sue en fit un bon usage . . ."

XII

LETTER TO PIERRE LESDAIN

May 3rd, 1950

MY DEAR PIERRE LESDAIN :

The idea has occurred to me, since reading your lengthy and most welcome letter of April 20th, to incorporate you into this book about books which I am writing. That is why this letter begins as of page 196 . . . There is no one to whom it gives me greater pleasure to impart my thoughts, particularly my *larval* thoughts. You are one of the most enthusiastic readers I know of. In your reviews you are often "against," but you are more often " for " the author. When you attack you reveal your love, not your rancor, envy, spite or jealousy. Often, when I think back to my early days, I think of you, and I always see you with book in hand or under your arm. Indeed, as I discover through reading your weekly column in *Volonté*,* I am certain now that we were often reading the same author, if not the same book by that author, at the same time.

It is over two weeks now since I have written anything, and my head is seething with thoughts. As I may have explained to you before, the reason I am in a continual state of bubble is because of the books I am rereading—mostly old favorites. Everything nourishes, stimulates me. Originally I planned to write a slim volume ; now it seems as if it will be a fat tome. Each day I jot down in my notebook a few more titles which I recollect. This is an exciting feature of my task, this exhuming from the unfathomable reservoir of memory a few new titles daily. Sometimes it takes two or three days for a book which is in the back of my head, or on the tip of my tongue, to announce itself completely—author, title, time and place. Once it becomes " fixed " in my memory,

---

* A weekly newspaper from Brussels. Since this was written it has folded up.

196

all sorts of associations crowd in and open up undreamed of realms of my dim past.

Thus I have already written what little I had to say about *Gil Blas* before ever receiving the copy you tell me you are sending. *Gil Blas* is one of the books I never read but about which there hangs a tale, and—for me, at least—the tale is always as important as the book. There are authors who intrigue me because of all I have heard and read about them, because their *lives* interest me, yet I cannot read their works. Stendhal is one, and the author of *Tristram Shandy* another. But perhaps the superb example in this respect is the Marquis de Sade. Everything I read about him, whether for or against, excites me enormously. I have actually read very little of all he has written, and this little I read without much pleasure or profit. Nevertheless, I believe in him, so to speak. I think him a most important writer, a great figure, *and* one of the most tragic wretches ever born. I am going to write about him, naturally, even though I shall never read the whole of him. (Who has ?) Incidentally, it may amuse you to know that I had great difficulty recalling the titles of so-called " obscene " works, both those I had read and those I had only heard about. This is one branch of literature with which I am only faintly acquainted. But is it a " branch " of literature or is it another category of misnomers ?

Here is a random thought *en passant*. Each time I pick up a volume of Elie Faure I undergo a great emotional conflict. Time and again, in speech and in writing, I have made mention of my indebtedness to this great individual. I ought to write a panegyric on him, but I doubt that I will, doubt that I can, any more than I can for Dostoievsky or Whitman. There are some authors who are at once too grand and too close to you. You never liberate yourself from the thrall of their enchantment. Impossible to tell where your own life and work separate or diverge from theirs. All is inextricably interwoven.

It seems, when I think of certain names, that my life began afresh a number of times. Doubtless because each time I rediscovered, through the instrumentality of these divine interpreters, my own being. You speak of having immersed yourself for three years in Nietzsche and in him alone. I understand, though I never did this with any author. But can you read Nietzsche today with the same fervor ? Ah, there's the miracle ! Whoso has the power to affect us more and more deeply each time we read him is indeed a master, no matter what his name, rank or status be. This is a thought which recurs as I reread my favorite authors. (I am certain, for instance, that if I were to pick up *The Birth of Tragedy*—the one book I have reread more than any other, I believe—I am certain, I say, that I would be "finished" for the day.) What is the meaning of this undying enthusiasm for so many authors ? I ask this frequently of myself. Does it mean I have not " evolved " ? Does it mean I am naïve ? *What ?* Whatever the answer, I assure you I regard this weakness as a singular blessing. And if, in picking up an old favorite, I should also happen to find in his book a quotation from another of my great favorites, then my joy is unbounded. Only yesterday, in glancing through *The Dance Over Fire and Water*,* this happened to me. On page six I found this from Walt Whitman : " The world will be complete for him who himself is complete." And on page eighty-four this, also from Whitman : " You look upon Bibles and religions as divine—and I say that they are divine. And I say that they have all come from you, can come again from you, and that it is not they who give life, but you who give life." (May I say, for once in my life, that I am proud it was an American who spoke thus !)

One of the reasons why I cannot write about these favorite authors at length is first because I cannot refrain from quoting them copiously, second because they have muscled so deep into my very fibres that the moment I begin talking about them I echo their language. It is not so much that I am ashamed of " plagiarizing " the masters as that I am fearful of ever being able to recover my own voice. Due to our slavish reading, we carry within us so many entities, so many voices, that rare indeed is the man who can say he speaks with his own voice. In the final analysis, is that iota of uniqueness which we boast of as " ours " really *ours* ? Whatever real or unique contribution we make stems from the same inscrutable source whence everything derives. We contribute nothing but our understanding, which is a way of saying—our acceptance. However, since we are all modelled upon previous models of which there is no end, let us rejoice if occasionally we

* By Elie Faure.

sound like the glorious ones, resound like those utterly emptied beings who can say nothing more than "Om."

And now to concentrate a few moments on the many issues raised in your letter . . . I cannot tell you how delighted I was that you should so speedily have made use of the citation I sent you from my old "master," John Cowper Powys. In the same mail I find the literary editor of *Combat* also quoting from the preface to *Visions and Revisions*. Soon I hope to find for you one of Powys' books of interpretation, which I am sure you will enjoy. I suppose he was never translated into French. To the French it would doubtless seem like "bringing coals to Newcastle." The other day, to gladden his heart and to make a long deferred obeisance, I addressed him as "mon très cher grand maître." Had Elie Faure been alive when I finally summoned the courage to approach his office, I would doubtless have knelt at his feet and kissed his hand.

You speak of having to conquer the sentiment of "revolt," where one's early idols are concerned. True enough, though I think this is a transitory phase. The first emotions, the first reactions, are the true and lasting ones, we usually discover. (To discover is to *recover*.) I must confess, however, that there are always a few authors for whom, once we have lost our affection or reverence, we are never again able to retrieve our original attitude. It is like a loss of grace. At this moment I cannot recall a single great author —"great" according to my definition—whom I have been deceived in. Indeed, the further back I wander among my idols, the more true and lasting seems my adoration. No deceptions. Particularly in the realm of "boys' authors." No, the astonishing thing to me is that, once my allegiance was given, I remained loyal. I remark on this because loyalty is not one of my strong points. The excep-tions are absolutely unimportant, altogether unworthy of note. I remain, where authors are concerned, "the constant lover."

It is this peculiar trait (devotion ? adoration ?) which is causing this book (hypothetically) to grow to astonishing proportions. How can I ever finish testifying ? How can I ever put an end to this song of love ? *And why should I ?* I, who have never kept a diary, begin to perceive how tempting and compelling is the desire to record the progress of one's inner voyage. I, moreover, who on several occasions swore that I was through with books, went so far once as to become a manual worker, worse than that—a veritable clodhopper—thinking thus (fatuously) to overcome the disease.

The other night, rereading *The Story of My Life* by Helen Keller, I came across the following lines by her teacher, Anne Mansfield Sullivan :

"Reading, I think, should be kept independent of the regular school exercises. Children should be encouraged to read for the pure delight of it. [Bravo !] The attitude of the child towards his books should be that of unconscious receptivity. The great works of the imagination ought to become a part of his life, as they were once of the very substance of the men who wrote them."

She adds : "Too often, I think, children are required to write before they have anything to say. Teach them to think and read and talk without self-repression, and they will write because they cannot help it."

In giving it as her opinion that "children will educate themselves under right conditions," that what they require are "guidance and sympathy far more than instruction," she made me think of Rousseau's *Emile*, and again when I came across the following passage on language :

Language grows out of life, out of its needs and experiences. At first my little pupil's mind was all but vacant. She had been living in a world she could not realize. *Language** and *knowledge* are indissolubly connected ; they are interdependent. Good work in language presupposes and depends on a real knowledge of things. As soon as Helen grasped the idea that everything had a *name*, and that by means of the manual alphabet these names could be transmitted from one to another, I proceeded to awaken her further interest in the *objects* whose names she learned to spell with such evident joy. *I never taught her language for the* PURPOSE *of teaching it ;* but invariably used language as a medium for the communication of *thought* ; thus the learning of language was *coincident* with the acquisition of knowledge. In order to use language intelligently, one must have something to talk *about*, and having something to talk about is the result of having had experiences ; no amount of language training will enable

* Italics throughout this passage are Miss Sullivan's own.

our little children to use language with ease and fluency
unless they have something clearly in their minds which
they wish to communicate, or unless we succeed in awakening in them a desire to know what is in the minds of
others.

All this leads me to your question about Lawrence—why I never
finished the study of him which I began in Paris some seventeen
years ago. But first let me reply to the other question—whether
I am not closer to Lawrence than to Joyce. Yes, indeed. Perhaps
too close, or rather I *was* too close when I began writing that *magnum
opus—The World of Lawrence*. Like the present book on which I
am engaged, it too began as a " small " volume. The publisher
of the *Tropic of Cancer*, Jack Kahane, had asked me if I would not
write for him a hundred pages or so on " my great favorite,"
D. H. Lawrence. His thought was to bring out this " plaquette "
before issuing the *Cancer* book, the publication of which had been
held up, for one reason and another, for three years or more. The
idea was certainly not to my liking, but I grudgingly consented.
By the time I had written a hundred pages I was so deep in the study
of Lawrence's work that I could no longer see the forest for the
trees. There remain of this abortive effort at least several hundred
finished pages. There are a few hundred more which need revision,
and there are, of course, voluminous notes. Two things worked
together to frustrate the completion of this work : one, the urgent
desire to get on with my own story ; two, the confusion which
arose in my mind as to what indeed Lawrence did actually represent.
" Before a man studies Zen," says Ch'ing-yuan, " to him mountains
are mountains and waters are waters ; after he gets an insight into
the truth of Zen, through the instruction of a good master, mountains
to him are not mountains and waters are not waters ; but after this,
when he really attains to the abode of rest, mountains are once
more mountains and waters are waters."* Something of the sort
applies to any approach to Lawrence. Today he is once again
what he was in the beginning, but knowing this, and being sure of
it, I no longer feel the need to air my views. All these critical and
interpretative studies of authors so vitally important (to us) are

* From *Zen*, by Alan W. Watts ; James Ladd Delkin, Stanford, California,
1948.

made in our own interest, I believe. Our labors only serve to make us better understand ourselves. Our subjects seldom need our defense or our brilliant interpretations. Usually they are dead by the time we get to them. As for the public, I am more and more convinced that " they " too need less and less assistance or instruction ; it is more important, I do believe, for them to struggle on their own.

As for Joyce, certainly I am indebted to him. Certainly I was influenced by him. But my affinity is more with Lawrence, obviously. My antecedents are the romantic, demonic, confessional, subjective types of writer. It is Joyce's gift for language which attracts me to him, but, as I pointed out in the essay called " The Universe of Death," *I prefer the language of Rabelais to that of Joyce. When all's said, however, Joyce remains the giant in this field. He has no equal ; he is virtually a " monster."

It is very, very difficult, I find, to distinguish the real from the imaginary influences. I have done my utmost to acknowledge *all* influences, yet I realize only too well that in appraising my work the writers to come will point out influences which I have ignored and will discount other influences which I have stressed. You mentioned in your letter *The Rime of the Ancient Mariner*. The author of that work is a man I seldom speak about. I read this work in school, of course, together with *The Lay of the Last Minstrel*. They are among the few books I enjoyed reading in school, I will tell you. But the book I remember best, from school days, the book which seems to have left an indelible impression upon me, though I have never reread it, is Tennyson's *Idylls of the King*. The reason ? King Arthur ! Only the other day, in reading a letter by the famous Gladstone to Schliemann, the discoverer of Troy and Mycenae, I noticed that he spoke of Schliemann as belonging to another age, an age of faith, an age of chivalry. Certainly this man, this very capable, practical-minded business man, did more for history than the whole gang of flatulent " historians." All because of a youthful love of and belief in Homer. I mention Gladstone's letter, a noble one, because whenever I touch upon the words faith, youth, chivalry, a flame lights up in me. I said a moment ago that my true arboreal

* From *The Cosmological Eye*, New Directions, New York, 1938. Editions Poetry London, London.

descent was such and such. But what is it that nourishes and sustains this species of writer ? The heroic, the legendary ! In a word, the literature of imagination and deed. When I mention the name King Arthur I think of a world which is still alive though sunk from sight ; I think of it, indeed, as the real, the eternal world, because in it imagination and deed are one, love and justice one. Today it would seem as if this world of Arthur's time belonged exclusively to the scholar, but it is resuscitated each time a boy or girl is inflamed by contact with it.

And this leads me to say how woefully mistaken are those who believe that certain books, because universally acknowledged as " masterpieces," are the books which alone have power to inspire and nourish us. Every lover of books can name dozens of titles which, because they unlock his soul, because they open his eyes to reality, are for him the golden books. It matters not what evaluation is made of these by scholars and critics, by pundits and authorities : for the man who is touched to the quick by them they are supreme. We do not ask of one who opens our eyes by what authority he acts ; we do not demand his credentials. Nor should we be forever grateful and reverent towards our benefactors, since each of us has the power in turn to awaken others and does in fact do so, often unwittingly. The wise man, the holy man, the true scholar, learns as much from the criminal, the beggar, the whore, as he does from the saint, the teacher, or the Good Book.

Yes, I would indeed be grateful if you would translate one or two tales from *the fabliaux*. I have read almost nothing of this literature. Which reminds me that, although I have received many books from the list I compiled, no one has yet sent me a good book on Gilles de Rais or on Saladin, two figures in whom I am tremendously interested. There are certain names one almost never encounters in our literary weeklies. The great difference between European literary weeklies and American ones lies in the emptiness with regard to literary names and events which characterizes them. In European weeklies the void is clustered or spangled with constellations : in a single column, for instance, of *Le Goéland* (published in Paramé-en-Bretagne) one can run across a dozen or more celebrated names, both past and contemporary, which we never hear of. Even in *Volonté*, which is not a strictly literary

203

periodical, I find articles about men, books, events that I never see mention of in our papers or reviews. In the days when I worked in the financial district of New York—for the Everlasting Cement Company—I recall what a pleasure it was, as I made my way to the elevated train at the Brooklyn Bridge, to see stacked up at the foot of that interminable flight of stairs the latest issue of *Simplicissimus*. In those days we had at least two excellent magazines in this country—*The Little Review* and *The Dial*. Today there is not one good magazine in the whole bloody country. Nor can I pass on without a word about *Transition* in whose pages I discovered the most exciting new foreign names, among them one I can never forget—Gottfried Benn.

But to come back to Saladin and Gilles de Rais, than whom there could hardly be two more opposite types—I have inquired of our libraries as to what books are available concerning them and I have gathered a few titles, mostly by English or American authors. These titles, however, do not incite me to look up the books ; they have that immediate, sensational appeal which is so eminently American. I am searching not so much for scholarly as for poetic interpretation. In the case of Gilles de Rais, I presume that the most serious studies have been made by the psychoanalysts. But I do not want a psychoanalytical study of Gilles de Rais. If I had to choose, I would prefer a Catholic inquiry into the workings of this strange soul.

Speaking of the books I am still searching for, I ought to add that I also want a book about the Children's Crusade. Do you know of a good one ? I remember reading about this altogether unique episode in history as a child ; I remember my extreme bewilderment accompanied by a feeling of pain such as I had never experienced. Since childhood I have stumbled only upon fleeting references to the subject. Now, with the reopening of my early past, I feel that I *must* look into it again.

As for Restif de la Bretonne—*Monsieur Nicolas* and *Les Nuits de Paris*—no one has yet sent me these either. I am expecting any day now a book about Restif by an American attaché stationed in Jidda ; he has written me several letters telling me of the remarkable affinities between the author of the *Tropics* and this singular French writer. You can imagine how curious I am to savor the blood of this strange creature.

In addition to books I have not asked for, I receive many that I do want ; in fact, by now I must have received about two-thirds of the titles listed. One that I pounced on immediately that I received it was a biography of George Alfred Henty, my favorite author when a boy. It is not a brilliant work (the author is G. Manville Fenn) but it serves the purpose. It afforded me, after waiting some forty odd years, the excruciating pleasure of gazing upon the face of my beloved author. I must say that the photo which serves as the frontispiece is in no wise disappointing or deceptive. There he is, my dear Henty (he was always just " Henty " to me), large as life, with a good massive head, flowing beard à la Whitman, a big broad nose, almost Russian, and a frank, genial, kindly gaze to his countenance. Though they do not resemble one another, he nevertheless reminds me strongly of another idol, Rider Haggard. They belong to the " manly " side of British men of letters. Rugged, stalwart, honest and honorable men, quite reticent about themselves, fair and upright in their dealings, capable in many ways, interested in many pursuits besides writing : active men, good, solid bulwarks, as we say. In demeanor and deportment, in the variety and scope of their activities, they had much in common. From an early age they both saw the rough side of life. Both were great travellers, spent considerable time in remote places. Even in their methods of work they had a great many points in common. Though they wrote fast and prodigiously, they devoted much time to the accumulation, preparation and analysis of their material. They both had the " chronicler " strain. They possessed imagination and intuition to a high degree. Yet no men were sterner realists, more immersed in life. Both enjoyed a certain affluence, too, on reaching middle life. And both had the good fortune to be aided by very capable secretaries, or amanuenses, to whom they dictated their books. (How I envy them that !)

I realize that Henty is a writer who may not be known to you at all ; but he *was* known to American and English boys, and was probably regarded as highly by them as Jules Verne, Fenimore Cooper, Captain Mayne Reid or Marryat. But let me quote you a few of Fenn's observations about this man Henty, his work, and the reasons for his great success. They strike a sympathetic note. A boy, he states, does not want *juvenile* literature. " His aim is to become a man and read what men do and have done. Hence the great success of George Henty's works. They are essentially manly, and he [Henty] used to say that he wanted his boys to be bold, straightforward and ready to play a young man's part, not to be milksops." (Henty was practically a confirmed invalid during early youth—he spent most of his days in bed. Which explains his early passion for books : he read everything that came to hand. It also explains the acute development of his imagination . . . *and* his good health in later life, for only the man who has started life as a weakling prizes good health and knows how to guard it.)

> " Unconsciously," says Fenn, " he was building up a greater success for his boys' books by enlisting on their behalf the suffrages of that great and powerful body of buyers of presents who has the selection of their gifts. By this body is meant our boys' instructors, who, in conning the publishers' lists, would come upon some famous name for the hero of the story and exclaim : ' Ha ! history—that's safe ! ' In this way Henty linked himself with the great body of teachers who joined with him hand in hand ; hence it was that the book-writer who kept up for so many years his wonderful supply of two, three and often four boys' books a year, full of solid interest and striking natural adventure, taught more lasting history to boys than all the schoolmasters of his generation."

But enough on this score. I find it strange, I must admit, to discover what " solid characters " my early idols possessed, to learn that they were men of affairs, interested in agrarian reforms, military strategy, yachting, big game hunting, political intrigues, archaeology, symbolism and so on. How startling to read of Henty, for example, that his motto could well have been : " God, the Sovereign, and the People ! " What a contrast to the characters who are later to influence me, so many of them " pathological," or, as Max Nordau would say—" degenerate." Even dear old Walt, the man of the great outdoors, the poet with a cosmic sweep, is now studied from the " pathological " side. Fenn saying that " the neurotic was as far from Henty as are the poles asunder " sounds almost comical to me now. The word " neurotic " was not even known in Henty's day. Hamsun used to flaunt the word "neurasthenic." Today it is "psychotic"—or else "schizophrenic." *Today !* Who writes for boys today ? *Seriously*, I mean. What do they feed on, the youths of today ? A most interesting question . . .

Last night I had great difficulty falling asleep. This happens to me frequently since I am engaged on this book. The reason is simple : I am inundated with such a flood of material, I have such a tremendous choice, that it is difficult for me to decide what *not* to write about. Everything seems pertinent. Everything I touch reminds me of the inexhaustible stream of contributory influences which have shaped my intellectual being. As I reread a book I think of the time, place and circumstances known to my former selves. Conrad says somewhere that a writer only begins to live after he has begun to write. A partial truth. I know what he meant, Conrad, but—the life of a creator is not the only life nor perhaps the most interesting one which a man leads. There is a time for play and a time for work, a time for creation and a time for lying fallow. And there is a time, glorious too in its way, when one scarcely exists, when one is a complete void. I mean—when boredom seems the very stuff of life.

Speaking of the Everlasting Cement Company a while ago got me to recalling the wonderful fellows who worked with me in that office at 30 Broad Street, New York. Suddenly I was so charged with recollections that I grabbed my notebook and began listing the names of these individuals and the trifling episodes connected with them. I saw them all clearly and distinctly—Eddie Rink, Jimmy Tierney, Roger Wales, Frank Selinger, Ray Wetzler, Frank McKenna, *Mister* Blehl (my bête noir), Barney something-or other (a mere mouse of a man), Navarro, the vice-president, whom we encountered only in going to the lavatory; Taliaferro, the peppery Southerner from Virginia, who would repeat over the phone a dozen times a day, "Not Taliaferro—*Tolliver !*" But the one on whom my memory fastened was a fellow I never once thought of from the day I left the company—at the age of twenty-one. Harold Street was his name. We were boon companions. Jotting down his name, I wrote alongside of it—for the record !—"vacant days." That is how I associate his name with mine—by the remembrance of blank, idle, happy days spent with him in the suburb called Jamaica. We must have had something in common, but what it was I no longer remember. I know definitely that he was not interested in books, nor in bicycle riding, as I was. I would go to his home, a large, rambling, lugubrious sort of faded mansion, where he lived with a grandmother, and the day would pass as in a dream. Not the faintest remembrance of what we talked about or how we passed the time. But to visit him in those quiet, sombre surroundings was a balm to me, that I do remember. I guess I envied him the quietude of his life. As far as I could detect, he had no problems. And that was utterly strange to me—because I was riddled with them. Harold was one of those calm, steady, poised young men who know how to get on in the world, how to adapt themselves, how to avoid pain and grief. It was that which attracted me to him. The deeper reasons for this attraction I will undoubtedly uncover when I go into this period more deeply—in *Nexus*—which, as you know, I have not even started to write. Enough, however, to call attention to those " vacant " periods in which, fortunately for us, we are not even concerned to know who we are, much less what we will do in life. I know one thing definitely, it was the prelude to my break with the family, my break with office routine ; the wanderlust had come over me and soon I was to say goodbye to all my friends as well as my family, to start out for the Golden West (of Puccini rather than the gold seekers). " No more books ! " I said to myself. " Done with the intellectual life." And then, on the fruit ranch at Chula Vista, California, whom do I pal up with but that cowboy, Bill Parr of Montana, who has an itch to read and who takes long walks with me after work to discuss our favorite authors. And it is because of my affection for Bill Parr that I happen upon Emma Goldman in San Diego and, without in the least intending it, am swung back again into the world of books, via Nietzsche first of all, then Bakunin, Kropotkin, Most, Strindberg, Ibsen, and all the celebrated European dramatists. So it turns, the wheel of destiny !

Last night I could not fall asleep. I had just been reading another old favorite—Edgar Saltus—an American author you probably never heard of. I was reading *The Imperial Purple*, one of those books which I thought had taught me something about " style." The night before I had finished Emil Ludwig's biography of Heinrich Schliemann, which made me dizzy, dizzy because it is almost incredible to think what this man accomplished in one lifetime. Yes, I know about Julius Caesar, Hannibal, Alexander, Napoleon, Thomas Edison, Rene Caillé (of Timbuctoo fame), and Gandhi and scores of other " active " men. They all led incredible lives. But somehow this man Schliemann, a grocer's boy who becomes a great merchant, who learns eighteen languages " on the side," as it were, and speaks and writes them fluently, this man who all his life conducted a heavy correspondence in his own hand—and made copies of each and every letter by hand !—this man who begins his career in Russia, as exporter and importer, who all his life is traveling between distant points, who rises at four in the morning usually, rides horseback to the sea (at Phaleron) takes a swim winter or summer, is at his desk or at the excavations having a second breakfast at eight A.M., who reads Homer in season and out, and towards the later years refuses to speak even modern Greek to his wife but insists on using the Greek of Homer's day, who writes his letters in the language of the man whom he is addressing, who unearths the greatest treasures any man has ever found, who, et cetera, et cetera, . . . well how can one sleep on putting such a book down ? Order, discipline, sobriety, perseverance, doggedness, authoritativeness, how German he was ! And this man had made himself a citizen of the United States, residing for a while in San Francisco and later in Indianapolis. Utterly cosmopolitan and yet thoroughly German. A Greek at heart and still a Teuton. The most amazing man imaginable. Uncovering the ruins of Troy, Mycenae, Tiryns and other places, and almost beating Sir Arthur Evans to the labyrinth of the Minotaur. Losing out because the peasant who was ready to sell him the site of Knossus had lied to him about the number of olive trees on the property. Only 888 instead of 2,500. What a man ! I waded through his fat tomes on Troy and Mycenae ; I read the autobiographical pages he inserted in one of these volumes. And then I decided on Ludwig's book for an over-all picture of the man.

What a task for the biographer ! Twenty thousand papers Herr Ludwig examined. Listen to his words :

> First of all, there was the long series of diaries and notebooks which he kept and wrote up almost continuously

from the twentieth year until the sixty-ninth and last year of his life. There were his business records and account books, family letters, legal documents, passports and diplomas, huge volumes of his linguistic studies, down to his very exercises in Russian and Arabic script. Besides all this, there were newspaper cuttings from all quarters of the globe, lists with historical data and dictionaries of his own compiling in a dozen languages. Since he preserved everything, I found, along with the most illuminating memoranda, an invitation to attend a concert in aid of a poor widow. Every paper was dated in his own handwriting.

I cannot leave the subject without reference to one humorous and pathetic incident concerning Agamemnon. Towards the end of his days, discussing for the thousandth time, perhaps, the question of whether it was or was not Agamemnon's body which he had exhumed, Schliemann exclaimed to his young assistant, Dörpfeld : " So this is not Agamemnon's body ; these are not his ornaments ? All right, let's call him Schulze ! "

Yes, each night I go to bed and digest the book or books I have been reading that evening. (I have only two hours at the most in a day to do all my reading.) One night it is Henty's life, the next Rider Haggard's two-volume autobiography, the next a little book on Zen, the next Helen Keller's life, the next a study of the Marquis de Sade, the next a book on Dostoievsky, either by Janko Lavrin (another old favorite and eye opener) or John Cowper Powys ; I go in rapid succession from one life to another—Rabelais, Aretino, Ouspensky—then Hermann Hesse (*Voyage en Orient*) and his *Siddhartha* (two English versions of it I am obliged to read and compare with the German and French), Elie Faure (*The Dance Over Fire and Water*), with sideswipes at certain passages in *The History of Art*, *The Black Death*, Boccaccio, *Le Cocu Magnifique*, et c'est bien magnifique, comme je vous ai dit par carte-postale. Let me stop a moment here. Crommelynck ! A Flemish genius. Another John Ford, in my eyes. A dramatist who has contributed something altogether original to the repertory of immortal drama. And on my favorite theme—jealousy. *Othello ?* You can have it ! I prefer Crommelynck. Proust was wonderful, in his labyrinthine way. But Crommelynck reaches the absolute. I don't see how it is possible to add anything more to this great theme. (My respect to your colleague, J. Dypreau, for his excellent review of the recent presentation of this play in Brussels. When will we see it here, I wonder, if ever?)

Yes, I cannot sleep nights after reading these marvelous books. Each one is sufficient to set a man's head spinning for a week. Some are new to me, others old. They overlap and intertwine. They complement one another, even when they seem most disparate. All is one. Ah, what was that line in Faure I wanted to remember? I have it. "The artist aims at a final order." True. Too true, alas. "The order is in us, and not elsewhere," he says. "And it does not reign elsewhere, only if we have the power to make it reign in us."

One of my readers, a young French psychoanalyst, sends me an excerpt from one of Berdyaev's books in which the latter speaks of the chaos in the present world which I have succeeded in rendering, and then adds that this chaos is also in me. As if I did not know! "The artist aims at a final order." Bien dit et vrai, même s'il essaie de ne rien donner que le chaos qui reside en lui-même. Ca, c'est mon avis. Aux autres à denicher ou la vérité ou le complexe. Là, je reste, moi.

To this let me add that, in writing several book-seller friends of mine for the books I wanted, I received in reply substantially the same gratuitous slap in the face from all : "Never saw such a fantastic medley of titles!" As if, in selecting from all the books I had read in the last forty years, I should have chosen for them a certain pleasing and intelligible sequence of titles! Where they see a farrago I see order and meaning. My order, my meaning. My continuity. Who is to say what I should have read, and in what order? How absurd! The more I uncover my past, as it reveals itself through the books I have read, the more logic, the more order, the more discipline I discover in my life. It makes grand sense, one's life, even when it resembles a quagmire. Certainly no Creator could have ordained the devious and manifold paths one treads, the choices and decisions one makes. Can you imagine a ledger in which the vagaries of every single mortal that ever lived were recorded? Would it not be insane to keep such a log book? No, I am sure that whatever difficulties we mortals have in finding our way, the Creator must have similar and more fantastic ones.

211

And if, as I solemnly believe, it all makes sense to Him, why can it not also make sense to us, at least as regards our own individual lives ?

If I cannot sleep nights it is not because of the books I am reading, for the extent of my reading is infinitesimal compared to what a bookworm devours in a day. (Think of Napoleon at St. Helena ordering up stacks of books each day, devouring them like a tapeworm, and calling for more, more !) No, it is not the books alone, it is the memories associated with them, the memories of former lives, as I said before. I can see these former selves as clearly as if I were looking at my many friends in turn. And yet, here is a fact I simply cannot get over—the man I was when I first read *Mysteries*, let us say, seems to be hardly a whit different from the man I was yesterday, the man I still am, let us suppose. At least I am no different in my appreciation of and enthusiasm for the author of this book. (That he was a " collaborator " during the last War, for example, means absolutely nothing to me.) Even if, as a writer, I am aware with each rereading of the "defects" or, to be more kind, " the weaknesses " of my favorite author, the man in me still responds to him, to his language, to his temperament, just as warmly. I may have grown—or I may not either !—in intellectual stature, but thank God, I say to myself, I have not altered in my essential being. It must be, I assume, that an appeal made to one's soul is final and irrevocable. And it is with the soul that we grasp the essence of another being, not with the mind, not even with the heart.

One day I read in the French paper *Combat* a letter dated as late as 1928 from H. G. Wells to James Joyce. It was a letter to make one blush with shame for a fellow author. It reminded me of a communication in the same vein, but in better spirit, from Strindberg to Gauguin, anent the latter's (new) Tahitian paintings. But listen to the tone of the pompous Englishman of letters : " Vous croyez sans doute à la chasteté, à la pureté et à un dieu personnel ; c'est pourquoi vous finissez toujours par vous repandre en cris de con, de merde et d'enfer."

" Oh, Henry, what beautiful *golden* teeth you have ! " exclaimed my four-year-old daughter the other morning on climbing into bed with me. C'est ainsi que je m'approche des œuvres de mes confrères.

I see how beautiful are their golden teeth, not how ugly or artificial they are . . .

But there are little things, trifling personal things, which also keep me awake nights after finishing a book. For example, time and again I am struck by the fact—and I hope you will not think this egotistical of me—that so many of the writers or artists I adore seem to have ended their lives just about the time I was being born. (Rimbaud, Van Gogh, Nietzsche, Whitman, to name just a few.) What do I make of this ? Nothing, actually. But it serves to bemuse me. So I was just making my way out of the womb, protestingly, when they were laying themselves to rest ! All that they fought and died for I have to repeat, in one way or another. Their experience, their wisdom of life, their teachings, nothing do I inherit by virtue of their immediate precedence. More, I must wait twenty, thirty, sometimes forty years before I even hear their names mentioned. Another thing about these figures—I am vitally interested in knowing how they came to their end ; whether through accident, illness, suicide or chagrin. Sometimes it is the circumstances attending their birth which fascinate me. (Jesus was not the only one to be born in a manger, I find. Nor was Swedenborg the only one to predict the day and hour of his own death.) The few who were comfortable and affluent during their lives are vastly outnumbered by the hordes who knew nothing but sorrow and misery, who were starved, tortured, persecuted, betrayed, reviled, imprisoned, banished, beheaded, hanged or drawn and quartered. Around almost every man of genius there clusters a constellation of similar geniuses ; rare are those who are born out of time. They all belong to and are part of bloody epochs. Those in the tradition, as we say, live and die according to tradition. I think of Nikolai V. Gogol for some reason—the one who wrote *The Diary of a Madman*, the author of the Cossack *Iliad*—who declares towards the end of one of his stories : " A gloomy place, this world, gentlemen ! " He, Gogol, settles down in Rome, of all places, fearing to remain in Holy Russia. (Have you noticed, incidentally, in what strange, foreign, and often remote and desolate places our scribes write their famous books ?) *Dead Souls* was completed in Rome. The second volume Gogol burned a few days before his death ; the third was never begun. Thus, in spite of a pilgrimage to Palestine as a holy penitent, this wretched, confused, despondent being, who had hoped to write a *Divine Comedy* for his people, one that would contain "a message," perishes miserably far from home. The man who has made millions laugh and weep, who had a most decided influence on the Russian (and other) writers to come, is labelled before his death as "a preacher of the knout, an apostle of ignorance, a defender of obscurantism and darkest oppression."* And by a former admirer! But how wonderful, how prophetic is that passage on the troika which ends the first volume! Janko Lavrin, from whom I have drawn the above observations, says that in this passage Gogol "addresses Russia with a question which all her great authors have been asking since—asking in vain." Here is the passage . . .

> Russia, are you not speeding along like a fiery and matchless troika? Beneath you the road is smoke, the bridges thunder, and everything is left far behind. At your passage the onlooker stops amazed as by a divine miracle. 'Was that not a flash of lightning?' he asks. What is this surge so full of terror? And what is this force unknown impelling these horses never seen before? Ah, you horses, horses—what horses! Your manes are whirlwind! And are your veins not tingling like a quick ear? Descending from above you have caught the note of the familiar song; and at once, in unison, you strain your chests of bronze and, with your hooves barely skimming the earth, you are transformed into arrows, into straight lines winging through the air, and on you rush under divine inspiration! . . . Russia, where are you flying? Answer me. There is no answer. The bells are tinkling and filling the air with their wonderful pealing; the air is rent and thundering as it turns to wind; everything on earth comes flying past and, looking askance at her, other peoples and States move aside and make way.†

Yes, it is a memorable passage, prophetic, indubitably so. But for me it evokes other emotions and reactions too. In these words —and especially when it comes to, "Answer me! There is no answer."—I seem to hear the sonorous music of so many famous exiles, all singing the same tune, even when they hated the father-

* See *From Pushkin to Mayakovsky*, by Janko Lavrin; Sylvan Press, London, 1948.
† Translation by George Reavey.

214

land or the motherland. " I am here. You are there." That is what they are saying. " I know my country better than you. I love it more, even though I spit upon it. I am the prodigal son and I shall return with honor one day—if it is not too late. But I shall not stir from here until you make me an honorary citizen of my home town. I am dying of loneliness but my pride is greater than any loneliness. I have a message for you, but it is not the time now to reveal it." And so on . . .

I know these hearts full of anguish, full of despair, full of such mingled love and hate as to burst a man asunder.

When I urged you to read with special attention the piece called " The Brooklyn Bridge " (in *The Cosmological Eye*), perhaps it was something of all this that I had in mind. You are right about *Black Spring*. You put your finger on the very line which illustrates my point : " I am grateful to America for having made me realize my needs . . ." But did I not say, too : " I am a man of the Old World ? " Those miserable, niggardly reviews you speak of— let us not waste time discussing them. Who will care fifty years from now what Robert Kemp said, or Edmund Wilson, or any of this gang ?

I am back in America. My days are full. Too full. At 6.20 sharp every morning the cock crows. The cock is Tony, my little son. From then on not a moment's rest. Often I begin the day by changing his diaper and fetching him a zwieback. Then comes Valentin—" the mystery of God," as she one day announced herself to be. Sometimes I am digging in the garden before breakfast, extending the interminable shallow trenches into which I put back what we have taken from the soil, like a good Chinese peasant. Breakfast over, I rush to my studio and begin answering the mail : every day fifteen or twenty letters to answer. Before the sun sets I usually take the children for a walk. If I go alone I come home on the trot, my head swarming with ideas. It is only when I enter the forest that I am truly alone, only then do I get the chance to empty my mind and recharge the battery. Some days are broken up by the arrival of visitors. Occasionally they pull up one after another, like railroad trains. I have hardly said goodbye to one van load than another pulls up. Many of these visitors have not even read my books. " We've heard about you ! " they say. As

if that constituted a warrant for encroaching upon a man's precious
time !

Between times, as it were, I write. If I can put in two to three
hours a day at my work I consider myself lucky. This letter to
you, for instance, I began yesterday, and will probably continue
tomorrow. It does me good to write a letter which is not a response
to a demand, a gratuitous letter, so to speak, which has accumulated
in me like the waters of a reservoir. I have owed you this letter
for a long time. You have evoked it without knowing it. How I
loathe those letters from college students who are about to write
a thesis on some aspect of my work, or on the work of some friend
of mine. The questions they ply, the demands they make ! And
to what end ? What could be more useless, more a waste of time
and energy, than a college thesis ? (It is not every day we get a
thesis such as Céline wrote on Semmelweiss !) Some, in utter
naïveté, have the cheek to ask me to explain my whole works to
them—in a few brief lines. Sometimes, resting on the spade, I look
up from the trench I am digging—it is beginning, by the way, to
look like those breastworks which were thrown up in the Balkan
wars !—sometimes, I say, looking up at the huge blue bowl of the
sky in which the vultures are careening, or looking out to sea where
perhaps not a ship is to be sighted, I wonder what is the use of it
all, why carry on this mad activity ? It is not that I feel lonely.
I doubt if I have known that feeling more than two or three times
in my whole life. No, I wonder simply—to what end ? You write,
others write me likewise, that my work should be disseminated,
that it contains something of value for the world. I wonder. How
good it would feel not to do anything at all for a while ! Just " set "
and ponder. Twiddle my thumbs. Nothing more. As it is, the
only way I can take a vacation is to trump up a dubious malaise
and take to bed for the day. I can lie for hours without looking
at a book. Just lie flat on my back and dream. What a luxury !
Sure, if I had the choice I would rather be spending my " vacation "
journeying to some distant realm—Timbuctoo, let us say, or Mecca,
or Lhasa. But since I cannot make the physical voyage I make
imaginary ones. As companions I choose a few after my own
heart—Dostoievsky, Ramakrishna, Elie Faure, Blaise Cendrars,
Jean Giono, or some unknown devil or saint whom I rout out

of his Himalayan fastness. Sometimes I get well of a sudden—all I needed was a change, an interlude—and jumping into my clothes I run down the line to visit my friend Schatz or my friend Emil White. (Both are painters, but the latter isn't aware of it yet. He doesn't know what to call himself, but every day he turns out another Persian miniature of Big Sur.) To see another American writer I would have to travel God knows how many miles.

Which reminds me that the other evening I read a most interesting and revelatory letter by Sherwood Anderson (January 2, 1936) to Theodore Dreiser. It was precipitated by the suicide of Hart Crane and Vachel Lindsay, two well-known American poets. "For the last year or two," Anderson begins, "I have had something in my mind that you and I should have spoken about and during the last year or two it has been sharpened in my mind by the suicide of fellows like Hart Crane, Vachel Lindsay and others, to say nothing of the bitterness of a Masters." (Edgar Lee Masters, author of *Spoon River Anthology*.) "If there has been a betrayal in America," he goes on to say, "I think it is our betrayal of each other. I do not believe that we—and by the word ' we ' I mean artists, writers, singers, etc.—have really stood by each other." He goes on to say that he has been thinking of putting his thoughts on the subject into a general letter or pamphlet to be called " American Man to American Man." He speaks of our loneliness for one another. He says that it might help for all of us " to return to the old habit of letter-writing between man and man that has at certain periods existed in the world." And then he adds this :

> For example, Ted, suppose that every morning when you go to your desk to work you would begin your day's work by writing, let's say, one letter to one other man working in the same field as you are. Suppose we did, by this effort, produce less as writers. There is probably too much being produced. I am suggesting this as the only way out I can see in the situation. It isn't that I want you to write to me. I could give you names and addresses of others who need you and whom you need. I think it possible to build up a kind of network of relationships, something closer say between writers and painters and songmakers, etc, etc . . . Further on—he continues this letter on the following day—he writes : Can you believe

that Vachel Lindsay would have taken . . . [suppression of text by the editor, not me !] if on that day he had got even two or three letters from some of the rest of us ?*

I don't know what you will think of this idea of Anderson's. It may strike you as jejune. But it appeals to me, being also an American. By that I mean that we Americans are always ready to try a thing out, even if we are not convinced beforehand that it will work. But as I was saying to a young writer who lives nearby and who is putting the idea into practice, it is a project better suited for young and unknown writers than older ones. Why shouldn't young and unknown writers communicate with one another about their needs, their desires, their hopes and dreams ? Why shouldn't they create a network of their own, a solid nucleus, a bulwark of defense against the indifference of the world, the indifference of older writers who have arrived, against the indifference, stupidity and blindness of editors and publishers particularly ? An older writer, I have noticed, is tempted to dissuade rather than encourage a young writer. He knows the traps, the pitfalls, the deceptions, the heart-aches which beset the novice. He is apt to be disillusioned about the value or necessity of any creative work, his own included.

I so firmly believe that the blind should aid the blind, the deaf the deaf, and the young writers the young writers. Moreover, we the older ones have more to learn from the young than they from us. "Fools rush in where angels fear to tread." Aye ! And lucky it be so. There was a pompous old scientist here the other day who, arguing with a young friend of mine about the coming voyage to the moon, insisted that it was not the time to think seriously about such ventures, that indeed to discuss such matters before the time was ripe, did more harm than good. What arrant nonsense ! As if we were to sit back and wait until the men of science had made full preparation and provision, until they said " Go ! " Would anything ever happen if that were the procedure ?

But to come back to Sherwood Anderson and his good friend Dreiser. I rather think I forgot to include these two men among my " influences," when I wrote on this subject earlier. I had the good fortune to meet Anderson just a few years before he died.

* *The Portable Sherwood Anderson ;* The Viking Press, New York, 1949.

It was shortly after my return from Europe. It happened that I was staying at the same hotel he was. I made a date to meet him at a nearby bar, and when I arrived I found to my delight that John Dos Passos was sitting with him. My first impression, on greeting them, was—how odd to be sitting with two celebrated American writers ! I felt as though I should study these " birds." (In Paris, of course, I had met a few American writers, but they were so close to me, so intimate, that I never regarded them as " men of letters." Before that, during my whole period of apprenticeship in America, I can hardly recall one writer of eminence, one of our own writers, I mean, that I had met and talked to.)

Of course this feeling of critical aloofness was immediately dissipated by the warmth and friendliness emanating from these two men. They were very, very human and at once put me at ease. I mention this because, finding myself back in America again, I also found myself back in my old attitude of the novice, the unknown writer. Neither of them had read my books, I am quite sure, but they knew my name. We got along splendidly. I was intoxicated especially by Anderson's storytelling gift. I was also impressed by his Americanism, though in appearance he was anything but the typical American. Dos Passos too struck me as very American, though he was quite a cosmopolite. The fact is, I soon observed that they were very much at home in their own country. They liked America. They had traveled over every part of it, too.

I say I was delighted to find Dos Passos there in the bar. Yes, because oddly enough it was the reading of one of his early contributions to a magazine—The Seven Arts, I think—that led me to believe I might also become a writer one day. I had of course read a number of his early books, such as Three Soldiers, Manhattan Transfer and Orient Express. I sensed the poet in him, as I had the born storyteller in Sherwood Anderson.

But before either of them had swum into my ken I had read and adored Theodore Dreiser. I read everything of his, in those early days, that I could lay hands on. I even modelled my first book on a book of his called Twelve Men. I loved his brother, too, whom he portrayed so tenderly in this book : Paul Dressler, the song writer. Dreiser, I need hardly tell you, gave a tremendous impetus to the young writers of his day. His big novels, like Jenny Gerhardt,

The Titan, The Financier—we call them "huge, cumbersome and unwieldy" today—carried a tremendous impact. They were sombre, realistic, dense, but never dull—at least to me. They were passionate novels, saturated with the color and the drama of American life ; they issued direct from the guts and were warmed by the very heart's blood of the man. So sincere do they seem now that men like Sinclair Lewis, Hemingway, even Faulkner, appear artificial by comparison. Here was a man who had anchored himself in midstream. As a reporter he had seen life close up—the seamy side, naturally. He was not bitter, he was honest. As honest as any American writer we have ever had. And that is what he taught me, if anything—the ability to look at life honestly. There was another quality he had and that was fullness. I know that Americans have the reputation of writing thick books, but they are not always fulsome books. I spoke a while back of the difference in "emptiness" between European writers and Americans. The emptiness of the European, as I feel it, is in the basic ore of his material ; the emptiness of the American is in his spiritual or cultural heritage. The "fullness of the void" which is so manifest in Chinese art seems to be unknown in the Western world, both in Europe and America. When I spoke of the thrill it gave me to glance at a European review or literary weekly, I meant to indicate the pleasure which the artist of the garret has when he watches a peasant stir a pot of thick stew, a stew which has been kept going, so to speak, for a week or more. It is nothing for a French writer to lard his article with dazzling names and references ; it is part of his daily literary fare. Our critical and interpretative essays are so meagre in this respect that one would think we emerged from barbarism only yesterday. But when it comes to the novel, to spilling out the raw experience of life, the American is apt to give the European a jolt. Perhaps the American writer lives closer to the roots, imbibes more of what is called experience. I am not sure. Besides, it is dangerous to generalize. I can cite a number of novels, by French writers particularly, the like of which for content, raw material, slag, rich ore, profusion and profundity of experience we have no counterpart for. In general, however, I have the impression that the European writer begins from the roof, or the firmament, if you like. *His* particular racial, cultural firmament—not *the* firmament. It's as though he worked with a triple-decked clavier. Sometimes he remains on the upper levels, his voice gets thin, his material is predigested. The great European, of course, works on all levels at once ; he knows how to pull every organ stop and he is a master with the pedals.

But let us approach the subject from another angle. Let us compare two men who ought really not to be compared, since one was a novelist and the other a poet : I mean Dostoievsky and Whitman. I choose them arbitrarily because for me they represent the peaks in modern literature. Dostoievsky was infinitely more than a novelist, of course, just as Whitman was greater than a poet. But the difference between the two, in my eyes at least, is that Whitman, though the lesser artist, though not as profound, saw bigger than Dostoievsky. He had the cosmic sweep, yes. We speak of him as " the great democrat." Now that particular appellation could never be given Dostoievsky—not because of his religious, political and social beliefs but because Dostoievsky was more and less than a " democrat." (I hope it is understood that when I use the word " democrat " I mean to signify a unique self-sufficient type of individual whose allegiance no government has yet arisen big enough, wise enough, tolerant enough, to include as citizen.) No, Dostoievsky was human in that " all too human " sense of Nietzsche. He wrings our withers when he unrolls his scroll of life. Whitman is impersonal by comparison ; he takes in the crowd, the masses, the great swarms of humanity. His eyes are constantly fixed on the potential, the divine potential, in man. He talks brotherhood ; Dostoievsky talks fellowship. Dostoievsky stirs us to the depths, causes us to shudder and grimace, to wince, to close our eyes at times. Not Whitman. Whitman has the faculty of looking at everything, divine or demonic, as part of the ceaseless Heraclitean stream. No end, no beginning. A lofty, sturdy wind blows through his poems. There is a healing quality to his vision.

We know that the great problem with Dostoievsky was God. God was no problem for Whitman ever. He was with God, just as the Word was with God, from the very beginning. Dostoievsky had virtually to create God—and what a Herculean task that was ! Dostoievsky rose from the depths and, reaching the summit, retained something of the depths about him still. With Whitman I have

221

the image of a man tossing like a cork in a turbulent stream ; he is submerged now and then but there is never any danger of his going down for good. The very substance of him prevented that. One may say, of course, that our natures are God-given. We may also say that the Russia of Dostoievsky's day was a far different world from the one Whitman grew up in. But, after acknowledging and giving due emphasis to all the factors which determine the development of character as well as the temperament of an artist, I come back to the question of vision. Both had the prophetic strain ; both were imbued with a message for the world. And both saw the world clearly ! Both mingled with the world too, let us not forget. From Whitman there exudes a largesse which is godlike ; in Dostoievsky there is an intensity and acuity almost superhuman. But the one emphasized the future and the other the present. Dostoievsky, like so many of the Nineteenth Century Russians, is eschatological : he has the Messianic strain. Whitman, anchored firmly in the eternal now, in the flux, is almost indifferent to the fate of the world. He has a hearty, boisterous, good-natured hail-fellow-well-met tone often. He knows au fond that all's well with the world. He knows more. He knows that if there is anything wrong with it, no tinkering on his part will mend it. He knows that the only way to put it to rights, if we must use the expression, is for every living individual to first put himself to rights. His love and compassion for the whore, the beggar, the outcast, the afflicted, delivers him from inspection and examination of social problems. He preaches no dogma, celebrates no Church, recognizes no mediator. He lives outdoors, circulating with the wind, observing the seasons and the revolutions of the heavens. His worship is implicit, and that is why he can do nothing better than sing hosanna the whole day long. He had problems, I know. He had his sore moments, his trials and tribulations. He had his moments of doubt too, perhaps. But they never obtrude in his work. He remains not so much the great democrat as the hail and hearty cosmocrator. He has abundant health and vitality. *There* perhaps I have put my finger on it. (Not that I mean to compare the two physically—the epileptic versus the man of the outdoors. No.) I am talking of the health and vitality which exudes from his language, which reflects, therefore, his inner state of being. Stress ing this, I mean to indicate that freedom from cultural cares, the lack of concern for the exacerbating problems of culture, probably had a great deal to do with this tonic quality of his poetry. It spared him those inroads which most European men of culture are at one time or another subject to. Whitman seems almost impervious to the ills of the day. He was not living in the times but in a condition of spiritual fullness. A European has much more difficulty maintaining such a " condition " when he attains it. He is beleaguered on all sides. He must be for or against. He must participate. It is almost impossible for him to be " a world citizen " : at the most he can be "a good European." Here too it is getting to be difficult to be above the mêlée, but not impossible. There is the element of chance here which in Europe seems altogether eliminated.

I wonder if I have made clear what I meant to bring out ? I was speaking of the fullness of life as it is reflected in literature. It is really the fullness of the world I am concerned with. Whitman is closer to the Upanishads, Dostoievsky to the New Testament. The rich cultural stew of Europe is one kind of fullness, the heavy ore of everyday American life another. Compared to Dostoievsky, Whitman is in a sense empty. It is not the emptiness of the abstract, either. It is rather a divine emptiness. It is the quality of the nameless void out of which sprang chaos. It is the emptiness which precedes creation. Dostoievsky is chaos and fecundity. Humanity, with him, is but a vortex in the bubbling maelstrom. He had it in him to give birth to many orders of humanity. In order to prescribe some livable order he had, one might almost say, to create a God. For himself ? Yes. But for all other men and women too. And for the children of this world. Dostoievsky could not live alone, no matter how perfect his life or the life of the world. Whitman could, we feel. And it is Whitman who is called the great democrat. He was that, to be sure. He was because he had achieved self-sufficiency . . . What speculations this thought opens up ! Whitman arrived, Dostoievsky still winging his way heavenward. But there is no question of precedence here, no superior or inferior. One is a sun, if you like, the other a star. Lawrence spoke somewhere of Dostoievsky striving to reach the moon of his being.*

* " He who gets nearer the sun is leader, the aristocrat of aristocrats, or he who, like Dostoievsky, gets nearest the moon of our not-being."

A typical Lawrencian image. Behind it lay a thesis which Lawrence was endeavoring to support. I have no axe to grind : I accept them both, Dostoievsky and Whitman, in essence and in utterance. I have put these two luminaries side by side merely to bring out certain differences. The one seems to me to glow with a human light, and he is thought of as a fanatic, as a demonic being ; the other radiates a cool cosmic light, and he is thought of as the brother of all men, as the man in the midst of life. They both *gave* light, that is the important thing. Dostoievsky is all passion, Whitman compassion. A difference in voltage, if you like. In Dostoievsky's work one has the feeling that the angel and the devil walk hand in hand ; they understand one another and they are tolerant of one another. Whitman's work is devoid of such entities : there is humanity in the rough, there is Nature grandiose and eternal, and there is the breath of the great Spirit.

I have often made mention of the celebrated photograph of Dostoievsky which I used to stare at years ago—it hung in the window of a bookshop on Second Avenue in New York. That will always be for me the real Dostoievsky. It is the man of the people, the man who suffered for them and with them. The eternal moujik. One does not care to know whether this man was a writer, a saint, a criminal or a prophet. One is struck by his universality. As for Whitman, the photo which I had always identified with his being, the one everyone knows, I discovered the other day that this photo no longer holds for me.

In the book on Whitman by Paul Jamati* I found a photo of Whitman taken in the year 1854. He is then thirty-five years of age and has just found himself. He has the look of an Oriental poet— I was almost going to say " sage." But there is something about the expression of the eyes which is not the look of a sage. There is just a tinge of melancholy in it. Or so it *seems* to me. He has not yet become that ruddy, bewhiskered bard of the famous photograph. It is a beautiful and arresting face, however, and there is deep quest in the eyes. But, if I may venture to say, judging from a mere photo,

---

* *Walt Whitman*, by Paul Jamati ; Editions Seghers, Paris, 1949.
    This same photo (from the collection of Hart Crane) serves as frontispiece to the 1949 reprint by The Bodley Press, New York, of *Walt Whitman the Wound Dresser*, edited by Richard M. Bucke and with an Introduction by Oscar Cargill.

there is also a remote stellar look in these light blue eyes. The
" veiled " look which they register, and which is contradicted by
the set of the lips, comes from looking at the world as though it
were "alien," as though he had been brought from above, or
beyond, to go through a needless (?) experience here below. This
is a strange statement to make, I know, and perhaps utterly without
support. A mere intuition, a flash in the pan. But the thought
haunts me, and no matter whether justifiable or not, it has altered
my conception of the way Whitman looked at the world and the
way he looked *to* the world. It conflicts disturbingly with the
image I had unquestioningly preserved, the one of the genial mixer,
the man who moved with the throng. This new image of Whitman
was captured six years before the outbreak of our Civil War, which
was for Whitman what Siberia was for Dostoievsky. In this look
of 1854 I read his unlimited capacity for sharing the sufferings of
his fellow man ; I can see why he nursed the wounded on the
battlefield, why destiny, in other words, did not place a sword
in his hand. It is the look of the ministering angel, an angel who
is also a poet and seer.

I must speak further of this arresting photo of the year 1854,
which is *not* the photo, by the way, that Jamati finds so remarkable.
I have just had a look at the photo Jamati dwells on, the daguerro-
type from which a steel engraving was made and which served
as the frontispiece to the first edition of *Leaves of Grass*. To me
there is nothing very remarkable about it ; thousands of young
Americans in that period might have passed for *this* Whitman.
What *is* amazing, to my mind, is that the same man could have
looked so different in two photos taken in the same year !

In search of an accurate physical description of Whitman, I
looked up the book by his friend, the Canadian doctor, Richard
Maurice Bucke.★ It is, unfortunately, a description of Whitman
at the age of sixty-one. However . . . Says Bucke : " The eye-
brows are highly arched, so that it is a long distance from the eye
to the center of the eyebrow. [This is the facial feature that strikes
one most at first sight.] The eyes themselves are light blue, not
large—indeed, in proportion to the head and face they seem rather

★ *Cosmic Consciousness*, 13th edition, 1947 ; E. P. Dutton & Co., New
York.

P

small ; they are dull and heavy, not expressive—what expression they have is kindness, composure, suavity." He goes on to say that " his cheeks are round and smooth. His face has no lines expressive of care, or weariness, or age . . . I have never seen his look, even momentarily, express contempt, or any vicious feeling. I have never known him to sneer at any person or thing, or to manifest in any way or degree either alarm or apprehension, though he has in my presence been placed in circumstances that would have caused both in most men." He speaks of the " well-marked rose color " of Whitman's body. And concludes thus : " His face is the noblest I have ever seen."

In the few pages which Bucke devotes to Whitman in this volume I find more of import than in whole books by the " professors of literature " who have made him an " object of study." But before I point out some of the salient passages let me say that, in pondering over the duality of Whitman, I forgot completely that he was a Gemini, probably the finest and fullest example of this type that ever lived, just as Goethe was the greatest example of a Virgo. Bucke has thrown the full power of his searchlight on the new and the old beings which Whitman managed to make compatible. Stressing the sudden change in the man's fundamental being, which occurred in his thirty-fourth or thirty-fifth year, he says : " We expect and always find a difference between the early and mature writings of the same man . . . But in the case of Whitman (*as in that of Balzac**) writings of absolutely no value were *immediately* followed (and, at least in Whitman's case, without practice or study) by pages across each of which in letters of ethereal fire are written the words ETERNAL LIFE ; pages covered not only by a masterpiece but by such vital sentences as have not been written ten times in the history of the race . . . "

And now for some of the observations which I find singularly interesting and significant . . .

> Walt Whitman, in my talks with him at that time, always disclaimed any lofty intention in himself or his poems. If you accepted his explanations they were simple and commonplace. But when you came to think about these explanations, and to enter into the spirit of them,

* Italics mine.

you found that the simple and the commonplace with him included the ideal and the spiritual.

He said to me one day (I forget now in what connection): 'I have imagined a life which should be that of the average man in average circumstances, and still grand, heroic.'

I beg you to keep this in mind ! We shall come back to it shortly. It is devastatingly important.

He seldom read any book deliberately through, and there was no more (apparent) system about his reading than in anything else that he did ; that is to say, there was no system about it at all.

He read no language but English, yet I believe he knew a great deal more French, German and Spanish than he would own to. But if you took his own word for it, he knew very little of any subject.

Perhaps, indeed, no man who ever lived liked so many things and disliked so few as Walt Whitman. All natural objects seemed to have a charm for him ; all sights and sounds, outdoor and indoor, seemed to please him. He appeared to like (and I believe he did like) all the men, women and children he saw (though I never knew him to say that he liked anyone), but each who knew him felt that he liked him or her, and that he liked others also . . . He was especially fond of children, and all children liked and trusted him at once.

For young and old his touch had a charm that cannot be described, and if it could the description would not be believed except by those who knew him either personally or through *Leaves of Grass*. This charm (physiological more than psychological), if understood, would explain the whole mystery of the man, and how he produced such effects not only upon the well, but among the sick and wounded.

He did not talk much . . . I never knew him to argue or dispute, and he never spoke about money. He always justified, sometimes playfully, sometimes quite seriously, those who spoke harshly of himself or his writings, and I often thought he even took pleasure in these sharp criticisms, slanders and the oppositions of his enemies. He said that his critics were quite right, that behind what his friends saw he was not at all what he seemed, and that, from the point of view of his foes, his book deserved all

the hard things they could say of it—and that he himself
undoubtedly deserved them and plenty more.

He said one day . . . ' After all, the great lesson is that
no special natural sights—not Alps, Niagara, Yosemite,
or anything else—is more grand or more beautiful than
the ordinary sunrise and sunset, earth and sky, the common
trees and grass.' Properly understood, I believe this suggests
the central teaching of his writings and life—namely, that
the commonplace is the grandest of all things ; that the
exceptional in any line is no finer, better or more beautiful
than the usual, and that what is really wanting is not that
we should possess something we have not at present, but
that our eyes should be opened to see and our hearts to
feel what we all have.

He never spoke deprecatingly of any nationality or
class of men, or time in the world's history, or (even)
feudalism, or against any trades or occupations—not even
against any animals, insects, plants or inanimate things,
nor any of the laws of nature, or any of the results of those
laws, such as illness, deformity or death. He never complained or grumbled either at the weather, pain, illness or
at anything else. He never in conversation, in any company,
or under any circumstances, used language that could be
thought indelicate (of course he has used language in his
poems which has been thought indelicate, but none that is
so.) . . . He never swore ; he could not very well, since
as far as I know he never spoke in anger, and apparently
never was angry. He never exhibited fear, and I do not
believe he ever felt it . . .

And now I come to the passage from Whitman's prose, to be
linked with the other one I signalled. Bucke says of it that it " seems
prophetical of the coming race." Howsoever that may be, I wish to
say to you, my dear Lesdain, that not only do I regard this passage
as the key to Whitman's philosophy, the very kernel of it, but—
and once again I beg you not to think this egotistical—I regard it as
expressing my own mature view of life. I will even go further and
say—and now indeed you may be surprised—that this view of
things strikes me as essentially American, or to put it another way,
as the underlying promise which inspired not only our best representatives but which is felt and understood by the so-called "common
man." And if I am right, if this broad, easy, genial, simple view of
life is reflected (even dimly) in both the highest and the lowest

strata of American society, there is indeed hope for a new race of
man to be born on this continent, hope for a new heaven and a
new earth. But let me not withhold the statement longer . . .

A fitly born and bred race, growing up in right conditions of outdoor as much as indoor harmony, activity
and development, would probably, from and in those
conditions, find it enough merely *to live*—and would,
in their relations to the sky, air, water, trees, etc., and to the
countless common shows, and in the fact of *life* itself,
discover and achieve happiness—with Being suffused night
and day by wholesome ecstasy, surpassing all the pleasures
that wealth, amusement, and even gratified intellect,
erudition, or the sense of art, can give.

You may think it presumptuous of me, insular, absurdly patriotic,
or what, but I insist that the tenor of this passage, the distinctive
note it strikes, its sweeping inclusiveness (and annihilation at the
same time), is absolutely American. I would say that it was on
this rock—temporarily forgotten—that America was founded.
For it *is* solid rock, this thought, this platform, and not a gaseous
abstraction of the intellect. It is what the highest representatives
of the human race have themselves believed and advocated, though
their thoughts have been sadly twisted and mutilated. That it is
the destiny of the common man, of every man, and not the way
of the elect, of the chosen few, is what makes it seem more true and
valid to me. I have always looked upon the " elect " as the pre-
cursors of a type to come. Viewed from an historical point of view,
they represent the peaks of the various pyramids which humanity
has thrown up. Viewed from the eternal point of view—and are
we not always face to face with the eternal ?—they represent the
seeds which will form the base of new pyramids to come. We
are always waiting for the revolution. The real revolution is taking
place constantly. And the name for this deeper process is emancipation—*self-liberation* in other words. What did Faure quote from
Whitman ? " The world will be complete for him who is himself
complete." Is it necessary to add that for such beings government
is superfluous ? There can only be government—that is, abdication
of the self, of one's own inalienable rights—where there are incomplete beings. The New Jerusalem can only be made of and by

emancipated individuals. That is community. That is " the absolute collective." *Are we to see it ever ?* If we see it now with our mind's eye we see it in the only actuality it will ever have.

" Zen is everyday life," you will find written in every book on the subject. " Nirvana is capable of attainment *now*," you will also find in every book on the subject. Attainment is hardly the word, because the " fulfilment " implied in such statements is something to be *realized* in the immediate present . . . How very like Zen is this from Whitman : " Is it lucky to be born ? It is just as lucky to die."

In summarizing his pages on Whitman, Bucke makes, among others, the following statements :

> In no man who ever lived was the sense of eternal life so absolute.
> Fear of death was absent. Neither in health nor in sickness did he show any sign of it, and there is every reason to believe he did not feel it.
> He had no sense of sin.

And what of Evil ? Suddenly it is Dostoievsky's voice I hear. If there be evil, there can be no God. Was that not the thought which plagued Dostoievsky ? Whoever knows Dostoievsky knows the torments he endured because of this conflict. But the rebel and doubter is silenced towards the end, silenced by a magnificent affirmation. (" Not resignation," as Janko Lavrin points out.)

> Love all God's creation and every grain of sand in it. Love every leaf, every ray of God's light. If you love everything, you will preserve the divine mystery of things. (Father Zosima, alias the real Dostoievsky.)

And what of Evil ?

Whitman answered thus, not once, but again and again : " And I say there is in fact no evil."

Twenty years after he had entered upon the new life, had taken the path in order to become the path, like Lao-tse, like Buddha, like Jesus, Whitman gives us the revolutionary poem, the *Prayer of Columbus*, ostensibly, as Bucke says, his own prayer, in which he describes in two immortal lines the illumination which had been vouchsafed him :

Light rare untellable, lighting the very light,
Beyond all signs, descriptions, languages.

He imagines himself to be on his deathbed ; his condition is, by worldly standards, pitiable. It would seem as if God had deserted him, or punished him. Does Whitman doubt ? The last two lines of the above-mentioned poem give the answer. Bucke writes of the moment thus : " What shall he say to God ? He says that God knows him through and through, and that he is willing to leave himself in God's hands." How could there be any doubt in the breast of a man who had written : " I feel and know that death is not the ending, as we thought, but rather the real beginning —and that nothing ever is or can be lost, nor even die, nor soul nor matter."

The questioning, the doubts, the denial and the negation even, which abound in Dostoievsky's works, expressed through the mouths of his various characters and revealing his obsession with the problem of certitude, stand in sharp contrast to Whitman's lifelong attitude. In some respects Dostoievsky reminds us of Job. He arraigns the Creator and life itself. To quote Janko Lavrin again . . . " Unable to accept life spontaneously, he was compelled to take it up as a problem." And he adds immediately : " But life as a problem demands a meaning which must satisfy our rational and irrational selves. At a certain stage the meaning of life may even become more important than life itself. One can reject life altogether, unless its meaning answers to the highest demands of our consciousness."

A few weeks ago, in going through my papers, I ran across an article I had torn out of the magazine *Purpose* (London, 1937). It was by Erich Gutkind, on Job. I was tremendously impressed by this new reading. I am sure I had never grasped the essential meaning of his words when I read it and put it carefully away in 1937. I mention this little essay, meaty and compact, because in it Gutkind gives an explanation of the problem such as I have never seen before. It connects, assuredly, with my preceding remarks about Dostoievsky.

" In the Book of Job," he says, " God is no longer measured by the world, by the order or disorder of the world. But the world is measured by God. The standard (just as it is light with Einstein) is here God. And that which changes is the world. The Book of Job leads us to a deeper understanding of the world." He then proceeds to explain that the Christian idea of sin as well as the doctrine of reincarnation with its notion of Karma, the idea, namely, that "everybody's suffering is explained by his own *sins*," is sharply rejected in the Book of Job.

"Suffering is not the payment of a debt," he says, "but rather a burden of responsibility. Job did not have to answer for sins which he had committed. He took upon himself the terrible problem of suffering." [Note how all this connects with Dostoievsky.] "The question with which he wrestled is a basic question of the order of the world, the struggle between God and Satan . . . It is the question of whether the world is meaningful or meaningless. Is the world good or evil ?"

And so on. Gutkind points out, *en passant*, that in the end everything was returned to Job—his wealth, his health, and his children also. "Job does not perish like the Greek heroes."

Then, diving into the heart of the problem, he says : "But let us ask with Job : What does the blind realm of Fate stand for ? What kind of strange sphere is this, in which God leaves everything to the operation of chance ? " He says that God's answer to Job does not appear to meet the cry of his soul. God answered Job cosmologically, he says. "Where wast thou, man, when I founded the cosmos ? " That was God's reply. He points out that "in the cosmos everything takes place according to law. There everything is weighed against everything else . . . All is balanced." Nature is the realm of Fate, he states. He says that Job, in seeking to understand God's ways, "takes God as a kind of cause, a natural force." "But," says he, "God is not only a principle whereby the universe can be explained or given meaning. That is the God of the theologians—an abstract God."

In the cosmos, man and God can never come together. The pantheistic idea, that God is to be found everywhere in nature, is one of the causes for the decline of the concept of God . . . Nothing has reality of itself. Nature is relative through and through. Every phenomenon is itself

part of an indescribably complicated net of relations.
Reality is not to be found there. The Jewish tradition
teaches that Abraham sought God in the cosmos. But he
did not find him there. And because he could not find
him there, he was driven to search for God where he
reveals himself, namely, in the direct conversation between
God and man.

Then follows this, which is what I have been leading up to :

One must always so conduct oneself as if there were no
God at all ! We may not explain the riddle of nature by
God : that would be the end of science. We may not
wait for succor from God : that would be the end of
human initiative. The less we concern ourselves with
the idea of God in our explanation of the world and in
our practical life, the more clearly will God appear. This
is what the Book of Job teaches when God asks : ' Where
wast thou when I founded the cosmos ? ' And even :
' Where art thou, when I direct the cosmos ? '

It is often said of Whitman that he had an inflated ego. I am
sure the same might be said of Dostoievsky, if we are to look at
them narrowly, because in Dostoievsky's extreme humility there
was an extraordinary arrogance. But we discover nothing by
examining the egos of such men. They transcended the ego : the
one through his ceaseless and almost unbearable questioning, the
other by his steady, clear affirmation of life. Dostoievsky undertook, as far as it was humanly possible, to assume the problems,
the torture and the anguish of all men—and especially, as we know
so well, the incomprehensible suffering of children. Whitman
answered man's problems, not by weighing them and examining
them, but by a continuous chant of love, of acceptance, in which
the answer was always implicit. The *Song of Myself* is no different,
fundamentally, than a hymn of creation.

D. H. Lawrence closes his *Studies in Classic American Literature*
with a chapter on Whitman. It is an incongruous piece of writing,
a mixture of shoddy balderdash and flashes of amazing acuity of
perception. To me it is the rock on which Lawrence shattered
himself. He had to come to Whitman eventually, and he did. He
cannot pay him out-and-out homage, no, not Lawrence. The truth
is, he cannot take the measure of the man. Whitman is a pheno-

233

menon to him, a very special kind of phenomenon—the *American* phenomenon.

But, despite all the fuming and ranting, despite the rather cheap song and dance with which his essay opens, Lawrence does succeed in saying things about Whitman which are imperishable. There is much in Whitman he fails to grasp, much he *could* not grasp, because, to be honest and candid, he was a lesser man, a man more-over who never achieved individuation. But Whitman's essential message he grasped, and the way he interprets it is a challenge to all interpreters to come.

> " Whitman's essential message," says Lawrence, " was the Open Road. The leaving of the soul free unto herself, the leaving of his fate to her and to the loom of the open road. Which is the bravest doctrine man has ever proposed to himself."

Declaring that the true rhythm of the American continent speaks out in Whitman, that he is the first white aboriginal, that he is the greatest and the first and the only American teacher (and no Savior !), he says also that he was a great changer of the blood in the veins of men. His true and earnest avowal of admiration, affection and reverence for Whitman begins at this point in the essay . . .

> Whitman, the great poet, has meant so much to me. Whitman, the one man breaking a way ahead. Whitman, the one pioneer. And only Whitman . . . Ahead of Whitman, nothing. Ahead of all poets, pioneering into the wilderness of unopened life, Whitman. Beyond him, none.

Singing the song of the soul himself, Lawrence grows ecstatic. He speaks of " a new doctrine, a new morality, a morality of actual living, not of salvation." Whitman's morality, he declares, " was a morality of the soul living her life, not saving herself . . . The soul living her life along the incarnate mystery of the open road."

Magnificent words, and Lawrence meant them undoubtedly. Towards the end of the essay, speaking of " the true democracy " which Whitman preached, speaking of how it makes itself known, he says, and with what unerringness! : " Not by a progression of piety, or by works of charity. Not by works at all. Not by anything but just itself. The soul passing unenhanced, passing on foot and being no more than itself. And recognized, and passing by or greeted according to the soul's dictate. If it be a great soul, it will be worshipped in the road."

" The only riches, the great souls." That is the closing sentence of the essay and the book. (Dated Lobos, New Mexico.)

And on this note I think I shall end my letter, my very dear Pierre Lesdain.

Big Sur, California
May 10th, 1950

Postscriptum

I can't bring my letter to a close at this point. There's more to say. What matter if it assumes elephantine proportions ? Unwittingly I am being led to disclose certain views and opinions I might never have released had I not embarked on this unintended excursus. You are probably the only man in Europe who will not wince or balk at anything I say, whom I cannot deceive or disillusion, no matter if I should act the idiot. You have been most modest and reticent about yourself. I know almost nothing about you. But I know that you are greater than you represent yourself to be, if only because of your unswerving faith, loyalty and devotion. These qualities are not found in combination in a nobody.

Anyway, I should like to amplify certain thoughts I threw out, reconcile certain " apparent " contradictions, and pick up some threads I left dangling in mid-air. First, then, let me dispose of the last-named, rapidly . . .

Opposite page 65 of Jamati's book is a photograph of Whitman which I never saw before. It might be taken, at first glance, for an early photo of Lincoln. The date is uncertain, it says below the photo, but it is definitely some years before the one of 1854 which I singled out for your attention and about which I may still have more to say. Parenthetically, speaking of Whitman's physical appearance, did I mention that in addition to having a rose-tinted skin, light-blue eyes, an aquiline nose, he also had black hair which, as you will note in the 1854 photo, is already turning gray ? Somehow, I never pictured him as having black hair and blue eyes ; it

235

is an irresistible combination, in man or woman. The Irish have it occasionally.

As for Lincoln, one of the homeliest men imaginable, if we are to believe his own words, I gather that, although their paths crossed a number of times, there were never any spoken words between them. Whitman had an uncommon veneration for Lincoln. A number of times during the latter years of his life he took part in commemorative services for Lincoln, sometimes at the risk of his health. Is it not curious, too, that Lincoln should use almost the same words about Whitman that Napoleon did about Goethe ? Both recognized *the man.*

Thinking of governments, of the excellent ones we might have had and still could have, despite all adverse conditions, I could not help but speculate between pauses in writing this letter on what America might be today if, directly after the Civil War, assuming Lincoln to be still alive, he had had in his cabinet—dead or alive— the following : Tom Paine, Thomas Jefferson, Robert E. Lee, John Brown, Ralph Waldo Emerson, Henry David Thoreau, Mark Twain, Walt Whitman.

I think of Whitman's funeral rites, as Jamati gives it, with Bob Ingersoll, of all men, pronouncing the last words. Who would have thought that these two should be linked together in death ? And not only that, not only the crowds which followed the funeral procession or lined the sidewalks, but the reading at the grave first from Whitman's own work and then from one after another of his peers. (" De ses pairs," says Jamati.) *Who were these ?* Buddha, Confucius, Zoroaster, Jesus, Plato, Mohammed! What American poet was ever given such a send-off ?

And then the admirable fortune, explicable and altogether justified, which attended Whitman's lifelong fight to gain recognition for his work. What a roster of names we find enlisted on his side ! Beginning with Emerson who, on receiving a copy of the first edition of *Leaves of Grass,* writes : " *Les Américaiūs qui sont a l'étranger peuvent rentrer ; il nous est né un artiste.*" Emerson, Thoreau, Bucke, Carlyle, Burroughs, William Douglas O'Connor, Horace Traubel, Mark Twain, the wonderful Anne Gilchrist, John Addington Symonds, Ruskin, Joaquin Miller (California's Whitman), the Rosettis, Swinburne, Edward Carpenter . . . what a roster!

And last but perhaps not least, Peter Doyle, the omnibus driver. As for Joaquin Miller*—we are getting close to home now!—it was this poet of the Sierras who, incensed by the outcries against Whitman, delivered himself thus : " Cet homme vivra, je vous le le dis! Cet homme vivra, soyez-en sûrs, lorsque le dôme puissant de votre Capitole là-bas, n'élévera plus ses épaules rondes contre les cercles du temps."

Let us not overlook another signal event in Whitman's career—his presence at the inauguration, in Baltimore, of the monument to the memory of Edgar Allen Poe. ("Le seul poète américain qui ait répondu à l'invitation du comité," says Jamati.)

Let us not overlook either the fact that, as his work began to draw attention in Europe—in England particularly, strange!—as one translation after another appeared in various countries, the first *French* translation (of fragments only) appears in *Provencal!* I find that a rather happy coincidence.

And Léon Bazalgette, the most devoted of Whitman's biographers! What a labor of love his was! What a tribute from the Old World! I remember reading Bazalgette's work in Paris ; I remember too, though my memory may be faulty, that in this same period I was also reading these strangely different works : The *Confessions* of St. Augustine and *The City of God* ; Nijinsky's *Diary* ; *The Absolute Collective*, by Erich Gutkind ; *The Spirit of Zen* by Alan Watts ; *Louis Lambert* and *Seraphita* of Balzac ; *La Mort d'un Quelconque*, of Jules Romains ; the life of the Tibetan saint, *Milarepa*, and *Connaissance de l'Est* by Paul Claudel. (No, I was never alone. At the worst, as I said somewhere, I was with God!)

There is a side of Whitman which I have not sufficiently stressed and which to me is extremely illuminating—I mean his quiet, steady, unruffled pursuit of the goal. How many editions of his opus are issued at his own expense! What a struggle to get those few " obnoxious," supposedly " obscene," poems included in a definitive edition! Notice that he never wastes himself in struggling against his enemies. He marches on, resolute, unwavering, unflinching. In his steadfast gaze they are overlooked, his enemies. As he follows " the open road," friends, supporters, champions spring

* His real name was Cincinnatus Heine Miller, and he was born in Indiana.

up everywhere. They issue forth in his wake. Observe the way
he handles Emerson when the latter endeavors to remonstrate
with him about the inclusion of these " offensive " poems in a
later edition. Is it not evident that Whitman is the superior of
the two ? Had Whitman capitulated on this issue the whole picture
would have been altered. (True, he made concession to his English
benefactors in omitting from the English editions the questionable
items, but he did so, I am sure, knowing that ultimately he would
win out in the homeland.) This fight against the powers that be,
taking place as it did in the middle and latter part of the Nineteenth
Century—the most conservative period in our history—cannot be
stressed too much. The whole course of American letters was
affected by it. (As it was again with the appearance of Dreiser's
Sister Carrie.) When it comes to the case of James Joyce, it is by
a sort of " generous revenge " that an American court absolves
the author of *Ulysses*. How much easier it was to sanction the free
circulation of *Ulysses*, in the second decade of the Twentieth Century,
than to grant Whitman full freedom of expression a half-century
earlier! It remains to be seen what the ultimate verdict will be,
by French, English and American authorities, in the case of my
own questionable works . . . However, I did not touch on this
theme to draw attention to my own case but rather to point out
that a sort of special providence seemed to guide the destiny of a
man like Whitman. He who had no doubts, he who never employed
the language of negation, nor mocked, sneered at, reviled or insulted
other human beings, was protected and preserved by staunch friends
and admirers. Jamati speaks of the astonishment which the recrimina-
tions against Whitman's outspoken poems aroused in Anne Gilchrist.

> Elle y voit une glorification, un respect, un amour de
> la vie tout religieux et elle se demande avec ingénuité, en
> s'apercevant qu'elle vibre si naturellement au diapason
> des Feuilles d'Herbe, si ces versets n'ont pas été écrits
> spécialement pour des femmes. He adds : Cette femme
> au grand cœur, cette mère accomplie, respectée, admirée,
> qui sait découvrir ' quelque chose de sacré dans tout,' quel
> témoin pour lui !

Her *"ingénuité,"* says Jamati. Her "perceptiveness," I would say.
Her courage. Her sublimity. Remember, she was an *Englishwoman!*

No, even though Whitman may not have written them "especially" for women, his words were addressed to women as well as to men. It is one of Whitman's rare virtues that throughout the poems woman receives the same exalted homage as man. He saw them as equals. He raised their manhood and their womanhood. He saw what was feminine in man and what was masculine in woman—long before Otto Weininger! He has been slandered *because* he proclaimed the duality of sex in all of us. In one of the few instances where he made a radical change in the original text it was to substitute a woman for a man—in order, it is said, to allay suspicion of "homosexual" tendencies. What filth has been written on this score! What absurdities the psychoanalysts have led us into! Whoso talks love, great love, falls under suspicion. These same gibes have been levelled against the greatest benefactors of the human race. Love which is all-inclusive seems to repel us. And yet, according to the deep-rooted legend of creation, man was originally bi-sexual. The first Adam was complete—or hermaphroditic. In his deepest being man will always be complete—that is, man *and* woman both.

When some pages back I referred to that veiled and distant look in Whitman's eyes, it was not, I hope, to give the impression that I think of him as cold, indifferent, aloof, a man living apart in "Brahmic splendor," and deigning, when the mood seizes him, to mingle with the crowd! The record of his years on the battlefield and in the hospitals should be enough to erase any such suspicion. What greater sacrifice, what greater renouncement of self, could any man have made ? He emerged from that experience shattered to the core.* He had witnessed more than is humanly demanded of a man. It was not the inroads upon his health that were so cruel, though a great tribulation, but rather the ordeal of too close communion. Much is related of his inexhaustible sympathy. *Empathy* is more nearly the word for it. But the word to describe this enlarged state of feeling is lacking in our tongue.

This experience, which, I repeat, must be compared with Dostoievsky's ordeal in Siberia, incites endless speculation. In both instances it was a Calvary. The inborn brotherly feeling of Dostoiev-

* See page xvii of Oscar Cargill's Introduction ("Walt Whitman as Saint") to *The Wound Dresser*.

sky, the natural comradely spirit in Whitman, were tested in the
fiery crucible by command of Fate. No matter how great the
humanity in them, neither would have *elected* for such an experience.
(I do not make this remark idly. There have been glorious instances
in man's history where individuals did elect to undergo some
awesome trial or test. I think of Jesus and Joan of Arc immediately.)
Whitman did not rush headlong to volunteer his services as a soldier
of the Republic. Dostoievsky did not fling himself into the "movement" in order to prove his capacity for martyrdom. In both
instances the situation was thrust upon them. But there, after all,
is the test of a man—how he meets the blows of Fate! It was in
exile that Dostoievsky really became acquainted with the teachings
of Jesus. It was on the battlefield, among the dead and wounded,
that Whitman discovered the meaning of abnegation, or better,
of service without thought of reward. Only heroic men could
have survived such ordeals. Only illuminated men could have
transformed these experiences into great messages of love and
benediction.

Whitman had seen the light, had received his illumination, some
few years before this crucial period in his life. Not so with Dostoievsky. Both had a lesson to learn, and they learned it in the
midst of suffering, sickness and death. That insouciant spirit of
Whitman underwent a change, a deepening. His " camaraderie "
developed into a more passionate acceptance of his fellowman.
That look of 1854, the look of a man who is a bit stunned by the
vision he has had, changes to a broader and deeper gleam which
embraces the whole universe of sentient beings—and the inanimate
world as well. His expression is no longer that of one coming
from afar but of one who is in the thick of it, who accepts his lot
completely, who rejoices in it, come what may. There may be
less of the divine in it, but there is more of the purely human.
Whitman had need of this humanization. If, as I firmly believe,
there took place in him an expansion of consciousness (in 1854 or
'55), there had also to take place, unless he were to go mad, a
revaluation of all human values. Whitman had to live as a man,
not as a god. We know, in Dostoievsky's case, how (via Solovyev
probably) this obsession with the idea of a " man-god " persisted.
Dostoievsky, illumined from the depths, had to humanize the god

in him. Whitman, receiving his illumination from beyond, sought to divinize the man in him. This fecundation of god and man—the man in god, the god in man—had far-reaching effects in both instances. Today it is common to hear that the prophecies of these two great figures have come to nought. Both Russia and America have become thoroughly mechanized, autocratic, tyrannical, materialistic and power mad. But wait! History must run its course. The negative aspect always precedes the positive.

Biographers and critics often take these crucial periods in the life of a subject and, dwelling on " brotherhood " and " universality of spirit," give the impression that it was the mere proximity to suffering and death which developed these attributes in their subjects. But what affected Whitman and Dostoievsky, if I read their characters rightly, was the ceaseless unbaring of the soul which they were made to witness. They were affected, *wounded* is the word, in their souls. Dostoievsky did not go to prison as a social worker, nor Whitman to the battlefield as nurse, doctor, or priest. Dostoievsky was obliged to live the lives of each one of his fellow prisoners because of utter lack of privacy : he lived like a beast, as we know from the records. Whitman had to become nurse, doctor, priest all in one, because there was no one else about who combined these rare gifts. His temperament would never have led him to choose any of these pursuits. But that same animal magnetism—or that same divinity in each—forced these two individuals, under similar stress, to go beyond themselves.* An ordinary man, after release from such a situation, might well devote himself for the rest of his days to the care of the unfortunate ; he might well conceive it to be his " mission " to thus dedicate his life. But Whitman and Dostoievsky go back to their writing. If they have a mission it will be incorporated in their " message " . .

If I have not made it clear already, let me say that it was precisely because they were artists first and foremost that these two men created the special conditions relating to their cruel experience, *and* conditioned themselves to transmute and ennoble the experience. Not all great men are capable of supporting the naked meeting of soul with soul, as was the case with these two. To witness not once,

* As in the case of Cabeza de Vaca.

Q

but again and again, the spectacle of a man unbaring his soul is almost beyond human endurance. We do not come forward with our souls ordinarily. A man may lay his heart bare, but not his soul. When a man does expose himself to another in this way there is demanded a response which few men, apparently, are capable of. In some ways I think that Dostoievsky's situation was even more trying than Whitman's. Performing for his fellow-sufferers all the services that Whitman did, he was nevertheless always regarded as one of them, that is, a criminal. Naturally he thought no more of " reward " than Whitman, but his dignity as a human being was ever deprived him. In another sense, of course, it could be said that this very fact made it easier for him to act the " ministering angel." It nullified all thought of *being* an angel. He could see himself as a victim and a sufferer because in fact he was one.

But the important point—let me not lose it!—is that, whether the rôles they assumed were deliberate or forced upon them, it was to these two beings that the anguished souls about them turned instinctively and unerringly. Acting as mediators between God and man, or if not mediators then intercessors, they surpassed the " experts " whose calling they had assumed. The one quality which they had strongly in common was their inability to reject *any* experience. It was their utter humanness which made them capable of accepting the great " responsibility " of suffering. They embraced more than their share because it was a " privilege," not because it was their duty or their mission in life. Thus, all that passed between them and their fellow sufferers went beyond the gamut of ordinary experience. Men saw into their souls and they saw into men's souls. The little self, in each instance, was burned away. When it was over they could not do other than resume their private tasks. They were no longer " men of letters," no, not even artists any more, but deliverers. We know only too well how their respective messages burst the frames of the old vehicles. How could it be otherwise? The revolutionizing of art which they helped bring about, which they initiated to an extent we are not yet properly aware of, was part and parcel of the greater task of trans-valuating all human values. Their concern with art was of a different order from that of other celebrated revolutionaries. It was a movement from the center of man's being outward, and the repercussions from that outer sphere (which is still veiled to us) we have yet to hear. But let us not for one moment believe that it was a vain or lost irruption of the spirit. Dostoievsky plunged deeper than any man before letting fly his arrows ; Whitman soared higher than any before tuning in to our antennae.

Still I cannot leave the subject of this very special ordeal they underwent. I must come back to it now in another way, my own personal way. There is something I am struggling to make absolutely clear . . .

You know that for almost five years I was the employment manager of a telegraph company. You know from the *Capricorn* book what the nature and extent of this experience was. Even a dullard could sense that from this glut of human contact something was bound to happen. I am aware that I have emphasized the matter of mere numbers, and not only of numbers but of the variety of types as well as the conditions of life which was my everyday fare. Fleetingly, too fleetingly, it seems to me now, I sketched the poignancy of these man-to-man situations into which I was plunged daily. But did I emphasize sufficiently *this* aspect of my daily experience—that men debased themselves before me, that they stripped themselves naked, that they withheld nothing, nothing ? They wept, they knelt at my feet, they snatched my hand to kiss it. Oh, to what lengths did they not go ? *And why ?* In order to get a job, or in order to thank me for giving them one ! As if I were God Almighty ! As if I controlled their private destinies. And I, the last man on earth who wished to interfere with the destiny of another, the last man on earth who wished to stand either above or below another man, who wanted to look each man in the face and greet him as a brother, as an equal, I was obliged, or I *believed* that I was obliged, to play this rôle for almost five years. (Because I had a wife and child to support ; because I could find no other job ; because I was thoroughly incapable, unfit, except in this accidental rôle. Accidental, yes ! because I had asked only to be a messenger, not the employment manager !) And so every day I found myself averting my gaze. I was in turn humiliated and exasperated. Humiliated to think that anyone should regard me as his benefactor, exasperated to think that human beings could beg so ignominiously for such a thing as a job. True, I myself had fought for the right to be " a messenger." Rejected, perhaps because they thought I was not in earnest, I stormed the president's office. Yes, I too had made a big thing of it—of this lousy, unmentionable messenger boy's job. (Twenty-eight years old I was. Rather mature for such a job.) Because my pride had been wounded I insisted on my rights. *I was to be rejected ?* I who had condescended to accept the lowest job on earth ? Incredible ! Thus, when I am returned from the president's office to the general manager's, knowing in advance that victory is in my palm—notice now the Dostoievskian touch !—nothing will do but to represent myself as *the supreme cosmodemoniacal messenger*—God's own, you might say. I know as well as the astute dud who is listening to me that it is no longer a question of taking a messenger boy's job. Had my listener told me that he was preparing to groom me to become the next president of the telegraph company, instead of the employment manager of the messenger department, my pride was then so inflated that I would not have blinked an eye. But, though I did not become a future candidate for the presidency, I nevertheless got more than I had bargained for. I never understood till that moment when I took over as employment manager, with the destinies of over a thousand individuals in my hands, what the prayers and entreaties of the unfortunate must sound like in God's ears. (That there is no such Being as these wretches imagine makes it all the more horrible and ironic.) For these poor " cosmococcic " messengers I was definitely God. Not Jesus the Christ, not his Holiness, the Pope, but God ! And to be God, if only as simulacrum, is about the most devastating situation a man can find himself in. These petty tyrants who call themselves dictators, these mice who think they alone can govern the world of men, I only wish to God these idiots might be permitted to play the rôle they imagine themselves suited for to the utter limit ! Why, in the knowledge of their utter fatuousness, why can we citizens of the world not surrender to them full and unlimited power for a brief interlude ? Nothing would shatter this bubble of pretense (which we all have to a degree) quicker than such a sanction. But if we are not even willing to commit ourselves to God's hands—I mean those who *believe* in Him—how can we ever hope to conduct such a drastic and humorous experiment ?

This God whom men imagine to be constantly cupping both ears in order to catch their entreaties, their blandishments, their beguilements, does he not blush, does he not wince, does he not squirm with anguish, chagrin and mortification when he listens in on this sickly caterwaul issuing from this tiny abode called the Earth ? (For we are not the one and only order of creation. Far from it ! What of the other stellar abodes ? Think of those long exploded as well as those which are not yet !)

My dear Lesdain, what I am trying to say is this . . . a man can be robbed of his human dignity by being put in a position above his fellow men, by being asked to do what no man has the right to do, namely, give and take dispensations, judge and condemn, or accept thanks for a favor which is not a favor but a privilege that every human being is entitled to. I don't know which was worse to endure—their shameless entreaties or their unmerited gratitude. I only know that I was torn apart, that I wanted more than any-thing in the world to live my own life and never again take part in this cruel scheme of master and slave. My solution was to write, and to do that necessitated another descent into the abyss. This time I am really underneath, not above, as before. Now I have to listen to what others want, what they think good or bad, above all, " what sells." But there is one comfort in this new rôle—I am not taking the bread out of anyone's mouth by plying my trade. If I have a boss, he is invisible. And I never pray to him, any more than I did to the Big Boss.

Then, when I think I have made myself into a capable worker, when I think I know my trade, when I think I can give satisfaction, when I am even reconciled to a long postponement of " my wages," I come face to face with the big bugaboo : Public Taste. You remember I said that if Whitman had capitulated on this issue, if he had obeyed the voice of his counselors, a totally different edifice would have reared itself. There are the friends and supporters who appear when you swim with the crowd ; there are the other kind of friends and supporters who rally round you when you are menaced. The latter are the only kind worthy of the name. It is strange but the only kind of support that means anything comes from those who believe in you to the hilt. The ones who go the whole hog. Let there be the slightest wavering, the slightest doubt, the slightest defection, and your would-be supporter turns into your worst enemy. For complete dedication there must be a corresponding total acceptance. Those who defend you *in spite of* your faults work against you in the long run. When you champion a man he must be all of a piece ; he must be that which he is through and through, and no doubts about it.

(There has been a lapse of about thirty-six hours. The thread is broken. But I will enter by the back door . . .)

When the illuminated individual is returned to the world, when his vision finally adjusts itself to re-embrace that view of the world which the ordinary mortal never loses, the round orb of the eye seems to grow fuller, deeper and more luminous. He takes time to readjust, to see the mountains as mountains again and the waters as waters. One not only sees himself seeing, one sees with added sight. That extra sight reveals itself by the serenity of the glance. The mouth too expresses that extra sight, if I may put it so. It does not shut firmly and tightly ; the lips remain always slightly parted. This serenity of the lips implies the abdication of useless struggle. The whole body, in fact, expresses the joy of surrender. The more it relaxes, the more it glows. The whole being becomes incandescent.

We know how impressed Balzac was when he read in Swedenborg that there are " solitary " angels. An extraordinary utterance, no gainsaying it. And did not Whitman say : " Sooner or later we come down to one single, solitary soul ? " Aye, eventually we get to bedrock, to the node which is as eternal in the human being as in God. And if, in the presence of such individuals, we have the impression . . .

(Another lapse of thirty-six hours—a very bad break, indeed. I no longer know what the thought was I was about to express. But it will doubtless come back. It is now May 15th !)

In the interim, despite all the fritting away, certain phrases remain lodged in the back of my head, the clue to the missing thread. One of these is : " Il faudra bien qu'un jour on soit l'humanité." (Jules Romains.) Another (my own) is : " The worm in the apple. Look for the worm ! ". With these came the command to look up the preface to *Looking Backward* (2000 to 1887 A.D.) by the son of Edward Bellamy. This book—I cannot find the edition

with his son's preface—had an unprecedented sale, one which
nearly rivaled the Bible.* It was translated into I don't know how
many languages. Today it is virtually forgotten. But here are a
few lines of Bellamy I find worth citing : " The long and weary
winter of the race is ended. Its summer has begun. Humanity
has burst the chrysalis. The heavens are before it." These words
were written before the end of the Nineteenth Century, just five
years, to be exact, before Whitman died. They follow not so very
long after these words of Whitman : " The poems of life are great,
but there must be the poems of the purport of life, not only in itself,
but beyond itself."

The worm in the apple . . I think that whenever or wherever the
worm makes its appearance it should be hailed as a sign of new life.
We ought to call it the " angel-worm." Au fond there is no such
thing as literature, no such thing as art, religion, civilization. There
is not even such a thing as humanity. Au fond there is nothing
but life, life manifesting itself in myriad inscrutable ways. To
live, to be alive, is to partake of the mystery. The other night I
encountered a line, undoubtedly famous, of Heraclitus, which
goes thus: "To live is to fight for life." That line set me to pondering. I could not believe that by " to fight for " Heraclitus
meant merely the continuance of the struggle for existence. I could
not believe that he was implying, like a stern realist, that the moment
we are born we are advancing towards death. I don't believe that
by " to fight for " he meant to defend or uphold life. I do not
know, I must admit, what the context was. But pondering over
these words I came to the conclusion that, whether Heraclitus
meant this or not, what he was saying was—life is the all, life is the
only privilege, life knows nothing, means nothing, but life ; the
fact of being alive means conscious allegiance, supreme faith, in
other words. From the moment we are born we wage a struggle
against undefinable things. Nearly everything we glorify is in the
nature of commemoration, commemoration of our heroic struggle.
We put the struggle above the flux, the past and future above the

---

* I have just found Paul Bellamy's preface. Here are his words : " *Looking
Backward*, first published in the winter of 1887–8, won such universal acceptance that in the middle Nineties it was said that more copies of the volume
had been sold than of any book hitherto written by an American author,
with the two exceptions of *Uncle Tom's Cabin* and *Ben Hur*."

present. But life bids us swim in the eternal stream. Cosmology is the myth of the mystery of creation. When God answers Job *cosmologically* it is to remind man that he is only a part of creation, that it is his duty to put himself in accord with it or perish. When man puts his head out of the stream of life he becomes self-conscious. And with self-consciousness comes arrest, fixation, symbolized so vividly by the myth of Narcissus.

The worm in the apple of human existence is consciousness. It steals over the face of life like an intruder. Seen through the mirror everything becomes the background of the ego. The seers, the mystics, the visionaries smash this mirror again and again. They restore man to the primordial flux, they put him back in the stream like a fisherman emptying his net. There is a line from *Tête d'Or* of Claudel which runs: "Mais rien n'empêchera que je meure de mal de la mort, à moins que je ne saisisse la joie . . ." A profound and beautiful utterance. The joy he speaks of is the joy of surrender. It could be no other.

In my study of Balzac I cited a number of utterances from the lips of Louis Lambert. I would like to give them again at this juncture . . . "My point is to ascertain the real relation that may exist between God and man. Is not this a need of the age ? . . . If man is bound up with everything, is there not something above him with which he again is bound up ? If he is the end-all of the unexplained transmutations that lead up to him, must he not be also the link between the visible and invisible creations ? The activity of the universe is not absurd ; it must tend to an end, and that end is surely not a social body constituted as ours is ! . . . It seems to me that we are on the eve of a great human struggle ; the forces are there, only I do not see the General . . ."

The Balzac who wrote these lines, and others even more discerning, more inspiring (in *Seraphita*), was not mistaken in his view of things. No more than Edward Bellamy or Dostoievsky or Walt Whitman.

I mentioned earlier in this letter that I had heard recently from the man whom I looked upon as a master in my youth, and whom I have written of in this book as " a living book " : John Cowper Powys. With this letter came a new book of his called *Obstinate Cymric*. In it is a chapter called Pair Dadeni, which is Welsh for

"The Cauldron of Rebirth." I find in this book, especially in this particular chapter, the same illuminating utterances which characterize the works of those mentioned above. Speaking of the change which is coming over humanity with the advent of our entry into Aquarius, speaking of the "new revelation" being granted us and which, he says, "may turn out to be the élan vital in the heart of all life," he states :

> Now what I am endeavouring to suggest in all this is that the secret underlying the cause of this great historic change coming over the human race, this change so closely connected with the movements of the heavenly bodies, this change which implies the passing forth out of the two thousand years of the sign *Pisces* into the sign *Aquarius*, this change which produces the effect of a living body slowly and dreadfully restored from death to life, or even of a living infant emerging from a dying mother's womb, may be nothing less than that very *change of heart* which the prophets have always spoken of and in which the *revivalists* have always believed, a "change of heart," however, not by any means on the lines which the "law" promulgated and the "prophets" predicted but on entirely different lines, on lines startling and unexpected, on lines in tune in fact with that "Stream of Tendency" in Nature which is steadily moving, and moving in defiance, not only of the Law and the Prophets, but of both God and the Devil.

Let me quote a few more lines, for they concern us, our part —or our refusal to take part—in this new vision of things, this new way of life.

> None of us realize the character of the hidden current, the occult wave, the unseen force, that is driving us forward. Our immediate purpose, our immediate destination, seems small and meagre compared with the driving force to which we are obscurely yielding. We are like somnambulists moving forward together, killing and being killed in a huge world migration from one climate of thought into another.
>
> In the old climate out of which we are moving perforce, whether we respond in blind faith or react in hostile dismay, we can see the wavering lineaments and cloudy shapes of the old totems and taboos that are disappearing. With angry desperation we cling to these fluctuant phan-

toms as they waver and undulate about us while we are swept on.

We ourselves are the dying body that is falling back, relaxed and faint, as the newborn utters its first cries, and we ourselves are the newborn.

Yes, and the more desperately we cling, the more angrily and recklessly we fling our wild accusations and imprecations against this *gravitational ground-tide*, the more surely are we forced on. "Fate leads the willing, drags the unwilling."

We are no longer " on the eve of a great human struggle," as Balzac wrote, we are in the very thick of it. And Powys is right in saying that it is *the human soul* which is in revolt. The soul is sick of this corpse-eating worship of life which humanity has celebrated for the last few thousand years.

There is an American astrologer, Dane Rudhyar, who has written of this change which is coming over us more lucidly and penetratingly than any one I know of. Many of his articles appeared in the columns of a popular magazine devoted to astrology. His books do not have a wide audience. If we were aware, if we were in accord with the deeper movement, we would not banish such a writer to the pages of a cheap magazine. That his name is associated with the " pseudoscience " of astrology is enough to make his utterances suspect. Such is the opinion of educated people—and of the uneducated. I mention him here only to say that he sees the coming age as " The Age of Plenitude." The cup will run over, it will fertilize and invigorate the whole earth, all humanity. The secret forces contained in this " golden vessel " will be the property of all men. The world is not coming to an end, as so many now seem to fear. What is coming to an end are the fetiches, superstitions, bigotries, the sterile forms of worship, the unjust terms of social contract, which have converted the miracle of life into a ceremony of death. We have nothing to lose but the corpse of life. The chains will fall away with the mummy which they hold fast to the earth. The slave does not free himself merely by hacking away the shackles which fetter him. Once his spirit is liberated he is free absolutely—and forever. The putrefaction has to be total before there can be new life. Freedom has to manifest itself at the roots before it can become universal.

America, like Russia, is hastening the process of putrefaction and decomposition. These two great peoples, like busy angel-worms, are tunneling through the very core of the apple in order to bring about, unconscious on their part, the vital transmogrification. All unconsciously, they are utilizing the new forces of life for their own destruction. Europe, ever more conscious of beginnings and ends, is appalled, paralyzed indeed, by the threat of extinction which the play of these slumbering Goliaths represents. Europe is for the conscious preservation of the old—and the timid, cautious trying out of the new. Europe is not a sleepwalker. Europe is a tired old man, weary of wisdom yet unable to show faith. Fear and anxiety are the ruling passions. If America is like a fruit rotting before it has ripened, Europe is like a valetudinarian living in a glass cage. Everything that happens in the outside world is a threat and a menace to this fragile self-made prisoner. This delicate, long-suffering creature has experienced so many upheavals and catastrophes that the very word " revolution," the very idea of an " end," makes it shudder with fright. It does not want to believe that " the winter of life is over." It prefers the freeze to the thaw. No doubt ice too hates to surrender its rigidity. In working its ceaseless transmutations Nature does not ask permission, even of ice, to break it up into fluid elements. And that, I feel, is at the bottom of the terror which has the European in its grip. He is not being asked if he wishes to participate in the new, nameless, terrifying order which is taking possession of the world. " If it is what I sense taking place in Russia," he says, " if it is like what is going on in China or America or India, then I would rather not have it." He is even ready to take his religion seriously, he thinks to himself, if only it will avert the panic in his soul. The idea that the new way of life may be a godless one, the idea that the responsibility may be wrested from God and conferred upon humanity as a whole, only adds to his terror. He sees no cause for rejoicing in the thought that the new dispensation may be man's. He is too human, yet not human enough, to believe that authority should rest with man, especially with " the common man." He has witnessed revolutions from the top and revolutions from the bottom, but no matter how they came about man always revealed himself as a beast. And if you say to him, as Powys does, " Now it

251

is the soul of man which is in revolt !" it is as if you said : " God has become the Fiend of Creation." He can recognize the soul in great works of art, he can detect its stirrings in the deeds of heroes, but he dare not look upon the soul as the autochthonous rebel situated at the very heart of the universe. To him creation is order, and what threatens that order is of the devil. But the soul aims to liberate itself from every thrall, even from the harmony of creation. The soul of art may be defined, but the soul itself remains undefinable. We are not to question the direction it takes, the aims or the tasks it sets itself. We are to obey its dictates.

> But nothing will prevent me from dying of the disease of death, unless I grasp joy . . .
> Unless I put it in my mouth like an eternal food, like a fruit that you crush between your teeth, and its juice gushes deep down in your throat . . .

That is the language of the soul. And this is the language of the soul's own wisdom :

> It is so clear that it takes long to see.
> You must know that the fire which you are seeking
> Is the fire in your own lantern,
> And that your rice has been cooked from the very beginning.

When I came to Europe I was so overjoyed that I had escaped from the homeland that I longed to remain in Europe forever. "This is my place," I said, "here is where I belong." And then I found myself in Greece, which has ever been a little out of Europe, and I thought I would remain there. But life seized me by the scruff of the neck and put me down again in America. Because of that brief sojourn in Greece, because of what happened to me there, I was able to say, truthfully at the time and truthfully still, I think : "I can feel at home anywhere in the world." For a type like myself, the hardest place to feel at home is home. You know that, I guess, and perhaps you understand it. It took me an infinite time to realize that "home" is a condition, a state of mind. I was ever in revolt against places and conditions of being. But when I discovered that "to be at home" was like being with God, the dread which had attached itself to the word fell away. It became my business, or better, *my privilege*, to make myself at home at home. It would have been easier for me to make myself at home anywhere on earth, I think, than here in America. I miss Europe and I yearn for Greece. And I am always dreaming of Tibet. I feel that I am much more than an American ; I feel that I am a good European, a potential Greek, Hindu, Russian, Chinese, and Tibetan too. And when I read of Wales and her twenty thousand years of direct descent from an earlier race of man, I feel like a born Welshman. I feel least of all like an American, though I am probably more an American than anything else. The American in me which I acknowledge and recognize, the American which I salute, if I must put it that way, is the aboriginal being, the seed and the promise, which took shape in "the common man" dedicating his soul to a new experiment, establishing on virgin soil "the city of brotherly love." This is not the man who ran away from something, but the man who ran *towards* something. The man destined no longer to seek but to fulfill himself. Not renunciation, but acceptance.

"What would you say to one who comes to you with nothing ? "
"Throw it away ! "

This "mondo" was used to illustrate the thought that "we must *walk on* even from spiritual poverty if this be used as a means to *grasp* the truth of Zen."

The spiritual poverty of America is perhaps the greatest in the world. It was not assumed to grasp the truth of Zen, that is a certainty. But the *Song of the Open Road* is altogether American, and it was sung by one who was not in any sense of the world impoverished. It sprang from the optimism, from the inexhaustible bounty, I might say, of one who was in complete accord with life. It completes the message of St. Francis of Assisi.

Walk on ! Let go ! Cease squirming!

Lawrence was frightened, nay horrified, to think that this man Whitman, in accepting everything, rejecting *nothing*, lived with *all* his sluices open—like some monstrous creature of the deep. But could there be a more salutary, comforting image than this human net adrift in the stream of life ? Where would you have man anchor ? Where would you have him take root ? Is he not divinely poised—in the eternal flux ?

Is there a road which eventually comes to an end ? Then it is
not the open road.

" We are such stuff as dreams are made of." Aye, and more.
Vastly more. Life is not a dream. Dreams and life intermarry,
and de Nerval has made of this fact the most haunting music. Dream
and dreamer are one. But that is not the all. That is not even
cardinal. The dreamer who knows in his dream that he is dreaming,
the dreamer who makes no divorce between the dreams he dreams
with eyes shut and the dreams he dreams with eyes open is nearer
to the supreme realization. But the one who passes from dream to
life, who ceases to sleep, even in the trance, who dreams no more
because he no longer hungers and thirsts, who remembers no more
because he has arrived at the Source, such a one is an Awakener.

My dear Lesdain, at this point I could conveniently bring my
letter to a close ; it has that " ultimate " ring which means the end.
But I prefer to reopen it and close on a more human and immediate
note.

You remember that I mentioned my Palestinian friend, Bezalel
Schatz, and how I visit him down the road occasionally. The other
day, going to town (Monterey), we fell to discussing the books
we had read and adored in our youth. It was not the first time we
had talked of such things. However, as he began to reel off the
titles of world-famous books which he had read in Hebrew, his
native tongue, I felt that I ought to tell you something of all this,
and through you the world.

I think the first time we opened this subject was when he discovered on my shelf Loti's *Disenchanted*. Beside it was Loti's
Jerusalem, which he had never read, never heard of, and he was
curious about it. You must know, of course, that we have had
many talks about Jerusalem, the Bible—especially the Old Testament—about characters like David, Joseph, Ruth, Esther, Daniel
and so on. Sometimes we spend the whole evening talking about
that strange desolate part of the world in which Mt. Sinai is located ;
sometimes it is about the accursed city of Petra, or about Gaza.
Sometimes it is about the wonderful Yemenite Jews who have in
Yemen (Arabia) one of the most interesting capitals in the world—
San'a. Or it may be about the Jews from Bokhara who settled in

Jerusalem centuries ago and still preserve their original tongue, their manners and customs, their strange head-dress and their wondrous colorful costumes. Sometimes we talk about Bethlehem and Nazareth, which to him are associated with very mundane experiences. Or it may be about Baalbec or Damascus, both of which he has visited.

Eventually we always return to literature. What started us off yesterday was his recollection of the first book he had ever read. And what do you suppose it might have been, considering that his language was Hebrew and his home Jerusalem? I almost fainted away when I heard the name—*Robinson Crusoe*! Another very early one was *Don Quixote*, also read in Hebrew. Everything he read was in Hebrew—until he grew older and learned English, German, French, Bulgarian, Italian, Russian and probably other tongues. (Arabic he knew from childhood. He still swears in Arabic—the richest language in the world for that, he maintains.)

"So *Robinson Crusoe* was the first book you ever read?" I exclaimed. "It came near being the first for me, too."

"What about *Gulliver's Travels*? You must have read that too."

"Of course!" he said, "and Jack London's books—*Martin Eden, The Call of the Wild* . . . all of them. But I remember *Martin Eden* particularly." (So do I. That book stuck long after his others had faded away. Many men have confessed the same to me. It must have struck home!)

Here he began to talk about Mark Twain. He had read quite a few of his books too. That surprised me. I couldn't quite conceive of Mark Twain's quaint, piquant Americanese being rendered in Hebrew. But apparently it had been done successfully.*

Suddenly he said : "But there was one thick book, a very thick book, which I read with sheer delight. I read it two or three times, in fact . . ." He had to rack his brain for the title. "Oh yes—*Pickwick Papers*!" We checked on this and I found that at the very same age I was poring over that book myself. Only *I* never got through it. I didn't like it nearly as well as *David Copperfield, Martin Chuzzlewit*, the *Tale of Two Cities*, or even *Oliver Twist*.

---

* To my astonishment, when speaking of *Babbit* later, he confessed that this book by Sinclair Lewis had given him a better picture of America than any of Mark Twain's. The Stockholm Royal Academy made a similar mistake in awarding the Nobel Prize to Lewis instead of Dreiser.

" And *Alice in Wonderland* ? " I cried. " Did you read that too ? "
He couldn't recall whether he had read it in Hebrew or not,
but he *had* read it, he was certain, though in which language he
couldn't say. (Imagine trying to recall in what language you had
read this unique book !)

We went down the list, the names rolling off our tongues like
maple syrup.

" *Ivanhoe* " ?

" You bet ! *And how !* That was a great book for me. Particularly the picture of Rebecca." I was thinking how strange
indeed must this novel have seemed to a little boy in far-off Jerusalem. I had the strangest feeling of gladness—for Sir Walter Scott,
long dead and no longer concerned as to where his books might
penetrate. I wondered how a boy from Pekin or Canton would
react to this book. (I can never forget that Chinese student I knew
in Paris—Mr. Tcheou, I think it was. One day, upon asking him
if he had ever read *Hamlet*, he answered : " You mean that novel
by Jack London ? ")

Ivanhoe led us into a long detour. We could not help but talk
of Richard the Lion-Hearted and of Saladin. " You're the only
American I ever heard mention Saladin's name," said Schatz.
" Why are you so interested in Saladin ? " I told him. " The Arabs
must have wonderful books about him," he concluded. Yes, I
thought, but where are they ? Why aren't we talking more about
Saladin ? Next to King Arthur, he's the most shining figure I can
think of.

By this time I was prepared for any title he might mention.
It did not surprise me to hear that he had read *The Last of the
Mohicans*, in Hebrew, or *The Arabian Nights* (a condensed version
for children—the only one I ever read !) ; it did not surprise me
any longer to learn that he had read Balzac, d'Annunzio, Schnitzler
(*Fraulein Elsa*), Jules Verne, Zola's *Nana*, *The Peasants* of Reymont,
or even *Jean Christophe*, though I was indeed glad to hear of this
last. (" I congratulate you, Lillik ! That must have been a wonderful experience.") Ah yes, to mention that book is to summon—
for every man and woman—some of the most soul-stirring hours
of youth. Whoever crosses the threshold of youth without having
read *Jean Christophe* has suffered an irreparable loss.

256

" But who wrote that book called *The Red Rose* ? "* he demanded. "It's by a French author, I'm certain." It had made a deep impression on him, apparently.

From this we skipped to *The Mysteries of Paris*, the works of de Maupassant, *Sapho Tartarin de Tarascon* (which he adored), the strange short story or novelette by Tolstoy to which Tolstoy gave two endings. (I know this one too, but I can't recall the title.) And then we came to Sienkiewicz. *That man!* (*That man Lincoln!* as some Southerners still say. Meaning : " That pest ! That impossible person ! ") Yes, no doubt every boy who first comes in contact with this passionate Pole must exclaim : " *That man! That Polish writer!* " What a volcano he was ! So Polish ! If as boys we could have spoken with the tongue of Amiel, might we not have rhapsodized over Sienkiewicz as Amiel did over Victor Hugo ? Do you remember, by chance, this astounding passage from Amiel's *Journal Intime* ? Let me remark, before I quote the passage, that we had been discussing *The Man Who Laughs*, which, if I am not mistaken, makes a more lasting impression on young people than *Les Misérables* . . .

His [Hugo's] ideal is the extraordinary, the gigantic, the overwhelming, the incommensurable. His most characteristic words are *immense, colossal, enormous, huge, monstrous.* He finds a way of making even child-nature extravagant and bizarre. The only thing which seems impossible to him is to be natural. In short, his passion is grandeur, his fault is excess ; his distinguishing mark is a kind of Titanic power with strange dissonances of puerility in its magnificence. Where he is weakest is in measure, taste, and sense of humor : he fails in *esprit*, in the subtlest sense of the word . . . His resources are inexhaustible, and age seems to have no power over him. What an infinite store of words, forms and ideas he carries about with him, and what a pile of works he has left behind him to mark his passage ! His eruptions are like those of a volcano ; and, fabulous workman that he is, he goes on forever raising, destroying, crushing, and rebuilding a world of his own creation, and a world rather Hindoo than Hellenic . . .

By a strange coincidence our talk of books switched to those

* Probably *The Red Lily* of Anatole France.

R

firebrands who sowed the whirlwind—Tamerlane, Genghis Khan, Attila—whose names, I discovered, were as thrilling and terrifying to Schatz as they are to everyone who reads of their bloody deeds. A coincidence, I say, because the only *long* passages I had marked in Amiel were on Hugo and these three scourges. Amiel records that he had been reading *La Bannière Bleue*. " It is a Turk, Ouïgour, who tells the story," he says. He continues thus :

" Genghis proclaimed himself the scourge of God, and he did in fact realize the vastest empire known to history, stretching from the Blue Sea to the Baltic, and from the vast plains of Siberia to the banks of the sacred Ganges." (This is what we had been dis- cussing, the fact that a *Mongol* had achieved this stupendous feat.) . . . " This tremendous hurricane, starting from the high Asiatic table- lands, felled the decaying oaks and worm-eaten buildings of the whole ancient world. The descent of the first yellow, flat-nosed Mongols upon Europe is a historical cyclone which devastated and purified our Thirteenth Century, and broke, at the two ends of the known world, through two great Chinese walls—that which protected the ancient empire of the Center, and that which made a barrier of ignorance and superstition round the little world of Christendom. Attila, Genghis Khan, Tamerlane, ought to range in the memory of men with Caesar, Charlemagne and Napoleon. They roused whole peoples into action, and stirred the depths of human life ; they powerfully affected ethnography, they let loose rivers of blood, and renewed the face of things . . . " A few lines farther, speaking of " the revilers of war [who] are like the revilers of thunder, storms and volcanoes," Amiel declares—and this is a line which must have sunk deep in me, for whenever I encounter it it resounds like a tocsin—"Catastrophes bring about a violent restoration of equilibrium ; they put the world brutally to rights." It is that last phrase which burns and sears : "*They put the world brutally to rights.*"

It is a long cry from Amiel to the Baron Munchausen tales and to Jerome K. Jerome's *Three Men in a Boat* (to say nothing of the dog!). Once again I was bowled over. So in far-off Palestine another young man had laughed himself silly over this stupid bit of humor ! Jerome K. Jerome in Hebrew ! I couldn't get over it. To think

that this atrociously funny book—funny only *once*, however !—
was just as funny in Hebrew !

" You *must* remember . . . please try ! . . . whether you read
Alice in Wonderland in Hebrew."

He tried, but he couldn't. Then, scratching his head, he said :
" Maybe I read it in Yiddish." (Put that in your pipe and smoke it !)

Anyway, suddenly he recalled that the original publisher of
most of these Hebrew translations was " Toshia," somewhere
in Poland. That seemed important to him at the moment. Like
when you suddenly recall not only the title of a child's book but
the feel of the cover, the smell of the paper, the very heft of the
volume.

Then he informed me that practically all the Russian writers
had been translated into Hebrew very early. " The whole works,"
he said. I thought of China, of the days of Sun Yat-sen, when the
same thing happened in that Celestial kingdom. And how, along
with Dostoievsky, Tolstoy, Gorky, Chekov, Gogol and the others,
the Chinese had swallowed Jack London and Upton Sinclair. It
is a wonderful moment in the life of a nation when it is first invaded
by foreign authors. (And to think that little Iceland reads more
authors, in translation, than any country in the world !)

Of course he had also read *The Three Musketeers*, *The Count
of Monte Cristo* and *The Last Days of Pompeii*, as well as *Sherlock
Holmes* and Poe's *The Gold Bug*. Suddenly he gave me another
warm thrill by mentioning Knut Hamsun's name. Yes, he had
read Hamsun, all he could lay hands on, and it was all golden.
(*Pan, Hunger, Victoria, Wanderers, Segelfoss Town, Women at the
Pump* . . .) Some titles he mentioned I had never heard of. A
pang of regret went through me, followed immediately by a touch
of joy, for, thought I to myself, I am still alive, I may yet find the
way to get these unknown books of Hamsun—even if I have to
read them in Norwegian !

" I read a number of authors from the Yiddish too," he suddenly
declared. " Read them in translation. Sholem Aleichem, of course.
But better than Sholem Aleichem, much better, was Mendele
Mocher-Sfarim ! "

" Do you remember Jacob Ben-Ami, the Jewish actor ? " I
asked. " Or Israel Zangwill ? "

"Israel Zangwill!" he exclaimed in amazement.

I told him I had read *Children of the Ghetto* and had seen the dramatization of *The Melting Pot*, of which Theodore Roosevelt was so enamored. He shook his head in amazement.

"I can name one book," I said, "that I bet you never read in Hebrew."

"What's that ?"

"*The Rivet in Grandfather's Neck!*"

"You got me there," he grinned. Then, to get even with me, he countered: "I know one book *you've* never read. It was the most wonderful book of all to me : *Memories of the House of David*. It was in many volumes, eight or ten at least."

"We ought to have a drink on that one," I suggested. But instead we got off on the subject of the "lamedvövnik." According to legend, "there are in the world not less than thirty-six (*lamed-vav*) righteous persons in every generation upon whom the Shekina (God's radiance) rests."

After this detour we came back to a book which he had spoken of several times before and always with the same passionate enthusiasm : *Ingeborg*, by a German named Kellermann. "He also wrote *The Tunnel*, a fascinating thing à la Jules Verne, don't forget that!" he shouted. "Maybe I haven't spelled it right, but it sounds like that—Ingeborg or Ingeburg. It was a love story. And what a love story ! Like that book *She* you're always talking about."

"I'll make a search for it," I promised. "Here, write the name down for me in my notebook." He wrote it down beside *Robinson* "*Kruso*" and "*Baalzac*" and "*Zenkewitz.*" (English spelling still baffles him. There's no logic in it, he insists, and he's damned right.)

"If you ever write anything about all this," he said, "don't overlook Joseph *Flauvius*. It's a thick book about the last days of the Jews . . ."

But it was about *Narcisse et Goldmund*—in Hebrew, of course—that we dwelt on at great length. In English, for some curious reason, it is called *Death and the Lover*. I had come upon this book of Hermann Hesse only a few years ago. It is one of those books which profoundly affect the artist. There is magic in it and great wisdom. "Life wisdom," as D. H. Lawrence would say. It is like a "cadenza" to the metaphysics of art. It is also "a heavenly

discourse" carried on in the lower octaves. It celebrates the pain
and the triumph of art. To my friend Schatz, who had witnessed
the revival of art in Palestine, who had been directly implicated
through his father's activities, it had made an enormous appeal,
naturally. Whoever reads this book must experience in himself a
great revival of the eternal truth of art.

Under the spell of *Narcisse et Goldmund* we rambled on—about
Jerusalem past and present, about the Arabs and how wonderful
they are when you know them intimately, about the banana
grove near Jericho which his father once owned together with
the Grand Mufti, about the Yemenites again and their incomparable
ways, and finally about his father, Boris Schatz, who had founded
the Bezalel School of Arts and Crafts in Jerusalem and who taught
his son all the arts, even as in days of old. Here he repeated the
anecdote about how his father succeeded in getting the first piano
into Palestine. This little story, so picaresque in its details, reminded
me of one of Cendrars' exotic passages (in *Bourlinguer*, I believe)
wherein he describes down to the last detail and with all the resources
of his amazing clavier the thousand and one articles of commerce
(pianos included) which, loaded on the backs of beasts, gods and
men, appeared one day over the ridge of the Andes (he was then
in some remote South American village) and were transported
slowly, tantalizingly, from morning to dusk, to sea level. To me
this passage has the flavor of a mysterious sunburst : the great
burning orb becomes metamorphosed into a huge cornucopia
shedding not heat but an assortment of the most incongruous
objects imaginable, emptied finally by some super-gravitational
Kriss Kringle—in the midst of nowhere !

In all these discussions the magic name for me is Jericho. For
Schatz, Jericho is a beautiful winter resort below sea level, to which
one descends from Jerusalem as on a toboggan slide. For me it is
not only " the walls " and the sound of the trumpet but an inconspicuous village on Long Island, whither, following the Jericho
Turnpike, I would race at top speed from Jamaica in preparation
for a workout with one of the famous six-day bike riders. How
different are the associations of names for different individuals !
I hardly dare tell you, for example, what Schatz associates with
the name Bethlehem. (" Always alive with whores ! ")

One of the lasting impressions I shall retain of Palestine is his story about the man who made Hebrew a living language once again.* Doubtless there is always a "first one" where the revival of a dead language is concerned. But who stops to think of that first man in connection with Basque, Gaelic, Welsh and such weird tongues ? (Perhaps these were never wholly "dead.") However, it was in our own generation that Hebrew was revived—and through the simple act of a man teaching it to his four-year-old son. Unquestionably there had been much *talk* of reviving it before this celebrated moment. It remained, however, for someone to put words into practice. Such an event is always in the nature of a miracle . . .

There is a sequel to this event, a little anecdote which Schatz relates with relish, that I cannot omit. It is about a member of the famous Habima troupe who, arriving for the first time in Palestine, from Russia, where Hebrew was spoken only on the stage (and in the synagogue), suddenly hears the urchins in the street cursing and swearing in the ancient tongue. "Now I *know* that it is a living language !" he exclaimed. I mention this to remark that every time a language is revitalized it is through the adoption and incorporation of the vulgar elements of that tongue. Everything is nourished from the roots.

"Tell me, Lillik," I asked as we were nearing home, "why did your father name his school *Bezalel* ? Did he name it after you or were you named after the school ? "

He laughed. "You know that it means ' in the shadow of God,' of course. But that is merely its literal meaning." He paused and a glowing smile spread over his face. Suddenly he burst into Hebrew. He went on and on—like an incantation it sounded.

"What are you doing ? " I asked.

"I'm reciting some verses from Exodus—*about Bezalel*. He was the first sculptor, didn't you know that ? He was more than that, really. The first *artist*, you might say. Read your Bible ! Find the part about the Ark of the Covenant. It's up your street. It's elaborate, poetic, precise and never-ending . . . "

Next morning I did as he had urged. And the first mention I

---

* Eliezer Ben-Yehuda, who also compiled the first Hebrew dictionary, containing about 50,000 words.

found of our cher Bezaleel was in Chapter 31 of Exodus, which
begins thus :

> And the Lord spake unto Moses, saying,
> See, I have called by name Bezaleel the son of Uri, the son
> of Hur, of the tribe of Judah ;
> And I have filled him with the spirit of God, in wisdom,
> and in understanding, and in knowledge, and in all manner
> of workmanship,
> To devise cunning works, to work in gold, and in silver,
> and in brass,
> And in cutting of stones, to set them, and in carving of
> timber, to work in all manner of workmanship . . .

I read on and on, about the building of the tabernacle, about
the Ark of the testimony, about the altar of burnt offering, about
keeping the Sabbath holy, about the writing of God graven upon
the tables . . . And I came upon the verse in Chapter 35 (Exodus)
which reads : " Take ye from among you an offering unto the
Lord ! whosoever is of a willing heart, let him bring it, an offering
of the Lord ; gold, and silver, and brass, and blue, and purple, and
scarlet, and fine linen, and goat's hair, and rams' skins dyed red,
and badgers' skins, and shittim wood, and oil for the light, and
spices for anointing oil . . . " As I read on and on I got drunk
with the music of the words, for it is indeed intricate and elaborate,
precise and poetic, fugitive and fixed, all this about the cunning
workmanship of Bezaleel and his " collaborators." And as I sat
there deep in reverie, I bethought me how deep was the vision of
Boris Schatz, the father of Bezalel, and with what loving patience,
with what heroic perseverance he labored to make the sons of
Israel capable, wise and cunning in the use of all the crafts, all the
arts, even the art of Juval. I saw that his son had imbibed this
knowledge and wisdom, this ability to devise curious works, even
from the cradle. And I whispered to myself : " Blessed be thy
name, Bezalel, for it is written into the very covenant between us ! "

And now, my dear Pierre Lesdain, this is really the end ! In
journeying back to the early books we have come at last to the
Book of Books, to the Ark and the Covenant. Here let us rest in
peace and contentment.

Your friend,

May 20th, 1950.   HENRY MILLER.

XIII

READING IN THE TOILET

THERE is one theme connected with the reading of books which I think worth dwelling on since it involves a habit which is widespread and about which, to my knowledge, little has been written— I mean, *reading in the toilet*. As a youngster, in search of a safe place wherein to devour the forbidden classics, I sometimes repaired to the toilet. Since that youthful period I have never done any reading in the toilet. Should I be in search of peace and quiet I take my book and go to the woods. I know of no better place to read a good book than in the depths of a forest. Preferably by a running stream.

I immediately hear objections. "But we are not all as fortunate as you ! We have jobs, we travel to and from work in crowded trams, buses, subways ; we have hardly a minute to call our own." I was a "worker" myself right up to my thirty-third year. It was in this early period that I did most of my reading. I read under difficult conditions, always. I remember getting the sack once when I was caught reading Nietzsche instead of editing the mail order catalogue, which was then my job. How lucky I was to have been fired, when I think of it now. Was not Nietzsche vastly more important in my life than a knowledge of the mail order business ?

For four solid years, on my way to and from the offices of the Everlasting Portland Cement Co., I read the "heaviest" books. I read standing up, squeezed on all sides by straphangers like myself. I not only read during these trips on the "El," I memorized long passages from these too-too-solid tomes. If nothing more, it was a valuable exercise in the art of concentration. At this job I often worked late into the night, and usually without eating lunch— not because I wanted to read during my lunch hour but because I had no money for lunch. Evenings, as soon as I had gulped down my meal, I left the house to join my pals. In those years, and for many a year to come, I rarely slept more than four or five hours a night. Yet I did a vast amount of reading. And, I repeat, I read

264

—for me, at least—the most difficult books, not the easiest ones.
I never read to kill time. I seldom read in bed, unless I was indisposed,
or pretending to be ill in order to enjoy a brief vacation. As I look
back it seems to me I was always reading in an uncomfortable position.
(Which is the way most writers write and most painters paint, I
find.) But what I read soaked through. The point is, if I must
stress it, that when I read I read with undivided attention and with
all the faculties I possessed. When I played it was the same thing.

Now and then I would go of an evening to the public library
to read. That was like taking a seat in heaven. Often, on leaving
the library, I would say to myself : " Why don't you do this
oftener ? " The reason I did not, of course, was that life came
between. One often says " life " when one means pleasure or any
foolish distraction.

From what I have gleaned through talks with intimate friends,
most of the reading which is done in the toilet is idle reading. The
digests, the picture magazines, the serials, detective stories, thrillers,
all the tag ends of literature, these are what people take to the
toilet to read. Some, I am told, have bookracks in the toilet. Their
reading matter awaits them, so to speak, as it does in the dentist's
office. Amazing with what avidity people comb through the
" reading matter," as it is called, which is piled high in the waiting
rooms of professional people. Is it to keep their minds off the painful
ordeal ahead ? Or is it to make up for lost time, " to catch up,"
as they say, with current events ? My own limited observations
tell me that these individuals have already absorbed more than
their share of " current events "—i.e. war, accidents, more war,
disasters, war again, murders, more war, suicides, war again, bank
robberies, war, and again war, hot and cold. Undoubtedly these
are the same individuals who keep the radio going most of the day
and night, who go to the movies as often as possible—where they
get more fresh news, more " current events "—and who buy
television sets for their children. All to be informed ! But what
do they really know that is worth knowing about these dreadfully
important, world-shaking events ?

People may insist that they devour the papers or glue their ears
to the radio (sometimes both at once !) in order to keep abreast
of world doings, but that is a sheer delusion. The truth is that the

moment these sorry individuals are not active, not busy, they become aware of an awesome, sickening emptiness in themselves. It doesn't matter much, frankly, on what pap they feed, just ˙o long as they can avoid coming face to face with themselves. To *meditate* on the issue of the day, or even on one's personal problems, is the last thing the normal individual wants to do.

Even in the toilet, where you would think it unnecessary to *do* anything, or to *think* anything, where once during the day at least one is alone with himself and whatever happens happens automatically, even this moment of bliss, for it *is* a minor sort of bliss, has to be broken by concentration on printed matter. Each one, I assume, has his own favorite kind of reading matter for the privacy of the toilet. Some wade through long novels, others read only the fluffiest, flimsiest crap. And some, no doubt, just turn the pages and dream. One wonders—what sort of dreams do they dream? With what are their dreams tinged?

There are mothers who will tell you that only in the toilet do they get the chance to read. Poor mothers! Life is indeed hard on you these days. Yet, compared to the mothers of fifty years ago, you have a thousand times more opportunity for self-development. In your complete arsenal of labor-saving devices you have what was lacking even to the empresses of old. If it was really " time " you were eager to save, in acquiring all these gadgets, then you have been cruelly deceived.

There are the children, of course! When all other excuses fail, there are always—" the children ! " You have kindergartens, playgrounds, baby-sitters, and God knows what all. You give the kids a nap after lunch and you put them to bed as early as you possibly can, all according to approved " modern " methods. *Bref*, you have as little to do with your young as possible. They get eliminated, just like the odious household chores. All in the name of science and efficiency.

("Francais, encore un tout petit effort . . . ! ")

Yes, dear mothers, we know that however much you do there is always more waiting to be done. It is true that your job is never finished. Whose is, I wonder? Who rests on the Seventh Day, except God? Who looks upon his work, when it *is* terminated, and finds it good? Only the Creator, apparently.

I wonder sometimes if these conscientious mothers who are always complaining that their work is never finished (an inverted form of self-praise), I wonder, as I say, do they ever think to take with them to the toilet, not reading matter, but the little jobs which they have left undone ? Or, to put it another way, does it ever occur to them, I wonder, to sit and meditate upon their lot during these precious moments of complete privacy ? Do they ever, in such moments, ask the good Lord for strength and courage to continue in the path of martyrdom ?

How did our poor impoverished and woefully handicapped ancestors ever accomplish all they did, is what I often wonder. Some mothers of old, as we know from the lives of great men, managed to do a powerful lot of reading despite these grave "handicaps." Some of them, it would almost seem, had time for everything. Not only did they take care of their own children, teach them all they knew, nurse them, feed them, clean them, play with them, make their clothes (and sometimes the material too), not only did they wash and iron everybody's clothes, but some at least also managed to give their husbands a hand, especially if they were plain country folk. Countless are the big and little things our forbears did unaided— before ever there were labor-saving devices, time-saving devices, before there were short cuts to knowledge, before there were kindergartens, nurseries, recreation centres, welfare workers, moving pictures and Federal relief bureaus of all kinds.

Perhaps the mothers of our great men were also addicted to reading in the toilet. If so, it is not commonly known. Nor have I read that omnivorous readers—like Macaulay, Saintsbury and Rémy de Gourmont, for example—cultivated this habit. I rather suspect that these Gargantuan readers were too active, too intent on the goal, to waste time in this fashion. The very fact that they were such prodigious readers would indicate that their attention was always undivided. It is true, we hear of bibliomaniacs who read while eating or while walking ; perhaps some have even been able to read and talk at the same time. There is a breed of men who cannot resist reading whatever falls within range of their eyes ; they will read literally anything, even the Lost and Found notices in the newspaper. They are obsessed, and we can only pity them.

A piece of sound advice at this juncture may not be amiss. If

your bowels refuse to function, consult a Chinese herb doctor !
Don't read in order to divert your mind from the business at hand.
What the autonomic system likes, what it responds to, is thorough
concentration, whether upon eating, sleeping, evacuating or what
you will. If you can't eat, can't sleep, it's because something is
bothering you. Something is " on your mind "—where it shouldn't
be, in other words. The same is true of the stool. Rid your mind
of everything but the business at hand. Whatever you do, tackle
it with a free mind and a clear conscience. That's old advice and
sound. The modern way is to attempt several things at one and
the same time, in order " to make the most of one's time," as it is
said. This is thoroughly unsound, unhygienic, and ineffectual.
Easy does it ! " Take care of the little things and the big ones will
take care of themselves." Everyone hears that as a child. Few ever
practice it.

If it is of vital importance to feed body and mind, it is of equal
importance to eliminate from body and mind what has served
the purpose. What is unused, "hoarded," becomes poisonous.
That's plain horse sense. It follows, therefore, as the night the day
that if you go to the toilet to eliminate the waste matter which
has accumulated in your system, you are doing yourself a disservice
by utilizing these precious moments in filling your mind with
"crap." Would you, to save time, think of eating and drinking
while using the stool ?

If every moment of life is so very precious to you, if you insist
on reasoning to yourself that it is no negligible portion of one's life
which is spent in the toilet each day—some people prefer the
" W.C." or " the John " to toilet—then ask yourself when reaching
for your favorite reading matter : " *Do I need this ? Why ?* "
(Cigarette smokers often do just this when trying to break the habit ;
so do alcoholics. It's a stratagem not to be despised.) Supposing—
and this is supposing a good deal !—that you are one who reads
only the "world's best literature" on the stool. Even so, I say it
will pay to ask yourself : " *Do I need this ?* " Let us assume that it is
The Divine Comedy which you are going to resist reading. Suppose
that instead of reading this great classic you meditated on what
little you *had* read of it, or on what you had heard about it. That
would mark a slight improvement. It would be still better, however,

not to meditate on literature at all but simply to keep your mind, as well as your bowels, open. If you must do something, why not offer up a silent prayer to the Creator, a prayer of thanks that your bowels still function ? Think what a plight you would be in if they were paralyzed ! It takes little time to offer up a prayer of this sort, and with it goes the advantage of being able to take Dante out in the sunlight, where you can commune with him on more equal terms. I am certain that no author, not even a dead one, is flattered by associating his work with the drainage system. Not even scatological works can be enjoyed to the fullest in the water closet. It takes a genuine coprophilist to make the most of such a situation.

Having said some harsh things about the modern mother, what of the modern father ? I will confine myself to the American father, because I know him best. This species of pater familias, we know only too well, looks upon himself as a slave-driven, unappreciated wretch. In addition to providing the luxuries, as well as the necessities, of life, he does his utmost to keep to the background as much as possible. Should he have an idle minute or two, he believes it his duty to wash dishes or sing the baby to sleep. Sometimes he feels so driven, so harried, so abused, that when his poor overworked, undernourished, lacklustre wife locks herself in the toilet—or " the John "—for an hour on end he is about ready to break down the door and murder her on the spot.

Let me recommend the following procedure, when such a crisis occurs, to these poor devils who are at a loss to know what their true rôle is. Let us say she has been " in there " a good half hour. She is not constipated, she is not masturbating, and she is not making herself pretty. " *Then what in hell is she doing in there ?* " Careful now ! I know how it is when you get to talking to yourself. Don't let your temper get the best of you. Just try to imagine that, sitting in there on the stool, is the woman you once loved so madly that nothing would do but hitch up with her for life. Don't be jealous of Dante, Balzac, Dostoievsky, if these be the shades she is communicating with in there. " *Maybe she's reading the Bible !* She's been in there long enough to have read the whole of Deuteronomy." I know. I know how you feel. But it's not the Bible she's reading, and you know it. It's probably not *The Possessed* either, nor *Seraphita*, nor Jeremy Taylor's *Holy Living*. Could be *Gone with the Wind*. But what matter ? The thing is—believe me, brother, it's always the thing !—to try a different tack. Try questions and answers. Like this, for example :

"What are you doing in there, *darling* ? "

" Reading."

" *What*, may I ask ? "

" About the Battle of the Marne."

(Pretend not to be fazed by this. Continue !)

" I thought perhaps you were brushing up on your Spanish."

" What was that, dear ? "

" I said—is it a good yarn ? "

" No, it's boring."

" Let me get you something else."

" What's that, dear ? "

" I said—would you like a cool drink while you're wading through that stuff ? "

"What stuff ? "

" The Battle of the Marne."

" Oh, I finished that. I'm on something else now."

" *Darling*, do you need any reference books ? "

" You bet I do. I'd like an abridged dictionary—Webster's, if you don't mind."

" *Mind ?* It's a pleasure. I'll fetch you the unabridged."

" No dear, the abridged will do. It's easier to hold."

(Here run up and down, as if searching for the dictionary.)

" Darling, I can't find either the abridged or the unabridged. Will the encyclopædia do ? What is it you're looking for—a word, a date, or . . . ? "

" *Dearest*, what I'm really looking for is peace and quiet."

" Yes, *dear*, of course. I'll just clear the table, wash the dishes, and put the children to bed. Then if you like I'll read to you. I've just discovered a wonderful book on Nostradamus."

" You're *so* thoughtful, dear. But I'd rather just go on reading."

" Reading *what* ? "

" It's called *The Memoirs of Marshal Joffre*, with a foreword by Napoleon and a detailed study of the major campaigns by a professor of military strategy—they don't give his name !—at West Point. Does that answer your question, dearest ? "

" Perfectly.

(At this point you make for the axe in the woodshed. If there is no woodshed, invent one. Make a noise with your teeth, as if you were grinding the axe—like Minutten in *Mysteries*.)

Here is an alternative suggestion. When she is not looking place a copy of Balzac's *About Catherine de Medici* in the water closet. Put a marker at page 169 and underscore the following passage :

> The Cardinal had just found himself deceived by Catherine. The crafty Italian had seen in the younger branch of the Royal Family an obstacle she could use to check the pretensions of the Guises ; and, in spite of the counsel of the two Gondis, who advised her to leave the Guises to act with what violence they could against the Bourbons, she had, by warning the Queen of Navarre, brought to nought the plot to seize Béarn concerted by the Guises with the King of Spain. As this State secret was known only to themselves and to Catherine, the Princes of Lorraine were assured of her betrayal, and they wished to send her back to Florence ; but to secure proofs of Catherine's treachery to the State—the House of Lorraine was the State—the Duke and Cardinal had just made her privy to their scheme for making away with the King of Navarre.

The advantage of giving her a text like this to wrestle with is that it will take her mind completely off her houshold duties and put her in a frame of mind to discuss history, prophecy or symbolism with you for the rest of the evening. She may even be tempted to read the introduction written by George Saintsbury, one of the world's greatest readers, a virtue or vice which did not prevent him from writing tedious and superfluous prefaces or introductions to other people's works.

I could, of course, suggest other absorbing books, notably one called *Nature and Man*, by Paul Weiss, a professor of philosophy and a logician, not of the first water merely, but of the " waters reglitterized," a ventriloquist able to twist the brains of a rabbinical pundit into a Gordian knot. One can read at random in this work and not lose a shred of his distillated logic. Everything has been predigested by the author. The text is comprised of nothing but pure thought. Here is a sample, from the section on " Inference " :

A necessary inference differs from a contingent one in that the premise alone suffices to warrant the conclusion. In a necessary inference there is only a logical relation between premise and conclusion ; there is no principle which provides content for the conclusion. Such an inference is derivable from a contingent inference by treating the contingent principle as a premise. C. S. Pierce seems to have been the first to discover this truth. ' Let the premises of any argument,' he said, ' be denoted by P, the conclusion by C, and the principle by L. Then if the whole principle be expressed as a premise the argument will become L and P $\therefore$ C. But this new argument must also have its principle which may be denoted by L'. Now, as L and P (supposing them to be true), contain all that is requisite to determine the probable or necessary truth of C, they contain L'. Thus L' must be contained in the principle, whether expressed in the premise or not. Hence every argument has, as portion of its principle, a certain principle which cannot be eliminated from its principle. Such a principle may be termed a *logical principle.*' Every principle of inference, Pierce's observation makes clear, contains a logical principle by which one can rigorously proceed from a premise and the original principle to the conclusion. Any result in nature or mind, therefore, is a necessary consequence of some antecedent and of some course which starts from that antecedent and terminates in that result.*

The reader may wonder why I have not suggested Hegel's *Phenomenology of Mind*, which is the acknowledged cornerstone of the whole nutcracker suite of intellectual hocus-pocus, or Wittgenstein, Korzybski, Gurdjieff & Co. Why not, indeed ! Why not Vaihinger's *Philosophy of As If* ? Or *The Alphabet* by David Diringer ? Why not *The Ninety-Five Theses* of Luther or Sir Walter Raleigh's *Preface to the History of the World* ? Why not Milton's *Areopagitica* ? All lovely books. So edifying, so instructive.

Ah me, if our poor American *pater familias* were to take this problem of reading in the toilet to heart, if he were to give serious thought to the most effective means of breaking this habit, what a list of books might he not devise for a Five-Foot Privy Shelf ! With a little ingenuity he would manage either to cure his wife of the habit or break her mind in the process.

* *Nature and Man*, by Paul Weiss ; Henry Holt & Co., New York, 1947.

If he were truly ingenious he might think up a substitute for this pernicious reading habit. He might, for example, line the walls of the " watterre," as the French call it, with paintings. How pleasant soothing, lenitive and *educational*, while answering the call of Nature, to let the eye roam over a few choice masterpieces of art ! For a starter—Romney, Gainsborough, Watteau, Dali, Grant Wood, Soutine, Breughel the Elder and the Albright brothers. (Works of art, incidentally, are no affront to the autonomic system.) Or, if her taste did not run in these directions, he could line the walls of the " watterre" with *Saturday Evening Post* covers or the covers of *Time*, than which nothing could be more " basic-basic," to use the language of dianetics. Or he might, in his off-moments, busy himself embroidering in many colored silks a quaint motto to be hung at the level of her eyes when she takes her accustomed place in the " watterre," a motto such as : *Home is wherever you hang your hat*. This, since it involves a moral, might captivate her in ways unimaginable. Who knows, it might free her from the cloying clutches of the stool in record time !

At this point I think it important to mention the fact that SCIENCE has just discovered the efficacy, the therapeutic efficacy, of Love. The Sunday supplements are full of this subject. Next to Dianetics, the Flying Saucers and Cybernetics, is is apparently the great discovery of the age. The fact that even psychiatrists now recognize the validity of love gives the stamp of approval which (seemingly) Jesus the Christ, *The Light of the World*, was unable to provide. Mothers, now awakened to this ineluctable fact, will no longer have a problem in dealing with their children, nor, " ipso facto," in dealing with their husbands. Wardens will be emptying the prisons of their inmates : generals will be ordering their men to throw away their arms. The millennium is just around the corner.

Nevertheless, and despite the approach of the millennium, human beings will still be obliged to repair to the water closet daily. They will still be confronted with the problem of how to use the time spent therein most profitably. This problem is virtually a metaphysical one. To give oneself up completely to the emptying of one's bowels would, at first blush, seem the easiest and the most natural thing in the world. To perform this function Nature asks nothing of us but complete abeyance. The only collaboration she

273

demands is the willingness on our part to let go. Evidently the Creator, when designing the human organism, realized that it were better for us if certain functions were allowed to take care of themselves ; it is only too obvious that if such vital functions as breathing, sleeping, defecating were left to our disposition, some of us would cease to breathe, sleep, or go to the toilet. There are plenty of people, and they are not all in the asylum either, who see no reason why we should eat, sleep, breathe or defecate. They not only question the laws which govern the universe, they question the intelligence of their own organism. They ask why, not to know, but to render absurd what is beyond their limited intelligence to grasp. They look upon the demands of the body as so much time wasted. How then do they spend their time, these superior beings ? Are they completely at the service of mankind ? Is it because there is so much " good work " to do that they cannot see the sense of spending time eating, drinking, sleeping and defecating ? It would indeed be interesting to know what these people mean when they speak of " wasting time."

Time, time . . . I have often wondered, if suddenly we were all privileged to function perfectly, what we *would* do with our time. For the moment we think of perfect functioning we can no longer retain the image of society as it is now constituted. We spend the greater part of our life in contending against maladjustments of all sorts ; everything is out of whack, from the human body to the body politic. Assuming the smooth functioning of the human body, with the correlative smooth functioning of the social body, I ask : " What *would* we do with our time ? " To limit the problem for the moment to one phase only—*reading*—try, I beg you, to imagine what books, what sort of books, one would then consider necessary or worth while giving time to. The moment one studies the reading problem from this angle almost the whole of literature falls away. We read now, as I see it, primarily for these reasons : one, to get away from ourselves ; two, to arm ourselves against real or imaginary dangers ; three, to " keep up " with our neighbors, or to impress them, one and the same thing ; four, to know what is going on in the world ; five, to enjoy ourselves, which means to be stimulated to greater, higher activity and richer being. Other reasons might be added, but these five appear to me to be the principal ones—and I have given them in the order of their *current* importance, if I know my fellow man. It does not take much reflection to conclude that, if one were right with himself and all was well with the world, only the last reason, the one which holds least sway at present, would be valid. The others would fade away, because there would be no reason for their existence. And even the last-named, given the ideal conditions mentioned, would have little or no hold over us. There are, and always have been, a few rare individuals who no longer have need of books, not even " holy " books. And these are precisely the enlightened, the awakened ones. They know full well what is going on in the world. They do not regard life as a problem or an ordeal but as a privilege and a blessing. They seek not to fill themselves with knowledge but with wisdom. They are not riddled with fear, anxiety, ambition, envy, greed, hatred or rivalry. They are deeply involved, and at the same time detached. They enjoy everything they do because they participate directly. They have no need to read sacred books or act in a holy way because they see life whole and are themselves thoroughly whole—and thus everything to them is whole and holy.

How do these unique individuals spend their time ?

Ah, there have been many answers given to this query, many. And the reason why there have been many answers is because whoever is able to put such a question to himself has a different type of " unique " individual in mind. Some view these rare individuals as passing their life in prayer and meditation ; some see them moving in the midst of life, performing any and all tasks, but never making themselves conspicuous. But no matter how one looks upon these rare souls, no matter how much or how little disagreement there may be as to the validity or the efficacy of their way of life, one quality these men have in common, one which distinguishes them utterly from the rest of mankind and gives the key to their personality, their raison d'être : *they have all time on their hands !* These men are never in a hurry, never too busy to respond to a call. The problem of time is simply nonexistent for them. They live in the moment and they are aware that each moment is an eternity. Every other type of individual that we know puts limits on his " free " time. These other men have nothing but free time.

If I could give you a thought to take with you daily to the water closet, it would be : " Meditate on free time ! " Should this thought bear no fruit, then go back to your books, your magazines, your newspapers, your digests, your comic strips, your thriller-dillers. Arm yourselves, inform yourselves, prepare yourselves, amuse yourselves, forget yourselves, divide yourselves. And when you have done all these things (including the burnishing of gold, as Cennini recommends), ask yourselves if you are stronger, wiser, happier, nobler, more contented beings. I know you will *not* be, but that is for *you* to discover . . .

It is a curious thing, but the best kind of water closet—according to the medicos—is one in which only an equilibrist could manage to read. I refer to the kind one finds in Europe, France especially, and which makes the ordinary American tourist quail. There is no seat, no bowl, just a hole in the floor with two footpads and a hand-rail on either side for support. One doesn't sit, one squats. (Les vraies chiottes, quoi !) In these quaint retreats the thought of reading never enters one's head. One wants to get done with it as soon as possible—and not get one's feet wet ! We Americans, through disguising whatever has to do with the vital functions, end up by making " the John " so attractive that we linger there long after we have done our business. The combination of toilet-and-bath is to us just ducky. To take a bath in a separate part of the house would strike us as absurd. It might not seem so to people with truly delicate susceptibilities.

Break . . . A few moments ago I was taking a nap outdoors in a heavy fog. It was a light sleep broken by the buzzing of a torpid fly. In one of my fitful starts, half-asleep half-awake, there came to me the remembrance of a dream, or to be exact, the fragment of a dream. It was an old, old dream, and a very wonderful one, which comes back to me—in parts—again and again. At times it comes back so vividly, even though through a chink, that I doubt if it ever was a dream. And then I begin to rack my brain to recall the title of a series of books which I once kept safely hidden away in a little vault. At this present moment the nature and content of this recurrent dream is not as clear as it has been on previous occasions. Nevertheless, the aura of it is still strong, as well as the associations which usually accompany the recall.

A moment ago I was wondering why it was that I thought of
this dream in connection with the toilet, but then suddenly I recalled
that in coming out of my fitful sleep, or half out of it, I brought
with me, so to speak, the frightful odor of the toilet which was
secreted in " the storm shed " at home in that neighborhood which
I always telescope into " the street of early sorrows." In winter
it was a veritable ordeal to take refuge in this air-tight, sub-zero
cubicle which was never illuminated, not even by a flickering wax
taper in sweet oil.

But there was something else which precipitated the remembrance
of these days long past. Just this morning I was glancing over the
index given in the last volume of The Harvard Classics, in order to
refresh my memory. As always, the mere thought of this collection
awakens memories of gloomy days spent in the parlor upstairs
with these bloody volumes. Considering the morose frame of
mind I usually was in when I retreated to this funereal wing of the
house, I cannot help but marvel that I ever waded through such
literature as *Rabbi Ben Ezra*, *The Chambered Nautilus*, *Ode to a Water-
fowl*, *I Promessi Sposi*, *Samson Agonistes*, *William Tell*, *The Wealth
of Nations*, *The Chronicles* of Froissart, John Stuart Mill's *Autobiography* and such like. I believe now that it was not the cold fog
but the leaden weight of those days upstairs in the parlor, when I
was struggling with authors for whom I had no relish, that made
me sleep so fitfully just a little while ago. If so, I must thank their
departed spirits for making me recall this dream which has to do
with a set of magic books I prized so highly that I hid them away—
in a little vault—and never have been able to find them again. Is
it not strange that these books, books belonging to my youth,
should be of more importance to me than anything I have read
subsequently ? Obviously I must have read them in my sleep,
inventing titles, contents, author, everything. Now and then, as
I mentioned before, with flashes of the dream there come sometimes
vivid recollections of the very texture of the narrative. At such
moments I go almost frantic, for there is one book among the series
which holds the clue to the entire work, and this particular book,
its title, contents, meaning, comes at times to the very threshold
of consciousness.

One of the hazier, fuzzier, more tormenting aspects connected

with the recall is that I am always reminded—by whom ? by what ?
—that it was in the neighborhood of Fort Hamilton (Brooklyn)
that I read these magic books. The conviction is forced upon me
that they are still secreted in the house wherein I read them, but
where this house is exactly, whom it belonged to, what business
brought me there, I have not the faintest notion. All that I can
recollect today about Fort Hamilton are the bike rides to and in
the vicinity which I took on lonely Saturday afternoons when
consumed with a forlorn love for my first sweetheart. Like a
ghost on wheels, I covered the same routine trajectory—Dyker
Heights, Bensonhurst, Fort Hamilton—whenever I left the house
thinking of her. So engrossed was I in thoughts of her that I was
absolutely unconscious of my body : I might be hugging the rear
right fender of a car at forty miles an hour or trailing along like
a somnambulist. I can't say that time hung heavy on my hands.
The heaviness was entirely in my heart. Occasionally I would be
roused from my reverie by the whizzing of a golf ball over my
head. Occasionally the sight of the barracks would bring me to,
for whenever I espy military quarters, quarters where men are
herded like cattle, I experience a feeling almost of nausea. But
there were also pleasant intermissions—or "remissions"—if you
like. Always, for instance, when swinging into Bensonhurst where,
as a boy, I had spent such marvelous days with Joey and Tony.
How time had changed everything ! I was now, on these Saturday
afternoons, a young man hopelessly in love, an absolute mooncalf
utterly indifferent to everything else in the world. If I threw myself
into a book it was only to forget the pain of a love which was
too much for me. The bike was my refuge. Astride the bike, I
had the sensation of taking my painful love for an airing. The
panorama which unrolled before me, or receded behind me, was
thoroughly dreamlike : I might just as well have been riding a
treadmill before a stage set. Whatever I looked at served only
to mind me of *her*. Sometimes, in order I suppose not to tumble
off the wheel in sheer despair and chagrin, I would encourage those
fatuous fancies which assail the lovelorn, the wisp of a hope, let
us say, that in making a bend in the road who should be standing
there to greet me—and with such a warm, gracious, lovely smile !
—but *she*. If she failed to "materialize" at this point I would lead

278

myself to believe that it would be at some other point, towards which, with prayers and propitiations, I would proceed to rush full speed, only to arrive there breathless and again deceived.

Undoubtedly the mysterious magical nature of those dream books had to do, and were inspired by, my pent-up longing for this girl I could never catch up with. Undoubtedly, somewhere in the neighbourhood of Fort Hamilton, in brief moments so black, so grief-ridden, so desolate, so uniquely my very own, my heart must have broken again and again. Yet—of this I am certain !—*those books had nothing to do with the subject of love.* They were beyond such . . . such what ? They dealt with unutterable things. Even now, foggy and time-bitten as the dream is in remembrance, I can recall such dim, shadowy, yet revelatory elements as these : a hoary, wizard-like figure seated on a throne (as in ancient stone chess pieces), holding in his hands a bunch of large, heavy keys (like ancient Swedish money), and he resembles neither Hermes Trismegistus nor Apollonius of Tyana, nor even dread Merlin, but is more like Noah or Methuselah. He is trying, it is so clear, to tell me something beyond my comprehension, something I have been longing and aching to know. (A cosmic secret, doubtless.) This figure is out of the key book which, as I have emphasized, is the missing link in the whole series. Up to this point in the narrative, if it may be called that—that is to say, throughout the preceding volumes of the dream collection—it has been a series of unearthly, interplanetary, and, for want of a better word, " forbidden " adventures of the most dazzling variety and nature. As if legend, history and myth, combined with supra-sensual flights beyond description, had been telescoped and compressed into one long sustained moment of godlike fancy. And of course—for my especial benefit ! *But*—what aggravates the situation, in the dream, is that I can always recall the fact that I *did* begin the reading of the missing volume but—ah, think of it !—for no obvious, apparent, or even hidden reason, certainly for no *good* reason, I dropped it. A sense of irreparable loss smothers, literally flattens out, any rising sense of guilt. Why, why, I ask myself, had I not continued the reading of this book ? Had I done so, the book would never have been lost, nor the others either. In the dream the double loss—loss of contents, loss of book itself—is accentuated and presented as one.

There is still another feature connected with this dream : my mother's part in it. In *The Rosy Crucifixion* I have described my visits to the old home, visits made expressly to recover my youthful belongings—particularly certain books which would, for some unaccountable reason, suddenly become on these occasions very precious to me. As I relate it, my mother seems to have taken a perverse delight in telling me that she had " long ago " given these old books away. " *To whom ?* " I would demand, beside myself. She could never remember, it was always so long ago. Or, if she did remember, the brats to whom she had given them had long since moved away, and of course she no longer knew where they lived, nor did she think—and this was ever gratuitous on her part—that they would have kept these childish books all this time. And so on. Some she had given, so she confessed, to the Good Will Society or to the Society of Saint Vincent de Paul. This sort of talk always drove me frantic. Sometimes, in waking moments, I would actually wonder to myself if those missing dream books whose titles had vanished from memory utterly were not real flesh-and-blood books which my mother had thoughtlessly, recklessly given away.

Of course, all the time I was up there in the parlor wading through the dreary five-foot shelf, my mother was just as baffled by this behavior as by everything which it struck me to do. She could not understand how I could " waste " a beautiful afternoon reading those soporific tomes. That I was miserable she knew, but as to why I was miserable she had never the faintest idea. Occasionally she would express the thought that it was the books which depressed me. And of course they did help to depress me more deeply—since they contained no remedy for what ailed me. I wanted to drown myself in my sorrows, and the books were like so many fat, buzzing flies keeping me awake, making my very scalp itch with boredom.

How I jumped the other day when I read in one of Marie Corelli's now forgotten books : " ' Give us something that will endure ! ' is the exclamation of weary humanity. The things we have pass, and by reason of their ephemeral nature are worthless. Give us what we can keep and call our own forever ! ' This is why we try and test all things that *appear* to give proof of the supersensual element in man, and when we find ourselves deceived by impostors

and conjurors, our disgust and disappointment are too bitter to
even find vent in words."

There is another dream, concerning another book, which I tell
of in *The Rosy Crucifixion*. It is a very, very strange dream, and
in it there appears a big book which this girl I loved (the same one !)
and another person (her unknown lover probably) are reading over
my shoulder. It is my own book—I mean a book which I wrote myself.
I mention it only to suggest that by all the laws of logic it *would*
come about that the missing dream book, the key to the whole
series—*what whole series ?*—was written by myself and no other.
If I had been able to write it in a dream why could I not rewrite it in
a waking dream ? Is one state so different from another ? Since I
have ventured to hazard this much, why not complete the thought and
add that my whole purpose in writing has been to clear up a mystery.
(What this mystery is I have never given overtly.) Yes, from the
time I began to write in earnest my one desire has been to unload
this book which I have carried about with me, deep under my belt,
in all latitudes and longitudes, in all travails and vicissitudes. To
dig this book out of my guts, make it warm, living, palpable—that
has been my whole aim and preoccupation . . . That hoary wizard
who appears in onirific flashes hidden away in a tiny vault—a
dream of a vault, you might say—who is he but myself, my most
ancient, ancient self ? He holds a bunch of keys in his hands, does
he not ? And he is situated in the key center of the whole mysterious
edifice. Well, what is that missing book, then, if not "the story of my
heart," as Jefferies so beautifully names it. Is there any other story a
man has to tell but this ? And is this not the most difficult one of all to
tell, the one which is most hidden, most abstruse, most mystifying ?

That we read even in our dreams is a signal thing. What are
we reading, what *can* we be reading in the darkness of unconscious-
ness, save our inmost thoughts ? Thoughts never cease to stir the
brain. Occasionally we perceive a difference between thoughts
and thought, between that which thinks and the mind which is all
thought. Sometimes, as if through a tiny crevice, we catch a glimpse
of our dual self. Brain is not mind, that we may be certain of.
If it *were* possible to localize the seat of mind, then it would be truer
to situate it in the heart. But the heart is merely a receptacle, or
transformer, by means of which thought becomes recognizable and

effective. Thought has to pass through the heart to be made active and meaningful.

There is a book which is part of our being, contained in our being, and is the record of our being. Our being, I say, and not our becoming. We commence the writing of this book at birth and we continue it after death. It is only when we are about to be reborn that we bring it to a close and write " Finis." Thus there is a whole series of books which, from birth to birth, continue the tale of identity. We are all authors, but we are not all heralds and prophets. What we bring to light of the hidden record we sign with our baptismal name, which is never the real name. But it is only a tiny, tiny fraction of the record which even the best of us, the strongest, the most courageous, the most gifted, ever bring to light. What cramps our style, what falsifies the narrative, are those portions of the record which we can no longer decipher. The art of writing we never lose, but what we do lose sometimes is the art of reading. When we encounter an adept in this art the gift of sight is restored to us. It is the gift for interpretation, naturally, for to read is always to interpret.

The universality of thought is supreme and paramount. Nothing is beyond comprehension or understanding. What fails us is the desire to know, the desire to read or interpret, the desire to give meaning to whatever thought be voiced. *Acedia :* the great sin against The Holy Ghost. Drugged by the pain of deprivation, in whatever form it manifests itself, and it assumes many, many forms, we take refuge in mystification. Humanity is, in the deepest sense, an orphan—not because it has been *abandoned*, but because it obstinately refuses to recognize its divine parentage. We terminate the book of life in the afterworld because we refuse to understand what we have written here and now . . .

But let us return to *les cabinets*, which is the French for toilet and, for some baffling reason, used always in the plural. Some of my readers may recall a passage, one in which I give tender reminiscences of France, concerning a hurried visit to the toilet and the wholly unexpected view of Paris which I had from the window of this tight place.* Would it not be fetching, some people think,

---

* See the chapter called " Remember to Remember " from my book, *Remember to Remember* ; New Directions, New York.

to so build one's home that from the toilet seat itself one could command a breath-taking panorama ? My thought is that it does not matter in the least what the view from the toilet may be. If, in going to the toilet, you have to take something else with you besides yourself, besides your own vital need to eliminate and cleanse the system, then perhaps a beautiful or a breath-taking view from the toilet window is a desideratum. In that case you may as well build a book shelf, hang paintings, and otherwise beautify this *lieu d'aisance*. Then, instead of going outdoors and seeking a bo-tree, one may as well sit in " the bathroom " and meditate. If necessary, build your whole world around " the John." Let the rest of the house remain subordinate to the seat of this supreme function. Bring forth a race which, highly conscious of the art of elimination, will make it its business to eliminate all that is ugly, useless, evil and " deleterious " in everyday life. Do that and you will raise the toilet to a heavenly place. But do not, while making use of this sacred retreat, waste your time reading *about* the elimination of this or that, nor even about elimination itself. The difference between the people who secrete themselves in the toilet, whether to read, pray or meditate, and those who go there only to do their business, is that the former always find themselves with unfinished business on hand and the latter are always ready for the next move, the next act.

The old saying is : " Keep your bowels open and trust in the Lord ! " There's wisdom in it. Broadly speaking, it means that if you keep your system free of poison you will be able to keep your mind free and clear, open and receptive ; you will cease worrying about matters which are not your concern—such as how the cosmos should be run, for example—and you will do what has to be done in peace and tranquillity. There is no hint or suspicion contained in this homely piece of advice that, in keeping your bowels open, you should also struggle to keep up with world events, or keep abreast of current books and plays, or familiarize yourself with the latest fashions, the most glamorous cosmetics, or the fundamentals of basic English. Indeed, the whole implication of this curt maxim is—the less done about it the better. I say " it," meaning the very serious—and neither absurd nor disgusting—business of going to the toilet. The key words are " open " and " trust." Now, if it be argued that to read while sitting on the stool is an aid to loosening the bowels, then I say—read the most lenitive literature possible. Read the Gospels, for the Gospels are of the Lord—and the second injunction is " to trust in the Lord." Myself, I am convinced that it is possible to have faith and trust in the Lord without reading Holy Writ in the toilet. Indeed, I am convinced that one is apt to have more faith and trust in the Lord if one reads nothing at all in the toilet.

When you visit your analyst does he ask you what you read when using the stool ? He should, you know. To an analyst it should make a great difference whether you read one kind of literature in the toilet and another elsewhere. It should even make a difference to him whether you read or do not read—in the toilet. Such matters are unfortunately not widely enough discussed. It is assumed that what one does in the toilet is one's own private affair. It is not. The whole universe is concerned. If, as we are led to believe more and more, there are creatures from other planets who are keeping tabs on us, be certain that they are prying into our most secret doings. If they are able to penetrate the atmosphere of this earth, what is to stop them from penetrating the locked doors of our toilets ? Give that a thought when you have nothing better to meditate upon—in there. Let me urge those who are experimenting with rockets and other interstellar means of communication and transportation to think for a brief moment of how they must appear to the denizens of other worlds when reading *Time* or *The New Yorker*, let us say, in " the John." What you read tells a good deal about your inmost being, but it does not tell everything. The fact, however, that you are *reading* when you should be *doing* has a certain importance. It is a characteristic which men alien to this planet would remark immediately. It might well influence their judgment of us.

And if, to change the tune, we limit ourselves to the opinion of merely terrestrial beings, but beings who are alert and discriminating, the picture does not alter much. There is not only something grotesque and ridiculous about poring over the printed page while seated on the stool, there is something mad about it. This pathological element evinces itself clearly enough when reading is combined with eating, for example, or with taking a promenade. Why is it not equally arresting when we observe it connected with the act of defecation ? Is there anything natural about doing these two things simultaneously ? Supposing that, though you never intended to become an opera singer, every time you went to the toilet you began practicing the scales. Supposing that, though singing was all in all to you, you insisted that the only time you could sing was when you went to "the John." Or supposing you simply said that you sang in the toilet because you had nothing better to do. Would that hold water in an alienist's cabinet ? But this is the sort of alibi people give when they are pressed to explain why they *must* read in the toilet.

To merely open the bowels, then, is not enough ? Must one include Shakespeare, Dante, William Faulkner and the whole galaxy of pocket-book authors ? Dear me, how complicated life has become ! Once upon a time any old place would do. For company one had the sun or the stars, the song of the birds or the hooting of an owl. There was no question of killing time, nor of killing two birds with one stone. It was just a matter of letting go. There wasn't even the thought of trust in the Lord. This trusting in the Lord was so implicit a part of man's nature that to connect it with the movement of the bowels would have seemed blasphemous and absurd. Nowadays it takes a higher mathematician, who is also a metaphysician and an astrophysicist, to explain the simple functioning of the autonomic system. Nothing is simple any more. Through analysis and experiment the slighest things have assumed such complicated proportions that it is a wonder any one can be said to know anything about anything. Even instinctive behavior now appears to be highly complex. Primitive emotions, such as fear, hate, love, anguish, all prove to be terribly complex.

And we are the people, heaven forbid, who in the next fifty years are going to conquer space ! We are the creatures who, though scorning to become angels, are going to develop into interplanetary beings ! Well, one thing is certainly predictable : even out there in space we shall have our water closets ! Wherever we go, "the John " accompanies us, I notice. Formerly we used to ask : " What if cows could fly ? " That joke has become antediluvian. The question which now imposes, in view of projected voyages beyond the gravitational pull, is : " How will our organs function when we are no longer subject to the sway of gravity ? " Traveling at a rate faster than the speed of thought—it has been hazarded that we may be able to accomplish this !—will we be able to read at all out there between the stars and planets ? I ask because I assume that the model space ship will be equipped with lavatories as well as laboratories, and, if so, our new time-space explorers will undoubtedly bring with them their toilet literature.

There is something to conjure upon—the nature of this interspatial literature ! We used to see questionnaires from time to time demanding to know what we would read if we were going to take refuge on a deserted island. No one, to my knowledge, has yet framed a questionnaire as to what would make good reading on the stool in space. If we are going to get the same old answers to this coming questionnaire, i.e., Homer, Dante, Shakespeare, et Cie, I shall indeed be cruelly disappointed.

That first ship to leave the earth, and possibly never return—what I would not give to know the titles of the books it will contain ! Methinks the books have not been written which will offer mental, moral and spiritual sustenance to these daring pioneers. The great possibility, as I see it, is that these men may not care to read at all, not even in the toilet : they may be content to tune in on the angels, to listen to the voices of the dear departed, to cock their ears to catch the ceaseless celestial song.

XIV

THE THEATRE

Drama is the one category of literature into which I have delved more than any other. My passion for the theatre goes so far back that it almost seems as if I were born backstage. From the age of seven I started going to the vaudeville house called The Novelty, on Drigg's Avenue, Brooklyn. I always went to the Saturday matinée. And alone. The price of admission to " nigger heaven " was then a dime. (It was the golden period when you really could get a good cigar for ten cents.) The doorman, Bob Maloney, an ex-pugilist with the broadest, squarest shoulders I have ever seen, stood guard over us with a stout rattan stick. I remember this individual better than any of the acts or actors I saw there. He was the villain who dominated my troubled dreams.

The first play I was taken to was *Uncle Tom's Cabin*. I was just a tiny tot and, as I recall it, the play made no impression upon me whatever. I do, however, recall that my mother wept copiously throughout the performance. My mother loved these tear jerkers. I don't know how many times I was dragged to see *The Old Homestead* (with Denman Thompson), *Way Down East*, and similar favorites.

There were two other theatres in this neighbourhood (The Fourteenth Ward) to which I was also taken by my mother at intervals : The Amphion and Corse Payton's. Corse Payton, often referred to as " the worst actor in the world," put on melodramas of the ten-twenty-thirty variety. Years later my father and he became drinking companions, something no one would have dreamed of in the days when Corse Payton's name was a byword throughout Brooklyn.

The first play to make an impression on me—I wasn't more than ten or eleven at the time—was *Wine, Woman and Song*. It was a jolly, bawdy performance, featuring the diminutive Lew Hearn and the ravishing Bonita. As I see it now, it must have been a glorified

burlesque show. ("Wer liebt nicht Wein, Weib und Gesang,
bleibt ein Narr sein Leben lang.") The most astonishing thing
connected with this event is that we occupied a box all to ourselves. The theatre, which I doubt if I ever entered again—it
reminded me somehow of an old French fortress—was called The
Folly, and stood at the corner of Broadway and Graham Avenue,
Brooklyn, of course.

By this time we had shifted from the glorious Fourteenth Ward
to the Bushwick Section ("The Street of Early Sorrows"). A little
distance from us, in the neighbourhood called East New York,
where everything seemed to come to a dead end, a stock company
gave performances in a theatre called The Gotham. Once a year
somewhere in this dismal vicinity Forepaugh & Sells spread their
huge circus tents. Not very far away were a Chinese cemetery, a
reservoir and a skating pond. The only play I seem to recall from
this no man's land is *Alias Jimmy Valentine*. But I undoubtedly saw
there such monstrosities as *Bertha, The Sewing Machine Girl* and
Nellie, the Beautiful Cloak Model. I was still going to grammar
school. The life of the open street was vastly more exciting to me
than the claptrap reality of the theatre.

It was during this period, however, in vacation time, that I would
visit my cousin in Yorkville where I was born. Here in the summer
evenings over a pint of ale my uncle would regale us with memories
of the theatre of his day. (*The Bowery After Dark* was probably still
running.) I can still see my uncle, a fat, lazy, jovial man with a
strong German accent, sitting at the bare round table in the kitchen,
always in a fireman's undershirt. I can see him spreading the
programs out—they were the long playbills printed on newspaper
stock, even then yellow with age, which were handed out at the
gallery entrances. Fascinating as were the names of the plays, the
names of the players were even more so. Such names as Booth,
Jefferson, Sir Henry Irving, Tony Pastor, Wallack, Ada Rehan,
Réjane, Lily Langtry, Modjeska, still ring in my ears. They were
the days when the Bowery was all the rage, when Fourteenth
Street was in its heyday, and when the great stage figures were
imported from Europe.

Every Saturday night, so my uncle said, he and my father used
to go to the theatre. (A pattern I was soon to follow with my

288

Henry Miller as a boy with his Parents and Sister

buddy, Bob Haase.) It seemed almost incredible to me, because from the time I came into the world my father had nothing more to do with that world. My uncle neither, for that matter. I mention this fact to emphasize my astonishment when one day, while working part-time for my father at the tailor shop—I was then about sixteen—he asked me if I would like to accompany him to the theatre that evening. Major Carew, one of his cronies from the Wolcott Bar, had bought tickets for a play called *The Gentleman from Mississippi*. He had suggested taking me along because of an actor whom he thought I would enjoy seeing, an actor who was just coming into prominence, and who was none other than Douglas Fairbanks. (Thomas Alfred Wise, of course, played the leading rôle.) But what was more thrilling to me than the prospect of seeing Douglas Fairbanks was the fact that I was about to enter a New York theatre for the first time, and in the evening ! Strange company to be in, too, my father and the dissolute Major Carew, who, from the time he arrived in New York, was never sober for an instant. It was only years later that I realized I had seen Douglas Fairbanks in his greatest stage success.

That same year, in company with my German teacher from High School, I made my second visit to a New York playhouse—the Irving Place Theatre. It was to see *Alt Heidelberg*. That event, which stands out in my mind as a thoroughly romantic one, for some strange reason, was soon overshadowed by my initiation into burlesque. I was still going to High School when an older boy (from the old Fourteenth Ward) asked me one day if I would not like to go with him to The Empire, a new burlesque theatre in our neighborhood. Fortunately I was already wearing long pants, though I doubt if my beard had yet begun to sprout. That first burlesque show I shall never forget.* From the moment the curtain rose I was trembling with excitement. Until then I had never seen a woman undressed in public. I had seen pictures of women in tights from childhood, thanks to Sweet Caporal cigarettes, in every package of which there used to be a little playing card featuring one of the famous soubrettes of the day. But to see one of these creatures *in life* on the stage, in the full glare of a spotlight, no, that I had never dreamed of. Suddenly I recalled the little theatre in

* *Krausemeyer's Alley*, with Sliding Billy Watson.

289

T

the old neighborhood, on Grand Street, called The Unique, or as *we* called it, " The Bum." Suddenly I saw again that long Saturday night queue outside, pushing and milling around to squeeze through the door and catch a glimpse of that naughty little soubrette, Mlle. de Leon (*we* called her *Millie* de Leon), the girl who flung her garters to the sailors at each performance. Suddenly I recalled those lurid billboards that flanked the entrance to the theatre, showing ravishing female figures of luxurious heft displaying all their billowy, sinuous curves. At any rate, from that momentous day when I first visited The Empire I became a devotee of burlesque. Before long I knew them all—Miner's on the Bowery, The Columbia, The Olympic, Hyde & Beeman's, The Dewey, The Star, The Gayety, The National Winter Garden—all of them. Whenever I was bored, despondent, or pretending to search for work, I headed either for the burlesque or the vaudeville house. Thank God, there were such glorious institutions in those days ! Had there not been, I might have committed suicide long ago.

But speaking of billboards . . . One of the strange recollections I have of this period is of passing a billboard announcing the play *Sapho*. I remember it for two reasons : first, because it was posted on the fence next to the old house where I knew my best days— shockingly close, so to speak—and second, because it was a lurid poster, openly revealing a man in the act of carrying a woman, clad only in a thin nightgown, up a long flight of stairs. (The woman was Olga Nethersole.) I knew nothing then of the scandal which the play had roused. Neither did I know that it was the dramatization of Daudet's famous book. I didn't read *Sapho* until I was eighteen or nineteen ; as for the celebrated Tartarin books, I must have been well in my twenties before I came upon them.

One of the most beautiful souvenirs of the theatre which I retain is the memory of the day my mother took me to the open air casino in Ulmer Park. Though it is highly improbable, I still have the notion that it was Adeline Patti I heard sing that day. At any rate, for a mere lad of eight or nine, just getting ready to witness the turn of the century, it was like a trip to Vienna. In " the good old summer time " it was, of a day so spankingly bright and gay that even a dog would remember it. (Poor Balzac, how I pity you, you who con- fessed that you had known only three or four happy days in all your life !) On this golden day even the awnings and parasols were brighter and gayer than ever before. The little round table at which we sat, my mother, sister and I, danced with golden reflections cast by brimming steins and mugs, by long slender glasses of Pilsener, by brooches, earrings, laveliers, lorgnettes, by gleaming belt buckles, by heavy gold watch chains, by a thousand and one trinkets so dear to the men and women of that generation. What good things there were to eat and drink ! And the program—so lively, so scintillating ! All headliners, doubtless. I couldn't get over the fact that boys my own age, or so it seemed, dressed in swaggering costumes, were employed to come out after each act and walk across the entire length of the stage—just to post the next number at each wing. They did it bowing and smiling. Very important adjuncts. The waiters, too, intrigued me, the way they balanced the heavy trays, the lightning-like way they made change, and with it all so polite, so cheerful, so utterly at ease. The whole atmosphere of the place was decidedly Renoir.

As soon as I was old enough to go to work—I started at seventeen —there began those wonderful Saturday afternoon and evening sprees at the beaches. Irene Franklin (" Red Head ") at the Brighton Beach Music Hall, another open-air theatre, stands out prominently in my memory. But more vivid still is the remembrance of an unknown zany who was then making " Harrigan " famous. It was again a hot day, with a beautiful breeze coming from the ocean, and I had on a new straw hat with a large polka dot band. To enjoy the song and dance cost only ten cents. But what I can't forget is the enclosure itself, a circular tier of benches exposed to the sky and hardly big enough for a monkey to do his stunts in. Here, on a rude, springy platform, this unknown minstrel gave one performance after another—from noon to midnight. I went back to hear him several times that day. I went back expressly to hear him sing :

> H . . . A . . . dooble R . . . I
> G . . . A . . . N spells Harrigan
> Divil a man can say a word agin me . . .

And so on. Ending with—

It's a name that a shame
Never has been connected with
Harrigan ! that's me !

Why this ditty should have infatuated me I don't know.
Undoubtedly it was the poor fried songbird, the vitality of the
man, the leer and flimflam, the delicious brogue he had, plus the
torture he was suffering.

A strange and roseate period, the turn of the century that refused
to come to an end. The Edison phonograph, Terry McGovern,
William Jennings Bryan, Alexander Dowie, Carrie Nation, Sandow
the Strong Man, Bostock's Animal Show, Mack Sennett comedies,
Caruso, Little Lord Fauntleroy, Houdini, Kid McCoy, the Hallroom
Boys, Battling Nelson, Arthur Brisbane, the Katzenjammer Kids,
Windsor McKay, the Yellow Kid, *The Police Gazette*, the Molineaux
Case, Theda Bara, Annette Kellerman, *Quo Vadis*, The Haymarket,
Ben Hur, Mouquin's, Considine's, *Trilby*, *David Harum*, *Peck's Bad
Boy*, the Gilsey House, the Dewey Theatre, Stanford White, the
Murray Hill Hotel, Nick Carter, Tom Sharkey, Ted Sloan, Mary
Baker Eddy, the Gold Dust Twins, Max Linder, *In the Shade of
the Old Apple Tree*, the Boer War, the Boxer Rebellion, " Remem-
ber the Maine," Bobby Walthour, Painless Parker, Lydia Pinkham,
Henry Miller in *The Only Way* . . .

When and where I first saw *Charley's Aunt* I no longer remember.
I know only this, that it remains in my mind as the funniest play
I ever saw. Not until the movie called *Turnabout* did I see anything
to make me laugh as hard. *Charley's Aunt* is one of those plays
which hit you below the belt. There's nothing you can do but
succumb to it. It has been playing off and on now for over fifty
years, and I presume it will go on being played for another fifty
years to come. No doubt it is one of the worst plays ever written,
but what matter ? To keep an audience in stitches for three full
acts is a feat. What amazes me is that the author, Brandon Thomas,
was British. In Paris, years later, I discovered a theatre on the
Boulevard du Temple—*Le Déjazet*—which specialized in broad,
sidesplitting farces. In this old barn of a place I had more belly
laughs than in any theatre except the famous Palace Theatre on
Broadway—" the home of vaudeville."

From the time I began going to High School until I was twenty or so I went regularly every Saturday night with my chum, Bob Haase, to the Broadway Theatre, Brooklyn, where the hits from the Manhattan stage would be shown after they had had their run. We usually stood up in the back of the orchestra. In this way I saw at least two hundred plays, among them such as *The Witching Hour*, *The Lion and the Mouse*, *The Easiest Way*, *The Music Master*, *Madame X*, *Camille*, *The Yellow Ticket*, *The Wizard of Oz*, *The Servant in the House*, *Disraeli*, *Bought and Paid For*, *The Passing of the Third Floor Back*, *The Virginian*, *The Man from Home*, *The Third Degree*, *Damaged Goods*, *The Merry Widow*, *The Red Mill*, *Sumurun*, *Tiger Rose*. My favorites then, among the stars, were Mrs. Leslie Carter, Lilly Maddern Fiske, Leonore Ulric, Frances Starr, Anna Held. Quite a motley company!

As soon as I started going to the New York theatres I branched out in all directions. I frequented all the foreign theatres as well as the little theatres, such as the Portmanteau, the Cherry Lane, The Provincetown, the Neighborhood Playhouse. And of course I went to the Hippodrome, the Academy of Music, the Manhattan Opera House and the Lafayette in Haarlem. I saw Copeau's group a number of times, at the Garrick, and the Moscow Art Players and the Abbey Theatre Players.

Curiously enough, a performance which stands out in my memory is that given by an unprofessional group, all youngsters, at the Henry Street Settlement. I was invited to attend the performance (an Elizabethan play) by a messenger then working for me at the telegraph company. He had only lately been released from prison, where he had served sentence for robbing a small post office in the South of a few stamps. To see him in doublet and hose—he played the leading rôle—declaiming with grace and distinction—was a most pleasurable shock. The whole evening stands out in my mind in much the same way as does the magical scene in Fournier's *The Wanderer* which I have mentioned so often. Time and again I went back to the Henry Street Settlement hoping to relive the enchantment of that first evening, but such things happen only once in a lifetime. Not so far away, on Grand Street, was the Neighborhood Playhouse which I visited frequently and where—another memorable occasion!—I saw Joyce's *Exiles* performed.

Whether it was the period or because I was young and impressionable, many of the plays I saw during the Twenties are unforgettable. I will mention just a few : *Androcles and the Lion, Cyrano de Bergerac, From Morn till Midnight, Yellow Jacket, The Playboy of the Western World, Him, Lysistrata, Francesca de Rimini, Gods of the Mountain, The Boss, Magda, John Ferguson, Fata Morgana, The Better 'Ole, Man of the Masses, Bushido, Juno and the Paycock.*

In the early days of The Deepthinkers and the Xerxes Society* I had the good fortune to be invited by a pal of mine to the " best " theatres, where we occupied " choice seats." My friend's boss was an inveterate theatre-goer. He had plenty of money and he enjoyed indulging his every whim. Sometimes he invited the whole gang of us—twelve healthy, jolly, rowdy, lusty youngsters—to accompany him to a "good show." If he got bored he would leave in the middle of the performance and go to another theatre. It was through him that I saw Elsie Janis, our great idol, for the first time, and also that little queen, Elsie Ferguson—" *Such a Little Queen !* " Bonnie days they were. Not only the best seats in the house but afterwards a cold snack at Reisenweber's, Bustanoby's or Rector's. Trotting from place to place in horse cabs. Nothing was too good for us. " Ah ! never to be forgotten days ! "

At the tailor shop, when I took to working full time for the old man—a sudden switch from the Savage School where I was training to become an athletic instructor (sic !)—I made the acquaintance of another wonderful prince, the eccentric Mr. Pach of Pach Brothers, photographers. This lovable old man never handled money. Everything he desired he got through barter, including the use of a car and a chauffeur. He had connections and affiliations everywhere, it seemed, not least of them being with the directors of the Metropolitan Opera, Carnegie Hall and such places. The result was that whenever I wished to attend a concert, an opera, a symphonic recital or a ballet, I had only to telephone old man Pach, as we called him, and a seat was waiting for me. Now and then my father made him a suit of clothes or an overcoat. In return we received photographs, all sorts of photographs, oodles of them. And so, in this peculiar way—rather miraculous to me !—I heard

* See *Plexus*, Book Two of *The Rosy Crucifixion*, for a full picture of these clubs which played such an important part in my early life.

in the space of a few years virtually everything of note in the realm of music. It was an invaluable education, worth far more than all the other pedagogic rigmarole I was put through.

As I said a while ago, I believe I have read more plays than novels or any other form of literature. I began this reading of plays via *The Harvard Classics*, that five-foot shelf recommended by old Dr. Foozlefoot Eliot. First ancient Greek drama, then Elizabethan drama, then Restoration and other periods. The real impetus, however, as I have remarked a number of times, was given me by Emma Goldman through her lectures on the European drama, in San Diego, back in 1913. Through her I launched heavily into Russian drama, which, with ancient Greek drama, I feel most at home in. The Russian drama and the Russian novel I took to with the same ease and sense of familiarity as I did Chinese poetry and Chinese philosophy. In them one always finds reality, poetry and wisdom. They are earth-bound. But the dramatists I envy, the ones I would imitate if I could, are the Irish. The Irish playwrights I can read over and over again, without fear of satiation. There is magic in them, together with a complete defiance of logic and a humor altogether unique. There is also darkness and violence, to say nothing of a natural gift for language which no other people seem to possess. Every writer employing the English language is indebted to the Irish. Through them we get glimmerings of the true language of the bards, now lost except for a remote corner of the world such as Wales. Once having savored the Irish writers, all other European dramatists seem pale and feeble in their expression. (The French more than any, perhaps.) The one man who still comes through, in translation, is Ibsen. A play like *The Wild Duck* is still dynamite. Compared to Ibsen, Shaw is just "a talking fool."

Aside from a few performances I attended during a short visit to America from France—*Waiting for Lefty*, *The Time of Your Life*, *Awake and Sing !* — I have not been to the theatre since that memorable production of Hamsun's *Hunger* (with Jean-Louis Barrault) given in Paris in 1938 or '39. It was rendered in expressionistic manner, à la Georg Kaiser, and remains a worthy end to my theatre-going days. Today I have not the least desire to enter a theatre. Finished, the whole business. I would rather see a second-rate movie than a play, though I must confess that the movies too have lost their hold over me.

It may seem strange that, despite my great interest in the theatre, I have never written a play. I tried my hand at it once, many years ago, but got no farther than the second act. It was obviously more important then for me to *live* the drama than to give expression to it. Besides, it is probably true that I have no talent in this direction, which I regret.

But even if I no longer go to the theatre, even if I have abandoned all thought of writing for the theatre, the theatre remains for me a realm of pure magic. In potency, the Elizabethan drama—excluding Shakespeare whom I cannot abide—ranks second only to the Bible. *For me.* Often in my mind I have compared this period with the age which produced the great Greek dramatists. What never fails to impress me is the utter contrast, in language, between these two periods of drama. The Greek is simple, straightforward language, understandable to anyone of intelligence ; the Elizabethan language is tumultuous and unbridled, meant for poets, though the audience (of that day) was largely made up of the mob. In Russian drama we again have the simplicity of the Greeks ; the machinery, however, is of another order.

What all good drama has in common, I find, is its readability. And this is the drama's supreme defect. The drama to come will lack this virtue. As " literature " it will be almost meaningless. The drama has yet to come into its own. And this cannot come about until the structure of our society is radically, fundamentally altered. Antonin Artaud, the French poet, actor, playwright, had illuminating ideas on this subject, some of which he exposed in a tract called *Le Théatre de la Cruauté.** What Artaud proposed was a new kind of participation by the audience. But this we shall never have until the whole conception of " theatre " is transformed.

Books tend to separate, the theatre to unite us. The audience,

* " Mais, et c'est ici la nouveauté, il y a un côté virulent et je dirai même dangéreux de la poésie et de l'imagination à retrouver. La poésie est une force dissociative et anarchique, qui par l'analogie, les associations, les images, ne vit que d'un bouleversement des rapports communs. Et la nouveauté sera de bouleverser ces rapports non seulement dans le domaine extérieur, dans le domaine de la nature, mais dans le domaine intérieur, c'est à dire, dans celui de la psychologie. Comment, c'est mon secret." (Antonin Artaud, in " Comoedia," September 21, 1932.)

like jelly in the hands of a capable playwright, never knows greater solidarity than during the brief hour or two which it takes to give a performance. Only during a revolution is there anything comparable to this togetherness. Used rightly, the theatre is one of the greatest weapons in the hands of man. That it has fallen into a state of decay is but another sign of the degenerate times. When the theatre lags it means that life is at a low ebb.

To me the theatre has always been like a bath in the common stream. To experience emotion in the company of a crowd is indeed tonic and therapeutic. Not only are the thoughts, deeds and personages materialized before one's eyes, but the effluvium in which all swims also envelops the audience. In identifying themselves with the players, the spectators re-enact the drama in their own minds. An invisible super-director is at work. Moreover, in each spectator there is another, unique drama going on parallel with the one which he is witnessing. All these reverberative dramas coalesce, heighten the visible, audible one, and charge the very walls with a psychic tension which is incalculable and, at times, almost unbearable.

Even to become acquainted with one's own language it is necessary to frequent the theatre. The talk of the boards is of a different order from the talk of books or the talk of the street. Just as the most indelible writing belongs to the parable, so the most indelible speech belongs to the theatre. In the theatre one hears what one is always saying to oneself. We forget how much silent drama we enact every day of our lives. What issues from our lips is infinitesimal compared to the steady stream of recitative which goes on in our heads. Similarly with deeds. The man of action, even the hero, lives out in deed but a fraction of the drama which consumes him. In the theatre not only are all the senses stimulated, enhanced, exalted, but the ear is tuned, the eye trained, in new ways. We are made alert to the unfailing significance of human actions. Everything which occurs on the stage is focused, as if through a distorting lens, to meet the angle of expectation. We not only sense what is called destiny, we experience it individually, each in his own way. In that narrow strip beyond the footlights we all find a common meeting place.

When I think of the numerous performances I have attended, and

297

in so many different tongues, when I think of the strange neighbor-
hoods in which these theatres were located and of my journeys
homeward, often on foot, often through bitter gales or through
slush and mud, when I think of the truly extraordinary personalities
that impinged on my being, of the multitudinous ideas which I
experienced vicariously, when I think of the problems of other
epochs, other peoples, and of the magical and mysterious denominator
which permitted me to grasp them and suffer them, when I think
of the effects which certain plays had upon me, and through me
upon my associates or even people unknown to me, when I think
of this tide of blood, of sap, of dark, mottled thought pumping itself
out in words, gestures, scenes, climaxes and ecstasies, when I think
how utterly, inexorably human was all this, so human, so salutary,
so remarkably universal, my appreciation of all that is connected
with plays, playwrights and play actors is augmented to the point of
extravagance.   To take one form of theatre alone, the Yiddish,
which seems so bizarre, so alien—how remarkably close and
intimate it is, now that I look back on it. In the Yiddish play there
is usually a little bit of everything which goes to make up life—
dancing, joking, horseplay, weddings, funerals, idiots, beggars,
feasts, to say nothing of the usual misunderstandings, problems,
anxieties, frustrations and so on which complicate modern drama.
(I am thinking, of course, of the ordinary Jewish play, intended for
the masses and therefore "concocted," like a good stew.) One
need not know a word of the language to enjoy the spectacle. One
laughs and weeps easily. One becomes thoroughly a Jew for the
nonce. Leaving the theatre, one asks : "Am I not also a Jew ? "
With the Irish, the French, the Russian, the Italian drama the same
thing occurs. One becomes all these alien creatures in turn, and
in doing so becomes more himself, more human, more like the
universal self. Through the drama we find our common and our
individual identity. We realize that we are star-bound as well as
earth-bound.

Sometimes, too, we find ourselves citizens of a world utterly
unknown, a world more than human, a world such as perhaps
only the gods inhabit. That the theatre can produce this effect,
with its very limited means, is worthy of note. The inveterate
theatre-goer, the person who enjoys being taken out of himself,

who imagines possibly that he has found a way to live other people's lives as well as his own, is inclined to forget that what he gets from the play which holds him so absorbed is only what he puts into it of himself. In the theatre so much has to be taken for granted, so very much has to be divined. One's own small life, if examined exteriorly, would never suffice to explain the close rapport between audience and players which every good dramatist establishes. In the exterior life of the humblest individual there is drama inexhaustible. It is from this inexhaustible reservoir that the playwright draws his material. This drama which goes on ceaselessly in every one's breast trickles through in mysterious ways, hardly ever formulating itself in spoken words or in deeds. Its overtones form a vast ocean, a vaporous ocean, on which here and there a frail bark of a play appears and disappears. In this vast ocean humanity is constantly sending forth signals, as if to the inhabitants of other planets. The great playwrights are no more than sensitive detectors flashing back to us, momentarily as it were, a line, a deed, a thought. The stuff of drama is not in the events of daily life ; drama lies in the very substance of life, embedded in every cell of the body, every cell of the myriad substances which envelop our bodies.

I am one of those individuals frequently accused of reading into things more than they contain, or more than was intended. This is a criticism levelled against me particularly where the theatre or the cinema is concerned. If it is a failing, it is one that I am not ashamed of. I have lived in the midst of drama from the time I was old enough to understand what was happening round and about me. I took to the theatre at an early age, as a duck takes to water. For me it was never just recreation, it was the breath of life. I went to the theatre to be restored and rejuvenated. With the rising of the curtain and the lowering of the lights I was prepared to accept implicitly what would be unfolded before my eyes. A play was not only as real to me as the life about me, the life in which I was immersed, it was more real. Looking backward, I must admit that much of it was " literature," much sheer claptrap. But at the moment it was life, life at its fullest. It colored and influenced my everyday life. It pervaded that life sensibly and irrevocably.

This faculty of overlooking—for it was an overlooking and not a failure to see properly—what the critical mind terms mere play-acting, this faculty which I deliberately nurtured, was born of a refusal to accept things at face value. At home, in school, in church, in the street, wherever I went, I was impregnated with drama. If it was to obtain a replica of daily life, then I had no need for the theatre. I went because from a tender age I shared, preposterous as this may sound, the secret intentions of the playwright. I sensed the everlasting presence of a universal drama which had deep, deep roots, vast and unending significance. I did not ask to be lulled or seduced ; I asked to be shocked and awakened.

On the stage, personality is everything. The great stars, whether comedians, tragedians, buffoons, impersonators, mountebanks or sheer zanies, are engraved as deeply in my memory as are the great characters in literature. Perhaps more so, since I knew them in the flesh. We are obliged to imagine how Stavrogin or the Baron de Charlus spoke, how they walked, gestured, and so on. Not so with the great dramatic personages.

There are literally hundreds of individuals I could speak of at length who once strode the boards and who still, if I but close my eyes, are declaiming their lines, working their mysterious magic. There were theatrical couples who exerted such a strong sentimental influence that they were nearer and dearer to us than the members of our own family. Noray Bayes and Jack Norworth, for example. Or James and Bonnie Thornton. Sometimes whole families endeared themselves to us, such as Eddie Foy's and George M. Cohan's. Actresses particularly took possession of our fancy as no other type possibly could. They were not always great actresses either, but their personalities were radiant, magnetic, hauntingly so. I think of a cluster of them immediately—Elsie Janis, Elsie Ferguson, Effie Shannon, Adele Ritchie, Grace George, Alice Brady, Pauline Lord, Anna Held, Fritzi Scheff, Trixie Friganza, Gertrude Hoffman, Minnie Dupree, Belle Baker, Alla Nazimova, Emily Stevens, Sarah Allgood—and of course that dark, blazing figure whose name I am sure no one will recall, Mimi Aguglia. The fact that they were flesh and blood, and not phantom creations of the screen, endeared them to us even more. Sometimes we saw them in their weak moments ; sometimes we watched them breathlessly, knowing that their hearts were really breaking.

The same pleasure one has in discovering his own books, his own authors, holds for the figures of the stage as well. We may have been told, as youngsters, that it was imperative to see (" before they die ") such as John Drew, William Faversham, Jack Barrymore, Richard Mansfield, David Warfield, Sothern and Marlowe, Sarah Bernhardt, Maude Adams—but our great joy came in discovering for ourselves such personalities as Holbrook Blinn, O. P. Heggie, Edward Breese, Tully Marshall, Mrs. Patrick Campbell, Richard Bennett, George Arliss, Cyril Maude, Elissa Landi, Olga Chekova, Jeanne Eagels and others, many, many others, now almost legendary.

The names, however, which are inscribed in *my* book of memory in letters of gold are those of the comedians, largely from vaudeville and burlesque. Let me mention—for old times' sake—just a few : Eddie Foy, Bert Savoy, Raymond Hitchcock, Bert Levy, Willie Howard, Frank Fay. Who could be immune to the powers of these spellbinders ? Better than any book, for me, was a matinée in which one of these appeared as a headliner. Often, at the Palace, there was an all-star program. I would no more have missed such an event than I would the weekly gathering of the Xerxes Society. Rain or shine, job or no job, money or no money, I was always there. To be with these " men of mirth " was the best medicine in the world, the best safeguard against melancholy, despair or frustration. I can never, never get over the reckless way they gave of themselves. Sometimes one of them would intrude upon the other fellow's act, creating with each irruption hysteria and pandemonium. The funniest book in the world* cannot rival, for me, a single performance of any of these individuals. There is not a single book I know of in the whole of literature which can keep one laughing throughout. The men I speak of could not only keep one chuckling, they could keep one in stitches. One laughed so hard and so continuously, in fact, that one felt like begging them to stop their antics for just a moment or two. Once they had the audience started it was scarcely necessary to do or say anything. A mere waggle of the fingers was sufficient to make one explode.

The man I liked best of all was Frank Fay. I adored him. I could see him of a matinée and go back in the evening to see him all over again, to laugh even harder the second or the third time. Frank

* What is the title, by the way ? I would give anything to know !

301

Fay impressed me as a man who could put on an act without the slightest preparation, a man who could hold the stage alone for ten or fifteen hours, if he chose. And who could vary the performance from day to day. To me he seemed possessed of inexhaustible wit, intention, intelligence. Like many another great comedian, he knew when and how to cross the borderline into the realm of the forbidden. He got away with murder, Frank Fay. He was irresistible, even to the censors, I imagine. Nothing, of course, can so rouse the risibilities of an audience as an incursion into the realm of the perverse and forbidden. But Frank Fay had a thousand tricks up his sleeve. He was indeed " a one-man show."

In passing I must make mention of an actor whom I saw only in one play, whom I never heard of again after his enormous success in *The Show Off*. I mean Louis John Bartels. Like *Charley's Aunt*, this play, which owed so much to Bartels' acting of it, remains a landmark in my memory. I can think of nothing quite like it. Again and again I went back to see it, especially to hear that raucous, blatant, infectious haw-haw-haw ! of Bartels, who was " the show off."

As far back as I can remember, I seem to be aware of voices speaking inside me. I mean by this that I was forever conducting conversation with these other voices. There was nothing "mystical" about this. It was a form of intercourse which ran concurrently with other forms of intercourse I indulged in. It could go on simultaneously while I held open conversation with another. Dialogue ! A constant dialogue. Before I began the writing of books I was writing them in my head—in this smothered sort of dialogue I speak of. One more capable of self-analysis than myself would have realized early in life that he was destined to write. Not I. If I thought about it at all—I mean this ceaseless, interior dialogue—it was merely to tell myself that I was reading too much, that I should stop chewing the cud. I never thought of it as unnatural or exceptional. Nor is it, except in the degree which it may attain. Thus it often happened that, while listening to some one, I heard his speech transmuted in varying ways, or, while giving close heed to his words, I would interpolate my own words, would embroider his words with others of my own, more piquant, more dramatic, more eloquent ; sometimes, indeed, after I had heard a person through, I would repeat the gist of his words in three or four ways, giving them back to him as if they were his own, and in doing so derive huge enjoyment in seeing him swallow his own words and marvel at their aptness, their acuteness, or their profundity and complexity. It was these performances which often endeared people to me, often people whom I had not the slightest interest in but who became attached to me much as they would to a clever mountebank or a sleight-of-hand artist. It was the mirror in which they saw themselves lucidly and flatteringly. It never occurred to me to deflate their egos : I enjoyed the game and was happy that they entered into it all unknowingly.

But what was this, or *it*, if not a sort of perambulating theatre in the first person ? What was I doing ? Creating character, drama, dialogue. Schooling myself, no doubt, and utterly without intention or prevision, for the task to come. And this task ? Not to mirror the world, not to render back *a* world, but to discover my own private world. The moment I say " private " world I realize that this is precisely what I have always lacked, what I have struggled more to obtain, or establish, than anything else in life. To unburden myself, therefore, is like writing another chapter of Revelation. The better part of my life I have spent in the theatre, though it may not have been a recognized playhouse. I have been author, actor, stage director and script itself. I have been so saturated with this never-ending drama, my own and others' combined, that just to take a walk alone is comparable to turning on Mozart or Beethoven.*

It was about eighteen years ago, sitting in the Café Rotonde in Paris, that I read Robinson Jeffers' *Women at Point Sur*, never dreaming that I would one day be living near Point Sur at a place called Big Sur, which I had never heard of. Dreams and life ! Little did I dream, when listening to the librarian of the Montague Street Library in Brooklyn tell of the marvels of the Cirque Medrano,

---

* In the preface to the first volume of his celebrated *roman-fleuve*, Jules Romain writes : " I wish that it will be understood that some episodes lead nowhere. There are destinies which finish none knows where. There are beings, enterprises, hopes, which one no longer hears about. Meteors which disintegrate, or aperiodic comets of the human firmament. A whole pathos of dispersion, of fading away, of which life is full, but which books nearly always ignore, preoccupied as they are, in the name of old rules, with beginning and finishing the game with the same cards." (*Hommes de bonne volonté*.)

that the first article I should write on arriving in Paris, the city of my dreams, would be on the Cirque Medrano, and that it would be accepted by Elliot Paul (of *Transition*) and published in the *Paris Herald*. Little did I realize, on the occasion of our brief meeting in Dijon—at the Lycée Carnot—that the man I was talking to would one day be the man to start me off on this book. Nor did I think, when at the Café du Dôme, Paris I was introduced to Fernand Crommelynck, the author of that celebrated and magnificent play, *Le Cocu Magnifique*, that it would be fifteen years or more before I would read his play. Little did I realize, when attending the performance of the *Duchess of Malfi* in Paris, that the man responsible for the superb translation of the play would soon become my translator and friend, that he and no other would lead me to the home of Jean Giono, his lifelong friend. Little did I imagine either, when seeing *Yellow Jacket* (written by the Hollywood actor, Charles Coburn), that I would encounter in Pebble Beach, California, the celebrated Alexander F. Victor (of the Victor Talking Machine Co.), who, talking of the thousand and one delightful experiences of his rich life, would end the conversation with a dithyramb on *Yellow Jacket*. How could I foresee that it would be in a far-off place called Nauplia, in the Peloponnesos, that I would see my first shadow play, and with such an astounding companion as Katsimbalis? Or, enamored as I was of burlesque (often following a troupe from town to town), how was I to surmise that in far-off Athens I would one day see the same type of performance, the same type of comedian, hear the same jokes, catch the same leer and banter? How could I possibly foresee that that same evening (in Athens), about two in the morning, to be exact, I should encounter a man I had seen only once before in my life, a man I had been merely introduced to, but whom I remembered as the one who came out of the stage door of the Theatre Guild after a performance of Werfel's *Goat Song*? And is this not a strange coincidence, that only now, just a few minutes ago, in glancing at my copy of *The Moon in the Yellow River*—a grand, grand play by Dennis Johnston—I notice for the first time that it was played by the Theatre Guild in New York, probably a year or two before my friend Roger Klein asked me to help him with the French translation of it. And though there may not be the least connection between the two, this also strikes me as curious and coincidental, that the first time I heard a French audience hiss was in a cinema in Paris during a showing of my beloved *Peter Ibbetson.* " Why are they hissing ? " I asked. " Because it is too unreal," my friend replied.

Ah yes, strange memories. Walking down the dusty streets of Heraklion, on my way to Knossos, what do I see but a huge poster announcing the coming of Charlie Chaplin at the Minoan cinema. Could anything be more incongruous ? The Minotaur and the Gold Rush ! Chaplin and Sir Arthur Evans. Tweedledum and Tweedledee. In Athens, some weeks later, I noticed the billboards advertising the coming of several American plays. One of them, believe it or not, was *Desire Under the Elms.* Another incongruity. At Delphi, a natural setting for *Prometheus Bound,* I sit in the amphitheatre listening to my friend Katsimbalis recite the last oracle delivered there. In a split second I am back in " The Street of Early Sorrows," upstairs in the parlor, to be precise, reading one after another of the Greek plays given in Dr. Foozlefoot's Five-Foot Shelf. It is my first acquaintance with that grim world. The real one follows much later, when at the foot of the citadel at Mycenae I inspect the graves of Clytemnestra and of Agamemnon . . . But that lugubrious parlor ! There, always alone, sad, forlorn, the last and the least of human kind, I not only tried to read the classics but I also listened to the voices of Caruso, Cantor Sirota, Mme. Schumann-Heink—even to Robert Hilliard, reciting " A Fool there was . . ."

As from some other existence there intrude now memories, rich, glorious memories, of that little theatre on the Boulevard du Temple (Le Déjazet), where I would laugh from beginning to end of the performance, my belly aching, the tears streaming down my face. Memories of Le Bobinot, rue de la Gaieté, where I listened to Damia or her numerous imitators, the theatre itself being only an aspect of a richer spectacle, for the street in which it stood, almost unique, even for Paris, was an endless passing show. And the Grand Guignol ! From hair-raising melodramas to the most riotous farces, all on one bill, with well-timed stampedes to the bar, a dream of a bar, hidden away in the lobby. But of all these strange, otherworldly memories, the best is of the Cirque Medrano. A world of

305

U

transmogrification. A world as old as civilization itself, one might say. For, certainly before the theatre, before the puppet show and the shadow play, there must have been the cirque intime with its saltimbanques, jongleurs, acrobats, sword swallowers, equestrians and clowns.

But to get back to that year 1913, in San Diego, where I heard Emma Goldman lecture on the European drama . . . Can it possibly be that long ago ? I ask myself. I was on my way to a whorehouse in company with a cowboy named Bill Parr from Montana. We were working together on a fruit ranch near Chula Vista and every Saturday evening we went to town for that one purpose. How strange to think that I was deflected, derouted, my whole life altered, by the chance encounter with a billboard announcing the arrival of Emma Goldman and Ben Reitman ! Through her, Emma, I came to read such playwrights as Wedekind, Hauptmann, Schnitzler, Brieux, d'Annunzio, Strindberg, Galsworthy, Pinero, Ibsen, Gorky, Werfel, von Hoffmansthal, Sudermann, Yeats, Lady Gregory, Chekov, Andreyev, Hermann Bahr, Walter Hasenclever, Ernst Toller, Tolstoy and a host of others. (It was her consort, Ben Reitman, who sold me the first book of Neitzsche's that I was to read—*The Anti-Christ*—as well as *The Ego and His Own* by Max Stirner.) Then and there my world was altered.

When, a little later, I began going to the Washington Square Players and the Theatre Guild, I became acquainted with more European dramatists—the Capek brothers, Georg Kaiser, Pirandello, Lord Dunsany, Benavente, St. John Ervine, as well as such Americans as Eugene O'Neill, Sidney Howard and Elmer Rice.

Out of this period there emerges the name of an actor who came originally from the Yiddish theatre—Jacob Ben-Ami. Like Nazimova, he had something indescribable. For years his voice and gestures haunted me. He was like a figure out of the Old Testament. But which figure ? I could never place him exactly. It was after one of his performances in some little theatre that a group of us repaired one night to a Hungarian restaurant where, after the other patrons had left, we closed the doors and listened till dawn to a pianist whose whole repertoire was Scriabin. These two names— Scriabin and Ben-Ami—are indissolubly connected in my mind.

Just as the title of Hamsun's novel, *Mysterium* (in German), is associated with another Jew, a Yiddish writer named Nahoum Yood. Whenever, wherever I met Nahoum Yood, he would begin talking about this mad book of Hamsun's. Similarly, in Paris, whenever I spent an evening with Hans Reichel, the painter, we would inevitably touch on Ernst Toller whom he had befriended and on whose account he had been thrown into prison by the Germans.

Whenever I think or hear of *The Cenci*, whenever I encounter the names Schiller and Goethe, whenever I see the word Renaissance (always connected with Walter Pater's book on the subject), I think of subway or elevated trains, either hanging on to a strap or standing on the platform looking down into dirty windows of filthy, woe-begone hovels, whilst committing to memory long passages from the works of these authors. Nor does it ever cease to seem remarkable to me that almost every day of my life, on entering the forest close by, where I strike an open glade, a golden glade, my mind immediately runs to those far-off performances of Maeterlinck's plays—*The Death of Tintagiles*, *The Blue Bird*, *Monna Vanna*, or else of the opera, *Pelléas et Mélisande*, the settings of which, almost as much as the music, have never ceased to haunt me.

It is the women of the theatre who seem to have left the greatest impression upon me, whether because of their great beauty, their singular personalities or their extraordinary voices.* Perhaps this is due to the fact that in everyday life women have so little chance to reveal themselves completely. Perhaps, too, the drama tends to enhance the rôles played by women. Modern drama is saturated with social problems, thereby reducing woman to a more human level. In ancient Greek drama the women are superhuman ; no modern has ever met such types in real life. In the Elizabethan drama they are also of startling proportions, not godlike, certainly, but of such magnification as to terrify and bewilder us. To get the full measure of woman one has to combine the properties of the female as given in ancient drama with those which only the burlesque theatre (in our time) has dared to reveal. I am alluding, of course,

---

* Pauline Lord's voice, for example, in *Anna Christie* : " O God, I am only a poor bum ! "—or the voice of Lucienne Lemarchand, the French actress, in *Dommage qu'elle soit putain !* Or our own dear Margo's.

W

to those so-called "degrading" comic bits in burlesque which derive from the commedia del' arte of the Middle Ages.

Since reading the life of de Sade, who spent some of his closing years at the insane asylum at Charenton, where he amused himself writing and directing plays for the inmates, I have often wondered what it would be like to witness the performance of a group of insane people. At the root of Artaud's ideas on the theatre was the thought of having the players so work upon the audience (with the aid of all manner of external devices) that the spectators would literally go mad and, participating with the actors in a frenzy of delirium, carry the drama to real and unthinkable excesses.

One thing about the theatre which has always impressed me is its power to overcome national and racial barriers. A few plays given by a group of foreign actors interpreting their native dramatists can do more, I have observed, than a cartload of books. Often the first reactions are anger, resentment, deception or disgust. But once the virus takes, what was absurd, preposterous, utterly alien, becomes accepted and approved, nay, enthusiastically endorsed. America has received wave after wave of such foreign influences, always to the betterment of our own native drama. But, like foreign cuisines, these infusions never seem to last. The American theatre remains within its own limited bounds, despite all the shocks which are administered to it from time to time.

Ah, but let me not overlook that strange figure, David Belasco ! About the time that my father added Frank Harris to his list of customers, thanks to his son's interest in literature, there came one day to the tailor shop this sombre, priest-like individual with dark, magnetic charm, who, like a clergyman, wore his collar backwards, who dressed always in black, yet was thoroughly alive, sensual, glowing, almost feline in his gestures and movements. David Belasco ! A name that Broadway will ever remember. He was not my father's customer but the client of one of my father's associates, a man named Erwin, who was mad about two things —boats and paintings. There were at that time four prominent figures—permanent fixtures, so to say—connected with the tailor shop : Bunchek, the cutter, this man Erwin, Rente, a sort of derelict boss tailor, and Chase, another boss tailor. No four men could differ more from one another than these did. Each one was an eccentric, and each one, with the exception of Bunchek, had his very personal and very peculiar assortment of customers—not many either, a mere handful, indeed, but sufficient, apparently, to keep them alive. Or perhaps it would be more accurate to say—"partially alive." Hal Chase, for example, who was from Maine and a Yankee to the core, a cantankerous one too, eked out the remainder of his income by playing billiards in the evening. Erwin, who was crazy about his "yacht" and always fretting because his customers failed to show up on time, thus preventing him from heading for Sheeps-head Bay where his boat lay at anchor—Erwin made little sums on the side by taking guests out for a sail. As for poor Rente, he had none of the mad or rash qualities of these two ; his solution was to work nights in a wealthy club, making sandwiches and serving beer and brandy to the card players. But what they all had in common was their propensity for dreaming life away. The greatest boon life offered for Chase was to duck out at noon —twelve sharp, if possible—and head for Coney Island or Rock-away Beach, where he would spend the entire afternoon swimming and baking himself in the broiling sun. He was a born storyteller, with a sort of Sherwood Anderson gift for hemming and hawing, but he was so damned full of character, so cocksure, so argumenta-tive, so pugnacious, so bull-headed, so eternally right, that he made himself obnoxious to every one, his customers included. As for these latter, his attitude was "take it or leave it." Erwin likewise. They gave their clients just one fitting ; if that didn't suit, they could go elsewhere. Which they usually did. Nevertheless, because of their eccentric natures, because of their peculiar, odd associates and the milieus in which they traveled, because of the language they talked, the figures they cut, they were constantly picking up new clients and often most astonishing ones. Belasco, as I said, was one of Erwin's customers. What these two men had in common I never could tell. Nothing, apparently. Sometimes my father's customers would collide with the customers of these other boss tailors as they were leaving the dressing room. General astonish-ment on the part of all. Many of my father's customers, as I have recounted in *Black Spring*, were his cronies, or became his cronies, through frequent meetings at the bar across the street. Some of them, men of parts (a number of them celebrated actors), found themselves delightfully at home in the back room of the tailor shop. Some of them were astute enough to engage Bunchek in conversation or argument, drawing him out about Zionism, the Yiddish poets and playwrights, the Kabbala, and such topics. Many an afternoon, when it seemed as if the combined clientèle of the establishment had utterly died away, we whiled away the weary hours at Bunchek's cutting table, discussing the most unheard of problems, religious, metaphysical, zodiacal and cosmological. Thus, Siberia, when I hear the word, is not the name of a vast, frozen tundra, but the name of a play by Jacob Gordin. Theodor Herzl, the father of Zionism, is even more of a father to me than the hatchet-faced George Washington.

One of the most beloved individuals who frequented the shop was a customer of my father's named Julian l'Estrange, who was then married to Constance Collier, the star of *Peter Ibbetson*. To hear Julian and Paul—Paul Poindexter—discussing the merits of Sheridan's plays or the histrionic virtues of Marlowe and Webster, for example, was almost like listening to Julian the Apostate versus Paul of Tarsus. Or then, as sometimes happened, to hear Bunchek (who caught their lingo only dimly and confusedly) disparage their talk, he who knew not a word of Sheridan, Marlowe, Webster, or even Shakespeare, was like turning on Fats Waller after a session at a Christian Science meeting room. Or, to top it all, listening to Chase, Rente, Erwin, Inc., tail off into their respective monologues on their respective, obsessive trivia. The whole atmosphere of the place was redolent of drink, discussion and dream. Each one was itching to retire into his own private world, a world, need I say it, which had absolutely nothing to do with tailoring. It was as if God, in his perverse way, had created them all tailors against their will. But it was just this atmosphere which gave me the necessary preparation for egress into the bizarre and unfathomable world of the solitary male, gave me strange, premature and premonitory notions of character, of passions, pursuits, vices, follies, deeds and intentions. Was it so extraordinary, therefore, that observing me with a book of Nietzsche's under my arm one day, the good Paul Poindexter should take me aside and give me a long lecture on Marcus Aurelius and Epictetus, whose works I had already read but dared not admit, because I hadn't the heart to let Paul down.

And Belasco ? I almost forgot about him. Belasco was always silent as a hermit. A silence which inspired respect rather than reverence. But this I do remember vividly about him—that I helped him on and off with his trousers. And I remember the illuminated smile he always gave in return for this little service : it was like receiving a hundred-dollar tip.

But before winding up the tailor shop I must say a word or two about the newspaper columnists of that day. You see, if clients were sometimes scarce, drummers were always plentiful. Not a day passed but three or four of them dropped in, not in hopes of taking an order, but to rest their weary bones, to chew the rag in friendly fashion. After they had discussed the news of the day they fastened on the columnists. The two reigning favorites were Don Marquis and Bob Edgren. Oddly enough, Bob Edgren, a sports writer, had a great influence upon me. I sincerely believe I am telling the truth when I say that it was through reading Bob Edgren's daily column that I cultivated what sense of fair play I have. Edgren gave every man his due ; after weighing all the pros and cons he would give his man the benefit of the doubt. I saw in Bob Edgren a sort of mental and moral referee. He was as much a part of my life then as Walter Pater, Barbey d'Aurevilly or James Branch Cabell. It was a period, of course, when I went frequently to the ringside, when I spent whole evenings with my pals discussing the relative merits of the various masters of fisticuffs. Almost my first idols were prizefighters. I had a whole pantheon of my own, which included among others such figures as Terry McGovern, Tom Sharkey, Joe Gans, Jim Jeffries, Ad Wolgast, Joe Rivers, Jack Johnson, Stanley Ketchel, Benny Leonard, Georges Carpentier and Jack Dempsey. Ditto for the wrestlers. Little Jim Londos was almost as much of a god to me as Hercules was for the Greeks. And then there were the six-day bike riders . . . Stop !

What I mean to point out by all this is that the reading of books, the going to plays, the heated discussions we waged, the sports contests, the banquets indoors and out, the musical fiestas (our own and those provided by the masters), were all merged and blended into one continuous, uninterrupted activity. On the way to the arena in Jersey the day of the Dempsey-Carpentier battle—an event, incidentally, almost equal in importance for us to the heroic, single-handed combats beside the walls of Troy—I remember discussing with my companion, a concert pianist, the contents, style and significance of *Penguin Island* and the *Revolt of the Angels*. A few years later, in Paris, while reading *La Guerre de Troie n'aura pas lieu*, I suddenly recalled this black day when I witnessed the sad defeat of my favorite, Carpentier. Again, in Greece, on the island of Corfu, reading the *Iliad*, or trying to—for it went against the grain —but anyhow, reading of Achilles, the mighty Ajax, and all the other heroic figures on one side or the other, I thought again of the beautiful godlike figure of Georges Carpentier, I saw him wilt and crumple, sink to the canvas under the crushing, sledgehammer blows of the Manassa mauler. It occurred to me then that his defeat was just as stunning, just as vivid, as the death of a hero or a demi-god. And with this thought came recollections of Hamlet, Lohengrin, and the other legendary figures whom Jules Laforgue had recreated in his inimitable style. Why ? Why ? But thus are books confounded with the events and deeds of life.

From eighteen to twenty-one or twenty-two, the period when the Xerxes Society flourished, it was a continuous round of feasting, drinking, play-acting, music-making (" I am a fine musician, I travel round the world ! "), broad farce and tall horseplay. There wasn't a foreign restaurant in New York which we did not patronize. Chez Bousquet, a French restaurant in the roaring Forties, we were so well liked, the twelve of us, that when they closed the doors the place was ours. (O fiddledee, O fiddledee, O fiddledum-dum-dee !) And all the while I was reading my head off. I can still recall the titles of those books I used to carry about under my arm, no matter where I was headed : *Anathema*, Chekov's *Short Stories*, *The Devil's Dictionary*, the complete Rabelais, the *Satyricon*, Lecky's *History of European Morals*, *With Walt in Camden*, Westermarck's *History of Human Marriage*, *The Scientific Bases of Optimism*, *The Riddle of the Universe*, *The Conquest of Bread*, Draper's *History of the Intellectual Development of Europe*, the *Song of Songs* by Sudermann, *Volpone*, and such-like. Shedding tears over the " convulsive beauty " of *Francesca da Rimini*, memorizing bits of *Minna von Barnhelm* (just as later, in Paris, I will memorize the whole of Strindberg's famous letter to Gauguin, as given in *Avant et Après*), struggling with *Hermann und Dorothea* (a gratuitous struggle, because I had

wrestled with it for a whole year in school), marveling over the
exploits of Benvenuto Cellini, bored with Marco Polo, dazed by
Herbert Spencer's *First Principles*, fascinated by everything from
the hand of Henri Fabre, plugging away at Max Muller's "philo-
logistica," moved by the quiet, lyrical charm of Tagore's poetic
prose, studying the great Finnish epic, trying to get through the
Mahabarrhata, dreaming with Olive Schreiner in South Africa,
reveling in Shaw's prefaces, flirting with Molière, Sardou, Scribe,
de Maupassant, fighting my way through the Rougon-Macquart
series, wading through that useless book of Voltaire's—*Zadig* . . .
What a life ! Small wonder I never became a merchant tailor.
(Yet thrilled to discover that *The Merchant Tailor* was the title of
a well-known Elizabethan play.) At the same time—and is this
not more wonderful, more bizarre ?—carrying on a kind of
"vermouth duckbill" talk with such cronies as George Wright,
Bill Dewar, Al Burger, Connie Grimm, Bob Haase, Charlie Sullivan, Bill Wardrop, Georgie Gifford, Becker, Steve Hill, Frank
Carroll—all good members of the Xerxes Society. Ah, what was
that atrociously naughty play we all went to see one Saturday
afternoon in a famous little theatre on Broadway ? What a great
good time we had, we big boobies ! A French play it was, *of course*,
and all the rage. So daring ! So risqué ! And what a night we made
of it afterwards at Bousquet's !

Those were the days, drunk or sober, I always rose at five A.M.
sharp to take a spin on my Bohemian racing wheel to Coney Island
and back. Sometimes, skeetering over the thin ice of a dark winter
morning, the fierce wind carrying me along like an iceboat, I would
be shaking with laughter over the events of the night before—just
a few hours before, to be exact. This, the Spartan regime, combined
with the feasts and festivities, the one-man study course, the pleasure
reading, the argument and discussions, the clowning and buffoonery,
the fights and wrestling bouts, the hockey games, the six-day races
at the Garden, the low dance halls, the piano-playing and piano
teaching, the disastrous love affairs, the perpetual lack of money,
the contempt for work, the goings-on in the tailor shop, the solitary
promenades to the reservoir, to the cemetery (Chinese), to the duck
pond where, if the ice were thick enough, I would try out my racing
skates—this unilateral, multilingual, sesquipedalian activity night

313

and day, morning, noon and night, in season and out, drunk or
sober, or drunk *and* sober, always in the crowd, always milling
around, always searching, struggling, prying, peeping, hoping,
trying, one foot forward, two feet backward, but on, on, on, completely gregarious yet utterly solitary, the good sport and at the same
time thoroughly secretive and lonely, the good pal who never had
a cent but could always borrow somehow to give to others, a
gambler but never gambling for money, a poet at heart and a
wastrel on the surface, a mixer and a clinker, a man not above pan-
handling, the friend of all yet really nobody's friend, well . . .
there it was, a sort of caricature of Elizabethan times, all gathered
up and played out in the shabby purlieus of Brooklyn, Manhattan
and the Bronx, the foulest city in the world, this place I sprang
from*—a cheese-box of funeral parlors, museums, opera houses,
concert halls, armories, churches, saloons, stadiums, carnivals,
circuses, arenas, markets Gansevoort and Wallabout, stinking
Gowanus canal, Arabian ice cream parlors, ferry houses, dry docks,
sugar refineries, Navy Yard, suspension bridges, roller skating rinks,
Bowery flophouses, opium dens, gambling joints, Chinatown,
Roumanian cabarets, yellow journals, open trolley cars, aquariums,
Saengerbunds, turn-vereins, newsboys' homes, Mills' hotels, peacock
alley lobbies, the Zoo, the Tombs, the Zeigfeld Follies, the Hippodrome, the Greenwich Village dives, the hot spots of Harlem, the
private homes of my friends, of the girls I loved, of the men I
revered—in Greenpoint, Williamsburg, Columbia Heights, Erie
Basin—the endless gloomy streets, the gaslights, the fat gas tanks,
the throbbing, colorful ghetto, the docks and wharves, the big ocean
liners, the banana freighters, the gun boats, the old abandoned
forts, the old desolate Dutch streets, Pomander Walk, Patchin
Place, United States Street, the curb market, Perry's drug store
(hard by the Brooklyn Bridge—such frothy, milky ice cream
sodas !), the open trolley to Sheepshead Bay, the gay Rockaways,
the smell of crabs, lobsters, clams, baked blue fish, fried scallops,

---

* " Ah ! blissful and never-to-be-forgotten age ! when everything was
better than it has ever been since, or ever will be again—when Buttermilk
Channel was quite dry at low water—when the shad in the Hudson were all
salmon, and when the moon shone with a pure and resplendent whiteness,
instead of that melancholy yellow light which is the consequence of her
sickening at the abominations she every night witnesses in this degenerate
city ! " (Washington Irving.)

the schooner of beer for five cents, the free lunch counters, and somewhere, anywhere, every old where, always one of Andrew Carnegie's " public " libraries, the books you so passionately wanted always " out " or not listed, or labelled, like Hennessy's whiskies and brandies, with three stars. No, they were not the days of old Athens, nor the days and nights of Rome, nor the murderous, frolicsome days of Elizabethan England, nor were they even the "good old 'Nineties"—but it was " little ole Manhattan " just the same, and the name of that little old theatre I'm trying so hard to remember is just as familiar to me as the Breslin Bar or Peacock Alley, but it won't come back, not now. But it was there *once*, all the theatres were there, all the grand old actors and actresses, including the hams such as Corse Payton, David Warfield, Robert Mantell, as well as the man my father loathed, his namesake, Henry Miller. They still stand, in memory at least, and with them the days long past, the plays long since digested, the books, some of them, still unread, the critics still to be heard from. (" *Turn back the universe and give me yesterday !* ")

And now, just as I am closing shop for the day, it comes to me, the name of the theatre ! *Wallack's !* Do you remember it ? You see, if you give up struggling (memoria-technica) it always comes back to you. Ah, but I see it again now, just as it once was, the dingy old temple façade of the theatre. And with it I see the poster outside. Shure, and if it wasn't—*The Girl from Rector's !* So naughty! So daring! So risqué!

A sentimental note to close, but what matter ? I was going to speak of the plays I had read, and I see I have hardly touched on them. They seemed so important to me once, and important they undoubtedly were. But the plays I laughed through, wept through, lived through, are more important still, though they were of lesser calibre. For then I was with others, with my friends, my pals, my buddies. Stand up, O ancient members of the Xerxes Society! Stand up, even if your feet are in the grave! I must give you a parting salute. I must tell you one and all how much I loved you, how often I have thought of you since. May we all be reunited in the beyond!

We were all such fine musicians. O fiddledee, O fiddledee, O fiddle-dum-dum-dee!

And now I take leave of that young man sitting alone upstairs in the lugubrious parlor reading the Classics. What a dismal picture! What could he have done with the Classics, had he succeeded in swallowing them ? The Classics! Slowly, slowly, I am coming to them—not by reading them, but by making them. Where I join with the ancestors, with my, your, our glorious predecessors, is on the field of the cloth of gold. *Bref,* daily life . . . Voltaire, though you are not precisely a classic, you gave me nothing, neither with your *Zadig,* nor with your *Candide.* And why pick on that miserable, vinegar-bitten skeleton, Monsieur Arouet ? Because it suits me at this moment. I could name twelve hundred different duds and dunderheads who likewise gave me nothing. I could let out a *pétarade. To what end ?* To indicate, to signify, to asseverate and adjudicate that, whether drunk or sober, whether with roller skates or without, whether with bare fists or six-ounce gloves, life comes first. Oui, en terminant ce fatras, d'événements de ma pure jeunesse, je pense de nouveau à Cendrars. De la musique avant toute chose! Mais, que donne mieux la musique de la vie que la vie elle-même ?

January to December, 1950,
Big Sur, California.

The Hundred Books Which Influenced Me Most*

AUTHOR	TITLE
——	Ancient Greek Dramatists
——	Arabian Nights Entertainment (for children)
——	Elizabethan Playwrights (excepting Shakespeare)
——	European Playwrights of the Nineteenth Century, including Russian and Irish
——	Greek Myths and Legends
——	Knights of King Arthur's Court
Abélard, Pierre	*The Story of My Misfortunes*
Alain-Fournier	*The Wanderer*
Andersen, Hans Christian	*Fairy Tales*
Anonymous	*Diary of a Lost One*
Balzac, Honoré de	*Seraphita*
——	*Louis Lambert*
Bellamy, Edward	*Looking Backward*
Belloc, Hilaire	*The Path to Rome*
Blavatsky, Mme. H. P.	*The Secret Doctrine*
Boccaccio, Giovanni	*The Decameron*
Breton, André	*Nadja*
Brontë, Emily	*Wuthering Heights*
Bulwer-Lytton, Edward	*The Last Days of Pompeii*
Carroll, Lewis	*Alice in Wonderland*
Céline, Louis-Ferdinand	*Journey to the End of the Night*
Cellini, Benvenuto	*Autobiography*
Cendrars, Blaise	Virtually the complete works
Chesterton, G. K.	*St. Francis of Assisi*
Conrad, Joseph	His works in general
Cooper, James Fenimore	*The Leatherstocking Tales*
Defoe, Daniel	*Robinson Crusoe*
De Nerval, Gérard	His works in general

* This list appeared in *Pour Une Bibliothèque Idéale;* Editions Gallimard, Paris, 1951.

AUTHOR	TITLE
Dostoievsky, Feodor	His works in general
Dreiser, Theodore	His works in general
Duhamel, Georges	*Salavin* Series
Du Maurier, George	*Trilby*
Dumas, Alexander	*The Three Musketeers*
Eckermann, Johann Peter	*Conversations with Goethe*
Eltzbacher, Paul	*Anarchism*
Emerson, Ralph Waldo	*Representative Men*
Fabre, Henri	His works in general
Faure, Elie	*The History of Art*
Fenollosa, Ernest	*The Chinese Written Character as a Medium for Poetry*
Gide, André	*Dostoievski*
Giono, Jean	*Refus d'Obéissance*
———	*Que ma joie demeure*
———	*Jean le Bleu*
Grimm, The Brothers	*Fairy Tales*
Gutkind, Erich	*The Absolute Collective*
Haggard, Rider	*She*
Hamsun, Knut	His works in general
Henty, G. A.	His works in general
Hesse, Hermann	*Siddhartha*
Hudson, W. H.	His works in general
Hugo, Victor	*Les Misérables*
Huysmans, Joris Karl	*Against the Grain*
Joyce, James	*Ulysses*
Keyserling, Hermann	*South American Meditations*
Kropotkin, Peter	*Mutual Aid*
Lao-tse	*Tao Teh Ch'ing*
Latzko, Andreas	*Men in War*
Long, Haniel	*Interlinear to Cabeza de Vaca*
M.	*Gospel of Ramakrishna*
Machen, Arthur	*The Hill of Dreams*
Maeterlinck, Maurice	His works in general
Mann, Thomas	*The Magic Mountain*
Mencken, H. L.	*Prejudices*
Nietzsche, Friedrich	His works in general
Nijinsky, Vaslav	*Diary*
Nordhoff & Hall	*Pitcairn Island*
Nostradamus	*The Centuries*
Peck, George Wilbur	*Peck's Bad Boy*
Percival, W. O.	*William Blake's Circle of Destiny*
Petronius	*The Satyricon*
Plutarch	*Lives*

AUTHOR	TITLE
Powys, John Cowper	*Visions and Revisions*
Prescott, William H.	*Conquest of Mexico*
————	*Peru*
Proust, Marcel	*Remembrance of Things Past*
Rabelais, Francois	*Garguanta and Pantagruel*
Rimbaud, Jean-Arthur	His works in general
Rolland, Romain	*Jean Christophe*
————	Prophets of the New India
Rudhyar, Dane	*Astrology of Personality*
Saltus, Edgar	*The Imperial Purple*
Scott, Sir Walter	*Ivanhoe*
Sienkiewicz, Henry	*Quo Vadis*
Sikelianos, Anghelos	*Proanakrousma* (in manuscript, translated)
Sinnett, A. P.	*Esoteric Buddhism*
Spencer, Herbert	*Autobiography*
Spengler, Oswald	*The Decline of the West*
Strindberg, August	*The Inferno*
Suarès, Carlo	*Krishnamurti*
Suzuki, Daisetz Teitaro	*Zen Buddhism*
Swift, Jonathan	*Gulliver's Travels*
Tennyson, Alfred	*Idylls of the King*
Thoreau, Henry David	*Civil Disobedience* and Other Essays
Twain, Mark	*Adventures of Huckleberry Finn*
Van Gogh, Vincent	*Letters to Theo*
Wassermann, Jacob	*The Maurizius Case* (Trilogy)
Weigall, Arthur	*Akhnaton*
Welch, Galbraith	*The Unveiling of Timbuctoo*
Werfel, Franz	*Star of the Unborn*
Whitman, Walt	*Leaves of Grass*

APPENDIX II

Books I Still Intend to Read

AUTHOR	TITLE
Anonymous	*My Secret Life*
Aquinas, Thomas	*Summa Theologica*
Aragon, Louis	*Le Paysan de Paris*
Bonaparte, Napoleon	*Memoirs*
Calas, Nicholas	*Foyers d'Incendie*
Casanova, Giacomo Giralamo	*Memoirs*
Chestov, Léon	*Athènes et Jérusalem*
Cleland, Dr. John	*Memoirs of Fanny Hill*
De Gourmont, Rémy	*Le Latin Mystique*
De la Bretonne, Restif	*Monsieur Nicholas*
———	*Les Nuits de Paris*
De Laclos, Choderlos	*Dangerous Acquaintances*
De Lafayette, Madame	*The Princess of Clèves*
De Sade, Marquis	*The Hundred and Twenty Days of Sodom*
Dickens, Charles	*Pickwick Papers*
Doughty, Charles	*Arabia Deserta*
Fielding, Henry	*Tom Jones*
Flaubert, Gustave	*Sentimental Education*
Gibbon, Edward	*The Decline and Fall of the Roman Empire*
Harrison, Jane	*The Orphic Myths*
———	*Prolegomena*
Hugo, Victor	*Toilers of the Sea*
Huizinga, H.	*The Waning of the Middle Ages*
James, Henry	*The Golden Bowl*
Maturin, Charles	*Melmoth the Wanderer*
Michelet, Jules	*History of the French Revolution*
Multatuli	*Max Havelaar*
Radcliffe, Ann Ward	*The Mysteries of Udolpho*
Rivière, Jacques & Alain-Fournier	*Correspondence*
Rousseau, Jean Jacques	*Emile*
Stendhal	*La Chartreuse de Parme*
Sullivan, Louis	*The Autobiography of an Idea*
Swift, Jonathan	*Letters to Stella*
Vaché, Jacques	*Lettres de Guerre*

And the works of the following authors :—Jean-Paul Richter, Novalis, Croce, Toynbee, Léon Bloy, Orage, Federov, Léon Daudet, Gerard Manley Hopkins, T. F. Powys, Ste. Thérèse, St. John of the Cross.

Friends Who Supplied Me With Books :

Ben Abramson	Mohegan Lake, New York
Graham Ackroyd	Sticklepath, England
Dr. Bruno Adriani	Carmel, California
Heinz Albers	Hamburg, Germany
Bruce Arliss	Monterey, California
William E. Ault	Phoenix, Arizona
Oscar Baradinsky	Yonkers, New York
René Barjavel	Paris, France
Roland Bartell	Monterey, California
Richard Beesley	Hollywood, California
Dr. Pierre Bélicard	Lyons, France
Hilary Belloc	Sausalito, California
Raoul Bertrand	Paris, France
Earl Blankinship	Seattle, Washington
André Breton	Paris, France
Robert A. Campbell	Kankakee, Illinois
Robert H. Carlock	Tucson, Arizona
Blaise Cendrars	Paris, France
J. Rives Childs	Jidda, Saudi Arabia
Hugh Chisholm	Big Sur, California
Cyril Connolly	London, England
Albert Cossery	Paris, France
Pascal Covici	New York City, New York
Frau Elisabeth Dibbern	Ohrigen, Germany
Lawrence Durrell	Belgrade, Yugoslavia
Jean Dutourd	London, England
David F. Edgar	Spring Valley, New York
Frank Elgar	Paris, France
Pete Fenton	Los Angeles, California
Robert Finkelstein	Los Angeles, California
J. H. Flagg	Chicago, Illinois
Mme. Geneviève Fondane	Paris, France
Wallace Fowlie	Bennington, Vermont
John Gildersleeve	Sacramento, California
Jean Giono	Manosque, France
Maurice Girodias	Paris, France
Raymond Guérin	Bordeaux, France
Jac. de Haan	The Hague, Holland
E. Haldeman-Julius	Girard, Kansas
Lars Gustav Hellström	Solna, Sweden
Walter Holscher	Hollywood, California
Andrew Horn	Los Angeles, California
Willard Hougland	Santa Fe, New Mexico

321

Claude Houghton	London, England
Louisa Jenkins	Pebble Beach, California
John Kidis	Sacramento, California
Pierre Laleure	Paris, France
James Laughlin	Norfolk, Connecticut
Janko Lavrin	Nottingham, England
Mme. H. Le Boterf	Paris, France
George Leite	Berkeley, California
Pierre Lesdain	Brussels, Belgium
Dr. Michael Lubtchansky	Paris, France
Pierre Mabille	Paris, France
Albert Maillet	Vienne, France
Rose K. Margoshes	New York City, New York
J. H. Masui	Paris, France
Gregory Mason	New York City, New York
Kathryn Mecham	Chicago, Illinois
H. L. Mermoud	Lausanne, Switzerland
Albert Mermoud	Lausanne, Switzerland
Sheldon Messinger	Los Angeles, California
H. W. Methorst, Jr.	Graveland, Holland
Maurice Nadeau	Paris, France
Gilbert Neiman	Denver, Colorado
Swami Nikhilananda	New York City, New York
Stan Noyes	Berkeley, California
Maud Oakes	Big Sur, California
Hugh O'Neill	Big Sur, California
Gordon Onslow-Ford	Sausalito, California
Kenneth Patchen	Old Lyme, Connecticut
Alfred Perlès	London, England
David Peery	Los Angeles, California
Lawrence Clark Powell	Los Angeles, California
John Cowper Powys	Corwen, Wales
Raymond Queneau	Paris, France
Paul Radin	Berkeley, California
Rajagopal	Ojai, California
Man Ray	Hollywood, California
Georges Ribemont-Dessaignes	Saint-Jeannet, France
John Rodker	London, England
Harrydick and Lillian Bos Ross	Big Sur, California
André Rousseaux	Paris, France
James S. Russell	Inverness, California
Mrs. Mark Saunders	Carmel, California
Tawfig Sayigh	Beirut, Lebanon
Bezalel Schatz	Big Sur, California
Dr. Olga Schatz	Berkeley, California

W. Schild	Lausanne, Switzerland
J. H. W. Schlamilch	Utrecht, Holland
Emil Schnellock	Fredericksburg, Virginia
Pierre Seghers	Paris, France
Henri Séguy	Sarlat, France
Jack W. Stauffacher	San Francisco, California
Frances Steloff	New York City, New York
Ruth Stephan	Westport, Connecticut
Irving Stettner	Paris, France
Carlo Suarès	Paris, France
W. T. Symons	London, England
Richard Thoma	Limona, Florida
Guy Tosi	Paris, France
Clara Urquhart	Johannesburg, South Africa
Jean Varda	Sausalito, California
Boris Vieren	Carmel, California
Alexander Victor	Carmel, California
Mme. Jean Voilier	Paris, France
Robert Vosper	Los Angeles, California
Kurt Wagenseil	Starnberg a/See, Germany
Alan W. Watts	Evanston, Illinois
Herbert F. West	Hanover, New Hampshire
Emil White	Big Sur, California
Walker Winslow	Topeka, Kansas
Bernhard Wolfe	New York City, New York
Kurt Wolff	New York City, New York
Jacob Yerushalmy	Berkeley, California
Dante T. Zaccagnini	Port Chester, New York